# Lecture Notes in Computer Science 5973

Commenced Publication in 1973
Founding and Former Series Editors:
Gerhard Goos, Juris Hartmanis, and Jan van Leeuwen

## Editorial Board

Kaoru Kurosawa (Ed.)

# Information Theoretic Security

4th International Conference, ICITS 2009
Shizuoka, Japan, December 3-6, 2009
Revised Selected Papers

 Springer

Volume Editor

Kaoru Kurosawa
Department of Computer
and Information Sciences
Ibaraki University
Hitachi, Ibaraki, Japan
E-mail: kurosawa@mx.ibaraki.ac.jp

Library of Congress Control Number: 2010932236

CR Subject Classification (1998): E.3, D.4.6, F.2.1, C.2, K.4.4, K.6.5

LNCS Sublibrary: SL 4 – Security and Cryptology

ISSN        0302-9743
ISBN-10     3-642-14495-0 Springer Berlin Heidelberg New York
ISBN-13     978-3-642-14495-0 Springer Berlin Heidelberg New York

springer.com

© Springer-Verlag Berlin Heidelberg 2010
Printed in Germany

Typesetting: Camera-ready by author, data conversion by Scientific Publishing Services, Chennai, India
Printed on acid-free paper        06/3180

# Preface

ICITS 2009 was held at the Shizuoka Convention and Arts Center "GRANSHIP" in Japan during December 3–6, 2009. This was the 4th International Conference on Information Theoretic Security.

Over the last few decades, we have seen several research topics studied requiring information theoretical security, also called unconditional security, where there is no unproven computational assumption on the adversary. (This is the framework proposed by Claude Shannon in his seminal paper.) Also, coding as well as other aspects of information theory have been used in the design of cryptographic schemes. Examples are authentication, secure communication, key exchange, multi-party computation and information hiding to name a few. A related area is quantum cryptography that predominantly uses information theory for modeling and evaluation of security. Needless to say, information theoretically secure cryptosystems are secure even if the factoring assumption or the discrete log assumption is broken. Seeing the multitude of topics in modern cryptography requiring information theoretical security or using information theory, it is time to have a regular conference on this topic. This was the fourth conference of this series, aiming to bring together the leading researchers in the area of information and/or quantum theoretic security.

There were 50 submissions of which 13 papers were accepted. Each paper was reviewed by at least three members of the Program Committee, while submissions co-authored by the Program Committee member were reviewed by at least five members. In addition to the accepted papers, the conference also included six invited speakers. These proceedings contain the accepted papers and the contribution by invited speakers. The invited speakers were: Yevgeniy Dodis "Leakage-Resilience and The Bounded Retrieval Model," Masato Koashi "Security of Key Distribution and Complementarity in Quantum Mechanics," Kazukuni Kobara "Code-Based Public-Key Cryptosystems and Their Applications," Prakash Narayan "Multiterminal Secrecy Generation and Tree Packing," Adi Shamir "Random Graphs in Security and Privacy" and Adam Smith "What Can Cryptography Do for Coding Theory?"

The conference received financial support from the Support Center for Advance Telecommunications Technology Research, Kayamori Foundation of Informational Science Advancement, and Research Center for Information Security (RCIS) of the National Institute of Advanced Industrial Science Technologies (AIST). We also received local support from the Shizuoka Convention and Visitors Bureau.

There are many people who contributed to the success of ICITS 2009. I would like to thank many authors from around the world for submitting their papers. I am deeply grateful to the Program Committee for their hard work to ensure that each paper received a thorough and fair review. I gratefully acknowledge the external reviewers listed on the following pages. I would like to thank Shai Halevi for developing and maintaining his very nice Web Submission and Review System. Finally, I would like to thank the general chair, Akira Otsuka, and the local organizer, Yukiko Ito, for organizing the conference. In particular, the unrelenting effort of Yukiko ensured the smooth running of the conference.

January 2010                                                            Kaoru Kurosawa

# ICITS 2009

The 4th International Conference on Information Theoretic Security

December 3–6, 2009, Shizuoka, Japan

In cooperation with
*International Association for Cryptologic Research (IACR) and
Technical Group on Information Security (ISEC) of IEICE, Japan*

Technical Co-sponsor: *IEEE Information Theory Society*

## General Chair

Akira Otsuka                    National Institute of Advanced Industrial
                                Science and Technology, Japan

## Program Chair

Kaoru Kurosawa                  Ibaraki University, Japan

## Program Committee

Carlo Blundo                    University of Salerno, Italy
Stefan Dziembowski              Universita La Sapienza, Italy
Paolo D'Arco                    University of Salerno, Italy
Serge Fehr                      CWI, The Netherlands
Juan Garay                      AT&T Labs-Research, USA
Goichiro Hanaoka                National Institute of Advanced Industrial
                                Science and Technology, Japan
Kaoru Kurosawa                  Ibaraki University, Japan
Hoi-Kwong Lo                    University of Toronto, Canada
Keith Martin                    Royal Holloway, University of London, UK
Ueli Maurer                     ETH, Switzerland
Jesper Buus Nielsen             University of Aarhus, Denmark
Renato Renner                   ETH, Switzerland
Rei Safavi-Naini                University of Calgary, Canada
Thomas Shrimpton                University of Lugano, Switzerland
Doug Stinson                    University of Waterloo, Canada
Stefan Wolf                     ETH, Switzerland
Moti Yung                       Google and Columbia University, USA
Yuliang Zheng                   University of North Carolina, USA

## Steering Committee

| | |
|---|---|
| Carlo Blundo | University of Salerno, Italy |
| Gilles Brassard | University of Montreal, Canada |
| Ronald Cramer | CWI, The Netherlands |
| Yvo Desmedt, Chair | University College London, UK |
| Hideki Imai | National Institute of Advanced Industrial Science and Technology, Japan |
| Kaoru Kurosawa | Ibaraki University, Japan |
| Ueli Maurer | ETH, Switzerland |
| Rei Safavi-Naini | University of Calgary, Canada |
| Doug Stinson | University of Waterloo, Canada |
| Moti Yung | Google and Columbia University, USA |
| Yuliang Zheng | University of North Carolina, USA |

## Local Organizer

| | |
|---|---|
| Yukiko Ito | National Institute of Advanced Industrial Science and Technology, Japan |

## Advisor

| | |
|---|---|
| Hideki Imai | National Institute of Advanced Industrial Science and Technology, Japan and Chuo University, Japan |

## External Reviewers

Johan Aaberg
Hadi Ahmadi
Susan Barwick
Zuzana
   Beerliova-Trubiniova
David Bernhard
Annalisa De Bonis
Niek Bouman
Cyril Branciard
Ashish Choudhary
Roger Colbeck
Yevgeniy Dodis
Matthias Fitzi
Philip Fong
Clemente Galdi

Peter Gaži
Clint Givens
Amin Aminzadeh Gohari
Yuval Ishai
Taichi Isogai
Yoshiyuki Kabashima
Hiroki Koga
Takeshi Koshiba
Kirill Morozov
Yusuke Naito
Siaw-Lynn Ng
Koji Nuida
Miyako Ookubo
Arpita Patra
Umberto Ferraro Petrillo

Krzysztof Pietrzak
Angel Perez Del Pozo
Dominik Raub
Bagus Santoso
Hongsong Shi
Thomas Sirvent
Björn Tackmann
Stefano Tessaro
Marco Tomamichel
Ivan Visconti
Douglas Wikström
Hong-Sheng Zhou
Vassilis Zikas

# Table of Contents

# Key Agreement from Common Randomness

# Random Graph and Group Testing

# Reliable Data Transmision and Computation

# Fingerprint and Watermarking

# Survey: Leakage Resilience and the Bounded Retrieval Model

Joël Alwen, Yevgeniy Dodis, and Daniel Wichs

Department of Computer Science, New York University
{jalwen,dodis,wichs}@cs.nyu.edu

**Abstract.** This survey paper studies recent advances in the field of *Leakage-Resilient Cryptography*. This booming area is concerned with the design of cryptographic primitives resistant to arbitrary side-channel attacks, where an attacker can repeatedly and adaptively learn information about the secret key, subject *only* to the constraint that the *overall amount* of such information is bounded by some parameter $\ell$. We start by surveying recent results in the so called *Relative Leakage Model*, where all the parameters of the system are allowed to depend on $\ell$, and the goal is to make $\ell$ large relative to the length of the secret key. We conclude by showing how to extend the relative leakage results to the *Bounded Retrieval Model* (aka "Absolute Leakage Model"), where only the secret key length is allowed to be slightly larger than $\ell$, but all other system parameters (e.g., public-key, communication, etc.) are independent of the absolute value of $\ell$. Throughout the presentation we will emphasize the information-theoretic techniques used in leakage-resilient cryptography.

## 1 Introduction

Traditionally, cryptographic systems rely on complete privacy of cryptographic keys. Unfortunately, in real systems, this idealized assumption is hard to meet perfectly. In many situations, the attacker might get some partial information about the secret keys through means which were not anticipated by the designer of the system and, correspondingly, not taken into account when arguing its security. Such attacks, typically referred to as *side-channel attacks*, come in a large variety (radiation, power, temperature, running time, fault detection, etc.), and often lead to a complete break of an otherwise "secure" system (e.g. [Koc96, BDL97, BS97, KJJ99, QS01, GMO01]). The situation becomes even worse if one also takes into account various computer viruses, internet worms and other malware, which might persist in a system inconspicuously for some time and leak private information to a remote attacker, until it is eventually detected.

Given that one cannot hope to eliminate the problem of side-channel and malware attacks altogether, it is natural to design cryptographic schemes which remain (provably) secure, even in the face of such attacks. To do so, we must first decide on an appropriate model of what information the adversary can learn during a side-channel attack. In this work, we assume that the attacker can repeatedly and adaptively learn *arbitrary functions* of the secret key sk, as long as the total number of bits leaked is bounded by some parameter $\ell$. Due to its generality, this model seems to include essentially all known side-channel attacks, and has recently attracted a lot of attention from

K. Kurosawa (Ed.): ICITS 2009, LNCS 5973, pp. 1–18, 2010.

the research community. In particular, this model simultaneously covers the following two typical scenarios, which seem to be treated differently in the existing literature.

RELATIVE LEAKAGE. Here, for a secret key of some particular length $s$, we assume that the leakage $\ell$ is bounded by some shrinking function of $s$; e.g., the attacker's leakage is less than half of the key-size. This assumption seems to be natural for modeling attacks where, no matter what the key-size is, the attacker gets some imperfect reading of the key. For example, this naturally models "memory" attacks [HSH+08] (where the attacker might get part of the key stored in RAM), "microwave" attacks (where the attacker manages to extract a corrupted copy of the key from a smart-card), or various power attacks (which repeatedly leak almost the same information about the secret, such as its hamming weight), among others.

ABSOLUTE LEAKAGE. Here we assume that there is a natural bound $\ell$ on the overall amount of information the attacker can learn throughout the lifetime of the system, particularly concentrating on the setting when $\ell$ can be extremely large. A prime example of this comes from most malware attacks, where a persistent virus may transmit a large amount of private data to a remote attacker. Nevertheless, in many situations it is either impossible, too time-consuming, or simply not cost-effective for the virus to download "too much data" (e.g. many gigabytes). In such situation one might resist side-channel attacks, but only by making the secret key *intentionally large*, to dominate the retrieval bound $\ell$. This *by itself* might not be a big problem for usability, given the extremely cheap price of storage nowadays. Therefore, the main goal of this setting, usually refereed to as the *Bounded Retrieval Model* (BRM) [CLW06, Dzi06], is to ensure that the *necessary* inefficiency in storage is essentially the *only* inefficiency that the users of the system incur. In particular, honest users should only have to read a small portion of the secret (this is called *locality*), and their computation and communication should not be much larger than in conventional cryptosystems.

To summarize, both leakage models – relative and absolute – study essentially the same technical question. However, the BRM setting additionally demands that: *users can increase their secret key size flexibly, so as to allow for an arbitrary large absolute leakage $\ell$, but without degrading other efficiency parameters, such as computation, communication and locality.* This is the perspective we will take in this paper, treating both settings together, while striving to allow for the above flexibility. Indeed, we will see that a natural paradigm for designing efficient BRM scheme often starts with designing a relative leakage scheme first, and then extending the basic scheme to the BRM model.

Another interesting feature of leakage-resilient cryptography is that information-theoretic techniques are often used even in the design of computationally secure schemes, such as password authentication, public-key encryption or digital signature schemes. We will try to emphasize these techniques throughout the presentation.

## 1.1 Related Work

WEAK SECRETS, SIDE-CHANNEL ATTACKS AND BRM. The model of side-channel attacks, as studied in this work, is very related to the study of cryptography with *weak secrets*. A weak secret is one which comes from some arbitrary distribution that has a sufficient level of (min-)entropy, and one can think of a secret key that has been partially compromised by side-channel attacks as coming from such a distribution. Most of the prior work concerning weak secrets is specific to the *symmetric key setting* and much of this work is *information-theoretic in nature*. For example, the study of privacy-amplification [BBR88, Mau92b, BBCM95] shows how two users who *share* a weak secret can agree on a uniformly random key in the presence of a passive attacker. The works of [MW97, RW03, DKRS06, KR09, DW09] extend this to active attacks, and the works of [Mau92a, AR99, ADR02, Lu02, Vad04] extended this to the case of *huge* secrets (motivated by the Bounded Storage Model, but also applicable to the BRM). Such information-theoretically secure schemes can only be used *once* to convert a shared secret, which may have been partially compromised by side-channel attacks, into a *single* uniform session-key.

In the computational setting, users can agree on *arbitrarily many* session-keys using Password Authenticated Key Agreement (PAKE) [BM93, BPR00, BMP00, KOY01, GL06], where they use their shared weak (or partially compromised) secret key as the password. However, these solutions do not scale to the BRM, as they do not preserve low locality when the secret is large. The Bounded Retrieval Model (BRM), where users have a huge secret key which is subject to large amounts of adversarial leakage, was introduced by [CLW06, Dzi06]. In particular, Dziembowski [Dzi06] constructed a *symmetric key* authenticated key agreement protocol for this setting in the Random Oracle model. This was later extended to the standard model by [CDD+07]. Other symmetric-key applications, such as password authentication and secret sharing, were studied in the BRM setting by [CLW06] and [DP07], respectively. We also note that *non-interactive* symmetric key encryption schemes using partially compromised keys were constructed implicitly in [Pie09] (based on weak pseudorandom functions) and explicitly in [DKL09] (based on "learning parity with noise").

The study of side-channel attacks in the *public-key* setting was initiated by Akavia et al. [AGV09], who showed that Regev's public-key encryption scheme [Reg05] (based on lattices) is secure against the side-channel attacks in the relative leakage model. Subsequently, Naor and Segev [NS09] presented several new constructions of public-key encryption schemes for this setting, based on other (non-lattice) assumptions, tolerating more leakage and achieving CCA2 security. Very recently, Alwen et al. [ADN+09] showed how to build the first public-key encryption in the BRM based on a variety of assumptions (lattices, quadratic residuosity, bilinear maps). Along the way, they also build identity-based encryption (IBE) schemes in the relative leakage model. The main drawback of these works is that (non-interactive) encryption schemes *inherently* only allow the adversary to perform side-channel attacks *prior to* seeing a ciphertext. This concern was addressed by Alwen et al. [ADW09] who showed how to construct public-key (interactive) key-exchange protocols both in the relative leakage-model and in the BRM, where the leakage was allowed to occur both before and after running the protocol. Along the way, the work of [ADW09] built leakage-resilient identification schemes (again, both in the relative leakage model and the BRM), used them to construct leakage-resilient signature schemes (in the random oracle model), and also developed general tools for converting schemes in the relative-leakage models into the more general BRM setting. Finally, Katz and Vaikuntanathan [KV09] recently developed leakage-resilient signature scheme in the standard model.

This survey article could be viewed as the digest of the main ideas and constructions from [ADW09, NS09, ADN+09, KV09], with the emphasis of trying to unify the different-looking techniques used in these works.

OTHER MODELS OF ADVERSARIAL KEY COMPROMISE. It is worth describing several related models for key compromise. One possibility is to restrict the *type* of information that the adversary can learn about the secret key. For example a line of work called *exposure resilient cryptography* [CDH+00, DSS01] studies a restricted class of adversarial leakage functions, where the adversary gets a *subset of the bits* of the secret key. In this setting, one can secure keys against leakage generically, by encoding them using an *all-or-nothing transform (AONT)*. We note that some natural side-channel attacks (e.g. learning the hamming weight of the key) and malware attacks are not captured by this model.

Another line of work, initiated by Micali and Reyzin [MR04] and studied further by [DP08, Pie09, FKPR09], designs various symmetric-key primitives and digital signatures under the axiom that "only computation leaks information". These models are incomparable to our setting, as they restrict the *type* of information the attacker can obtain, but can allow a greater overall *amount* of such information to be leaked. While quite reasonable in some application scenarios, such as power/radiation attacks, the above axiom does not seem to apply to many other natural attacks, such as the memory/microwave attacks or virtually all malware/virus attacks. A related model, where the adversary can learn/influence the values on some subset of wires during the evaluation of a circuit, was studied by Ishai et al. [ISW03, IPSW06], and recently generalized by [FRT09].

Lastly, the recent works [DKL09, DGK+09] study *auxiliary input*, where the adversary can learn functions $f(\mathsf{sk})$ of the secret key $\mathsf{sk}$ subject only to the constraint that such a function is *hard to invert*. Technically, this is a strictly stronger model than the one considered in this work as such functions $f$ can have output length larger than the size of the secret key.

## 2   Preliminaries

ENTROPY.   The *min-entropy* of a random variable $W$ is $\mathbf{H}_\infty(W) \stackrel{\text{def}}{=} - \log(\max_w \Pr[W = w])$. This is a standard notion of entropy used in cryptography, since it measures the worst-case predictability of $W$. We also review a generalization from [DORS08], called *average conditional min-entropy* defined by

$$\widetilde{\mathbf{H}}_\infty(W|Z) \stackrel{\text{def}}{=} - \log \left( \mathbb{E}_{z \leftarrow Z} \left[ \ \max_w \Pr[W = w | Z = z] \ \right] \right) = - \log \left( \mathbb{E}_{z \leftarrow Z} \left[ 2^{-\mathbf{H}_\infty(W|Z=z)} \right] \right).$$

This measures the worst-case predictability of $W$ by an adversary that may observe a correlated variable $Z$. We will use the following lemmas to reason about entropy.

**Lemma 1 ([DORS08]).** *Let $W, X, Z$ be random variables where $Z$ takes on values in a set of size at most $2^\ell$. Then $\widetilde{\mathbf{H}}_\infty(W|(X, Z)) \geq \widetilde{\mathbf{H}}_\infty((W, X)|Z) - \ell \geq \widetilde{\mathbf{H}}_\infty(W|X) - \ell$ and, in particular, $\widetilde{\mathbf{H}}_\infty(W|Z) \geq \mathbf{H}_\infty(W) - \ell$.*

In [ADW09], the authors define a more general notion of conditional min-entropy $\widetilde{\mathbf{H}}_\infty(W \mid \mathcal{E})$, where $\mathcal{E}$ can denote any arbitrary experiment (and not just some "one-time" random variable $Z$). Intuitively, this measures the (log of the) best prediction probability for $W$ after running the experiment $\mathcal{E}$. We refer to [ADW09] for the details.

REVIEW OF $\Sigma$-PROTOCOLS. Let $\mathcal{R}$ be a relation consisting of *instance, witness* pairs $(x, w) \in \mathcal{R}$ and let $L_R = \{x \mid \exists w, (x, w) \in \mathcal{R}\}$ be the *language* of $\mathcal{R}$. A $\Sigma$-protocol for $\mathcal{R}$ is a protocol between a PPT ITM prover $\mathcal{P}(x, w)$ and a PPT ITM verifier $\mathcal{V}(x)$, which proceeds in three rounds where: (1) the prover $\mathcal{P}(x, w)$ sends an initial message $a$, (2) the verifier $\mathcal{V}(x)$ sends a uniformly random challenge $c$, (3) the prover $\mathcal{P}(x, w)$ sends a response $z$. The verifier $\mathcal{V}(x)$ either *accepts* or *rejects* the conversation by computing some predicate of the instance $x$ and the conversation $(a, c, z)$. We require that $\Sigma$-protocols satisfy the following three properties:

1. *Perfect Completeness:* For any $(x, w) \in \mathcal{R}$, the execution $\{\mathcal{P}(x, w) \rightleftharpoons \mathcal{V}(x)\}$ is always accepting.
2. *Special Soundness:* There is an efficient algorithm such that, given an instance $x$ and two accepting conversations for $x$: $(a, c, z)$, $(a, c', z')$ where $c \neq c'$, the algorithm outputs $w$ such that $(x, w) \in \mathcal{R}$.
3. *Perfect Honest Verifier Zero Knowledge (HVZK):* There is a PPT simulator $\mathcal{S}$ such that, for any $(x, w) \in \mathcal{R}$, the simulator $\mathcal{S}(x)$ produces conversations $(a, c, z)$ which are *identically distributed* to the conversations produced by an honest execution $\{\mathcal{P}(x, w) \rightleftharpoons \mathcal{V}(x)\}$.

As was shown in [CDS94], the HVZK property implies *witness indistinguishability*. Here, we rephrase essentially the same property in a slightly different manner. We show that, oracle access to a prover $\mathcal{P}(x, w)$ does not decrease the entropy of $w$ *in any experiment* in which $x$ is given to the predictor.

**Lemma 2.** *Let $(\mathcal{P}, \mathcal{V})$ be an HVZK protocol for the relation $\mathcal{R}$, and let $(X, W)$ be random variables over $\mathcal{R}$. Let $\mathcal{E}_1$ be an arbitrary experiment in which $\mathcal{A}$ is given $X$ at the start of the experiment, and let $\mathcal{E}_2$ be the same as $\mathcal{E}_1$, except that $\mathcal{A}$ is also given oracle access to $\mathcal{P}(X, W)$ throughout the experiment. Then $\widetilde{\mathbf{H}}_\infty(W|\mathcal{E}_2) = \widetilde{\mathbf{H}}_\infty(W|\mathcal{E}_1)$.*

ONE-WAY FUNCTIONS (OWF) AND SECOND-PREIMAGE RESISTANCE (SPR). We review these two standard notions. In the full generality, the index $i$ for the OW/SPR function $f_i$ is sampled by a special index generation procedure $\mathsf{Gen}(1^\lambda)$ (where $\lambda$ is the security parameter), which also defines the domain $D_i$ and the range $R_i$ for the function.

**Definition 1 (One Way Functions (OWF)).** *A family of functions $\mathcal{F} = \{f_i : D_i \to R_i\}$ is one-way if:*

- *Easy to generate, sample and compute: There exist efficient algorithms for key generation $i \leftarrow \mathsf{Gen}(1^\lambda)$, sampling $w \leftarrow D_i$ and for computing $f_i(w)$ in time $\mathrm{poly}(\lambda)$.*
- *Hard to invert: For any PPT algorithm $\mathcal{A}$, we have $\Pr[f_i(\mathcal{A}(i, f_i(w))) = f_i(w)] \leq \mathrm{negl}(\lambda)$, where the probability is over random $i \leftarrow \mathsf{Gen}(1^\lambda)$, $w \leftarrow D_i$ and the random coins of $\mathcal{A}$.*

**Definition 2 (Second Pre-Image Resistant Functions (SPR)).** *A family of functions* $\mathcal{F} = \{f_i \; : \; D_i \to R_i\}$ *is* second-preimage resistant *(SPR) if $\mathcal{F}$ is easy to generate, sample and compute (defined the same way as for OWF) and, for any PPT algorithm $\mathcal{A}$,* $\Pr[w' \neq w \wedge f_i(w') = f_i(w) \mid w' = \mathcal{A}(i, f_i(w), w)] \leq \mathrm{negl}(\lambda)$, *where the probability is over random $i \leftarrow \mathsf{Gen}(1^\lambda)$, $w \leftarrow D_i$ and the random coins of $\mathcal{A}$. We define the* loss *of $f_i$ to be $\mathcal{L}(f_i) \stackrel{def}{=} (\log(|D_i|) - \log(|R_i|))$.*

In theory, it is known [Rom90] that for any polynomial $p(\lambda)$, the existence of OWFs implies the existence of SPR functions with $D_i = \{0,1\}^{p(\lambda)}$, $R_i = \{0,1\}^\lambda$. In practice, it is easy to construct SPR functions from most natural number-theoretic assumptions. For example, if the discrete log problem is hard in some group $G$ of prime order $q$, the following is a simple SPR function from $\mathbb{Z}_q^n \to G$: $(w_1 \ldots w_n) \mapsto \prod_{j=1}^n g_j^{w_j}$, where $g_1 \ldots g_n$ are random generators of $G$ (forming part of the function index $i$).

As we shall see, SPR functions will play a critical role in the design of leakage-resilient schemes, but first we need to model leakage-resilience.

LEAKAGE ORACLE. We model adversarial side-channel attacks on a secret key sk, by giving the adversary access to a *side-channel oracle*, which the adversary can (periodically) query to gain information about sk. Intuitively, we would like to capture the fact that the adversary can compute arbitrary efficient functions of the secret key as long as the *total* number of bits learned is *bounded* by some parameter $\ell$. In general, these *leakage functions* can be chosen adaptively, based on the results of prior leakage attacks and any other events that may take place during the attack game. The following definition formalizes the above concept.

**Definition 3.** *A leakage oracle $\mathcal{O}_{sk}^{\lambda,\ell}(\cdot)$ is parameterized by a secret key sk, a leakage parameter $\ell$ and a security parameter $\lambda$. A query to the oracle consists of (a description of) a leakage function $h \; : \; \{0,1\}^* \to \{0,1\}$. The oracle computes the function $h(sk)$ for at most $\mathrm{poly}(\lambda)$ steps and, if the computation completes, responds with the output, and otherwise, outputs 0. A leakage oracle $\mathcal{O}_{sk}^{\lambda,\ell}(\cdot)$ responds to at most $\ell$ queries, and ignores all queries afterwards.*

## 3   Relative Leakage Model

We start with the relative leakage model, where the goal is to design a cryptographic scheme allowing one to tolerate relative leakage $\ell$ as close to the length of the secret key of the system as possible.

### 3.1   Password Authentication and OWF

Password authentication is, perhaps, the most basic cryptographic problem. A client Alice has a secret key sk and wishes to authenticate herself to a server Bob, who stores some function pk of Alice's key. It is assumed the the communication channel between Alice and Bob is secure, but server Bob's storage pk is not. Thus, it must be the case that no valid sk can be computed from pk. Therefore, it is clear that a necessary and sufficient primitive for the problem of password-authentication is a OWF. Namely, the key generation algorithm KeyGen sets sk $= w$ and pk $= (i, f_i(w))$, where $i$ is the index of a OWF from $D_i$ to $R_i$. In the setting of leakage, the adversary $\mathcal{A}$ is also given oracle access to $\mathcal{O}_{\text{sk}}^{\lambda,\ell}(\cdot)$. Notice, in this setting adaptive access to the leakage oracle is equivalent to choosing a single leakage function $h(\text{sk})$ whose output is $\ell$ bits. We call the resulting OWF family $\mathcal{F}$ $\ell$-leakage-resilient ($\ell$-LR).

The first hope of building LR-OWFs is to hope that all OWF's are LR. The good news is that it is true for $\ell(\lambda) = O(\log \lambda)$, since one can always guess the proper leakage with probability $\frac{1}{2^\ell} \geq \frac{1}{poly(\lambda)}$. The bad news is that it is unlikely we can say more about it. As an example, consider $f(x_1, x_2) = f'(x_1)$ where $|x_1| = \lambda^{0.01}$, $|x_2| = (\lambda - \lambda^{0.01})$ and $f'$ is some auxiliary OWF. Clearly, $f$ is not even ($\lambda^{0.01}$)-LR. The next hope is to try some natural OWF's and hope that they happen to be leakage-resilient. Unfortunately, this is also problematic. For example, consider the modular exponentiation function $f(w) = g^w$ over some group $G$ of order $q$. It turns out that we do not have any attacks on this $f$, and, yet, we cannot prove the leakage-resilience of this function based on the discrete log assumption either. The difficulty is in simulating the leakage oracle: given only $f(w) = g^w$, there does not appear to be any way to compute (with any decent probability) $h(w)$ for an adversarially chosen function $h : \mathbb{Z}_q \to \{0,1\}^\ell$, when $\ell = \omega(\log \lambda)$.

This is where the SPR functions come to the rescue. In the SPR attack on a function $f$, the SPR attacker $\mathcal{A}$ is given a valid pre-image $w$ of $x = f(w)$. Thus, it is easy to simulate the correct value $z = h(w)$ for the leakage attacker $\mathcal{B}$. However, if both $z$ and $x$ are much shorter than $w$, the leakage attacker $\mathcal{B}$ still has a lot of uncertainty about the original value $w$ used by $\mathcal{A}$. Hence, there is a good chance that $\mathcal{B}$ will compute a different pre-image $w' \neq w$ of $x$, therefore violating the SPR security of $f$. This easy observation is formalized below, but will form the basis for building more complicated leakage-resilient primitives.

**Theorem 1.** *If $\mathcal{F}$ is an SPR family with loss $\ell = \ell(\lambda)$ (see Definition 2), then $\mathcal{F}$ is $(\ell - \omega(\log \lambda))$-LR-OWF.*

*Proof.* Assume that $f_i$ is not a $\ell'$-LR-OWF, where $\ell' = (\ell - \omega(\log \lambda))$. So there exists an inverter $\mathcal{B}$ which inverts $f_i(w)$ (given $f_i(w)$ and leakage $h(w)$) with probability $\varepsilon$ which is non-negligible. We construct an algorithm $\mathcal{A}$ which breaks the SPR security with non-negligible advantage (analyzed below).

On input $(i, w, x = f_i(w))$, $\mathcal{A}$ invokes $\mathcal{B}(i, x)$. When $\mathcal{B}$ makes a leakage query $h$, $\mathcal{A}$ responds with $h(w) \in \{0,1\}^{\ell'}$. If $\mathcal{B}$ then returns a valid pre-image $w'$ such that $f_i(w') = x$, $\mathcal{A}$ returns $w'$ iff $w' \neq w$. It is clear that $\mathcal{A}$ simulated $\mathcal{B}$ perfectly. Hence,

$$\Pr(\mathcal{A} \text{ succeeds}) \geq \Pr(\mathcal{B} \text{ succeeds} \wedge w \neq w') \geq \varepsilon - \Pr(w = w')$$

Let $W$ be the random variable corresponding to sampling $w$ from $D_i$, and denote by $X = f_i(W)$, $Z = h(W)$. It is clear that even if $\mathcal{B}$ is infinitely powerful, its best chance to predict $W$ from $X$ and $Z$ is $2^{-\tilde{\mathbf{H}}_\infty(W|X,Z)}$. However, using Lemma 1, we know that $\tilde{\mathbf{H}}_\infty(W \mid X, Z) \geq \tilde{\mathbf{H}}_\infty(W) - (\log |R_i| + \ell') = \log(|D_i|/|R_i|) - \ell' = \ell - \ell'$, which gives $\Pr(w = w') \leq 2^{\ell'-\ell}$. Setting $\ell' = (\ell - \omega(\log \lambda))$, we get that $\mathcal{A}$ succeeds with non-negligible probability ($\varepsilon - \text{negl}(\lambda)$). $\qquad\square$

As an example, recall the SPR function $f(w_1, \ldots, w_n) = \prod_{j=1}^{n} g_j^{w_j}$ defined over some group $G$ of prime order $q$. We conclude that if the discrete logarithms in $G$ are hard, then $f$ is $\ell$-LR-OWF for $\ell = (n \log q - \log |G| - \omega(\log \lambda))$. For large $n$, this value of $\ell$ approaches the length $(n \log q)$ of the secret key $w = (w_1 \ldots w_n)$.

### 3.2 Identification Schemes

Recall, (public-key) identification (ID) schemes are similar to password authentication schemes, except the communication between the client Alice and the server Bob is no longer assumed secure. As a result, ID schemes must be interactive. We informally recall two main notions of security for ID schemes: *passive* security and *active* security. Both notions proceed in two stages. In the *learning stage*, the attacker $\mathcal{A}(\mathsf{pk})$ gets access to the communication channel between Alice and the verifier. In the passive attack, this is modeled by giving $\mathcal{A}$ oracle access to the transcript oracle $\mathcal{T}$, which returns an honestly generated communication transcript between Alice and Bob. In the active attack, $\mathcal{A}$ is actually allowed to play the role of the verifier with Alice (and possibly deviate from the honest verifier behavior). Formally, $\mathcal{A}$ is given oracle access to polynomially many "copies of Alice". After the end of the learning stage, $\mathcal{A}$ enters the *impersonation stage* and loses its "learning oracle" (either $\mathcal{T}$ or Alice herself). In this stage $\mathcal{A}$ tries to impersonate Alice to the honest verifier Bob, and wins the game if it succeeds.

LEAKAGE-RESILIENT ID SCHEMES. In the setting of leakage, the adversary $\mathcal{A}$ is also given oracle access to the leakage oracle $\mathcal{O}_{\mathsf{sk}}^{\lambda, \ell}(\cdot)$. Not very surprisingly, it is easier to handle leakage calls made during the learning stage than the leakage calls made during the impersonation stage (which might depend on the actual challenges received). For this reason, we will call the ID scheme $(\ell_1, \ell_2)$-*leakage-resilient* (LR) if the attacker can learn up to $\ell_1$ bits in the learning stage, and up to $\ell_2$ bits in the impersonation stage. For simplicity of exposition, from now now we assume that the attacker calls the leakage oracle precisely once in each stage, learning $\ell_1$ and $\ell_2$ bits respectively.

CONSTRUCTIONS. Recall, in the leak-free setting, a $\Sigma$-protocol for proving the knowledge of a pre-image of any OWF immediately gives a passively secure ID scheme. Namely, setting $\mathsf{sk} = w$, $\mathsf{pk} = (i, x = f_i(w))$, let $\mathcal{R} = \{(x = f(w), w)\}$ and $\Pi$ be a $\Sigma$-protocol for $\mathcal{R}$ with challenge size $|c| = k = \omega(\log \lambda)$. Then $\Pi$ is a passively secure ID scheme. Intuitively, the HVZK property of $\Pi$ enables us to perfectly simulate the transcript queries in the learning stage. On the other hand, if an attacker $\mathcal{A}$ can respond to a random challenge $c$ with probability $\varepsilon$ in the impersonation stage, then by rewinding the attacker with a new (random) challenge $c'$, one can obtain two accepting conversations $(a, c, z), (a, c', z')$ with $c \neq c'$ with probability $\varepsilon(\varepsilon - \frac{1}{2^k})$,[1] which is non-negligible if $\varepsilon$ is non-negligible and $k = \omega(\log \lambda)$. Then, the special soundness of $\Pi$ implies that we can extract a valid witness $w'$ from the attacker, contradicting the one-wayness of $f_i$.

It is easy to see that this analysis easily extends to the leakage-resilient setting, provided that: (a) one uses a *leakage-resilient* OWF instead of any OWF; and (b) the leakage threshold $\ell$ of this OWF is greater than $\ell_1 + 2\ell_2$, since we need to rewind the attacker in the impersonation stage, and hence double the leakage to $2\ell_2$ bits.

---

[1] We omit this standard derivation.

**Theorem 2.** *Assume $\Pi$ is a $\Sigma$-protocol for $(\ell_1 + 2\ell_2)$-LR-OWF with challenge size $\omega(\log \lambda)$. Then $\Pi$ is $(\ell_1, \ell_2)$-LR passively secure ID scheme.*

Using Theorem 1, this means we can use an SPR function with loss $\ell = (\ell_1 + 2\ell_2 + \omega(\log(\lambda))$. It turns out, however, that this will immediately give an actively secure ID scheme! The reason is that, in the SPR reduction, the SPR adversary actually knows the pre-image $w$, so it can easily simulate the leakage oracle, as well as play the role of the prover in the active learning stage. Moreover, since $\Sigma$-protocols are witness indistinguishable, Lemma 2 implies that, information-theoretically, the oracle access to the prover does not reduce the min-entropy of $w$ conditioned on the leakage. Namely, all the information the ID attacker learns about $w$ comes from the leakage queries. Overall, we get the following result:

**Theorem 3.** *Assume $\Pi$ is a $\Sigma$-protocol with challenge size $\omega(\log \lambda)$ for an SPR function with loss $\ell(\lambda) = (\ell_1 + 2\ell_2 + \omega(\log \lambda))$. Then $\Pi$ is $(\ell_1, \ell_2)$-LR actively secure ID scheme.*

We notice that, in principle, any SPR function has a $\Sigma$-protocol with challenge size $\omega(\log \lambda)$ if OWFs exist [FS89, GMW91]. However, concrete SPR functions often have very efficient protocols. For example, such an efficient $\Sigma$-protocol for the SPR function $f(w_1, \ldots, w_n) = \prod_{j=1}^{n} g_j^{w_j}$ is given by Okamoto [Oka92]. This gives a very efficient $(\ell_1, \ell_2)$-LR active ID scheme where $\ell_1 + 2\ell_2$ approaches the length of the secret key $w$ as $n$ grows.

### 3.3 Signatures

Recall, a signature scheme consists of a key-generation procedure $(\mathsf{pk}, \mathsf{sk}) \leftarrow \mathsf{KeyGen}(1^\lambda)$, a signing procedure $\sigma \leftarrow \mathsf{Sign}(m, \mathsf{pk})$ which produces a signature $\sigma$ for the message $m$, and a verification procedure $\mathsf{Ver}(m, \sigma, \mathsf{sk})$, which uses the secret key $\mathsf{sk}$ to assess the (in)validity of the signature $\sigma$ of $m$. The standard existential unforgeability (UF) against the chosen message attack (CMA) of the signature scheme states that no efficient attacker $\mathcal{A}(\mathsf{pk})$, given oracle access to the signing procedure $\mathsf{Sign}(\cdot, \mathsf{sk})$, should be unable to forge a valid signature $\sigma$ of some message $m$ not queried to the signing oracle. In the setting of leakage, the usual UF-CMA security is augmented and the attacker $\mathcal{A}$ is also given oracle access to $\mathcal{O}_{\mathsf{sk}}^{\lambda, \ell}(\cdot)$. The resulting signature scheme is called $\ell$-*leakage-resilient (LR)*.

$t$-TIME LEAKAGE-RESILIENT SIGNATURES. In general, the forger $\mathcal{A}$ is allowed to make an arbitrary polynomial number of oracle calls to the signing oracle. For the special case where this number is a-priori bounded by a constant $t \geq 1$, we call the resulting signature scheme a $t$-*time* signature scheme. In the leak-free setting, such $t$-time schemes are easier to construct [Lam79] and can be more efficient then general schemes. Further, Naor and Yung [NY89] show how to construct general UF-CMA secure signatures from any such 1-time scheme. Although this transformation does not work in the setting of leakage, [FKPR09] show a similar transformation turns any 3-time $\ell$-LR signature into and $\ell$-LR signature in the "only computation leaks information" model of [MR04]. Thus, it is still interesting to build *leakage-resilient $t$-time signatures* for a small constant $t$. Two such constructions are given by Katz and

Vaikuntanathan [KV09]. One general construction is a variant of Lamport's $t$-time signatures [Lam79] with $\ell \approx |\mathsf{sk}|/4$, and the other is a much more efficient construction from any sufficiently shrinking "homomorphic collision-resistant hash function" (which can be built from a variety of specific assumptions) with $\ell \approx |sk|/2$. We refer to [KV09] for the details.

LEAKAGE-RESILIENT SIGNATURES VIA FIAT-SHAMIR. Recall, the standard Fiat-Shamir transformation [FS86, AABN02] builds a secure signature scheme from any passively-secure, public-coin, 3-round ID scheme, such as the ID schemes originating from $\Sigma$-protocols. To sign the message $m$, the signer generates the first flow $a$, sets the challenge $c = H(a, m)$, where $H$ is modeled as a random oracle, and finally computes the third flow $z$. The signature consists of the tuple $(a, z)$. Not surprisingly, the construction generalizes to the setting of leakage [ADW09, KV09], modulo the following two caveats: (a) the ID scheme must be $(0, \ell)$-LR (i.e., leakage should be allowed in the impersonation stage); and (b) the leakage oracle cannot depend on the random oracle. Luckily, using the construction of passively (in fact, even actively) secure LR ID schemes from SPR functions given in Theorem 3, we satisfy the requirement (a) and can easily eliminate the restriction (b) by direct analysis, obtaining the following result:

**Theorem 4.** *Assume $\Pi$ is a $\Sigma$-protocol with challenge size $\omega(\log \lambda)$ for an SPR function with loss $\ell(\lambda) = (2\ell + \omega(\log \lambda))$. Then, applying the Fiat-Shamir heuristics to $\Pi$, we obtain an $\ell$-LR signature scheme in the random oracle model.*

STANDARD MODEL LEAKAGE-RESILIENT SIGNATURE. On an abstract level, the construction in Theorem 4 can be viewed as choosing a secret key $\mathsf{sk} = w$, $\mathsf{pk} = (i, x = f_i(w))$, and letting the signature of $m$ be a "$m$-dependent, non-interactive, zero-knowledge proof of knowledge (NIZK-POK) of $w$, in the Random Oracle Model". Katz and Vaikuntanathan [KV09] observed that one can instead use NIZK-POKs in the common-reference string (CRS) model, as opposed to the Random Oracle model. Formalizing this idea, they showed how to obtain a leakage-resilient signature scheme in the standard model. Unfortunately, this is mainly a feasibility result, since existing (so called simulation-sound) NIZK-POKs are extremely inefficient in the CRS model. Constructing practical LR signatures in the standard model remains an important open question.

### 3.4  Encryption and KEM

We will concentrate on leakage-resilient *public-key* encryption (PKE) schemes, noticing only that leakage-resilient symmetric-key schemes were constructed implicitly in [Pie09] (based on weak pseudorandom functions) and explicitly in [DKL09] (based on "learning parity with noise"). In fact, for our use it will be more convenient to use the notion of a *key-encapsulation mechanism* (KEM) [CS04], which implies PKE (see below). Recall, a KEM consists of a key-generation procedure $(\mathsf{pk}, \mathsf{sk}) \leftarrow \mathsf{KeyGen}(1^\lambda)$, an encapsulation procedure $(c, k) \leftarrow \mathsf{Encap}(\mathsf{pk})$ which produces ciphertext/randomness pairs $(c, k)$, and a decapsulation procedure $k = \mathsf{Decap}(c, \mathsf{sk})$, which uses the secret key $\mathsf{sk}$ to recover the randomness $k$ from a ciphertext $c$. A KEM allows a sender that knows $\mathsf{pk}$, to securely agree on randomness $k$ with a receiver that possesses $\mathsf{sk}$, by sending an encapsulation-ciphertext $c$. Once this is done, one can use the randomness $k$ to symmetrically encrypt the message $m$, giving a trivial way to get PKE from KEM.

The standard *chosen plaintext attack* (CPA) security of a KEM requires that the distribution $(\mathsf{pk}, c, k)$, where $(c, k) \leftarrow \mathsf{Encap}(\mathsf{pk})$, is computationally indistinguishable from $(\mathsf{pk}, k^*, c)$, where $k^*$ is truly random and independent of $c$. One can naturally define $\ell$-*leakage-resilient (LR) KEMs*, where the attacker $\mathcal{A}(\mathsf{pk})$ gets access to the leakage oracle $\mathcal{O}_{\mathsf{sk}}^{\lambda, \ell}(\cdot)(\mathsf{sk})$ *before* the challenge encapsulation $c$ is produced. Notice, in this setting adaptive access to the leakage oracle is equivalent to choosing a single leakage function $h(\mathsf{sk})$ whose output is $\ell$ bits.

HASH PROOF SYSTEMS AND LEAKAGE-RESILIENT KEMS. As with the other primitives we studied, not every KEM is leakage-resilient. However, Naor and Segev [NS09] showed that a special class of KEMs, called *hash proof systems* (HPS) [CS02, KPSY09], can be used to easily construct leakage-resilient KEMs.[2] Informally, am HPS is a KEM with the following two properties:

- There exists an *invalid-encapsulation procedure* $c \leftarrow \mathsf{Encap}^*(\mathsf{pk})$, so that ciphertexts generated by $\mathsf{Encap}^*(\mathsf{pk})$ are computationally indistinguishable from those generated by $\mathsf{Encap}(\mathsf{pk})$, *even given the secret key* $\mathsf{sk}$.
- For a fixed $\mathsf{pk}$ and *invalid ciphertext* $c$ generated by $\mathsf{Encap}^*(\mathsf{pk})$, the output of $\mathsf{Decap}(c, \mathsf{sk})$ is *statistically* uniform, over the randomness of $\mathsf{sk}$. This property can only hold if a fixed $\mathsf{pk}$ leaves statistical entropy in $\mathsf{sk}$.

Notice the difference between valid and invalid ciphertexts. For a fixed $\mathsf{pk}$, a *valid* $c$, produced by $(c, k) \leftarrow \mathsf{Encap}(\mathsf{pk})$, always decapsulated to the same value $k$, no matter which secret key $\mathsf{sk}$ is used to decapsulate it. On other hand, an invalid $c$ produced by $c \leftarrow \mathsf{Encap}^*(\mathsf{pk})$, decapsulated to a statistically random value based on the randomness of $\mathsf{sk}$.

The above two properties are sufficient to prove leak-free KEM security, showing that for $(c, k) \leftarrow \mathsf{Encap}(\mathsf{pk})$, an attacker given $c$ cannot distinguish $k$ from uniform. The proof by contradiction proceeds as follows. As the first step, we replace the honestly generated $(c, k) \leftarrow \mathsf{Encap}(\mathsf{pk})$ with $c' \leftarrow \mathsf{Encap}^*(\mathsf{pk})$ and $k' \leftarrow \mathsf{Decap}(c', \mathsf{sk})$. Since valid ciphertexts are indistinguishable from invalid ciphertexts even given the secret key $\mathsf{sk}$, the attacker must still distinguish $(\mathsf{pk}, c', k')$ from $(\mathsf{pk}, c', k^*)$. As the second step, this is argued impossible, since $k' = \mathsf{Decap}(c', \mathsf{sk})$ is *statistically uniform* over the choice of $\mathsf{sk}$, which is unknown to the adversary.

As Naor and Segev noticed in [NS09], this proof also works in the presence of leakage, since the first argument of replacing $(c, k)$ by $(c', k')$ holds even if the adversary saw *all of* $\mathsf{sk}$, and the second argument is *information-theoretic*, so we can argue that $\ell$ bits of leakage about $\mathsf{sk}$ will only reduce the statistical entropy of $k'$ by at most $\ell$ bits. Thus, as long as decapsulation $k'$ of the invalid ciphertext has $m > \ell$ bits of entropy without leakage, it will still have at least $(m - \ell)$ bits of entropy after the leakage (see Lemma 1). To agree on a uniform value $k$ in the presence of leakage, we just compose the HPS KEM with a randomness extractor [NZ96], such as a universal hash function.

---

[2] Our informal description and definition of HPS here is a simplified version of the standard one. Although the two are *not* technically equivalent, the standard definition implies ours, which is in-turn sufficient for leakage-resilience and captures the main essence of HPS.

The main benefit of this proof strategy is that, after switching valid/invalid ciphertexts in the first step, we can argue about leakage using a purely information-theoretic analysis.

Since HPS KEMs can be constructed from a variety of assumptions (see [NS09]), we can construct leakage-resilient KEMs and PKEs from many assumptions as well. We also mention that Alwen et al. [ADN+09] recently generalized the notion of HPS to the identity-based setting, which allowed them to construct leakage-resilient identity-based encryption (IBE) schemes in a similar manner (generalizing the prior LR-IBE construction from [AGV09]).

## 4    Bounded Retrieval Model

Now that we saw how to build many leakage-resilient primitives in the *relative-leakage model*, we would like to extend the constructions to the bounded retrieval model as well. In the BRM, we want to have the flexibility to allow for arbitrarily large leakage-bounds $\ell$, just by increasing the size of the secret, but without any other unnecessary affect on efficiency. The main question that we address in the BRM is one of *leakage-resilience amplification*: assuming we start with some $\ell$-leakage-resilient primitive in the relative-leakage model, how can we construct an $L$-leakage-resilient primitive for arbitrary values of $L \gg \ell$. Ideally, we would like to achieve leakage-resilience amplification with minimal efficiency degradation: even though the "secrets" of the scheme will need to be made potentially huge so that $L$ bits of leakage does not reveal the entire value, we want to make sure that the computational effort and public-key sizes *do not need to grow proportionally*. Following similar discussion in [ADN+09], we consider several approaches, and hone in on the right one. We put most of our discussion into the "toy example" of password authentication. However, this will be the simplest way to showcase the methodology, and the ideas used to construct identification schemes, signatures and public-key encryption in the BRM will be analogous.

### 4.1    Password Authentication in the BRM

Let us start with the question of building a leakage-resilient "password authentication scheme" (as described in Section 3.1) in the BRM. We now want to build such a scheme where, for any leakage bound $L$, we have a KeyGen() procedure that outputs a (pk, sk) pair where the client's password sk is made potentially *huge* depending on the leakage bound $L$. As a security guarantee, we would like to ensure that, given pk and $L$ bits of leakage about sk, it is infeasible to come up with any value sk' for which Verify(pk, sk') = 1. In addition, the efficiency requirements of the BRM dictate that the size of pk and the computation time of Verify(pk, sk) are *independent of* $L$. We start with the question of leakage-amplification and then address efficiency.

BAD APPROACH: ARTIFICIALLY INFLATING THE SECURITY PARAMETER. As we saw, many of the leakage-resilient primitives in the *relative-leakage model* have leakage-bounds $\ell(\lambda)$ being a large portion of the key-size $s(\lambda)$ which, in turn, depends on a security parameter $\lambda$. Therefore, one solution to leakage-amplification is to simply artificially inflate the security parameter $\lambda$ sufficiently, until $s(\lambda)$ and, correspondingly, $\ell(\lambda)$ reach the desired level of leakage $L$ we would like to tolerate. Unfortunately, it is clear that this approach gets extremely inefficient very fast – e.g. to allow for Gigabytes worth of leakage, we may need to perform exponentiations on group elements with Gigabyte-long description sizes.

NEW APPROACH: PARALLEL REPETITION. As an improvement over the previous suggestion, we propose an alternative which we call *parallel-repetition*. Assume we have a leakage-resilient scheme in the relative-leakage model, tolerating $\ell$-bits of leakage, for some small $\ell$. We can create a new "parallel-repetition scheme", by taking $n$ independent copies of the original scheme so that the new secret key $\overline{\text{sk}} = (\text{sk}_1, \ldots, \text{sk}_n)$ and the public key $\overline{\text{pk}} = (\text{pk}_1, \ldots, \text{pk}_n)$ consists of $n$ independently sampled keypairs of the original scheme. To run verify in the new scheme, the server simply runs Verify$(\text{pk}_i, \text{sk}_i)$ for each of the component keys individually and accepts if all runs are accepting. One may hope to show that, if the original scheme is $\ell$-leakage-resilient than the new construction is $L$-leakage resilient for $L = n\ell$. Intuitively, if an adversary gets $\leq L = n\ell$ bits of leakage in the new scheme, than there should be many values $\text{sk}_i$ for which the adversary learned less than $\ell$ bits and hence will be unable to come up with any "good value" $\text{sk}_i'$ that verifies for the $i$th position.

Unfortunately, it is far from clear how to prove the above intuition, if we only assume that the underlying scheme is $\ell$-leakage resilient. In particular, we would need a reduction showing how to use an adversary that expects $L$ bits of leakage on $\overline{\text{sk}}$ to break the underlying scheme given $\ell$ bits of leakage on some $\text{sk}_i$. Unfortunately, this seems impossible in general: if the adversary expects to learn the output of some complicated leakage function (for example a hash function) $H(\overline{\text{sk}})$ with $L$ bit output, it is unlikely that we can evaluate this function correctly by learning only some $h(\text{sk}_i)$ with $\ell$ bit output (even if we know all of $\text{sk}_j$ for $j \neq i$).

PARALLEL REPETITION OF SPR FUNCTIONS. To make leakage amplification via parallel repetition work, let us look more specifically at some concrete examples of leakage-resilient password authentication schemes. One such example (Theorem 2) consisted of using $\ell$-leakage-resilient OWF where each $\text{pk}_i = f(\text{sk}_i)$ for a uniformly random $\text{sk}_i$. In addition, we showed (Theorem 1) that SPR functions $f$ with loss $\mathcal{L}(f) \geq \ell + \omega(\log(\lambda))$ are $\ell$-leakage-resilient OWFs. It is fairly easy to see that $n$-wise parallel repetition of such a scheme based on an SPR function $f : D \to R$ yields a new SPR function $f' : D^n \to R^n$ with loss $\mathcal{L}(f') = n(\mathcal{L}(f))$. Therefore, we can show directly that parallel-repetition amplifies leakage in this special case, producing an $L = n\ell$-leakage-resilient "passwords authentication scheme".

EFFICIENCY IMPROVEMENT: RANDOM SUBSET SELECTION. To decrease the computational effort of the verification procedure, we have Verify$^*(\overline{\text{pk}}, \overline{\text{sk}})$ selects some random subset $\{r_1, \ldots, r_t\} \subseteq \{1 \ldots n\}$ of $t$ indices, and only run the original verification procedure Verify$(\text{pk}_{r_i}, \text{sk}_{r_i})$ for the $t$ selected key-pairs at indices $\{r_1, \ldots, r_t\}$. Here $t$ will be only proportional to the security parameter $\lambda$, and can be much smaller than the keys size (which depends on $n$).

EFFICIENCY IMPROVEMENT: PUBLIC-KEY SIZE REDUCTION. Using parallel-repetition and random-subset selection, we get a "password authentication scheme" which can be made $L$-leakage-resilient for arbitrarily large $L$, with the computational effort of verification only proportional to the security parameter $\lambda$ and not proportional to $L$. Unfortunately, the public-key size $\overline{\mathsf{pk}}$ is still large and proportional to the leakage-bound $L$. We can reduce the public-key in the following way:

- The new KeyGen$^*$ procedure of the BRM scheme generates $n$ pairs $(\mathsf{pk}_1, \mathsf{sk}_1), \ldots,$ $(\mathsf{pk}_n, \mathsf{sk}_n)$ of the underlying scheme in the relative-leakage model. It also generates a signing/verification key $(\mathsf{sigk}, \mathsf{verk})$ for a (standard, non-leakage-resilient) signature scheme and computes signatures $\sigma_i = \mathsf{Sign}_{\mathsf{sigk}}(\mathsf{pk}_i)$ for each $i = 1, \ldots, n$. It outputs $\mathsf{pk} = \mathsf{verk}$ and $\mathsf{sk} = (\mathsf{sk}_1, \ldots, \mathsf{sk}_n, \sigma_1, \ldots, \sigma_n)$.
- The new verification procedure Verify$^*(\mathsf{pk}, \mathsf{sk})$ of the BRM scheme selects $t$ random indices $r_i$ and, for each one verifies that $\mathsf{Verify}(\mathsf{pk}_{r_i}, \mathsf{sk}_{r_i}) = 1$ and also $\mathsf{Ver}_{\mathsf{verk}}(\mathsf{pk}_{r_i}, \sigma_i) = 1$.

The security of this scheme follows from that of the previous paragraph, given the unforgeability of the signature scheme (note that the signing key sigk is never stored by the client or server).

### 4.2 Identification Schemes and Signatures in the BRM

Recall that our main construction of leakage-resilient ID schemes was based on $\Sigma$-protocols for SPR functions. We can essentially use both techniques from the previous section to build leakage-resilient ID schemes in the BRM. This leads to the main construction given in [ADW09]. Essentially, the only difference between the identification scheme and the "password authentication" scheme from the previous section is that, instead of having the client simply "hand over" the secret keys $\mathsf{sk}_{r_i}$, the client runs $\Sigma$-protocols for the relation $\{(\mathsf{pk}, \mathsf{sk}) : \mathsf{pk} = f(\mathsf{sk})\}$. We leverage the fact that the $\Sigma$-protocol is Witness Indistinguishable, to argue that observing executions of the $\Sigma$-protocol does not reduce the entropy of sk from the point of view of the attacker.

Once we have ID schemes in the BRM, we can just use the Fiat-Shamir transform to get signature schemes in the BRM, as we showed in Section 3.3. We notice that Fiat-Shamir preserves the efficiency properties (public-key size, computational effort, communication complexity) of the ID scheme. However, to maintain short signatures and allow for large leakage, one must relax the standard notion of existential unforgeability to a slightly weaker notion of *entropic unforgeability*. As illustrated by [ADW09], this (necessarily) weaker notion is still sufficient for many applications, such as bulding a signature-based key exchange protocol in the BRM.

In [ADW09], it was shown that for some specific schemes, one can get additional efficiency improvements in the communication complexity (res. signature size) of BRM ID schemes (resp. signatures) by "compacting" the $t$ parallel runs of the $\Sigma$-protocol.

### 4.3 Public-Key Encryption in the BRM

The recent work of [ADN$^+$09] constructs public-key encryption and IBE schemes in the BRM. Again, one of the main components is to show that (a variant) of parallel-repetition can be used to amplify leakage-resilience for PKE schemes constructed out of Hash Proof Systems. Also, a variant of "random-subset selection" can be used to reduce encryption/decryption times and ciphertext sizes to be independent of the leakage bound $L$. It turns out that the main difficulty, however, is in reducing the public-key size. It is clear that our previous idea of signing the public-keys with a signature scheme and storing the signed values as part of the secret-key, will not work with PKE, where the encryptor needs to encrypt non-interactively, without talking to the decryptor. The difficulty is resolved using the idea of Identity Based Encryption (IBE), where there is a single master-public-key and many secret-keys for various identities. However, we still need the IBE to have the structure of an HPS scheme to prove leakage-resilience of the scheme and leakage-amplification via parallel repetition. Interestingly (variants of) several IBE schemes in the literature have an HPS-like structure. Such schemes can therefore be used to construct Public-Key Encryption schemes in the BRM. We refer to [ADN+09] for the details.

# References

[AABN02] Abdalla, M., An, J.H., Bellare, M., Namprempre, C.: From identification to signatures via the fiat-shamir transform: Minimizing assumptions for security and forward-security. In: Knudsen, L.R. (ed.) EUROCRYPT 2002. LNCS, vol. 2332, pp. 418–433. Springer, Heidelberg (2002)

[ADN+09] Alwen, J., Dodis, Y., Naor, M., Segev, G., Walfish, S., Wichs, D.: Public-key encryption in the bounded-retrival model (2009), http://eprint.iacr.org/2009/512

[ADR02] Aumann, Y., Ding, Y.Z., Rabin, M.O.: Everlasting security in the bounded storage model. IEEE Transactions on Information Theory 48(6), 1668–1680 (2002)

[ADW09] Alwen, J., Dodis, Y., Wichs, D.: Leakage-resilient public-key cryptography in the bounded-retrieval model. In: Halevi, S. (ed.) Advances in Cryptology - CRYPTO 2009. LNCS, vol. 5677, pp. 36–54. Springer, Heidelberg (2009)

[AGV09] Akavia, A., Goldwasser, S., Vaikuntanathan, V.: Simultaneous hardcore bits and cryptography against memory attacks. In: Reingold, O. (ed.) TCC 2009. LNCS, vol. 5444. Springer, Heidelberg (2009)

[AR99] Aumann, Y., Rabin, M.O.: Information theoretically secure communication in the limited storage space model. Wiener [Wie99], pp. 65–79 (1999)

[BBCM95] Bennett, C.H., Brassard, G., Crépeau, C., Maurer, U.M.: Generalized privacy amplification. IEEE Transactions on Information Theory 41(6), 1915–1923 (1995)

[BBR88] Bennett, C.H., Brassard, G., Robert, J.-M.: Privacy amplification by public discussion. SIAM J. Comput. 17(2), 210–229 (1988)

[BDL97] Boneh, D., DeMillo, R.A., Lipton, R.J.: On the importance of checking cryptographic protocols for faults (extended abstract). In: Fumy, W. (ed.) EUROCRYPT 1997. LNCS, vol. 1233, pp. 37–51. Springer, Heidelberg (1997)

[BM93] Bellovin, S.M., Merritt, M.: Augmented encrypted key exchange: A password-based protocol secure against dictionary attacks and password file compromise. In: ACM Conference on Computer and Communications Security, pp. 244–250 (1993)

[BMP00] Boyko, V., MacKenzie, P.D., Patel, S.: Provably secure password-authenticated key exchange using diffie-hellman. In: Preneel, B. (ed.) EUROCRYPT 2000. LNCS, vol. 1807, pp. 156–171. Springer, Heidelberg (2000)

[Bon03] Boneh, D. (ed.): CRYPTO 2003. LNCS, vol. 2729. Springer, Heidelberg (2003)

[BPR00] Bellare, M., Pointcheval, D., Rogaway, P.: Authenticated key exchange secure against dictionary attacks. In: Preneel, B. (ed.) EUROCRYPT 2000. LNCS, vol. 1807, pp. 139–155. Springer, Heidelberg (2000)

[Bri93] Brickell, E.F. (ed.): CRYPTO 1992. LNCS, vol. 740. Springer, Heidelberg (1993)

[BS97] Biham, E., Shamir, A.: Differential fault analysis of secret key cryptosystems. In: Jr. [Jr.97], pp. 513–525 (1997)

[CDD+07]  Cash, D., Ding, Y.Z., Dodis, Y., Lee, W., Lipton, R.J., Walfish, S.: Intrusion-resilient key exchange in the bounded retrieval model. In: Vadhan, S.P. (ed.) TCC 2007. LNCS, vol. 4392, pp. 479–498. Springer, Heidelberg (2007)

[CDH+00]  Canetti, R., Dodis, Y., Halevi, S., Kushilevitz, E., Sahai, A.: Exposure-resilient functions and all-or-nothing transforms. In: Preneel, B. (ed.) EUROCRYPT 2000. LNCS, vol. 1807, pp. 453–469. Springer, Heidelberg (2000)

[CDS94]  Cramer, R., Damgård, I., Schoenmakers, B.: Proofs of partial knowledge and simplified design of witness hiding protocols. In: Desmedt, Y.G. (ed.) CRYPTO 1994. LNCS, vol. 839, pp. 174–187. Springer, Heidelberg (1994)

[CLW06]  Di Crescenzo, G., Lipton, R.J., Walfish, S.: Perfectly secure password protocols in the bounded retrieval model. In: Halevi, Rabin (eds.) [HR06], pp. 225–244 (2006)

[CS02]  Cramer, R., Shoup, V.: Universal hash proofs and a paradigm for adaptive chosen ciphertext secure public-key encryption. In: Knudsen, L.R. (ed.) EUROCRYPT 2002. LNCS, vol. 2332, pp. 45–64. Springer, Heidelberg (2002)

[CS04]  Cramer, R., Shoup, V.: Design and analysis of practical public-key encryption schemes secure against adaptive chosen ciphertext attack. SIAM J. Comput. 33(1), 167–226 (2004)

[DGK+09]  Dodis, Y., Goldwasser, S., Kalai, Y., Peikert, C., Vaikuntanathan, V.: Public-key encryption schemes with auxiliary inputs (2009)

[DKL09]  Dodis, Y., Kalai, Y.T., Lovett, S.: On cryptography with auxiliary input. In: STOC, pp. 621–630 (2009)

[DKRS06]  Dodis, Y., Katz, J., Reyzin, L., Smith, A.: Robust fuzzy extractors and authenticated key agreement from close secrets. In: Dwork, C. (ed.) CRYPTO 2006. LNCS, vol. 4117, pp. 232–250. Springer, Heidelberg (2006)

[DORS08]  Dodis, Y., Ostrovsky, R., Reyzin, L., Smith, A.: Fuzzy extractors: How to generate strong keys from biometrics and other noisy data. SIAM J. Comput. 38(1), 97–139 (2008)

[DP07]  Dziembowski, S., Pietrzak, K.: Intrusion-resilient secret sharing. In: FOCS, pp. 227–237. IEEE Computer Society, Los Alamitos (2007)

[DP08]  Dziembowski, S., Pietrzak, K.: Leakage-resilient cryptography. In: FOCS, pp. 293–302. IEEE Computer Society, Los Alamitos (2008)

[DSS01]  Dodis, Y., Sahai, A., Smith, A.: On perfect and adaptive security in exposure-resilient cryptography. In: Pfitzmann, B. (ed.) EUROCRYPT 2001. LNCS, vol. 2045, pp. 301–324. Springer, Heidelberg (2001)

[DW09]  Dodis, Y., Wichs, D.: Non-malleable extractors and symmetric key cryptography from weak secrets. In: STOC (2009), Full version, http://eprint.iacr.org/2008/503

[Dzi06]  Dziembowski, S.: Intrusion-resilience via the bounded-storage model. In: Halevi, Rabin (eds.) [HR06], pp. 207–224 (2006)

[FKPR09]  Faust, S., Kiltz, E., Pietrzak, K., Rothblum, G.: Leakage-resilient signatures (2009), http://eprint.iacr.org/2009/282

[FRT09]  Faust, S., Reyzin, L., Tromer, E.: Protecting circuits from computationally-bounded leakage. Cryptology ePrint Archive, Report 2009/379 (2009), http://eprint.iacr.org/

[FS86]  Fiat, A., Shamir, A.: How to prove yourself: Practical solutions to identification and signature problems. In: Odlyzko, A.M. (ed.) CRYPTO 1986. LNCS, vol. 263, pp. 186–194. Springer, Heidelberg (1987)

[FS89]  Feige, U., Shamir, A.: Zero Knowledge Proofs of Knowledge in Two Rounds. In: Brassard, G. (ed.) CRYPTO 1989. LNCS, vol. 435, pp. 526–544. Springer, Heidelberg (1990)

[GL06]    Goldreich, O., Lindell, Y.: Session-key generation using human passwords only. J. Cryptology 19(3), 241–340 (2006)

[GMO01]   Gandolfi, K., Mourtel, C., Olivier, F.: Electromagnetic analysis: Concrete results. In: Koç, Ç.K., Naccache, D., Paar, C. (eds.) CHES 2001. LNCS, vol. 2162, pp. 251–261. Springer, Heidelberg (2001)

[GMW91]   Goldreich, O., Micali, S., Wigderson, A.: Proofs that yield nothing but their validity for all languages in np have zero-knowledge proof systems. J. ACM 38(3), 691–729 (1991)

[HR06]    Halevi, S., Rabin, T. (eds.): TCC 2006. LNCS, vol. 3876, pp. 1–20. Springer, Heidelberg (2006)

[HSH$^+$08]  Alex Halderman, J., Schoen, S.D., Heninger, N., Clarkson, W., Paul, W., Calandrino, J.A., Feldman, A.J., Appelbaum, J., Felten, E.W.: Lest we remember: Cold boot attacks on encryption keys. In: van Oorschot, P.C. (ed.) USENIX Security Symposium, pp. 45–60. USENIX Association (2008)

[IPSW06]  Ishai, Y., Prabhakaran, M., Sahai, A., Wagner, D.: Private circuits ii: Keeping secrets in tamperable circuits. In: Vaudenay, S. (ed.) EUROCRYPT 2006. LNCS, vol. 4004, pp. 308–327. Springer, Heidelberg (2006)

[ISW03]   Ishai, Y., Sahai, A., Wagner, D.: Private circuits: Securing hardware against probing attacks. In: Boneh [Bon03], pp. 463–481 (2003)

[Jr.97]   Kaliski Jr., B.S. (ed.): CRYPTO 1997. LNCS, vol. 1294, pp. 1–15. Springer, Heidelberg (1997)

[KJJ99]   Kocher, P.C., Jaffe, J., Jun, B.: Differential power analysis. In: Wiener [Wie99], pp. 388–397 (1999)

[Koc96]   Kocher, P.C.: Timing attacks on implementations of diffie-hellman, RSA, DSS, and other systems. In: Koblitz, N. (ed.) CRYPTO 1996. LNCS, vol. 1109, pp. 104–113. Springer, Heidelberg (1996)

[KOY01]   Katz, J., Ostrovsky, R., Yung, M.: Efficient password-authenticated key exchange using human-memorable passwords. In: Pfitzmann, B. (ed.) EUROCRYPT 2001. LNCS, vol. 2045, pp. 475–494. Springer, Heidelberg (2001)

[KPSY09]  Kiltz, E., Pietrzak, K., Stam, M., Yung, M.: A new randomness extraction paradigm for hybrid encryption. In: Ghilardi, S. (ed.) EUROCRYPT 2009. LNCS, vol. 5479, pp. 590–609. Springer, Heidelberg (2009)

[KR09]    Kanukurthi, B., Reyzin, L.: Key agreement from close secrets over unsecured channels. In: Joux, A. (ed.) EUROCRYPT 2009. LNCS, vol. 5479. Springer, Heidelberg (2009), Full version, http://eprint.iacr.org/2008/494

[KV09]    Katz, J., Vaikuntanathan, V.: Signature schemes with bounded leakage resilience. In: Matsui, M. (ed.) ASIACRYPT 2009. LNCS, vol. 5912. Springer, Heidelberg (2009), http://www.mit.edu/ vinodv/papers/asiacrypt09/KV-Sigs.pdf

[Lam79]   Lamport, L.: Constructing digital signatures from a one-way function. Technical report, SRI International (October 1979)

[Lu02]    Lu, C.-J.: Hyper-encryption against space-bounded adversaries from on-line strong extractors. In: Yung, M. (ed.) CRYPTO 2002. LNCS, vol. 2442, pp. 257–271. Springer, Heidelberg (2002)

[Mau92a]  Maurer, U.M.: Conditionally-perfect secrecy and a provably-secure randomized cipher. J. Cryptology 5(1), 53–66 (1992)

[Mau92b]  Maurer, U.M.: Protocols for secret key agreement by public discussion based on common information. In: Brickell [Bri93], pp. 461–470 (1993)

[MR04]    Micali, S., Reyzin, L.: Physically observable cryptography (extended abstract). In: Naor, M. (ed.) TCC 2004. LNCS, vol. 2951, pp. 278–296. Springer, Heidelberg (2004)

[MW97]    Maurer, U.M., Wolf, S.: Privacy amplification secure against active adversaries. In: Jr. [Jr.97], pp. 307–321 (1997)

[NS09]    Naor, M., Segev, G.: Public-key cryptosystems resilient to key leakage. In: Halevi, S. (ed.) Advances in Cryptology - CRYPTO 2009. LNCS, vol. 5677, pp. 18–35. Springer, Heidelberg (2009), http://eprint.iacr.org/2009/105

[NY89]    Naor, M., Yung, M.: Universal one-way hash functions and their cryptographic applications. In: STOC, pp. 33–43. ACM, New York (1989)

[NZ96]    Nisan, N., Zuckerman, D.: Randomness is linear in space. J. Comput. Syst. Sci. 52(1), 43–52 (1996)

[Oka92]    Okamoto, T.: Provably secure and practical identification schemes and corresponding signature schemes. In: Brickell[Bri93], pp. 31–53 (1993)

[Pie09]    Pietrzak, K.: A leakage-resilient mode of operation. In: Eurocrypt 2009, Cologne, Germany, pp. 462–482 (2009)

[QS01]    Quisquater, J.-J., Samyde, D.: Electromagnetic analysis (ema): Measures and counter-measures for smart cards. In: Attali, S., Jensen, T. (eds.) E-smart 2001. LNCS, vol. 2140, pp. 200–210. Springer, Heidelberg (2001)

[Reg05]    Regev, O.: On lattices, learning with errors, random linear codes, and cryptography. In: Gabow, H.N., Fagin, R. (eds.) STOC, pp. 84–93. ACM, New York (2005)

[Rom90]    Rompel, J.: One-way functions are necessary and sufficient for secure signatures. In: STOC, pp. 387–394. ACM, New York (1990)

[RW03]    Renner, R., Wolf, S.: Unconditional authenticity and privacy from an arbitrarily weak secret. In: Boneh[Bon03], pp. 78–95 (2003)

[Vad04]    Vadhan, S.P.: Constructing locally computable extractors and cryptosystems in the bounded-storage model. J. Cryptology 17(1), 43–77 (2004)

[Wie99]    Wiener, M. (ed.): CRYPTO 1999. LNCS, vol. 1666. Springer, Heidelberg (1999)

# A Lower Bound on the Key Length of Information-Theoretic Forward-Secure Storage Schemes

Stefan Dziembowski*

Department of Computer Science
University of Rome, *La Sapienza*

**Abstract.** *Forward-Secure Storage* (FSS) was introduced by Dziembowski (CRYPTO 2006). Informally, FSS is an encryption scheme (Encr, Decr) that has the following non-standard property: even if the adversary learns the value of some function $h$ of the ciphertext $C = \mathrm{Encr}(K, M)$, he should have essentially no information on the corresponding plaintext $M$, even if he knows the key $K$. The only restriction is that $h$ is *input-shrinking*, i.e. $|h(R)| \leq \sigma$, where $\sigma$ is some parameter such that $\sigma \leq |C|$.

We study the problem of minimizing the length of the secret key in the IT-secure FSS, and we establish an almost optimal lower bound on the length of the secret key. The secret key of the FSS scheme of Dziembowski has length $|M| + O(\log \sigma)$. We show that in every FSS the secret key needs to have length at least $|M| + \log_2 \sigma - O(\log_2 \log_2 \sigma)$.

## 1 Introduction

*Forward-Secure Storage* (FSS) was introduced by Dziembowski in [5]. Informally, FSS is an encryption scheme (Encr, Decr) that has the following non-standard property: if the adversary has only partial information about the ciphertext $C = \mathrm{Encr}(K, M)$, he should have essentially no information on the corresponding plaintext $M$, even if he learns the key $K$. Here, "partial information" means that the adversary knows some value $U = h(C)$, where $h$ is chosen by him. The only restriction is that $h$ is *input-shrinking*, i.e. $|U| \leq \sigma$, where $\sigma$ is some parameter such that $\sigma \leq |C|$. In the security definition one assumes that $h$ has to be chosen *before* the adversary learns $K$ (as otherwise he could simply choose $h$ to be the function that decrypts $M$ from $C$). Since usually one wants to construct schemes that are secure for large values of $\sigma$, and since obviously $\sigma < |C|$, therefore normally $\mathrm{Encr}(K, M)$ is much longer than $M$.

Originally FSS was proposed in the context of the so-called *Bounded-Storage Model (BSM)*[1] [4,3,5,7,10,2] as a tool for increasing security of data stored on

---

* The European Research Council has provided financial support under the European Community's Seventh Framework Programme (FP7/2007-2013) / ERC grant agreement no 207908.

[1] In [5] this model was called a *Limited Communication Model*.

the machines that can be attacked by internet viruses. In this model one assumes that the ciphertext $C$ is stored on a PC on which the adversary can install a virus. The virus may perform any computation on $C$ but he can communicate to the adversary only a value $|h(C)| \leq \sigma$. The practical relevance of this assumption comes from the fact that in many cases it may be hard to retrieve large amounts of data from an infected machine. Since in practice the length of $C$ needs to be huge (several gigabytes) it is often required that it should be possible to decrypt $M$ just by reading a small number of the bits of $C$.

Another application of FSS is to use it for storing data on hardware that can leak information via the so-called side-channel attacks, which are the attacks based on measuring the power consumption, electromagnetic radiation, timing information, etc. As before, one can model such an attack by allowing the adversary to compute some input-shrinking function on ciphertext (this method was also used, in a different context in [8,1,11]). The only difference is that usually the size of the secret data stored on the device is much smaller, and hence there is no need to require that only a small portion of $C$ has to be read to decrypt the message.

In this paper we study the problem of constructing FSS schemes that are information-theoretically (IT) secure, which means that the computing power of the adversary is not limited, and there is no restriction on the computational complexity of the function $h$. Such an IT-secure FSS scheme was already constructed in [5] (besides of this, [5] considers also computationally-secure and so-called hybrid-secure schemes).

*Our contribution:* In this paper we revisit the IT-secure FSS construction of [5], and establish an almost optimal lower bound on the length of the secret key. The secret key of the FSS scheme of [5] has length $|M| + O(\log \sigma)$ (if built using an appropriate randomness extractor). Obviously, since FSS has to be secure as an information-theoretically encryption scheme, by Shannon's theorem the length of the key has to be at least $|M|$, one may ask, however, if the $O(\log \sigma)$ term is necessary. In this paper we show that that the construction of [5] is essentially optimal, by proving (cf. Corollary 1) that in every secure FSS the secret key needs to have length at least $|M| + \log_2 \sigma - O(\log_2 \log_2 \sigma)$.

## 2   FSS — The Formal Definition

Formally, a *Forward-Secure Storage (FSS)* scheme is a pair of randomized algorithms $\Phi = (\mathrm{Encr}, \mathrm{Decr})$. The algorithm Encr takes as input a *key* $K \in \mathcal{K}$ and a *plaintext* $M \in \mathcal{M}$ and outputs a *ciphertext* $C \in \mathcal{C}$. The algorithm Decr takes as input a key $K$ and a ciphertext $C$, and it outputs a string $M'$. The following correctness property has to be satisfied with probability 1: $\mathrm{Decr}(K, \mathrm{Encr}(K, M)) = M$.

To define the security of an FSS scheme consider a $\sigma$-*adversary* $\mathcal{A}$ (that we model as a Turing Machine), that plays the following game against an oracle $\Omega$.

---

FSS - distinguishing game

1. The adversary produces two messages $M^0, M^1 \in \{0,1\}^\mu$ and sends them to $\Omega$.
2. $\Omega$ selects a random key $K \in \{0,1\}^\kappa$, a random bit $b \in \{0,1\}$ and computes $C = \text{Encr}(K, M^b)$.
3. The adversary gets access to $C$ and can compute an arbitrary value $U = h(C)$ such that $|U| \leq \sigma$. The adversary can store $U$, but he is not allowed to store any other information.
4. The adversary learns $K$ and has to guess $b$.

We say that an adversary $\mathcal{A}$ *breaks the scheme* $\Phi$ *with an advantage* $\epsilon$ if his probability of winning the game is $1/2 + \epsilon$. We say that an FSS scheme $\Phi$ is $(\epsilon, \sigma)$-*IT-secure* if every $\sigma$-adversary $\mathcal{A}$ breaks $\Phi$ with advantage at most $\epsilon$. Without loss of generality we can assume that $\mathcal{A}$ is deterministic. This is because a computationally-unlimited deterministic adversary can always compute the optimal randomness for the randomized adversary.[2]

## 3    FSS — The Construction of [5]

### 3.1    Probability-Theoretic Preliminaries

Let random variables $X_0, X_1, X_2$ be distributed over some set $\mathcal{X}$ and let $Y$ be a random variable distributed over $\mathcal{Y}$. Define the *statistical distance between* $X_0$ *and* $X_1$ as $\delta(X_0; X_1) = \frac{1}{2} \sum_{x \in \mathcal{X}} |P(X_0 = x) - P(X_1 = x)|$. If $X$ is distributed over $\mathcal{X}$ then let $d(X) := \delta(X; U_\mathcal{X})$ denote the *statistical distance of $X$ from a uniform distribution (over $\mathcal{X}$)*. Moreover, $d(X_0|X_1) = \delta((X_0, X_1); (U_\mathcal{X}, X_1))$ denotes the statistical distance of $X_0$ from a uniform distribution *given* $X_1$. It is easy to verify that

$$d(X_0|X_1) = \sum_x d(X_0|X_1 = x) \cdot P(X_1 = x), \tag{1}$$

and that the triangle inequality $(\delta(X_0, X_1) \leq \delta(X_0, X_2) + \delta(X_2, X_1))$ holds. We will overload the symbols $\delta$ and $d$ and sometimes apply them to the probability distributions instead of the random variables. A *min-entropy* $\mathbf{H}_\infty$ *of a random variable* $R$ is defined as

$$\mathbf{H}_\infty(R) := \min_r \log_2(P(R = r)).$$

A function $\text{ext} : \{0,1\}^\rho \times \{0,1\}^\kappa \to \{0,1\}^\mu$ is an $(\epsilon, n)$-*extractor* if for any $R$ with $\mathbf{H}_\infty(R) \geq n$ and $K$ distributed uniformly over $\{0,1\}^\kappa$ we have that $d(\text{ext}(R, K)|K) \leq \epsilon$ (see e.g. [14] for an introduction to the theory of extractors).

---

[2] More precisely suppose that $\mathcal{A}$ takes some random input $\varrho_\mathcal{A}$ and the oracle takes some random input $\varrho_\Omega$. Let $p$ denote the probability (taken over $\varrho_\mathcal{A}$ and $\varrho_\Omega$) that $\mathcal{A}(\varrho_\mathcal{A})$ wins the game. Then there has to exist randomness $r$ such that $\mathcal{A}(r)$ wins with probability $p$. A computationally-unlimited adversary can find this $r$.

## 3.2   The Construction

The construction of the IT-secure FSS scheme of [5] used as a building-block a special type of randomness extractors called BSM-secure-functions, where BSM stands for the *Bounded-Storage Model* (see [13,6,12,15]). The need to use this special type of extractors came from the fact that originally FSS was proposed as a primitive in the Bounded-Retrieval Model, were it is crucial that the decryption function does not need to read the entire ciphertext. To be more general, in this paper we drop this assumption, and build an FSS scheme using any randomness extractor.

For completeness, in this section we review the construction [5], and prove that it is secure (this security argument appeared already implicitly in [5]). Let $\mu$ denote the length of the plaintext $M$ and let $\text{ext} : \{0,1\}^\rho \times \{0,1\}^\kappa \to \{0,1\}^\mu$ be an $(\epsilon, \rho - \sigma - \alpha)$-extractor (for any parameter $\alpha$). The key for an FSS scheme is a pair $(K_0, K_1)$, where $|K_0| = \kappa$ and $|K_1| = \mu$, and the encryption procedure is defined as $\text{Encr}((K_0, K_1), M) := (R, \text{ext}(R, K_0) \oplus K_1 \oplus M)$, where $R \in \{0,1\}^\rho$ is uniformly random. The decryption is defined as $\text{Decr}((K_0, K_1), (R, X)) = \text{ext}(R, K_0) \oplus K_1 \oplus X$.

**Lemma 1.** *The* $(\text{Encr}, \text{Decr})$ *scheme constructed above is* $(2\epsilon + 2^{-\alpha}, \sigma)$-*IT-secure.*

Before proving this lemma we show the following.

**Lemma 2.** *Modify the distinguishing game from Sect. 2 in the following way. The adversary (that we will call a* weak *adversary), instead of getting access to the entire ciphertext* $C = (R, \text{ext}(R, K_0) \oplus K_1 \oplus M)$ *(in Step 3) gets only access to* $R$*, and then in Step 4 he gets* $K_0$ *and* $\text{ext}(R, K_0) \oplus M^b$*. Then any* $\sigma$-*adversary wins this game (i.e. guesses* $b$ *correctly) with probability at most* $1/2 + 2^{-\alpha} + 2\epsilon$.

*Proof.* Let $y = h(R)$ be the value that the adversary retrieves in Step 3. We first show that

$$P\left(\mathbf{H}_\infty(R|h(R = y) \leq \rho - \sigma - \alpha\right) \leq 2^{-\alpha}. \tag{2}$$

Since $|h(R)| \leq \sigma$, hence the number of all $y$'s is at most equal to $2^\sigma$. Therefore the number of $r$'s for which there exists some $y$ such that

$$|\{r : h(r = y)\}| \leq 2^{\rho - \sigma - \alpha} \tag{3}$$

is at most $2^{\rho - \sigma - \alpha} \cdot 2^\sigma = 2^{\rho - \alpha}$. Hence the probability that it exists for a *random* $r \in \{0,1\}^\rho$ is at most $2^{\rho - \alpha}/2^\rho = 2^{-\alpha}$. Clearly, since $R$ is distributed uniformly, we have that if $y$ is such that (3) holds then

$$\mathbf{H}_\infty(R|h(R = y)) \leq \rho - \sigma - \alpha. \tag{4}$$

Thus (2) is proven. Now, since ext in an $(\epsilon, \rho - \sigma - \alpha)$-extractor, we have that if $y$ is such that $\mathbf{H}_\infty(R|h(R = y)) \leq \rho - \sigma - \alpha$ then $d(\text{ext}(R, K_0)|K, h(R) = y) \leq \epsilon$. Therefore in this case from the point of view of the adversary $M^b$ is simply encrypted with a one-time pad $X = \text{ext}(R, K_0)$ such that $d(X) \leq \epsilon$. In [6] (Lemma 7) it is shown that if this is the case then the adversary can distinguish between the ciphertexts $M^0 \oplus X$ and $M^1 \oplus X$ (for any messages $M^0$ and $M^1$) with an advantage at most $2d(X)$. Therefore the total advantage of the adversary is at most

$$P\left(\mathbf{H}_\infty(R|h(R=y) \le \rho - \sigma - \alpha\right) \cdot 1 + 2d(X)$$
$$\le 2^{-\alpha} + 2\epsilon.$$

We are now ready for the proof of Lemma 1.

*Proof (of Lemma 1).* We show that if there exists an adversary $\mathcal{A}$ that breaks (Encr, Decr) with probability $\xi$ then there exists a weak adversary $\mathcal{A}'$ that breaks (Encr, Decr) with probability $\xi$. Clearly by Lemma 2, showing this will finish the proof.

The adversary $\mathcal{A}'$ simulates $\mathcal{A}$ in the following way. First, he starts $\mathcal{A}$ and forwards to the oracle the messages $M^0$ and $M^1$ that $\mathcal{A}$ produces. Then, when he gets access to $R$ he chooses a uniformly random string $Z \in \{0,1\}^\mu$ and gives $(R, Z)$ to $\mathcal{A}$. Later (in Step 4), when he receives $K$ and $X = \text{ext}(R, K_0) \oplus M^b$ he sets $K_0 = K$ and $K_1 = X \oplus Z$ (hence: $K_1 = \text{ext}(R, K_0) \oplus M^b \oplus Z$) and gives $(K_0, K_1)$ to $\mathcal{A}$. At the end $\mathcal{A}'$ outputs the bit $b$ that $\mathcal{A}$ outputs.

Set $T := \text{ext}(R, K_0) \oplus M^b$ and observe that in the original game $\mathcal{A}$ can see the following random variables

$$R, K_0, K_1, T \oplus K_1 \tag{5}$$

(where $K_0, K_1, R$ are uniformly random and independent) and in our simulation we have

$$R, K_0, T \oplus Z, Z \tag{6}$$

(where $K_0, R, Z$ are uniformly random and independent). Obviously the variables in (5) and (6) have an identical joint distribution, and therefore the simulated $\mathcal{A}$ guesses $b$ correctly with the same probability as $\mathcal{A}$ in a normal execution. Hence the probability that $\mathcal{A}$ wins is equal to the probability that $\mathcal{A}'$ wins.  □

Since randomness extractors with seed of length $O(\log k)$ are known (see e.g. [14]), in particular the non-explicit extractor that extracts almost all the entropy has seed of length $\log k + O(1)$, therefore we can conclude that there exists a $(\delta, \sigma)$-IT-secure FSS scheme with key of length $|M| + O(\log |R|)$ and $\delta$ being a small constant. Since one can also construct extractors where $\sigma$ is a constant fraction of $|R|$ we get that one can construct a $(\delta, \sigma)$-IT-secure FSS scheme with key of length $|M| + O(\log \sigma)$.

## 4   The Lower Bound

In this section we present the main result of the paper. We start with the following lemma.

**Lemma 3.** *Let $\Phi = (\mathrm{Encr}, \mathrm{Decr})$ be an FSS scheme. Suppose the set $\mathcal{K}$ of the keys is equal to $\{0,1\}^\kappa$, for some parameter $\kappa$. There exists a $\sigma$-adversary $\mathcal{A}$ that breaks $\Phi$ with advantage at least $1/4$, for*

$$\sigma = \frac{\kappa \cdot 2^{\kappa+1}}{|\mathcal{M}|} + 1. \tag{7}$$

*Proof.* We construct $\mathcal{A}$ as follows. For every message $M$ and a ciphertext $C$ let

$$\mathcal{K}_{M,C} := \{K : P\left(\mathrm{Encr}(K, M) = C\right) > 0\}.$$

Of course a computationally-unlimited machine can always compute $\mathcal{K}_{M,C}$ for given $M, C$, by just examining all possible $K$'s and all possible random inputs of the Encr algorithm. Clearly, from the correctness of the decryption, for any $C$ and any two distinct messages $M^0$ and $M^1$ we have that

$$\mathcal{K}_{M^0,C} \cap \mathcal{K}_{M^1,C} = \emptyset. \tag{8}$$

Set $x := (\sigma - 1)/\kappa$. Therefore from (7) we have

$$x = 2^{\kappa+1}/|\mathcal{M}|. \tag{9}$$

The strategy of $\mathcal{A}$ is as follows. First, he chooses two messages $M^0$ and $M^1$ (such that $M^0 \neq M^1$) uniformly at random. He sends $M^0, M^1$ to the oracle. After receiving $C = \mathrm{Encr}(K, M^b)$ the adversary determines $\mathcal{K}_{M^0,C}$ and $\mathcal{K}_{M^1,C}$ and checks if for some $b' \in \{0,1\}$ it is the case that $|\mathcal{K}_{M^{b'},C}| \leq x$ (if it holds for both $b' = 0, 1$ then he chooses $b'$ arbitrarily). Denote this even with $\mathcal{E}$. If such $b'$ does not exist then he sets $U$ to be equal to an empty string. Otherwise he sets $U$ to be equal to $(\tilde{U}, b')$ where $\tilde{U}$ is the binary representation of $\mathcal{K}_{M^{b'},C}$. Clearly, $\mathcal{K}_{M^{b'},C}$ can be represented (just by listing all its elements) with $|\mathcal{K}_{M^{b'},C}| \cdot \kappa = \sigma - 1$ bits, so $U$ has length at most $\sigma$.

After learning $K$ the adversary does the following:

1. if $\mathcal{E}$ did not occurr, i.e. $U$ is an empty string then he outputs $b$ uniformly at random,
2. otherwise suppose $U = (\tilde{U}, b')$. The adversary checks if $K$ is a member of the set that $\tilde{U}$ represents. If yes, then he outputs $b'$, otherwise he outputs $1 - b'$.

Clearly in the first case the probability that the adversary guesses $b$ correctly is equal to $1/2$. It follows from (8) that in second case the probability that he guesses $b$ correctly is equal to $1$. Hence, the total probability that the adversary guesses $b$ correctly is equal to

$$1/2 \cdot (1 - P\left(\mathcal{E}\right)) + 1 \cdot P\left(\mathcal{E}\right)$$
$$= 1/2 + 1/2 \cdot P\left(\mathcal{E}\right)$$

Therefore he wins the game with advantage $1/2 \cdot P\left(\mathcal{E}\right)$. Thus it remains to give a bound on the probability of $\mathcal{E}$, or in other words, to bound the following probability:

$$P\left(\text{there exists } b' \text{ such that } |\mathcal{K}_{M^{b'},C}| \leq x\right). \tag{10}$$

From (8) it follows that for every $C$ we have that

$$\sum_{M \in \mathcal{M}} |\mathcal{K}_{M,C}| = \left| \bigcup_M \mathcal{K}_{M,C} \right| \leq 2^\kappa.$$

Hence, for a randomly chosen $M$ the probability that $|\mathcal{K}_{M,C}| \geq x$ is at most equal to $2^\kappa/(x \cdot |\mathcal{M}|)$, which, from (9) is at most equal to $1/2$. We now observe that $M^{1-b}$ is distributed completely uniformly given $C$ (since $C$ is a function of $M^b$ and $K)^3$. Therefore the probability that $|\mathcal{K}_{M^{1-b},C}| \geq x$ is at most equal to $2^\kappa/(x \cdot |\mathcal{M}|)$. This implies that the (10) is at least $1/2$. Hence, the adversary wins the game with advantage at least $1/4$.                                □

**Corollary 1.** *For every $\sigma$ consider a family of FSS schemes that is $(1/4, \sigma)$-secure. Suppose $\mathcal{M} = \{0,1\}^\mu$ (where $\mu$ is constant) and $\mathcal{K} = \{0,1\}^\kappa$. Then*

$$\kappa \geq \mu + \log_2 \sigma - O(\log_2 \log_2 \sigma). \tag{11}$$

*Proof.* From Lemma 3 we get that

$$\sigma \leq \frac{\kappa \cdot 2^{\kappa+1}}{2^\mu} + 1.$$

This implies that:

$$\kappa \geq \mu + \underbrace{\log_2(\sigma - 1) - 1}_{\log_2(\sigma) + O(1)} - \underbrace{\log_2 \kappa}_{(*)} \tag{12}$$

Since we can assume that $\kappa \leq \mu + \log_2 \sigma$ (as otherwise (11) is proven), we get that $(\star)$ is $O(\log_2 \log_2 \sigma)$. Hence (11) is proven.                                □

# References

1. Akavia, A., Goldwasser, S., Vaikuntanathan, V.: Simultaneous hardcore bits and cryptography against memory attacks. In: Reingold, O. (ed.) TCC 2009. LNCS, vol. 5444, pp. 474–495. Springer, Heidelberg (2009)
2. Cash, D., Ding, Y.Z., Dodis, Y., Lee, W., Lipton, R.J., Walfish, S.: Intrusion-resilient key exchange in the bounded retrieval model. In: Vadhan, S.P. (ed.) TCC 2007. LNCS, vol. 4392, pp. 479–498. Springer, Heidelberg (2007)
3. Di Crescenzo, G., Lipton, R.J., Walfish, S.: Perfectly secure password protocols in the bounded retrieval model. In: Halevi, S., Rabin, T. (eds.) TCC 2006. LNCS, vol. 3876, pp. 225–244. Springer, Heidelberg (2006)
4. Dziembowski, S.: Intrusion-resilience via the bounded-storage model. In: Halevi, S., Rabin, T. (eds.) TCC 2006. LNCS, vol. 3876, pp. 207–224. Springer, Heidelberg (2006)
5. Dziembowski, S.: On forward-secure storage. In: Dwork, C. (ed.) CRYPTO 2006. LNCS, vol. 4117, pp. 251–270. Springer, Heidelberg (2006)

---

[3] Note that this does not necessarily hold for $M^b$, since $M^b$ can slightly depend on $C$.

6. Dziembowski, S., Maurer, U.M.: On generating the initial key in the bounded-storage model. In: Cachin, C., Camenisch, J.L. (eds.) EUROCRYPT 2004. LNCS, vol. 3027, pp. 126–137. Springer, Heidelberg (2004)
7. Dziembowski, S., Pietrzak, K.: Intrusion-resilient secret sharing. In: FOCS, pp. 227–237 (2007)
8. Dziembowski, S., Pietrzak, K.: Leakage-resilient cryptography. In: 49th Annual IEEE Symposium on Foundations of Computer Science, FOCS 2008, Philadelphia, PA, USA, October 25-28, pp. 293–302. IEEE Computer Society, Los Alamitos (2008)
9. Halevi, S., Rabin, T. (eds.): TCC 2006. LNCS, vol. 3876. Springer, Heidelberg (2006)
10. Alwen, Y.D.J., Wichs, D.: Leakage resilient public-key cryptography in the bounded retrieval model. In: Halevi, S. (ed.) Advances in Cryptology - CRYPTO 2009. LNCS, vol. 5677, pp. 36–54. Springer, Heidelberg (2009)
11. Katz, J.: Signature schemes with bounded leakage resilience. Cryptology ePrint Archive, Report 2009/220 (2009), http://eprint.iacr.org/
12. Lu, C.-J.: Encryption against storage-bounded adversaries from on-line strong extractors. J. Cryptology 17(1), 27–42 (2004)
13. Maurer, U.M.: Conditionally-perfect secrecy and a provably-secure randomized cipher. J. Cryptology 5(1), 53–66 (1992)
14. Shaltiel, R.: Recent developments in explicit constructions of extractors. Bulletin of the EATCS 77, 67–95 (2002)
15. Vadhan, S.P.: Constructing locally computable extractors and cryptosystems in the bounded-storage model. J. Cryptology 17(1), 43–77 (2004)

# Security of Key Distribution and Complementarity in Quantum Mechanics

Masato Koashi

Division of Materials Physics, Graduate School of Engineering Science,
Osaka University, Toyonaka, Osaka 560-8531, Japan
koashi@mp.es.osaka-u.ac.jp

**Abstract.** Complementarity is one of the fundamental properties of quantum mechanics, which prohibits the control of both of a pair of physical quantities even if either one alone is accessible. This property is useful in understanding the relation between quantum communication and secret communication: It gives a simple explanation why basic quantum key distribution protocols are secure against any eavesdropping attack. The imperfection in the final secret key is determined through the failure probabilities of a pair of complementary tasks, which have a clear operational meaning. It also serves as a powerful tool for proving the security under the use of practical imperfect devices. Finally, it gives a comprehensive understanding of how quantum correlations provide the ability of secret communication, since one can prove that for every case in which a secret key is obtained though quantum communication, there exists an explanation in terms of complementarity.

K. Kurosawa (Ed.): ICITS 2009, LNCS 5973, p. 27, 2010.

# Free-Start Distinguishing: Combining Two Types of Indistinguishability Amplification

Peter Gaži[1,2] and Ueli Maurer[1]

[1] ETH Zürich, Switzerland
Department of Computer Science
{gazipete,maurer}@inf.ethz.ch
[2] Comenius University, Bratislava, Slovakia
Department of Computer Science

**Abstract.** The term indistinguishability amplification refers to a setting where a certain construction combines two (or more) cryptographic primitives of the same type to improve their indistinguishability from an ideal primitive. Various constructions achieving this property have been studied, both in the information-theoretic and computational setting. In the former, a result due to Maurer, Pietrzak and Renner describes the amplification achieved by a very general class of constructions called neutralizing. Two types of amplification are observed: a product theorem (bounding the advantage in distinguishing the construction by twice the product of individual advantages) and the amplification of the distinguisher class (the obtained construction is secure against a wider class of distinguishers).

In this paper, we combine these two aspects of information-theoretic indistinguishability amplification. We derive a new bound for the general case of a neutralizing construction that keeps the structure of a product theorem, while also capturing the amplification of the distinguisher class. This improves both bounds mentioned above.

The new technical notion we introduce, central to our analysis, is the notion of free-start distinguishing of systems. This describes the setting where the distinguisher is allowed to choose any common state for both systems and then it is supposed to distinguish these systems starting from that chosen state.

**Keywords:** Information-theoretic cryptography, indistinguishability amplification, neutralizing constructions, projected systems, free-start distinguishing.

## 1 Introduction

**Indistinguishability Amplification.** An important goal of cryptography is to provide real objects (e.g. functions, permutations) such that their behavior is indistinguishable from the corresponding ideal object (e.g. a truly random function or permutation) by a distinguisher interacting with these objects. One reasonable way to approach this task is to devise constructions that allow us

K. Kurosawa (Ed.): ICITS 2009, LNCS 5973, pp. 28–44, 2010.

to combine objects of the same type to obtain a new one, with provably better indistinguishability properties. This is called *indistinguishability amplification.*

A natural candidate for such an indistinguishability-amplifying construction for permutations is the composition, while for random functions it is the quasi-group combination of the outputs (e.g. XOR of the output bitstrings). Both these constructions are widely used in the design of practical cryptographic primitives, such as blockciphers. Therefore, the indistinguishability amplification achieved by these constructions deserves being studied in detail. Both these examples as well as other natural constructions are special cases of the general concept of a *neutralizing construction*, introduced in [6].

In the information-theoretic setting, the most general treatment of indistinguishability amplification is due to Maurer, Pietrzak and Renner [6]. In their work, two different types of indistinguishability amplification are presented. Both are proved for the general class of neutralizing constructions, but for simplicity we describe their contribution on the special case of the XOR of random functions $\mathbf{F} \oplus \mathbf{G}$. First, a product theorem is proved, stating that the advantage in distinguishing $\mathbf{F} \oplus \mathbf{G}$ from the uniform random function $\mathbf{R}$ is upper-bounded by twice the *product* of the individual distinguishing advantages for these functions. Second, an amplification of the distinguishing class is observed, proving that the advantage in distinguishing $\mathbf{F} \oplus \mathbf{G}$ from $\mathbf{R}$ adaptively is upper-bounded by the *sum* of advantages in distinguishing $\mathbf{F}$ and $\mathbf{G}$ from $\mathbf{R}$ non-adaptively.

**Our Contribution.** First, we extend the random system framework from [3], in which we perform our analysis. We introduce the concept of a system *projected to a specific state.* Loosely speaking, any properly defined discrete system $\mathbf{S}$ and a transcript $t$ of interaction with this system together define a new system, which behaves as the original system $\mathbf{S}$ would behave after this interaction $t$. We refer to this new system as $\mathbf{S}$ projected to the state described by $t$. In particular, any one-player game can be modelled as a special type of a discrete system. Therefore, we are also able to model the intuitive situation where a player can continue playing a given game from a specific position (where the game is not won yet) or where it can pick an arbitrary such position in the game tree and try to win the game from there.

This leads to the central new notion in this paper, *free-start distinguishing.* Informally, the free-start distinguishing advantage of two systems is the best advantage a distinguisher can achieve, assuming that it is allowed to project both the distinguished systems to any one state consistent with both of them and then try to distinguish the resulting systems.

This concept, besides giving an interesting new viewpoint on the distinguishing of random systems, allows us to perform a more careful analysis of the indistinguishability amplification achieved by neutralizing constructions in the information-theoretic setting. We use the notion of free-start distinguishing to combine the two types of amplification described in [6]. We derive a new bound which keeps the structure of a product theorem, while involving also the non-adaptive distinguishing advantages, thus describing the amplification of the distinguisher class.

**Motivation and Intuition.** As observed in [6], there is a tight correspondence between distinguishing systems and winning an appropriately defined game. Distinguishing $\mathbf{F} \oplus \mathbf{G}$ from $\mathbf{R}$ can be reduced (by a factor of 2) to winning two games constructed from $\mathbf{F}$ and $\mathbf{G}$, while obtaining only the XOR of their outputs. As long as none of the games is won, the output of the construction is useless to the player, hence one of the games has to be won non-adaptively first. After achieving this, the player still has to win the other game, this time with access to some (possibly useful) outputs. Since winning each of these games is as hard as distinguishing the corresponding system from $\mathbf{R}$, one could conjecture a bound like

$$\Delta_k(\mathbf{F} \oplus \mathbf{G}, \mathbf{R}) \leq 2\left(\Delta_k^{\mathsf{NA}}(\mathbf{F}, \mathbf{R}) \cdot \Delta_k(\mathbf{G}, \mathbf{R}) + \Delta_k^{\mathsf{NA}}(\mathbf{G}, \mathbf{R}) \cdot \Delta_k(\mathbf{F}, \mathbf{R})\right),$$

where $\Delta_k(\mathbf{S}, \mathbf{T})$ and $\Delta_k^{\mathsf{NA}}(\mathbf{S}, \mathbf{T})$ denote the adaptive and non-adaptive advantage in distinguishing $\mathbf{S}$ from $\mathbf{T}$ with $k$ queries, respectively.

However, this is not correct, since winning the first game may involve getting the second game into a state where winning it becomes much easier than if played from scratch. We model this by allowing the player to choose the starting position in the second game freely, with the only restriction being that the game is not won yet in the chosen position. Translated back into the language of systems distinguishing, this gives us a valid bound

$$\Delta_k(\mathbf{F} \oplus \mathbf{G}, \mathbf{R}) \leq 2\left(\Delta_k^{\mathsf{NA}}(\mathbf{F}, \mathbf{R}) \cdot \Lambda_k(\mathbf{G}, \mathbf{R}) + \Delta_k^{\mathsf{NA}}(\mathbf{G}, \mathbf{R}) \cdot \Lambda_k(\mathbf{F}, \mathbf{R})\right), \qquad (1)$$

where $\Lambda_k(\mathbf{S}, \mathbf{T})$ denotes the free-start distinguishing advantage for systems $\mathbf{S}$ and $\mathbf{T}$, as described above. In this paper we prove a general theorem for neutralizing constructions, of which the bound (1) is a simple corollary.

**Related Work.** There has been a lot of previous research on indistinguishability-amplifying constructions, both in the information-theoretic and the computational setting.

In the former, a product theorem for the composition of stateless permutations was proved by Vaudenay using the decorrelation framework [11]. The amplification of the distinguisher class was proved in [5] for a class of constructions and in [4] also for the four-round Feistel network. As mentioned above, the paper [6] addressed both these types of indistinguishability amplification for any neutralizing construction.

On the other hand, computational product theorems for various constructions were proved by Luby and Rackoff [2], Myers [8,9] and Dodis et al. [1]. For the general case of a neutralizing construction a product theorem was proved by Maurer and Tessaro [7]. The second type of amplification considered here, amplification of the distinguisher class, does not in general translate to the computational setting, as observed by Pietrzak [10].

# 2   Preliminaries

## 2.1   Basic Notation

Throughout the paper, we denote sets by calligraphic letters (e.g. $\mathcal{S}$). A $k$-tuple is denoted by $u^k = (u_1, \ldots, u_k)$, and the set of all $k$-tuples of elements of $\mathcal{U}$ is denoted by $\mathcal{U}^k$. The tuples can be concatenated, which we write as $u^k v^l = (u_1, \ldots, u_k, v_1, \ldots, v_l)$. By ms($i$) we denote the set of monotone binary sequences of length $i$ where zeroes are preceding ones, i.e., $\mathrm{ms}(i) = \{0^i, 0^{i-1}1, \ldots, 1^i\}$.

We usually denote random variables and concrete values they can take on by capital and small letters, respectively. Naturally, for any binary random variable $B$, we denote the event that it takes on the value 1 also by $B$. The complement of an event $A$ is denoted by $\overline{A}$. For events $A$ and $B$ and random variables $U$ and $V$ with ranges $\mathcal{U}$ and $\mathcal{V}$, respectively, we denote by $\mathsf{P}_{UA|VB}$ the corresponding conditional probability distribution, seen as a function $\mathcal{U} \times \mathcal{V} \to \langle 0, 1 \rangle$. Here the value $\mathsf{P}_{UA|VB}(u, v)$ is well-defined for all $u \in \mathcal{U}$ and $v \in \mathcal{V}$ such that $\mathsf{P}_{VB}(v) > 0$ and undefined otherwise. Two probability distributions $\mathsf{P}_U$ and $\mathsf{P}_{U'}$ on the same set $\mathcal{U}$ are equal, denoted $\mathsf{P}_U = \mathsf{P}_{U'}$, if $\mathsf{P}_U(u) = \mathsf{P}_{U'}(u)$ for all $u \in \mathcal{U}$. Conditional probability distributions are equal if the equality holds for all arguments for which both of them are defined. To emphasize the random experiment $\mathcal{E}$ in consideration, we usually write it in the superscript, e.g. $\mathsf{P}^{\mathcal{E}}_{U|V}(u, v)$. By a lower-case $\mathsf{p}$ we denote (conditional) probability distributions that by themselves do not define a random experiment.

## 2.2   Random Systems

In this subsection, we present the basic notions of the random systems framework introduced in [3], following the notational changes in [6]. The input-output behavior of any discrete system can be described by a *random system* in the spirit of the following definition.

**Definition 1.** *An $(\mathcal{X}, \mathcal{Y})$-random system $\mathbf{S}$ is a (generally infinite) sequence of conditional probability distributions $\mathsf{p}^{\mathbf{S}}_{Y_i|X^i Y^{i-1}}$ for all $i \geq 1$.*

The behavior of the random system is specified by the sequence of conditional probabilities $\mathsf{p}^{\mathbf{S}}_{Y_i|X^i Y^{i-1}}(y_i, x^i, y^{i-1})$ (for $i \geq 1$) of obtaining the output $y_i \in \mathcal{Y}$ on query $x_i \in \mathcal{X}$ given the previous $i - 1$ queries $x^{i-1} = (x_1, \ldots, x_{i-1}) \in \mathcal{X}^{i-1}$ and their corresponding outputs $y^{i-1} = (y_1, \ldots, y_{i-1}) \in \mathcal{Y}^{i-1}$.

We shall use boldface letters (e.g. $\mathbf{S}$) to denote both a discrete system and a random system corresponding to it. This should cause no confusion. We emphasize that although the results of this paper are stated for random systems, they hold for arbitrary systems, since the only property of a system that is relevant here is its input-output behavior. It is reasonable to consider two discrete systems equivalent if their input-output behaviors are the same, even if their internal structure differs.

**Definition 2.** *Two systems* $\mathbf{S}$ *and* $\mathbf{T}$ *are* equivalent, *denoted* $\mathbf{S} \equiv \mathbf{T}$, *if they correspond to the same random system, i.e., if* $\mathsf{p}_{Y_i|X^iY^{i-1}}^{\mathbf{S}} = \mathsf{p}_{Y_i|X^iY^{i-1}}^{\mathbf{T}}$ *for all* $i \geq 1$.

A random system can also be defined by a sequence of conditional probability distributions $\mathsf{p}_{Y^i|X^i}^{\mathbf{S}}$ for $i \geq 1$. This description is often convenient, but is not minimal: the distributions $\mathsf{p}_{Y^i|X^i}^{\mathbf{S}}$ must satisfy a consistency condition for different $i$. The conversion between these two forms can be described by

$$\mathsf{p}_{Y^i|X^i}^{\mathbf{S}} = \prod_{j=1}^{i} \mathsf{p}_{Y_j|X^jY^{j-1}}^{\mathbf{S}} \qquad \text{and} \qquad \mathsf{p}_{Y_i|X^iY^{i-1}}^{\mathbf{S}} = \frac{\mathsf{p}_{Y^i|X^i}^{\mathbf{S}}}{\mathsf{p}_{Y^{i-1}|X^{i-1}}^{\mathbf{S}}}. \tag{2}$$

A *random function* is a special type of random system that answers consistently, i.e., it satisfies the condition $X_i = X_j \Rightarrow Y_i = Y_j$. For example, $\mathbf{R}$ denotes a *uniform random function*, which answers every new query with an element uniformly chosen from its (finite) range. A *random permutation* on $\mathcal{X}$ is a random function $\mathcal{X} \to \mathcal{X}$ mapping distinct inputs to distinct outputs: $X_i \neq X_j \Rightarrow Y_i \neq Y_j$. For example, $\mathbf{P}$ denotes a *uniform random permutation*, which for a domain and range $\mathcal{X}$ realizes a function chosen uniformly at random from all bijective functions $\mathcal{X} \to \mathcal{X}$. Following [7], we say that a random function is *convex-combination stateless* (*cc-stateless*) if it corresponds to a random variable taking on as values function tables $\mathcal{X} \to \mathcal{Y}$. For example, both $\mathbf{R}$ and $\mathbf{P}$ are cc-stateless.

We can define a *distinguisher* $\mathbf{D}$ for an $(\mathcal{X}, \mathcal{Y})$-system as a $(\mathcal{Y}, \mathcal{X})$-system which is one query ahead, i.e., it is defined by the conditional probability distributions $\mathsf{p}_{X_i|X^{i-1}Y^{i-1}}^{\mathbf{D}}$ for all $i \geq 1$. In particular, the first query of $\mathbf{D}$ is determined by $\mathsf{p}_{X_1}^{\mathbf{D}}$. After a certain number of queries (say $k$), the distinguisher outputs a bit $W_k$ depending on the transcript $X^kY^k$. For a random system $\mathbf{S}$ and a distinguisher $\mathbf{D}$, let $\mathbf{DS}$ be the random experiment where $\mathbf{D}$ interacts with $\mathbf{S}$. The distribution of $X^kY^k$ in this experiment can be expressed by

$$\mathsf{P}_{X^kY^k}^{\mathbf{DS}}(x^k, y^k) = \prod_{i=1}^{k} \mathsf{p}_{X_i|X^{i-1}Y^{i-1}}^{\mathbf{D}}(x_i, x^{i-1}, y^{i-1}) \mathsf{p}_{Y_i|X^iY^{i-1}}^{\mathbf{S}}(y_i, x^i, y^{i-1})$$

$$= \mathsf{p}_{X^k|Y^{k-1}}^{\mathbf{D}}(x^k, y^{k-1}) \cdot \mathsf{p}_{Y^k|X^k}^{\mathbf{S}}(y^k, x^k), \tag{3}$$

where the last equality follows from (2).

We consider two special classes of distinguishers. By $\mathsf{NA}$ we denote the class of all (computationally unbounded) non-adaptive distinguishers which select all queries $X_1, \ldots, X_k$ in advance, i.e., independent of the outputs $Y_1, \ldots, Y_k$. By $\mathsf{RI}$ we denote the class of all (computationally unbounded) distinguishers which cannot select queries but are given uniformly random values $X_1, \ldots, X_k$ and the corresponding outputs $Y_1, \ldots, Y_k$. These distinguisher classes correspond to the attacks $\mathsf{nCPA}$ (non-adaptive chosen-plaintext attack) and $\mathsf{KPA}$ (known-plaintext attack) from the literature, respectively.

For two $(\mathcal{X}, \mathcal{Y})$-systems $\mathbf{S}$ and $\mathbf{T}$, the *distinguishing advantage* of $\mathbf{D}$ in distinguishing systems $\mathbf{S}$ and $\mathbf{T}$ by $k$ queries is defined as

$$\Delta_k^{\mathbf{D}}(\mathbf{S}, \mathbf{T}) = \left| \mathsf{P}^{\mathbf{DS}}(W_k = 1) - \mathsf{P}^{\mathbf{DT}}(W_k = 1) \right|.$$

We shall denote by $\Delta_k^{\mathcal{D}}(\mathbf{S}, \mathbf{T})$ and $\Delta_k(\mathbf{S}, \mathbf{T})$ the maximal advantage over the class $\mathcal{D}$ of distinguishers and over all distinguishers issuing at most $k$ queries, respectively. On the other hand, we define

$$\delta_k^{\mathbf{D}}(\mathbf{S}, \mathbf{T}) := ||\mathsf{P}_{X^k Y^k}^{\mathbf{DS}} - \mathsf{P}_{X^k Y^k}^{\mathbf{DT}}|| = \frac{1}{2} \sum_{x^k y^k} |\mathsf{P}_{X^k Y^k}^{\mathbf{DS}}(x^k, y^k) - \mathsf{P}_{X^k Y^k}^{\mathbf{DT}}(x^k, y^k)|$$

to be the *statistical distance of transcripts* when $\mathbf{D}$ interacts with $\mathbf{S}$ and $\mathbf{T}$, respectively. Again, $\delta_k^{\mathcal{D}}(\mathbf{S}, \mathbf{T})$ and $\delta_k(\mathbf{S}, \mathbf{T})$ denote the maximal value over the class $\mathcal{D}$ of distinguishers and over all distinguishers, respectively. The statistical distance of transcripts is closely related to the distinguishing advantage: in general we have $\Delta_k^{\mathbf{D}}(\mathbf{S}, \mathbf{T}) \leq \delta_k^{\mathbf{D}}(\mathbf{S}, \mathbf{T})$, but for a computationally unbounded distinguisher $\mathbf{D}$ that chooses the output bit optimally, we have $\Delta_k^{\mathbf{D}}(\mathbf{S}, \mathbf{T}) = \delta_k^{\mathbf{D}}(\mathbf{S}, \mathbf{T})$. In particular, we have $\Delta_k(\mathbf{S}, \mathbf{T}) = \delta_k(\mathbf{S}, \mathbf{T})$, $\Delta_k^{\mathsf{NA}}(\mathbf{S}, \mathbf{T}) = \delta_k^{\mathsf{NA}}(\mathbf{S}, \mathbf{T})$ and $\Delta_k^{\mathsf{RI}}(\mathbf{S}, \mathbf{T}) = \delta_k^{\mathsf{RI}}(\mathbf{S}, \mathbf{T})$. Finally, using (3) to expand the definition of $\delta_k^{\mathbf{D}}(\mathbf{S}, \mathbf{T})$, we obtain

$$\delta_k^{\mathbf{D}}(\mathbf{S}, \mathbf{T}) = \frac{1}{2} \sum_{x^k y^k} \mathsf{p}_{X^k | Y^{k-1}}^{\mathbf{D}}(x^k, y^{k-1}) \cdot \left| \mathsf{p}_{Y^k | X^k}^{\mathbf{S}}(y^k, x^k) - \mathsf{p}_{Y^k | X^k}^{\mathbf{T}}(y^k, x^k) \right|$$

$$= \sum_{x^k y^k} \mathsf{p}_{X^k | Y^{k-1}}^{\mathbf{D}}(x^k, y^{k-1}) \cdot \left( \mathsf{p}_{Y^k | X^k}^{\mathbf{S}}(y^k, x^k) - \mathsf{p}_{Y^k | X^k}^{\mathbf{T}}(y^k, x^k) \right), \quad (4)$$

where the last summation goes only over all $x^k y^k$ such that $\mathsf{p}_{Y^k | X^k}^{\mathbf{S}}(y^k, x^k) > \mathsf{p}_{Y^k | X^k}^{\mathbf{T}}(y^k, x^k)$ holds.

For two $(\mathcal{X}, \mathcal{Y})$-systems $\mathbf{S}$ and $\mathbf{T}$ and a uniform random bit $B$, $\langle \mathbf{S}/\mathbf{T} \rangle_B$ denotes the random system which is equal to $\mathbf{S}$ if $B = 0$ and equal to $\mathbf{T}$ otherwise. If mentioning the random variable $B$ explicitly is not necessary, we only write $\langle \mathbf{S}/\mathbf{T} \rangle$. The following simple lemma comes from [6].

**Lemma 1.** *For every distinguisher* $\mathbf{D}$, *we have:*

*(i)* $\Delta_k^{\mathbf{D}}(\mathbf{S}, \mathbf{T}) = 2 \left| \mathsf{P}^{\mathbf{D}\langle \mathbf{S}/\mathbf{T} \rangle_B}(W_k = B) - \frac{1}{2} \right|$,

*(ii)* $\Delta_k^{\mathbf{D}}(\mathbf{S}, \langle \mathbf{S}/\mathbf{T} \rangle_B) = \frac{1}{2} \Delta_k^{\mathbf{D}}(\mathbf{S}, \mathbf{T})$.

We denote by $\mathbf{C}(\cdot, \cdot)$ a *construction* that invokes two other systems as its subsystems. If we instantiate these subsystems by $\mathbf{S}_1$ and $\mathbf{S}_2$, we denote the resulting system by $\mathbf{C}(\mathbf{S}_1, \mathbf{S}_2)$. Upon each query to $\mathbf{C}(\cdot, \cdot)$, the construction may adaptively issue 0 or more queries to its subsystems. A construction is *neutralizing* for pairs of systems $(\mathbf{F}, \mathbf{I})$ and $(\mathbf{G}, \mathbf{J})$ if $\mathbf{C}(\mathbf{F}, \mathbf{J}) \equiv \mathbf{C}(\mathbf{I}, \mathbf{G}) \equiv \mathbf{C}(\mathbf{I}, \mathbf{J})$. Moreover, let $k'$ and $k''$ denote the maximal number of queries made to the first and second subsystem, respectively, during the first $k$ queries issued to the construction (if defined). There are two important examples of neutralizing constructions that we shall consider in this paper:

**Quasi-group combination.** For $(\mathcal{X}, \mathcal{Y})$-random systems $\mathbf{F}$ and $\mathbf{G}$ and for a quasi-group[1] operation $\star$ on $\mathcal{Y}$, the construction $\mathbf{F} \star \mathbf{G}$ feeds any query it

---

[1] A binary operation $\star$ on $\mathcal{X}$ is a quasi-group operation if for every $a, c \in \mathcal{X}$ (every $b, c \in \mathcal{X}$) there is a unique $b \in \mathcal{X}$ ($a \in \mathcal{X}$) such that $a \star b = c$.

receives to both subsystems and then combines their outputs using $\star$ to determine its own output. This is a neutralizing construction for random functions $\mathbf{F}$, $\mathbf{G}$ and $\mathbf{I} \equiv \mathbf{J} \equiv \mathbf{R}$.

**Composition.** For a $(\mathcal{X}, \mathcal{Y})$-random system $\mathbf{F}$ and a $(\mathcal{Y}, \mathcal{Z})$-random system $\mathbf{G}$, $\mathbf{F} \triangleright \mathbf{G}$ denotes the serial composition of systems: every input to $\mathbf{F} \triangleright \mathbf{G}$ is fed to $\mathbf{F}$, its output is fed to $\mathbf{G}$ and the output of $\mathbf{G}$ is the output of $\mathbf{F} \triangleright \mathbf{G}$. This is a neutralizing construction for a permutation $\mathbf{F}$, a cc-stateless permutation $\mathbf{G}$ and $\mathbf{I} \equiv \mathbf{J} \equiv \mathbf{P}$.

## 2.3   Monotone Boolean Outputs and Games

Among random systems, we shall be in particular interested in systems having a monotone bit as a part of their output, in the sense of the following definition from [6].

**Definition 3.** *For a $(\mathcal{X}, \mathcal{Y} \times \{0,1\})$-system $\mathbf{S}$ the binary component $A_i$ of the output $(Y_i, A_i)$ is called a* monotone binary output (MBO)*, if $A_i = 1$ implies $A_j = 1$ for all $j > i$. For convenience, we define $A_0 = 0$. For a system $\mathbf{S}$ with MBO we define two derived systems:*

*(i) $\mathbf{S}^-$ is the $(\mathcal{X}, \mathcal{Y})$-system obtained from $\mathbf{S}$ by ignoring the MBO.*
*(ii) $\mathbf{S}^\dashv$ is the $(\mathcal{X}, \mathcal{Y} \times \{0,1\})$-system which masks the $\mathcal{Y}$-output to a dummy symbol $(\perp)$ as soon as the MBO turns to 1. More precisely, the following function is applied to the outputs of $\mathbf{S}$:*

$$(y, a) \mapsto (y', a) \quad \text{where} \quad y' = \begin{cases} y & \text{if } a = 0 \\ \perp & \text{if } a = 1. \end{cases}$$

The reason for studying this particular type of systems is that any one-player game can be seen as a $(\mathcal{X}, \mathcal{Y} \times \{0,1\})$-system $\mathbf{S}$ with a monotone binary output. Here the player makes moves $X_1, X_2, \ldots$ and receives game outputs $Y_1, Y_2, \ldots$. Additionally, the game after each move also outputs a monotone bit indicating whether the game has already been won. The goal of the player[2] is to provoke the change of this bit, which is initially 0. Note that it is irrelevant whether the player can see this bit, so we can think of it interacting only with the system $\mathbf{S}^-$.

For a $(\mathcal{X}, \mathcal{Y} \times \{0,1\})$-system $\mathbf{S}$ with an MBO called $A_i$ and for a player $\mathbf{D}$, we denote by $\nu_k^{\mathbf{D}}(\mathbf{S})$ the probability that $\mathbf{D}$ wins the game $\mathbf{S}$ within $k$ queries, i.e., $\nu_k^{\mathbf{D}}(\mathbf{S}) = \mathsf{P}_{A_k}^{\mathbf{DS}}(1)$. As usually, $\nu_k^{\mathcal{D}}(\mathbf{S})$ and $\nu_k(\mathbf{S})$ denote the maximal winning probability over the class $\mathcal{D}$ of players and over all players, respectively.

The relationship between distinguishing two systems and winning an appropriately defined game was studied in [3] and later in [6], where the following lemma was proved.

**Lemma 2.** *For any two $(\mathcal{X}, \mathcal{Y})$-systems $\mathbf{S}$ and $\mathbf{T}$ there exist $(\mathcal{X}, \mathcal{Y} \times \{0,1\})$-systems $\hat{\mathbf{S}}$ and $\hat{\mathbf{T}}$ such that*

---

[2] Note that a player is formally the same type of object as a distinguisher, hence we shall use both terms, depending on the context.

(i) $\hat{\mathbf{S}}^- \equiv \mathbf{S}$

(ii) $\hat{\mathbf{T}}^- \equiv \mathbf{T}$

(iii) $\hat{\mathbf{S}}^{\dashv} \equiv \hat{\mathbf{T}}^{\dashv}$

(iv) $\delta_k^{\mathbf{D}}(\mathbf{S}, \mathbf{T}) = \nu_k^{\mathbf{D}}(\hat{\mathbf{S}}) = \nu_k^{\mathbf{D}}(\hat{\mathbf{T}})$ for all $\mathbf{D}$.

Intuitively, Lemma 2 states that any two systems $\mathbf{S}$ and $\mathbf{T}$ can be extended by adding an MBO to each of them that "signals" whether the system has deviated from the common behavior of both $\mathbf{S}$ and $\mathbf{T}$. The systems are equivalent as long as the MBOs are 0 and the probability that a distinguisher $\mathbf{D}$ turns one of these MBOs to 1 is equal to the statistical distance of transcripts of the experiments $\mathbf{DS}$ and $\mathbf{DT}$.

Moreover, it was proved in [6] that if any $(\mathcal{X}, \mathcal{Y} \times \{0,1\})$-systems $\hat{\mathbf{S}}$ and $\hat{\mathbf{T}}$ satisfy for every $i \geq 1$ the conditions (for $\hat{\mathbf{T}}$, the conditions are analogous)

$$
\begin{aligned}
\mathsf{p}_{Y^i A_i | X^i}^{\hat{\mathbf{S}}}(y^i, 0, x^i) &= m_{x^i, y^i}^{\mathbf{S}, \mathbf{T}} \\
\mathsf{p}_{Y^i A_i | X^i}^{\hat{\mathbf{S}}}(y^i, 1, x^i) &= \mathsf{p}_{Y^i | X^i}^{\mathbf{S}}(y^i, x^i) - m_{x^i, y^i}^{\mathbf{S}, \mathbf{T}}
\end{aligned}
\tag{5}
$$

where

$$
m_{x^i, y^i}^{\mathbf{S}, \mathbf{T}} = \min\{\mathsf{p}_{Y^i | X^i}^{\mathbf{S}}(y^i, x^i), \mathsf{p}_{Y^i | X^i}^{\mathbf{T}}(y^i, x^i)\},
$$

then they also satisfy the properties stated in Lemma 2. In fact, Lemma 2 was proved in [6] by demonstrating that the systems $\hat{\mathbf{S}}$ and $\hat{\mathbf{T}}$ satisfying (5) can always be constructed.

## 3  Projected Systems

Any system $\mathbf{S}$ and a transcript of the initial part of a possible interaction with it together define a new system that simulates the behavior of $\mathbf{S}$ from the state at the end of this interaction onwards. This is formalized in the following definition.

**Definition 4.** *For an $(\mathcal{X}, \mathcal{Y})$-random system $\mathbf{S}$ and $(\overline{x}^j, \overline{y}^j) \in \mathcal{X}^j \times \mathcal{Y}^j$, let $\mathbf{S}[\overline{x}^j, \overline{y}^j]$ denote the system $\mathbf{S}$ projected to the state $\overline{x}^j \overline{y}^j$, i.e. the random system that behaves like $\mathbf{S}$ would behave after answering the first $j$ queries $\overline{x}^j$ by $\overline{y}^j$. Formally, $\mathbf{S}[\overline{x}^j, \overline{y}^j]$ is defined by the distributions*

$$
\mathsf{p}_{Y_i | X^i Y^{i-1}}^{\mathbf{S}[\overline{x}^j, \overline{y}^j]}(y_i, x^i, y^{i-1}) := \mathsf{p}_{Y_{j+i} | X^{j+i} Y^{j+i-1}}^{\mathbf{S}}(y_i, \overline{x}^j x^i, \overline{y}^j y^{i-1})
$$

*if $\mathsf{p}_{Y^j | X^j}^{\mathbf{S}}(\overline{y}^j, \overline{x}^j) > 0$ and undefined otherwise.*

This is most intuitive if we consider a game (i.e., a special type of system with an MBO), where the transcript represents a position in this game. For a $(\mathcal{X}, \mathcal{Y} \times \{0,1\})$-system $\mathbf{S}$ representing a game, the MBO bits are also a part of the output, therefore we have to specify them when describing its answers to the first $j$ queries. To denote a position where the game is not won yet, we set these bits to 0, obtaining the system $\mathbf{S}[\overline{x}^j, \overline{y}^j 0^j]$.

**Definition 5.** *Let* $\mathbf{S}$ *be a* $(\mathcal{X}, \mathcal{Y} \times \{0,1\})$*-system with the MBO* $A_i$ *and let* $\mathbf{D}$ *be a compatible player. Let* $j \leq k$ *be non-negative integers. For any* $x^j \in \mathcal{X}^j$ *and* $y^j \in \mathcal{Y}^j$ *such that* $\mathsf{p}^{\mathbf{S}}_{Y^j A_j | X^j}(y^j, 0, x^j) > 0$*, we call* $\nu^{\mathbf{D}}_{k-j}(\mathbf{S}[x^j, y^j 0^j])$ *the probability of* $\mathbf{D}$ *winning the game* $\mathbf{S}$ *from the position* $x^j y^j$ *within the remaining* $k - j$ *queries. Moreover, we also define the probability of winning* $\mathbf{S}$ *within* $k$ *queries with a free start to be*

$$\lambda_k(\mathbf{S}) := \max_{j, x^j, y^j} \nu_{k-j}(\mathbf{S}[x^j, y^j 0^j]),$$

*where the maximization[3] goes over all* $j \leq k, x^j, y^j$ *such that the projected system* $\mathbf{S}[x^j, y^j 0^j]$ *is defined.*

Intuitively, if a player starts playing the game $\mathbf{S}$ from the position $x^j y^j$ (assuming the game is not won yet), $\nu_{k-j}(\mathbf{S}[x^j, y^j 0^j])$ describes the probability that it wins the game within the remaining $k - j$ queries if he plays optimally from now on. On the other hand, if the player is allowed to choose *any* position in the game tree within the first $k$ queries (where the game is not won yet) and play from that position, it can win with probability $\lambda_k(\mathbf{S})$. Obviously $\lambda_k(\mathbf{S}) \geq \nu_k(\mathbf{S})$.

Let us now consider a construction $\mathbf{C}(\mathbf{S}_1, \mathbf{S}_2)$. In this section, we assume that $\mathbf{S}_1$ and $\mathbf{S}_2$ are two $(\mathcal{X}, \mathcal{Y} \times \{0,1\})$-systems (games) with MBOs $A_i$ and $B_i$, respectively. Moreover, we assume that $\mathbf{C}(\mathbf{S}_1, \mathbf{S}_2)$ is a $(\mathcal{X}, \mathcal{Y} \times \{0,1\})$-construction and it combines the last binary outputs of its subsystems using the AND operation to determine its own binary output $C_i$. Note that although the construction may determine the number and ordering of the queries to its subsystems adaptively, we can assume that the order of the queries to the subsystems is well-defined for every run of the experiment. This justifies the following definition.

**Definition 6.** *In the experiment* $\mathbf{DC}(\mathbf{S}_1, \mathbf{S}_2)$*, let* $F^i_j$ *denote the event that the game* $\mathbf{S}_i$ *was won during the first* $j$ *queries to* $\mathbf{C}(\mathbf{S}_1, \mathbf{S}_2)$ *and it was the first of the games* $\mathbf{S}_1, \mathbf{S}_2$ *that was won.*

Note that if both games are to be won, one of them always has to be won first. Afterwards, the adversary needs to also win the second game in order to provoke the MBO of the whole construction. This is captured by the following lemma.

**Lemma 3.** *Let* $\mathbf{S}$ *denote the system* $\mathbf{C}(\mathbf{S}_1, \mathbf{S}_2)$ *with MBO as described above. Then we have*

$$\nu^{\mathbf{D}}_k(\mathbf{S}) \leq \mathsf{P}^{\mathbf{DS}}(F^1_k) \cdot \lambda_{k''}(\mathbf{S}_2) + \mathsf{P}^{\mathbf{DS}}(F^2_k) \cdot \lambda_{k'}(\mathbf{S}_1).$$

*Proof.* Since the MBO of $\mathbf{S}$ is the AND of the MBOs of the subsystems, we have

$$\begin{aligned} \nu^{\mathbf{D}}_k(\mathbf{S}) &\leq \mathsf{P}^{\mathbf{DS}}(F^1_k \wedge B_{k''}) + \mathsf{P}^{\mathbf{DS}}(F^2_k \wedge A_{k'}) \\ &= \mathsf{P}^{\mathbf{DS}}(F^1_k) \cdot \mathsf{P}^{\mathbf{DS}}(B_{k''}|F^1_k) + \mathsf{P}^{\mathbf{DS}}(F^2_k) \cdot \mathsf{P}^{\mathbf{DS}}(A_{k'}|F^2_k). \end{aligned}$$

---

[3] Note that depending on the game $\mathbf{S}$, any $j \in \{0, \ldots, k-1\}$ may maximize the term $\nu^{\mathbf{D}}_{k-j}(\mathbf{S}[x^j, y^j 0^j])$.

It remains to upper-bound the terms $\mathsf{P}^{\mathbf{DS}}(B_{k''}|F_k^1)$ and $\mathsf{P}^{\mathbf{DS}}(A_{k'}|F_k^2)$. Let $X_i$ and $Y_i$ be the random variables corresponding to the $i$-th input and $\mathcal{Y}$-output of $\mathbf{S}$, respectively; and let $M_i$ and $N_i$ ($U_i$ and $V_i$) be the random variables corresponding to the $i$-th input and $\mathcal{Y}$-output of $\mathbf{S}_1$ ($\mathbf{S}_2$), respectively. Let $T$ denote the random variable corresponding to the initial part of the transcript of the experiment from its beginning until the MBO $A$ is provoked or until the end of the experiment, whichever comes first. This transcript contains all the queries $X_i$ to the construction, all the corresponding answers $(Y_i, C_i)$, as well as all the query-answer pairs $(M_i, (N_i, A_i))$ and $(U_i, (V_i, B_i))$ of the subsystems, in the order as they appeared during the execution. Conditioning over all possible values of $T$, we have

$$\mathsf{P}^{\mathbf{DS}}(B_{k''}|F_k^1) = \sum_t \mathsf{P}^{\mathbf{DS}}_{T|F_k^1}(t) \cdot \mathsf{P}^{\mathbf{DS}}_{B_{k''}|TF_k^1}(t). \tag{6}$$

Let now $t$ be fixed such that $\mathsf{P}^{\mathbf{DS}}_{T|F_k^1}(t) > 0$, we need to prove $\mathsf{P}^{\mathbf{DS}}_{B_{k''}|TF_k^1}(t) \leq \lambda_{k''}(\mathbf{S}_2)$. Let us consider a player $\mathbf{D}'$ defined as follows: it simulates the behavior of the player $\mathbf{DC}(\mathbf{S}_1, \cdot)$. However, as long as the MBO $A$ is not provoked, all its choices are fixed to follow the transcript $t$. After these "cheated" choices, as soon as the MBO $A$ is provoked (and $t$ ends), it simulates $\mathbf{D}$, $\mathbf{C}$ and $\mathbf{S}_1$ faithfully. Let $j$ denote the number of queries issued to $\mathbf{S}_2$ in $t$, let $u^j$ and $v^j$ denote these queries and the corresponding answers, respectively. For the described player $\mathbf{D}'$, we have

$$\begin{aligned}
\mathsf{P}^{\mathbf{DS}}_{B_{k''}|TF_k^1}(t) &= \mathsf{P}^{\mathbf{D}'\mathbf{S}_2}_{B_{k''}|U^j V^j \overline{B_j}}(u^j, v^j) \\
&\leq \max_{\mathbf{D}} \mathsf{P}^{\mathbf{DS}_2}_{B_{k''}|U^j V^j \overline{B_j}}(u^j, v^j) \\
&= \nu_{k''-j}(\mathbf{S}[u^j, v^j 0^j]) \\
&\leq \lambda_{k''}(\mathbf{S}_2),
\end{aligned}$$

and since $\sum_t \mathsf{P}^{\mathbf{DS}}_{T|F_k^1}(t) = 1$, from (6) we have $\mathsf{P}^{\mathbf{DS}}(B_{k''}|F_k^1) \leq \lambda_{k''}(\mathbf{S}_2)$. The same argument gives us a symmetric bound for $\mathsf{P}^{\mathbf{DS}}(A_{k'}|F_k^2)$ and concludes the proof. □

## 4   Free-Start Distinguishing

The notion of winning a game with a free start, captured by the quantity $\lambda_k(\mathbf{S})$, has a counterpart in the language of systems indistinguishability, which we now define formally.

**Definition 7.** *For any random systems $\mathbf{S}$ and $\mathbf{T}$, we define the free-start distinguishing advantage of $\mathbf{S}$ and $\mathbf{T}$ to be*

$$\Lambda_k(\mathbf{S}, \mathbf{T}) := \max_{j, x^j, y^j} \Delta_{k-j}(\mathbf{S}[x^j, y^j], \mathbf{T}[x^j, y^j]),$$

*where the maximization goes over all $j \in \{0, \ldots, k-1\}$ and all $x^j, y^j$ such that the systems on the right side are defined.*

Informally, suppose that the distinguisher is allowed to choose an arbitrary transcript $x^j y^j$ compatible with both the systems it is supposed to distinguish, project them to the states described by this transcript and then try to distinguish the resulting systems with the remaining $k - j$ queries. Then the quantity $\Lambda_k(\mathbf{S}, \mathbf{T})$ denotes the optimal advantage it can achieve.

To demonstrate the relationship between $\lambda_k$ and $\Lambda_k$, we exploit the connection between distinguishing two systems and winning an appropriately defined game described in [6]. Let us consider the setting with a real system $\mathbf{F}$ (e.g. a random function) and an ideal system $\mathbf{I}$ (e.g. a uniform random function). Using Lemma 2 (and, in particular, condition (5)), we can add MBOs to the systems $\mathbf{F}$ and $\mathbf{I}$ to obtain systems $\hat{\mathbf{F}}$ and $\hat{\mathbf{I}}$ such that $\nu_k(\langle \hat{\mathbf{F}}/\hat{\mathbf{I}} \rangle) = \Delta_k(\mathbf{F}, \mathbf{I})$ and the systems behave identically as long as the MBO is not provoked. Since provoking this MBO corresponds to distinguishing the systems, one can expect $\nu_{k-j}(\langle \hat{\mathbf{F}}/\hat{\mathbf{I}} \rangle [x^j, y^j 0^j])$ to be related to the advantage in distinguishing $\mathbf{F}$ and $\mathbf{I}$ projected to the state described by the transcript $x^j y^j$ on the remaining $k - j$ queries. In the following, we capture this intuition.

**Lemma 4.** *Let $\mathbf{F}$ and $\mathbf{I}$ be two random systems, let $\hat{\mathbf{F}}$, $\hat{\mathbf{I}}$ be the systems obtained from $\mathbf{F}$, $\mathbf{I}$ by adding the MBOs according to Lemma 2 and condition (5). Then we have*

$$\nu_k(\langle \hat{\mathbf{F}}/\hat{\mathbf{I}} \rangle [\overline{x}^j, \overline{y}^j 0^j]) = \Delta_k(\hat{\mathbf{F}}[\overline{x}^j, \overline{y}^j 0^j]^-, \hat{\mathbf{I}}[\overline{x}^j, \overline{y}^j 0^j]^-)$$

*for any $\overline{x}^j, \overline{y}^j$ such that the system on the left side is defined.*

*Proof.* First note that $\nu_k(\langle \hat{\mathbf{F}}/\hat{\mathbf{I}} \rangle [\overline{x}^j, \overline{y}^j 0^j]) = \nu_k(\hat{\mathbf{F}}[\overline{x}^j, \overline{y}^j 0^j])$, hence it suffices to prove $\nu_k(\hat{\mathbf{F}}[\overline{x}^j, \overline{y}^j 0^j]) = \Delta_k(\hat{\mathbf{F}}[\overline{x}^j, \overline{y}^j 0^j]^-, \hat{\mathbf{I}}[\overline{x}^j, \overline{y}^j 0^j]^-)$. We prove this claim by showing that the MBO of $\hat{\mathbf{F}}[\overline{x}^j, \overline{y}^j 0^j]$, originally defined to capture the differences between $\mathbf{F}$ and $\mathbf{I}$, keeps the properties guaranteed by Lemma 2 also with respect to the systems $\hat{\mathbf{F}}[\overline{x}^j, \overline{y}^j 0^j]^-$ and $\hat{\mathbf{I}}[\overline{x}^j, \overline{y}^j 0^j]^-$. We achieve this by showing that the system $\hat{\mathbf{F}}[\overline{x}^j, \overline{y}^j 0^j]$ satisfies the condition (5) with respect to the systems $\hat{\mathbf{F}}[\overline{x}^j, \overline{y}^j 0^j]^-$ and $\hat{\mathbf{I}}[\overline{x}^j, \overline{y}^j 0^j]^-$. Seeing this, the claim follows from Lemma 2.

Throughout the proof let $p$ denote the probability $\mathsf{p}^{\hat{\mathbf{F}}}_{Y^j A^j | X^j}(\overline{y}^j, 0^j, \overline{x}^j) = \mathsf{p}^{\hat{\mathbf{I}}}_{Y^j A^j | X^j}(\overline{y}^j, 0^j, \overline{x}^j)$ (by the assumptions of the lemma, $p > 0$). We first show that the relevant probabilities describing the behavior of the random system $\hat{\mathbf{F}}[\overline{x}^j, \overline{y}^j 0^j]$ (and $\hat{\mathbf{I}}[\overline{x}^j, \overline{y}^j 0^j]$) correspond to the probabilities describing the original system $\hat{\mathbf{F}}$ (and $\hat{\mathbf{I}}$) scaled by the factor $1/p$. More precisely, we have

$$\mathsf{p}^{\hat{\mathbf{F}}[\overline{x}^j, \overline{y}^j 0^j]}_{Y^i | X^i}(y^i, x^i) = \sum_{a^i \in \mathrm{ms}(i)} \mathsf{p}^{\hat{\mathbf{F}}[\overline{x}^j, \overline{y}^j 0^j]}_{Y^i A^i | X^i}(y^i, a^i, x^i)$$

$$= \frac{1}{p} \cdot \sum_{a^i \in \mathrm{ms}(i)} \mathsf{p}^{\hat{\mathbf{F}}}_{Y^{j+i} A^{j+i} | X^{j+i}}(\overline{y}^j y^i, 0^j a^i, \overline{x}^j x^i)$$

$$= \frac{1}{p} \cdot \mathsf{p}^{\hat{\mathbf{F}}}_{Y^{j+i} A^j | X^{j+i}}(\overline{y}^j y^i, 0^j, \overline{x}^j x^i)$$

and similarly $\mathsf{p}_{Y^i|X^i}^{\hat{\mathbf{I}}[\overline{x}^j,\overline{y}^j0^j]}(y^i,x^i) = \frac{1}{p}\cdot\mathsf{p}_{Y^{j+i}A^j|X^{j+i}}^{\hat{\mathbf{I}}}(\overline{y}^jy^i,0^j,\overline{x}^jx^i)$. We can use this to express the quantity $m_{x^i,y^i}^{\hat{\mathbf{F}}[\overline{x}^j,\overline{y}^j0^j]^-,\hat{\mathbf{I}}[\overline{x}^j,\overline{y}^j0^j]^-}$ as

$$
\begin{aligned}
m_{x^i,y^i}^{\hat{\mathbf{F}}[\overline{x}^j,\overline{y}^j0^j]^-,\hat{\mathbf{I}}[\overline{x}^j,\overline{y}^j0^j]^-} &= \min\left\{\mathsf{p}_{Y^i|X^i}^{\hat{\mathbf{F}}[\overline{x}^j,\overline{y}^j0^j]^-}(y^i,x^i),\mathsf{p}_{Y^i|X^i}^{\hat{\mathbf{I}}[\overline{x}^j,\overline{y}^j0^j]^-}(y^i,x^i)\right\} \\
&= \frac{1}{p}\cdot\min\Big\{\mathsf{p}_{Y^{j+i}A^j|X^{j+i}}^{\hat{\mathbf{F}}}(\overline{y}^jy^i,0^j,\overline{x}^jx^i), \\
&\qquad\qquad \mathsf{p}_{Y^{j+i}A^j|X^{j+i}}^{\hat{\mathbf{I}}}(\overline{y}^jy^i,0^j,\overline{x}^jx^i)\Big\} \\
&= \frac{1}{p}\cdot\mathsf{p}_{Y^{j+i}A^{j+i}|X^{j+i}}^{\hat{\mathbf{F}}}(\overline{y}^jy^i,0^{j+i},\overline{x}^jx^i) \qquad (7)\\
&= \frac{1}{p}\cdot m_{\overline{x}^jx^i,\overline{y}^jy^i}^{\hat{\mathbf{F}},\hat{\mathbf{I}}}.
\end{aligned}
$$

To justify the step (7), note that from the condition (5), which is satisfied for $\hat{\mathbf{F}}$ and $\hat{\mathbf{I}}$, we have $\mathsf{p}_{Y^{j+i}A^{j+i}|X^{j+i}}^{\hat{\mathbf{F}}}(\overline{y}^jy^i,0^{j+i},\overline{x}^jx^i) = \mathsf{p}_{Y^{j+i}A^{j+i}|X^{j+i}}^{\hat{\mathbf{I}}}(\overline{y}^jy^i,0^{j+i},\overline{x}^jx^i)$ and also $\mathsf{p}_{Y^{j+i}A^j|X^{j+i}}(\overline{y}^jy^i,0^j,\overline{x}^jx^i) = \mathsf{p}_{Y^{j+i}A^{j+i}|X^{j+i}}(\overline{y}^jy^i,0^{j+i},\overline{x}^jx^i)$ for at least one of the systems $\hat{\mathbf{F}}$ and $\hat{\mathbf{I}}$.

Now we can verify that the condition (5) is satisfied also for the system $\hat{\mathbf{F}}[\overline{x}^j,\overline{y}^j0^j]$ with respect to the systems $\hat{\mathbf{F}}[\overline{x}^j,\overline{y}^j0^j]^-$ and $\hat{\mathbf{I}}[\overline{x}^j,\overline{y}^j0^j]^-$. For the first equation of (5), we have

$$
\begin{aligned}
\mathsf{p}_{Y^iA_i|X^i}^{\hat{\mathbf{F}}[\overline{x}^j,\overline{y}^j0^j]}(y^i,0,x^i) &= \frac{1}{p}\cdot\mathsf{p}_{Y^{j+i}A_{j+i}|X^{j+i}}^{\hat{\mathbf{F}}}(\overline{y}^jy^i,0,\overline{x}^jx^i) \\
&= \frac{1}{p}\cdot m_{\overline{x}^jx^i,\overline{y}^jy^i}^{\hat{\mathbf{F}},\hat{\mathbf{I}}} = m_{x^i,y^i}^{\hat{\mathbf{F}}[\overline{x}^j,\overline{y}^j0^j]^-,\hat{\mathbf{I}}[\overline{x}^j,\overline{y}^j0^j]^-}
\end{aligned}
$$

and since clearly $\mathsf{p}_{Y^i|X^i}^{\hat{\mathbf{F}}[\overline{x}^j,\overline{y}^j0^j]}(y^i,x^i) = \mathsf{p}_{Y^i|X^i}^{\hat{\mathbf{F}}[\overline{x}^j,\overline{y}^j0^j]^-}(y^i,x^i)$, the second equation of (5) is satisfied as well. Therefore, by Lemma 2(iv), we have $\nu_k(\hat{\mathbf{F}}[\overline{x}^j,\overline{y}^j0^j]) = \Delta_k(\hat{\mathbf{F}}[\overline{x}^j,\overline{y}^j0^j]^-,\hat{\mathbf{I}}[\overline{x}^j,\overline{y}^j0^j]^-)$. $\qquad\square$

Lemma 4 involves the systems $\hat{\mathbf{F}}$ and $\hat{\mathbf{I}}$ projected to a specific state, but it is more desirable to consider the original systems $\mathbf{F}$ and $\mathbf{I}$ instead. This is achieved by the following lemma.

**Lemma 5.** *In the setting described in Lemma 4, we have*

$$
\Delta_k(\hat{\mathbf{F}}[\overline{x}^j,\overline{y}^j0^j]^-,\hat{\mathbf{I}}[\overline{x}^j,\overline{y}^j0^j]^-) \le \Delta_k(\mathbf{F}[\overline{x}^j,\overline{y}^j],\mathbf{I}[\overline{x}^j,\overline{y}^j])
$$

*for any $\overline{x}^j,\overline{y}^j$ such that the systems on the left side are defined.*

*Proof.* To prove the lemma, we show that for any distinguisher $\mathbf{D}$ we have $\delta_k^{\mathbf{D}}(\hat{\mathbf{F}}[\overline{x}^j,\overline{y}^j0^j]^-,\hat{\mathbf{I}}[\overline{x}^j,\overline{y}^j0^j]^-) \le \delta_k^{\mathbf{D}}(\mathbf{F}[\overline{x}^j,\overline{y}^j],\mathbf{I}[\overline{x}^j,\overline{y}^j])$. Without loss of generality, let us assume $\mathsf{p}_{Y^j|X^j}^{\mathbf{F}}(\overline{y}^j,\overline{x}^j) \ge \mathsf{p}_{Y^j|X^j}^{\mathbf{I}}(\overline{y}^j,\overline{x}^j)$, otherwise the proof would be symmetric. This assumption implies $\hat{\mathbf{I}}[\overline{x}^j, \overline{y}^j 0^j]^- \equiv \mathbf{I}[\overline{x}^j, \overline{y}^j]$, hence it suffices to prove

$$\delta_k^{\mathbf{D}}(\hat{\mathbf{F}}[\overline{x}^j, \overline{y}^j 0^j]^-, \mathbf{I}[\overline{x}^j, \overline{y}^j]) \leq \delta_k^{\mathbf{D}}(\mathbf{F}[\overline{x}^j, \overline{y}^j], \mathbf{I}[\overline{x}^j, \overline{y}^j]).$$

Using (4) to express both sides of this inequality, we see that we only need to prove that for all $x^k \in \mathcal{X}^k$ and $y^k \in \mathcal{Y}^k$,

$$\mathsf{p}_{Y^k|X^k}^{\hat{\mathbf{F}}[\overline{x}^j, \overline{y}^j 0^j]^-}(y^k, x^k) < \mathsf{p}_{Y^k|X^k}^{\mathbf{I}[\overline{x}^j, \overline{y}^j]}(y^k, x^k) \Rightarrow \mathsf{p}_{Y^k|X^k}^{\mathbf{F}[\overline{x}^j, \overline{y}^j]}(y^k, x^k) \leq \mathsf{p}_{Y^k|X^k}^{\hat{\mathbf{F}}[\overline{x}^j, \overline{y}^j 0^j]^-}(y^k, x^k). \tag{8}$$

In the systems $\mathbf{I}[\overline{x}^j, \overline{y}^j]$, $\mathbf{F}[\overline{x}^j, \overline{y}^j]$ and $\hat{\mathbf{F}}[\overline{x}^j, \overline{y}^j 0^j]^-$, the conditional distributions $\mathsf{p}_{Y^k|X^k}(y^k, x^k)$ are given by the following expressions, respectively:

$$\mathsf{p}_{Y^k|X^k}^{\mathbf{I}[\overline{x}^j, \overline{y}^j]}(y^k, x^k) = \frac{\mathsf{p}_{Y^{j+k}|X^{j+k}}^{\mathbf{I}}(\overline{y}^j y^k, \overline{x}^j x^k)}{\mathsf{p}_{Y^j|X^j}^{\mathbf{I}}(\overline{y}^j, \overline{x}^j)} \tag{9}$$

$$\mathsf{p}_{Y^k|X^k}^{\mathbf{F}[\overline{x}^j, \overline{y}^j]}(y^k, x^k) = \frac{\mathsf{p}_{Y^{j+k}|X^{j+k}}^{\mathbf{F}}(\overline{y}^j y^k, \overline{x}^j x^k)}{\mathsf{p}_{Y^j|X^j}^{\mathbf{F}}(\overline{y}^j, \overline{x}^j)} \tag{10}$$

$$\mathsf{p}_{Y^k|X^k}^{\hat{\mathbf{F}}[\overline{x}^j, \overline{y}^j 0^j]^-}(y^k, x^k) = \frac{\mathsf{p}_{Y^{j+k}A^j|X^{j+k}}^{\hat{\mathbf{F}}}(\overline{y}^j y^k, 0^j, \overline{x}^j x^k)}{\mathsf{p}_{Y^j A^j|X^j}^{\hat{\mathbf{F}}}(\overline{y}^j, 0^j, \overline{x}^j)} \tag{11}$$

Informally, the conditional distributions $\mathsf{p}_{Y^k|X^k}$ of the systems $\mathbf{I}[\overline{x}^j, \overline{y}^j]$, $\mathbf{F}[\overline{x}^j, \overline{y}^j]$ and $\hat{\mathbf{F}}[\overline{x}^j, \overline{y}^j 0^j]^-$ are again related to the conditional distributions $\mathsf{p}_{Y^{j+k}|X^{j+k}}$ of the original systems ($\mathbf{I}$, $\mathbf{F}$, and $\hat{\mathbf{F}}$ with $A_j = 0$, respectively) by some scaling factors (the denominators in the above equations). The factor turns out to be the same for $\mathbf{I}[\overline{x}^j, \overline{y}^j]$ and $\hat{\mathbf{F}}[\overline{x}^j, \overline{y}^j 0^j]^-$, however for $\mathbf{F}[\overline{x}^j, \overline{y}^j]$ it may be different. This results into a different scaling of the distributions for $\hat{\mathbf{F}}[\overline{x}^j, \overline{y}^j 0^j]^-$ and $\mathbf{F}[\overline{x}^j, \overline{y}^j]$ and allows us to show that (8) is indeed satisfied. A more detailed argument follows.

Let us fix $x^k$ and $y^k$ such that $\mathsf{p}_{Y^k|X^k}^{\hat{\mathbf{F}}[\overline{x}^j, \overline{y}^j 0^j]^-}(y^k, x^k) < \mathsf{p}_{Y^k|X^k}^{\mathbf{I}[\overline{x}^j, \overline{y}^j]}(y^k, x^k)$. By the definition of $A_i$ we have $\mathsf{p}_{Y^j|X^j}^{\mathbf{I}}(\overline{y}^j, \overline{x}^j) = \mathsf{p}_{Y^j A^j|X^j}^{\hat{\mathbf{F}}}(\overline{y}^j, 0^j, \overline{x}^j)$, hence by comparing the equations (9) and (11) we get $\mathsf{p}_{Y^{j+k}A^j|X^{j+k}}^{\hat{\mathbf{F}}}(\overline{y}^j y^k, 0^j, \overline{x}^j x^k) < \mathsf{p}_{Y^{j+k}|X^{j+k}}^{\mathbf{I}}(\overline{y}^j y^k, \overline{x}^j x^k)$. This in turn implies $\mathsf{p}_{Y^{j+k}A^{j+k}|X^{j+k}}^{\hat{\mathbf{F}}}(\overline{y}^j y^k, 0^{j+k}, \overline{x}^j x^k) < \mathsf{p}_{Y^{j+k}|X^{j+k}}^{\mathbf{I}}(\overline{y}^j y^k, \overline{x}^j x^k)$. Now, recalling that the MBO $A_i$ is defined to satisfy the properties (5), we see that $\mathsf{p}_{Y^{j+k}|X^{j+k}}^{\mathbf{F}}(\overline{y}^j y^k, \overline{x}^j x^k) < \mathsf{p}_{Y^{j+k}|X^{j+k}}^{\mathbf{I}}(\overline{y}^j y^k, \overline{x}^j x^k)$ and therefore also $\mathsf{p}_{Y^{j+k}A^{j+k}|X^{j+k}}^{\hat{\mathbf{F}}}(\overline{y}^j y^k, 0^{j+k}, \overline{x}^j x^k) = \mathsf{p}_{Y^{j+k}|X^{j+k}}^{\mathbf{F}}(\overline{y}^j y^k, \overline{x}^j x^k)$. This in turn implies $\mathsf{p}_{Y^{j+k}A^j|X^{j+k}}^{\hat{\mathbf{F}}}(\overline{y}^j y^k, 0^j, \overline{x}^j x^k) = \mathsf{p}_{Y^{j+k}|X^{j+k}}^{\mathbf{F}}(\overline{y}^j y^k, \overline{x}^j x^k)$, hence the numerators in (10) and (11) are the same. The denominators are easy to compare, it obviously holds $\mathsf{p}_{Y^j|X^j}^{\mathbf{F}}(\overline{y}^j, \overline{x}^j) \geq \mathsf{p}_{Y^j A^j|X^j}^{\hat{\mathbf{F}}}(\overline{y}^j, 0^j, \overline{x}^j)$, hence from (10) and (11) we obtain $\mathsf{p}_{Y^k|X^k}^{\mathbf{F}[\overline{x}^j, \overline{y}^j]}(y^k, x^k) \leq \mathsf{p}_{Y^k|X^k}^{\hat{\mathbf{F}}[\overline{x}^j, \overline{y}^j 0^j]^-}(y^k, x^k)$, completing the proof of (8). $\qquad\square$

Note that combining the technical Lemmas 4 and 5 gives us

$$\lambda_k(\langle \hat{\mathbf{F}}/\hat{\mathbf{I}}\rangle) = \max_{j,\overline{x}^j,\overline{y}^j} \Delta_{k-j}\left(\hat{\mathbf{F}}[\overline{x}^j,\overline{y}^j 0^j]^-, \hat{\mathbf{I}}[\overline{x}^j,\overline{y}^j 0^j]^-\right) \le \Lambda_k(\mathbf{F},\mathbf{I}) \qquad (12)$$

for the systems described above.

## 5   Connection to Indistinguishability Amplification

We are now ready to prove our main theorem. First we define some intuitive notation: by $\mathcal{D}\mathbf{C}(\cdot,\mathbf{J})$ we denote the class of distinguishers obtained by connecting any distinguisher to $\mathbf{C}(\cdot,\mathbf{J})$ and placing the system to be distinguished as the first subsystem. The class of distinguishers $\mathcal{D}\mathbf{C}(\mathbf{I},\cdot)$ is defined analogously.

**Theorem 1.** *Let $\mathbf{C}(\cdot,\cdot)$ be a neutralizing construction for the pairs $(\mathbf{F},\mathbf{I})$ and $(\mathbf{G},\mathbf{J})$ of systems. Let $\mathbf{Q}$ denote the system $\mathbf{C}(\mathbf{I},\mathbf{J})$. Then, for all $k$,*

$$\Delta_k(\mathbf{C}(\mathbf{F},\mathbf{G}),\mathbf{Q}) \le 2\left(\delta_{k'}^{\mathcal{D}\mathbf{C}(\cdot,\mathbf{J})}(\mathbf{F},\mathbf{I}) \cdot \Lambda_{k''}(\mathbf{G},\mathbf{J}) + \delta_{k''}^{\mathcal{D}\mathbf{C}(\mathbf{I},\cdot)}(\mathbf{G},\mathbf{J}) \cdot \Lambda_{k'}(\mathbf{F},\mathbf{I})\right).$$

*Proof.* We use the technique from the proof of Theorem 1 in [6] to transform the task of distinguishing $\mathbf{C}(\mathbf{F},\mathbf{G})$ from $\mathbf{Q}$ to the task of provoking the MBO of the system $\mathbf{S} := \hat{\mathbf{C}}(\langle \hat{\mathbf{F}}/\hat{\mathbf{I}}\rangle_{Z_1}, \langle \hat{\mathbf{G}}/\hat{\mathbf{J}}\rangle_{Z_2})$, where $\hat{\mathbf{F}}$, $\hat{\mathbf{I}}$ and $\hat{\mathbf{G}}$, $\hat{\mathbf{J}}$ are obtained using Lemma 2 from $\mathbf{F}$, $\mathbf{I}$ and $\mathbf{G}$, $\mathbf{J}$, respectively; and $\hat{\mathbf{C}}$ is the same construction as $\mathbf{C}$ except that it also has an MBO, which is defined as the AND of the two internal MBOs. Then we use a different approach to bound the value $\nu_k(\mathbf{S})$, exploiting the concept of free-start distinguishing.

First, by Lemma 1 (ii) we have $\Delta_k(\mathbf{C}(\mathbf{F},\mathbf{G}),\mathbf{Q}) = 2 \cdot \Delta_k(\langle \mathbf{C}(\mathbf{F},\mathbf{G})/\mathbf{Q}\rangle_Z, \mathbf{Q})$ and by Lemma 1 (i) $\Delta_k(\langle \mathbf{C}(\mathbf{F},\mathbf{G})/\mathbf{Q}\rangle_Z, \mathbf{Q})$ is the optimal advantage in guessing the uniform random bit $Z'$ in the system $\langle\langle \mathbf{C}(\mathbf{F},\mathbf{G})/\mathbf{Q}\rangle_Z/\mathbf{Q}\rangle_{Z'}$. However, thanks to the neutralizing property of $\mathbf{C}(\cdot,\cdot)$. it can be easily verified that $\langle\langle \mathbf{C}(\mathbf{F},\mathbf{G})/\mathbf{Q}\rangle_Z/\mathbf{Q}\rangle_{Z'} \equiv \mathbf{C}(\langle \mathbf{F}/\mathbf{I}\rangle_{Z_1}, \langle \mathbf{G}/\mathbf{J}\rangle_{Z_2})$ for independent uniformly random bits $Z_1 := Z$ and $Z_2 := Z \oplus Z'$. Hence, $\Delta_k(\langle \mathbf{C}(\mathbf{F},\mathbf{G})/\mathbf{Q}\rangle_Z, \mathbf{Q})$ is also the optimal advantage in guessing the bit $Z' = Z_1 \oplus Z_2$ in $\mathbf{C}(\langle \mathbf{F}/\mathbf{I}\rangle_{Z_1}, \langle \mathbf{G}/\mathbf{J}\rangle_{Z_2})$.

We can now extend the systems $\mathbf{F}$ and $\mathbf{I}$ by adding MBOs satisfying the equations (5) to obtain the systems $\hat{\mathbf{F}}$ and $\hat{\mathbf{I}}$ with the properties guaranteed by Lemma 2. Similarly, we can extend $\mathbf{G}$ and $\mathbf{J}$ and obtain the systems $\hat{\mathbf{G}}$ and $\hat{\mathbf{J}}$. Since the MBO in $\mathbf{S}$ can always be ignored, the task of guessing $Z_1 \oplus Z_2$ can only be easier in $\mathbf{S}$ compared to $\mathbf{C}(\langle \mathbf{F}/\mathbf{I}\rangle_{Z_1}, \langle \mathbf{G}/\mathbf{J}\rangle_{Z_2})$. However, as long as one of the MBOs in the subsystems of $\mathbf{S}$ is 0, the advantage in guessing the corresponding bit $Z_i$ is 0 and hence also the advantage in guessing $Z_1 \oplus Z_2$ is 0. Therefore the latter advantage can be upper-bounded by $\nu_k(\mathbf{S})$.

Using Lemma 3, for any distinguisher $\mathbf{D}$ we have

$$\nu_k^{\mathbf{D}}(\mathbf{S}) \le \mathsf{P}^{\mathbf{DS}}(F_k^1) \cdot \lambda_{k''}(\langle \hat{\mathbf{G}}/\hat{\mathbf{J}}\rangle) + \mathsf{P}^{\mathbf{DS}}(F_k^2) \cdot \lambda_{k'}(\langle \hat{\mathbf{F}}/\hat{\mathbf{I}}\rangle).$$

Let us first bound the term $\mathsf{P}^{\mathbf{DS}}(F_k^1)$. Since $\langle \hat{\mathbf{F}}/\hat{\mathbf{I}}\rangle^{\dashv} \equiv \hat{\mathbf{F}}^{\dashv}$ and $\langle \hat{\mathbf{G}}/\hat{\mathbf{J}}\rangle^{\dashv} \equiv \hat{\mathbf{J}}^{\dashv}$, we have $\mathsf{P}^{\mathbf{DS}}(F_k^1) = \mathsf{P}^{\mathbf{D}\hat{\mathbf{C}}(\hat{\mathbf{F}},\hat{\mathbf{J}})}(F_k^1)$. Moreover, $\mathsf{P}^{\mathbf{D}\hat{\mathbf{C}}(\hat{\mathbf{F}},\hat{\mathbf{J}})}(F_k^1) \le \nu_k^{\mathbf{D}}(\mathbf{C}(\hat{\mathbf{F}},\mathbf{J}))$

since on the left side, we only consider the MBO of $\hat{\mathbf{F}}$ being provoked first, while on the right side is the probability of it being provoked at any time. Obviously $\nu_k^{\mathbf{D}}(\mathbf{C}(\hat{\mathbf{F}}, \mathbf{J})) \le \nu_{k'}^{\mathbf{DC}(\cdot, \mathbf{J})}(\hat{\mathbf{F}})$ and by Lemma 2 we have $\nu_{k'}^{\mathbf{DC}(\cdot, \mathbf{J})}(\hat{\mathbf{F}}) = \delta_{k'}^{\mathbf{DC}(\cdot, \mathbf{J})}(\mathbf{F}, \mathbf{I})$. By a symmetric reasoning we obtain $\mathsf{P}^{\mathbf{DS}}(F_k^2) \le \delta_{k''}^{\mathbf{DC}(\mathbf{I}, \cdot)}(\mathbf{G}, \mathbf{J})$.

Finally, using (12) we obtain the bounds $\lambda_{k''}(\langle \hat{\mathbf{G}}/\hat{\mathbf{J}}\rangle) \le \Lambda_{k''}(\mathbf{G}, \mathbf{J})$ and $\lambda_{k'}(\langle \hat{\mathbf{F}}/\hat{\mathbf{I}}\rangle) \le \Lambda_{k'}(\mathbf{F}, \mathbf{I})$, which together conclude the proof.     □

For the two particular neutralizing constructions that motivate our analysis, we obtain the following corollaries.

**Corollary 1.** *Let* $\mathbf{F}$ *and* $\mathbf{G}$ *be* $(\mathcal{X}, \mathcal{Y})$-*random functions, let* $\star$ *be a quasi-group operation on* $\mathcal{Y}$. *Then, for all* $k$,

$$\Delta_k(\mathbf{F} \star \mathbf{G}, \mathbf{R}) \le 2\left(\Delta_k^{\mathsf{NA}}(\mathbf{F}, \mathbf{R}) \cdot \Lambda_k(\mathbf{G}, \mathbf{R}) + \Delta_k^{\mathsf{NA}}(\mathbf{G}, \mathbf{R}) \cdot \Lambda_k(\mathbf{F}, \mathbf{R})\right).$$

*Proof.* Applying Theorem 1 to the neutralizing construction $\mathbf{F} \star \mathbf{G}$, it only remains to prove that $\mathcal{D}(\cdot \star \mathbf{R})$ corresponds to the class of non-adaptive distinguishers. This is indeed the case, since any distinguisher will only receive random outputs from $\mathbf{F} \star \mathbf{R}$. It could simulate these outputs itself, ignoring the actual outputs, thus operating non-adaptively. The same holds for the class of distinguishers $\mathcal{D}(\mathbf{R} \star \cdot)$. Recalling that $\delta_k^{\mathsf{NA}}(\mathbf{S}, \mathbf{T}) = \Delta_k^{\mathsf{NA}}(\mathbf{S}, \mathbf{T})$ for any systems $\mathbf{S}, \mathbf{T}$ completes the proof.     □

**Corollary 2.** *Let* $\mathbf{F}$ *and* $\mathbf{G}$ *be* $(\mathcal{X}, \mathcal{X})$-*random permutations, let* $\mathbf{G}$ *be cc-stateless. Then, for all* $k$,

$$\Delta_k(\mathbf{F} \triangleright \mathbf{G}, \mathbf{P}) \le 2\left(\Delta_k^{\mathsf{NA}}(\mathbf{F}, \mathbf{P}) \cdot \Lambda_k(\mathbf{G}, \mathbf{P}) + \Delta_k^{\mathsf{RI}}(\mathbf{G}, \mathbf{P}) \cdot \Lambda_k(\mathbf{F}, \mathbf{P})\right).$$

*Proof.* Again, when applying Theorem 1 to the neutralizing construction $\mathbf{F} \triangleright \mathbf{G}$, we need to justify that the distinguisher classes $\mathcal{D}(\cdot \triangleright \mathbf{P})$ and $\mathcal{D}(\mathbf{P} \triangleright \cdot)$ correspond to $\mathsf{NA}$ and $\mathsf{RI}$, respectively. In the first case, the distinguisher only receives random outputs, so it can again simulate them itself and hence corresponds to a non-adaptive distinguisher. In the second case, the distinguisher $\mathbf{D}(\mathbf{P} \triangleright \cdot)$ can only provide random inputs to the distinguished system, with the possibility of repeating an input. However, since both $\mathbf{G}$ and $\mathbf{P}$ are cc-stateless permutations, repeated inputs will only produce repeated outputs and hence cannot help the distinguisher.     □

# 6   Conclusion and Further Research

Our main theorem unifies the claims of both Theorem 1 and Theorem 2 in [6] under reasonable assumptions. To see this, let us focus for example on the natural case of random functions, assuming $\mathbf{F} \equiv \mathbf{G}$ and $\mathbf{I} \equiv \mathbf{J} \equiv \mathbf{R}$. Our theorem gives a better bound than Theorem 2 in [6] as long as $\Lambda_k(\mathbf{F}, \mathbf{R}) < 1/2$. It also improves the bound from Theorem 1 in [6] as long as

$$\frac{\Lambda_k(\mathbf{F}, \mathbf{R})}{\Delta_k(\mathbf{F}, \mathbf{R})} < \frac{1}{2} \cdot \frac{\Delta_k(\mathbf{F}, \mathbf{R})}{\Delta_k^{\mathsf{NA}}(\mathbf{F}, \mathbf{R})}.$$

This means, loosely speaking, that the improvement occurs as long as the ratio of advantage gained from the free choice of state is smaller than the ratio of advantage gained from extending the distinguisher class.

This improvement is significant for any random function $\mathbf{F}$ that satisfies the conditions

$$\Delta_k^{\mathsf{NA}}(\mathbf{F}, \mathbf{R}) \ll \Delta_k(\mathbf{F}, \mathbf{R}) \approx \Lambda_k(\mathbf{F}, \mathbf{R}) \ll 1.$$

As an example, consider the simple cc-stateless random function $\mathbf{F} \colon \{0,1\}^n \to \{0,1\}^n$ that behaves as follows: with probability $2^{-n/2}$ it satisfies the (adaptively verifiable) condition $\mathbf{F}(\mathbf{F}(0)) = 0$ and the remaining values (including $\mathbf{F}(0)$) are chosen uniformly at random, in the rest of the cases (with probability $1 - 2^{-n/2}$) $\mathbf{F}$ behaves exactly like $\mathbf{R}$.

In general, a small $\Delta_k(\mathbf{F}, \mathbf{R})$ does not necessarily imply a small $\Lambda_k(\mathbf{F}, \mathbf{R})$, since it is easy to construct a counterexample where some specific initial transcript leads to a behavior that is easy to distinguish from the ideal system. However, a small value of $\Lambda_k(\mathbf{F}, \mathbf{R})$ may be considered a desirable requirement for a good quasi-random function.

Although it is not difficult to define the concept of free-start distinguishing in the computational setting, our main result does not translate to this setting. This is because such a translation would imply that for example composition of non-adaptively secure pseudo-random permutations is adaptively secure, which would contradict the results in [10] under standard assumptions. Therefore, the implications of our result for the computational setting remain an open question.

**Acknowledgements.** This research was partially supported by the Swiss National Science Foundation (SNF) project no. 200020-113700/1 and by the grants VEGA 1/0266/09 and UK/385/2009.

# References

1. Dodis, Y., Impagliazzo, R., Jaiswal, R., Kabanets, V.: Security Amplification for Interactive Cryptographic Primitives. In: Reingold, O. (ed.) TCC 2009. LNCS, vol. 5444, pp. 128–145. Springer, Heidelberg (2009)
2. Luby, M., Rackoff, C.: Pseudo-random Permutation Generators and Cryptographic Composition. In: STOC 1986, pp. 356–363 (1986)
3. Maurer, U.: Indistinguishability of Random Systems. In: Knudsen, L.R. (ed.) EUROCRYPT 2002. LNCS, vol. 2332, pp. 110–132. Springer, Heidelberg (2002)
4. Maurer, U., Oswald, Y.A., Pietrzak, K., Sjödin, J.: Luby-Rackoff Ciphers with Weak Round Functions. In: Vaudenay, S. (ed.) EUROCRYPT 2006. LNCS, vol. 4004, pp. 391–408. Springer, Heidelberg (2006)
5. Maurer, U., Pietrzak, K.: Composition of Random Systems: When Two Weak Make One Strong. In: Naor, M. (ed.) TCC 2004. LNCS, vol. 2951, pp. 410–427. Springer, Heidelberg (2004)
6. Maurer, U., Pietrzak, K., Renner, R.: Indistinguishability Amplification. In: Menezes, A. (ed.) CRYPTO 2007. LNCS, vol. 4622, pp. 130–149. Springer, Heidelberg (2007)

7. Maurer, U., Tessaro, S.: Computational Indistinguishability Amplification: Tight Product Theorem for System Composition. In: Halevi, S. (ed.) Advances in Cryptology - CRYPTO 2009. LNCS, vol. 5677, pp. 355–373. Springer, Heidelberg (2009)
8. Myers, S.: On the Development of Blockciphers and Pseudo-random Function Generators Using the Composition and XOR Operators, M.Sc. Thesis (1999)
9. Myers, S.: Efficient Amplification of the Security of Weak Pseudo-random Function Generators. Journal of Cryptology 16(1), 1–24 (2003)
10. Pietrzak, K.: Composition Does Not Imply Adaptive Security. In: Shoup, V. (ed.) CRYPTO 2005. LNCS, vol. 3621, pp. 55–65. Springer, Heidelberg (2005)
11. Vaudenay, S.: Decorrelation: A Theory for Block Cipher Security. Journal of Cryptology 16(4), 249–286 (2003)

# Code-Based Public-Key Cryptosystems and Their Applications

Kazukuni Kobara

Research Center for Information Security (RCIS), National Institute of Advanced Industrial Science and Technology (AIST), 11F 1003, Akihabara-Daibiru, 1-18-13, Soto-Kanda, Tiyoda-ku, Tokyo, 101-0021, Japan
kobara_conf@m.aist.go.jp

**Abstract.** Code-based public-key cryptosystems are based on the hardness of a decoding problem. Their advantages include: 1) quantum tolerant, i.e. no polynomial time algorithm is known even on quantum computers whereas number theoretic public-key cryptosystems, such as RSA, Elliptic Curve Cryptosystems, DH, DSA, are vulnerable against them. 2) arithmetic unit is small for encryption and signature verification since they consists mostly of exclusive-ors that are highly parallelizable. The drawback is, however, that the public-key size is large, which is around some hundreds KB to some MB for typical parameters. Several attempts have been conducted to reduce the public-key size. Most of them, however, failed except one, which is Quasi-Dyadic (QD) public-key (for large extention degrees). While an attack has been proposed on QD public-key (for small extension degrees), it can be prevented by making the extension degree $m$ larger, specifically by making $q^{(m(m-1))}$ large enough where $q$ is the base filed and $q = 2$ for a binary code. QD approach can be improved further by using the method proposed in this paper. We call it "Flexible" Quasi-Dyadic (FQD) since it is flexible in its parameter choice, i.e. FQD can even achieve the maximum code length $n = 2^m - t$ with one shot for given error correction capability $t$ whereas QD must hold $n << 2^m - t$ (at least $n \leq 2^{m-1}$) and the key generation is performed by trial and error. Achieving $n = 2^m - t$ or more loosely $n = 2^m - 2^{\lceil \log_2 t \rceil}$) is crucial for code-based digital signatures since they must make $2^{mt}/\binom{n}{t}$ small enough and without making $n$ close to $2^m - t$ it cannot be satisfied. FQD can also be applied to code-based digital signatures.

**Keywords:** Public-key, digital signature, lightweight, ubiquitous, linear code.

## 1 Introduction

Public-key cryptosystems (PKCs) can be divided into the categories[1] shown in Fig. 1 and 2, respectively. Almost all of the currently deployed ones are based only on a small class of hard problems, namely Integer Factoring Problem (IFP) or Discrete Logarithm Problem (DLP). They are referred to as number theoretic problems. The number theoretic problem based PKCs have the following disadvantages that should be solved in

---

[1] Multivariate polynomial based ones may be included, but all of them have been broken and no relief method is known so far.

K. Kurosawa (Ed.): ICITS 2009, LNCS 5973, pp. 45–55, 2010.

**Integer Factoring Based:**
- RSA
- Rabin
- Okamoto-Uchiyama
- Paillier

**Discrete Logarithm Based:**
- Diffie-Hellman
- ElGamal
- ECC
- XTR
- Cramer-Shoup
- Kurosawa-Desmedt

**Code Based:**
- McEliece
- Niederreiter

**Lattice Based:**
- NTRU
- Ajtai-Dwork
- Goldreich-Goldwasser-Halevi
- Ajtai
- Regev
- Peikert

**Subset Sum Based:**
- Okamoto-Tanaka-Uchiyama

**Fig. 1.** Examples of PKCs Based on Number Theoretic (Cyclic) Problem

**Fig. 2.** Examples of PKCs Based on Combinatorial Problem

short term and long term, respectively. The long term problem is the lack of quantum tolerance. The number theoretic problems are closely related to a problem to determine the cycle (hence they may be referred to as a cyclic problem) and they will be solved in (probabilistic) polynomial-time after the emergence of quantum computers [27] though several breakthroughs are needed to realize quantum computers. The short term problem is the requirement of heavy multiple precision modular exponentiations that are not easy to deploy with low cost on low-computational power devices, such as RFID (Radio Frequency Identity), sensors and SCADA (Supervisory Control And Data Acquisition) devices.

On the other hand, combinatorial-problems are quantum tolerant and only small arithmetic units, e.g. addition in a small field or ring, are required for encryption and signature verification. Furthermore, among the combinatorial-problem based PKCs, code-based PKCs are advantageous in redundancy, i.e. (Plaintext Size) − (Ciphertext Size), and in the arithmetic unit, i.e. encryption and signature verification consists mostly on exclusive-ors that are highly parallelizable.

The strongest security notion for PKCs is IND-CCA2 (Indistinguishability against Adaptive Chosen Ciphertext Attack) and it can be achieved by applying "appropriate" conversion scheme to the primitive code-based PKEs as long as it satisfies OW-CPA (One-Wayness against Chosen Plaintext Attack). For the McEliece primitive PKC, specific conversion scheme [17] makes the redundancy smallest while maintaining provable security in the random oracle model. For the Niederreiter primitive PKC, either OAEP++ [16] for a long plaintext or OAEP+ [28] for a small plaintext can achieve them. Not only in the random oracle model, provable security of IND-CPA and IND-CCA2 have been achieved in the standard model in [25] and [11] respectively even though the constructions in the standard model are less efficient compared to those in the random oracle model. Anyway, secure constructions are available as long as the underlying primitive code-based PKCs satisfy OW-CPA and the parameters meeting OW-CPA are estimated in [13] against the most powerful attacks (Optimized) Information Set Decoding (OISD$^2$) and Generalized Birthday Attack (GBA).

---

$^2$ In [13], it is referred to as ISD but in this paper we call it OISD to distinguish it from classical ISDs.

The drawback of code-based PKCs is, however, that the publick-key size is large, which is $k(n-k)$ bits if a binary code of length $n$ with information rate $k/n$ is used. To overcome this problem, several attempts have been conducted. They are summarized as follows.

**(Potential approaches for reducing public-key size for code-based PKCs)**
**Enhancement of error correction capability:**
- Capacity Approaching Codes
  - LDPC codes
  - QC-LDPC codes [4]
- List Decoding
  - Exhaustive search
  - List decoding for Goppa Code [7]
- Error expansion/hold [20]

**Compression of public-key:**
- Quasi-Cyclic Construction [5]
- Quasi-Dyadic Construction [23]
- Flexible-Quasi-Dyadic Construction (proposal)

Unfortunately, LDPC (Low-Density Parity Check) code approach has been broken in [24,14] where [24] works if the density of the random nonsingular secret matrix $S$ is low and [14] works for any $S$. Error expansion/hold approach has been broken in [18]. Quasi-Cyclic and QC-LDPC approaches have been broken in [2,32]. Quasi-Dyadic approach has been broken in [32], but only for small extension degrees [22]. Hence the remaining approaches are list decoding and Quasi-Dyadic approach for large extension degrees. While list decoding works, its effect is small since it can correct only a couple of more errors for practical parameters within practical decoding complexity. Hence the last resort is the quasi-dyadic approach with large extension degrees.

## 2   Quasi-Dyadic Construction

I will skip the preliminary of code-based PKCs, but you can find a lot of contents to explain them, e.g. in the surveys section of [6] or in [10].

Quasi-Dyadic construction was proposed in [23]. It uses the inter section between dyadic matrices and Goppa codes in Cauchy form. A $2^v \times 2^v$ dyadic matrix $M$ is in this form:

$$M = \begin{bmatrix} A & B \\ B & A \end{bmatrix} \tag{1}$$

where $A$ and $B$ are $2^{v-1} \times 2^{v-1}$ dyadic matrices, respectively. The advantage of a dyadic matrix is that the whole matrix can be constructed from its one row or one column. This is the trick to reduce the public matrix.

Due to the following Theorem, it is possible to make a parity check matrix of the Goppa code Cauchy from.

**Table 1.** Sample parameters of plain code-based PKE estimated in [13]

| $m$ | $t$ | $n$ | BWF OISD $(p.l)$ | Public-key size | Plaintext/Ciphertext |
|---|---|---|---|---|---|
| 11 | 32 | 2,048 | $2^{86.8}$ $(4, 24)$ | 72.9KB | 233/352 [bits] |
| 12 | 41 | 4,098 | $2^{128.5}$ $(10.54)$ | 216.5KB | 327/492 [bits] |

**Table 2.** Sample parameters of Quasi-Dyadic (QD) code-based PKE [23]

| $m$ | $t$ | $n$ | BWF OISD $(p.l)$ | Public-key size | Plaintext/Ciphertext |
|---|---|---|---|---|---|
| 16 | 64 | 2,560 | $2^{91.3}$ $(1, 12)$ | 3.0KB | 427/1024 [bits] |
| 16 | 64 | 3,072 | $2^{108.0}$ $(2, 17)$ | 4.0KB | 445/1024 [bits] |
| 16 | 128 | 4,096 | $2^{135.8}$ $(2, 18)$ | 4.0KB | 817/1024 [bits] |

**Theorem 1 (Goppa Codes in Cauchy Form [31,21]).** *The Goppa code generated by a monic polynomial* $g(x) = (x - z_0) \cdots (x - z_{t-1})$ *without multiple zeros admits a parity-check matrix* $H$ *whose i-th row and j-th column is* $H_{ij} = 1/(z_i - L_j)$ *for* $0 \le i < t$ *and* $0 \le j < n$.

The Cauchy matrix can be dyadic by choosing distinct $z_i$ and $L_j$ meeting the following conditions:

$$\frac{1}{h_{i \oplus j}} = \frac{1}{h_i} + \frac{1}{h_j} + \frac{1}{h_0} \tag{2}$$

$$z_i = \frac{1}{h_i} + \omega \tag{3}$$

$$L_j = \frac{1}{h_j} + \frac{1}{h_0} + \omega \tag{4}$$

The construction algorithm proposed in [23] generates a sequence of $h_i$ for $0 \le i \le N$ where $n < N$ at random meeting (2) to (4). If they are not satisfied, it discards $h_i$ and regenerates them until the conditions are satisfied. Using the generated $h_i$, a $N \times N$ full dyadic matrix can be constructed. It finally picks up a $t \times n$ sub-matrix from the full $N \times N$ dyadic matrix.

This algorithm is, however, restrictive on its parameter choice, i.e. $n << 2^m - t$ must hold otherwise it eventually fails to generate a distinct set of $z_i$ and $L_j$, or takes a lot of time since it generates them by trial-and-error. This restriction prevents it from generating parameters for digital signatures since in digital signatures $2^{mt}/\binom{n}{t}$ must be small enough and without making $n$ close to $2^m - t$, $2^{mt}/\binom{n}{t}$ cannot be small.

## 3   Flexible-Quasi-Dyadic Construction

To overcome the problems in QD, we propose a more flexible and efficient construction, which we call Flexible-Quasi-Dyadic (FQD) construction. FQD does not use trial-and-error approach and generates distinct $z_i$ and $L_j$ with one shot even for $n = 2^m - t$. FQD does not have any restriction such as $n << 2^m - t$.

**Table 3.** Sample parameters of Flexible-Quasi-Dyadic (FQD) code-based PKE (proposal)

| m | t | n | BWF | | Public-key size | Plaintext/Ciphertext |
|---|---|---|---|---|---|---|
| | | | OISD $(p.l)$ | UL | | |
| 11 | 32 | 2,016 | $2^{86.0}$ $(4,24)$ | - | 2.2KB | 224/352 [bits] |
| 11 | 37 | 1,984 | $2^{90.3}$ $(4,24)$ | - | 2.1KB | 262/407 [bits] |
| 11 | 64 | 1,984 | $2^{103.1}$ $(4,25)$ | - | 1.7KB | 404/704 [bits] |
| 11 | 96 | 1,920 | $2^{91.0}$ $(2,16)$ | - | 1.2KB | 546/1056 [bits] |
| 11 | 112 | 1,920 | $2^{80.0}$ $(2,16)$ | - | 0.92KB | 546/1056 [bits] |
| 12 | 19 | 4,064 | $2^{81.0}$ $(8,44)$ | - | 5.6KB | 171/228 [bits] |
| 12 | 23 | 4,064 | $2^{91.4}$ $(8,44)$ | - | 5.5KB | 202/276 [bits] |
| 12 | 32 | 4,064 | $2^{111.6}$ $(10,53)$ | - | 5.4KB | 266/384 [bits] |
| 12 | 42 | 4,032 | $2^{129.3}$ $(9,49)$ | - | 5.2KB | 333/504 [bits] |
| 12 | 64 | 4,032 | - | $2^{157.4}$ | 4.8KB | 470/768 [bits] |
| 12 | 128 | 3,968 | - | $2^{156.4}$ | 3.6KB | 811/1536 [bits] |
| 12 | 186 | 3,840 | - | $2^{155.9}$ | 2.4KB | 1069/2232 [bits] |
| 12 | 256 | 3,840 | $2^{91.3}$ $(1,13)$ | - | 1.1KB | 1352/3072 [bits] |
| 12 | 256 | 3,728 | $2^{80.0}$ $(1,13)$ | - | 0.96KB | 1340/3072 [bits] |

**Table 4.** Sample parameters of plain code-based signature (CFS signature [8])

| m | t | n | BWF | | Public-key size | Iteration | Signature Size |
|---|---|---|---|---|---|---|---|
| | | | GBA | OISD $(p.l)$ | | | |
| 19 | 11 | 524,288 | $2^{83.6}$ | - | 13,370.7KB | $2^{25.3}$ | 209 (234.3) [bits] |
| 15 | 12 | 32,768 | $2^{81.5}$ | - | 716.0KB | $2^{28.8}$ | 180 (208.8) [bits] |
| 15 | 13 | 32,768 | $2^{84.8}$ | - | 775.4KB | $2^{32.5}$ | 195 (227.5) [bits] |
| 14 | 14 | 16,384 | - | $2^{84.0}$ $(11,66)$ | 387.3KB | $2^{36.4}$ | 196 (232.4) [bits] |
| 14 | 15 | 16,384 | - | $2^{89.2}$ $(11,67)$ | 414.6KB | $2^{40.3}$ | 210 (250.3) [bits] |
| 13 | 16 | 8,192 | - | $2^{83.5}$ $(9,52)$ | 202.7KB | $2^{44.3}$ | 208 (252.3) [bits] |

FQD construction is as follows. It firstly generates one small $u \times u$ dyadic matrix using $\delta_i$ for $0 \leq i < \log_2 u$. We call them "inner delta" since they define the inner structure of the $u \times u$ full dyadic matrix. Then FQD generates the other $u \times u$ full dyadic matrices by duplicating the inner structure of the first $u \times u$ full dyadic matrix but shifting them using both $\Delta_{j_1}$ and $\Delta'_{i_1}$ for $0 \leq j_1 < \lceil n/u \rceil$ and $1 \leq i_1 < \lceil t/u \rceil$, respectively. We call $\Delta_{j_1}$ and $\Delta'_{i_1}$ "outer delta" since they define the relationship among the full $u \times u$ dyadic matrices. FQD can also remove the block-wise permutation and removal in the key generation phase of QD since the choice of $\Delta_{j_1}$ and $n$ already includes them. This is another advantage of FQD.

I will explain how to choose $\delta_i$, $\Delta_{j_1}$ and $\Delta'_{i_1}$ later on, but once they are determined, $z_i$ and $L_j$ are given as follows:

$$z_{i_0} = \oplus_{b=0}^{\log_2 u - 1} i_0[b] \cdot \delta_b \qquad \text{for} \quad 0 \leq i_0 < u \qquad (5)$$

$$z_{i_1 \cdot u + i_0} = z_{i_0} \oplus \Delta'_{i_1} \qquad \text{for} \quad 1 \leq i_1 < \lceil t/u \rceil \qquad (6)$$

$$L_{j_1 \cdot u + j_0} = z_{j_0} \oplus \Delta_{j_1} \qquad \text{for} \quad 0 \leq j_1 < \lceil n/u \rceil \qquad (7)$$

**Table 5.** Sample parameters of Flexible-Quasi-Dyadic (FQD) code-based digital signature (proposal)

| $m$ | $t$ | $n$ | BWF | | Public-key size | Iteration | Signature Size |
|---|---|---|---|---|---|---|---|
| | | | GBA | OISD $(p.l)$ | | | |
| 19 | 11 | 524,272 | $2^{83.6}$ | - | 1,215.5KB | $2^{25.3}$ | 209 (234.3) [bits] |
| 15 | 12 | 32,752 | $2^{81.5}$ | - | 59.6KB | $2^{28.8}$ | 180 (208.8) [bits] |
| 15 | 13 | 32,752 | $2^{84.8}$ | - | 59.6KB | $2^{32.5}$ | 195 (227.5) [bits] |
| 14 | 14 | 16,368 | $2^{84.1}$ | - | 27.6KB | $2^{36.4}$ | 196 (232.4) [bits] |
| 14 | 15 | 16,368 | - | $2^{89.2}$ (11,67) | 27.6KB | $2^{40.3}$ | 210 (250.3) [bits] |
| 13 | 16 | 8,176 | - | $2^{83.4}$ (9,52) | 12.6KB | $2^{44.3}$ | 208 (252.3) [bits] |

where $\oplus$ denotes exclusive-or, $i[b]$ and $j[b]$ denote $(b+1)$-th bit of $i$ and $j$ in the binary form, respectively. One can easily verify that $h_{i,j} = 1/(z_i \oplus L_j)$ makes a quasi-dyadic matrix. When $t \leq u$, $z_{i_1 \cdot u + i_0}$ can be ignored. When $\lceil t/u \rceil \cdot u > t$ and/or $\lceil \cdot n/u \rceil u > n$, by removing $\lceil t/u \rceil u - t$ rows and $\lceil n/u \rceil u - n$ columns respectively, the size can be $t \times n$. Another option is to add removed $z_i$ as $L_j$. This is useful to achieve $n = 2^m - t$ when $t \neq 2^x$ for any positive integer $x$.

The variables $\delta_i$, $\Delta_{j_1}$ and $\Delta'_{i_1}$ must be chosen at random while making all the $z_i$ for $0 \leq i < t$ and $L_j$ for $0 \leq j < n$ distinct, i.e.

$$
\begin{aligned}
z_i \oplus z_{i'} &\neq 0 & \text{for } i \neq i' && (8) \\
L_j \oplus L_{j'} &\neq 0 & \text{for } j \neq j' && (9) \\
z_i \oplus L_j &\neq 0 &&& (10)
\end{aligned}
$$

These conditions are equivalent to the following conditions:

1.  $\delta_b$ for $0 \leq b < \log_2 u$ are linearly independent.
2.  $\forall r \in \{0,1\}^{\log_2 u}$,

$$ \Delta'_{i_1}, \Delta_{j_1}, (\Delta'_{i_1} \oplus \Delta_{j_1}), (\Delta'_{i_1} \oplus \Delta'_{i'_1}), (\Delta_{j_1} \oplus \Delta_{j'_1}) \notin \oplus_{b=0}^{\log_2 u - 1} r[b] \cdot \delta_b \qquad (11) $$

where $r[b]$ denotes the $(b+1)$-th bit of $r$ in the binary form.

$\delta_b$, $\Delta'_{i_1}$ and $\Delta_{j_1}$ satisfying the above conditions can be generated by the following algorithm:

1.  Generate a $m \times m$ random binary nonsingular matrix $M$.
2.  Let the $(b+1)$-th row from the top of $M$ denote $\delta_b$ for $0 \leq b \leq (\log_2 u) - 1$.
3.  Choose distinct $\Delta'_{i_1}$ and $\Delta_{j_1}$ from a linear combination of the bottom $m - \log_2 u$ rows of $M$.

The cardinality of a nonsingular matrix $M$ is around $\pi \cdot 2^{(m(m-1))}$, which is one of the secrets of FQD construction. Other secrets include permutation among $\Delta_{j_1}$, random scalar multiplication with each $u \times u$ full dyadic block and multiplication of non-singular random dyadic matrix $S$.

We show some sample parameters for binary codes in Table 1 to 5, but the idea of FQD construction can easily be extended to non-binary codes, too. In these tables, $m$,

$t$ and $n$ are parameters of the underlying code. $m$ is the extension degree, $t$ is the error correction capability and $n$ is the code length. In plain (non-quasi-dyadic) schemes, $n = 2^m$ or $n < 2^m$, in QD, $n << 2^m - t$ and in FQD, $n = 2^m - t$ (or $n < 2^m - t$). BWF is the minimal binary workfactor to break the system, which is either Optimized Information Set Decoding (OISD), Generalized Birthday Attack (GBA) or the attack in [32] on QD/FQD (we call it UL attack). The values of OISD and GBA follow the estimation in [13]. $p$ and $l$ are optimum parameters for OISD. In [32], the BWF of UL, $\text{BWF}_{\text{UL}}$ is estimated as $q^2 \times (\log_2 q^2)^3 (v^2 + 3v + b)^2 v(v + b)$ where $v = \log_2 u$ and $b = \lceil n/u \rceil$, but this estimation is for $m = 2$. For $m \geq 2$, it is

$$\text{BWF}_{\text{UL}} = q^{m(m-1)} \times (\log_2 q^2)^3 (v^2 + 3v + b)^2 v(v + b) \qquad (12)$$

In the columns of BWF "-" means the corresponding attack is less powerful. In the column of public-key size, KB$= 1024 \times 8$ bits. Plaintext/Ciphertext is the plaintext size and the ciphertext size in bits in the Niederreiter form. Iteration shows the signature generation cost, i.e. the number of trials to decode an error pattern corresponding to given syndromes. The signature size in () is when the error pattern is expressed as the positions of $t$ errors. This increases the signature size but decreases the signature verification cost compared with the case where an error pattern is expressed as an integer between 0 and $\binom{n}{t} - 1$. The signature size can be reduced further by using the same technique in [8], i.e. by removing some error positions in the signature even though this increases the verification cost.

## 4    Applications of Code-Based Primitives

Not only, PKEs and digital signatures, code-based primitives can be used to construct ZKIP (Zero Knowledge Interactive Proof) [29], Hash functions [3], OT (Oblivious Transfer) [19,12] and so on.

In the code-based PKCs, encryption and signature verification do not require heavy multiple precision modular exponentiations that are not easy to deploy with low cost on low-computational devices, such as RFID, sensors and SCADA devices. Code-based PKCs require mostly xors that are highly parallelizable. Hence, code-based PKCs are suitable for heterogeneous applications where one side may have a reasonable computational power, but that of the other side is limited.

As such heterogeneous applications, we introduce Lightweight Broadcast Authentication for Emergency (LBAE) and Privacy-Preserving RFID.

### 4.1    Lightweight Broadcast Authentication for Emergency

Lightweight Broadcast Authentication is a scenario where one broadcasts a same message to a huge number of light weight devices and then the devices verify the authenticity and data integrity of the received message. The message may be mission-critical commands, update packages and so on. Reasonable delay may be acceptable in these cases. On the other hand, Lightweight Broadcast Authentication for Emergency (LBAE) is intended for the cases where delay is not acceptable. E.g. such cases include disaster warning for earthquake, tsunami, flood, tornado, thunderbolt, fire and so on.

**Table 6.** Comparison Among Solutions for Lightweight Broadcast Authentication for Emergency

| | MAC with one master key | MAC with pair-wise keys | TESLA | Digital Signature Conventional | Digital Signature Code-based |
|---|---|---|---|---|---|
| Authenticity and Data Integrity | × | ○ | ○ | ○ | ○ |
| Computational Cost | ○ | ○ | ○ | × | ○ |
| Header Size | ○ | × | ○ | ○ | ○ |
| Latency | ○ | × | × | × | ○ |

In LBAE system, light weight devices may be deployed in anywhere, e.g. houses, buildings, hospitals, (nuclear) power plants, public transport control systems, and then take appropriate quick actions against disasters to mitigate the damages of them. E.g., in houses they may stop gas and/or open the doors when they receive earthquake early warning broadcast[3]. In some cases, a few seconds are enough to mitigate serious damages, and delay is crucial in LBAE. On the other hand, such system may be abused unless authentication and integrity of messages are not verified.

Table 6 shows the comparison among potential solutions for LBAE. In the "MAC (Message Authentication Code) with one master key" solution, a master key is shared among a broadcaster and its receivers. In LBAE, however, a huge number of lightweight devices may be deployed anywhere and some of them must be cracked. Once a master key is revealed the system can be abused completely. Hence this approach is not recommended (though this must be the simplest way to achieve LBAE). In the "MAC with pair-wise keys" solution, each pair between a receiver and a broadcaster shares a unique key. This overcomes the above problem, but the broadcaster must broadcast a huge number of MACs.[4] This increases the header size in the broadcast data and latency until the device's MAC is delivered.

TESLA (Timed Efficient Stream Loss-tolerant Authentication) [26] uses hash-chain and provides delayed authentication, i.e. the MAC key in the current time slot is released in the next time slot. Hence each device must wait until the MAC key is released and this causes latency. Duration of the time slot may be shortened but the drawback is that the hash-chain is consumed rapidly or each device must update the hash-chain frequently.

The drawback of the conventional digital signatures including RSA, DSA, ECDSA is the computational complexity for low cost lightweight devices and this causes latency. This drawback can be removed by employing a code-based digital signature and by tuning up to speed up the signature verification.

### 4.2   Privacy-Preserving RFID

Privacy-Preserving RFID provides unlinkability among IDs sent by tags against adversaries. It is necessary to prevent adversaries to trace a person who carries RFIDs that may be read remotely. The solutions can categorized as follows[30].

---

[3] The Earthquake Early Warning (EEW) broadcasts have already been deployed in Japan[1].

[4] The number can be reduced by the techniques used in the broadcast encryptions, but they still require certain amount of header size and/or complexity.

**(Privacy-Preserving RFIDs)**
**Tag disabling solutions (permanently):**
- Manually removal or destruction
- Kill command

**Tag disabling solutions (temporally):**
- Faraday cage
- Access password
- Hash lock
- Blocker tag
- Mode switch

**Tag enabling solutions:**
- Randomized hash lock [33]
- HB+ [15] and its variants
- Code-Based Unlinkable-ID [9]

Tag disabling solutions disable RFID functions whereas tag enabling solutions enable them while providing unlinkability among IDs. Previous tag enabling solutions, such as randomized hash lock [33], HB+ [15] and its variants, require exhaustive search of candidate secret keys to identify the tag. Hence they are not scalable against the number of tags to manage. On the other hand, the tag identification cost of the code-based unlinkable-ID [9] is constant regardless of the number of managing tags. It logically uses the code-based PKE to send its ID but the server pre-computes the ID part and then assigns it to the corresponding tag in advance. This reduces both the encryption complexity and the public-key size, and makes the tag identification complexity independent of the number of tags. Application of code-based unlinkable-ID is not limited to RFID. It may be used in any application where anonymity and/or privacy is required. It may even be used in PAKE (Password-Authenticated Key Exchange) to hide the ID that must be sent in a plaintext in PAKE.

## 5   Conclusion

This paper reviewed code-based PKCs. While secure constructions are available for them, public-key size was their drawback. This drawback can be improved using Quasi-Dyadic (QD) construction and Flexible Quasi-Dyadic (FQD) construction. Advantage of FQD is that it can achieve the maximum code length $n = 2^m - t$ with one shot whereas QD must hold $n << 2^m - t$ and its parameter generation is performed by trial-and-error. The condition of $n << 2^m - t$ prevents QD from applying it to digital signatures, but FQD can be applied to them.

Code-based PKCs are suitable for heterogeneous applications where one side may have a reasonable computational power and the other side consists of low-computational power devices. Such application includes Broadcast Authentication and Unlinkable-ID for low-computational power devices, such as RFID, sensors, SCADA devices, but not limited to them.

Research themes left in this area include, further reduction of public-key sizes, new attacks (especially on QD and FQD), new primitives/applications, implementation and side-channel attacks, provable security and so on. There are a lot of interesting research themes left in this area and new comers are welcome.

## Acknowledgment

The author would like to thank Paulo S. L. M. Barreto, Rafael Misoczki and Yang Cui for fruitful discussions on the attacks on Quasi-Dyadic public-keys.

## References

1. Earthquake early warning,
   http://en.wikipedia.org/wiki/Earthquake_Early_Warning_Japan
2. Dallot, L., Otmani, A., Tillich, J.P.: Cryptanalysis of two McEliece cryptosystems based on quasi-cyclic codes (2008), http://arxiv.org/abs/0804.0409
3. Augot, D., Finiasz, M., Gaborit, P., Manuel, S., Sendrier, N.: SHA-3 proposal: FSB. SHA-3 NIST competition (2008)
4. Baldi, M., Chiaraluce, F.: Cryptanalysis of a new instance of McEliece cryptosystem based on QC-LDPC codes. In: Proc. of IEEE International Symposium on Information Theory, ISIT 2007, pp. 2591–2595 (2007)
5. Berger, T., Cayrel, P.-L., Gaborit, P., Otmani, A.: Reducing key length of the McEliece cryptosystem. In: Preneel, B. (ed.) Progress in Cryptology – AFRICACRYPT 2009. LNCS, vol. 5580, pp. 77–97. Springer, Heidelberg (2009)
6. Bernstein, D.J.: Code-based public-key cryptography,
   http://pqcrypto.org/code.html
7. Bernstein, D.J.: List decoding for binary Goppa codes (2008),
   http://cr.yp.to/codes/goppalist-20081107.pdf
8. Courtois, N.T., Finiasz, M., Sendrier, N.: How to achieve a McEliece-based digital signature scheme. In: Boyd, C. (ed.) ASIACRYPT 2001. LNCS, vol. 2248, pp. 157–174. Springer, Heidelberg (2001)
9. Cui, Y., Kobara, K., Matsuura, K., Imai, H.: Lightweight privacy-preserving authentication protocols secure against active attack in an asymmetric way. IEICE Trans. E91-D(5), 1457–1465 (2008)
10. Schmidt, A., Engelbert, D., Overbeck, R.: A summary of McEliece-type cryptosystems and their security. Journal of Mathematical Cryptology, 1 (2007), Previous version, http://eprint.iacr.org/2006/162
11. Dowsley, R., Muller-Quade, J., Nascimento, A.C.A.: A CCA2 secure public key encryption scheme based on the McEliece assumptions in the standard model (2008), http://eprint.iacr.org/2008/468
12. Dowsley, R., van de Graaf, J., Quade, J.M., Nascimento, A.: Oblivious transfer based on the McEliece assumptions. In: Safavi-Naini, R. (ed.) ICITS 2008. LNCS, vol. 5155, pp. 107–117. Springer, Heidelberg (2008)
13. Finiasz, M., Sendrier, N.: Security bounds for the design of code-based cryptosystems. In: Matsui, M. (ed.) ASIACRYPT 2009. LNCS, vol. 5912, pp. 88–105. Springer, Heidelberg (2009)
14. Hagiwara, M., Kobara, K., Imai, H.: On the security of McEliece public key cryptosystem with LDPC code (in japanese). In: The 2007 Symposium on Cryptography and Information Security: 2C1-1 (January 2007)
15. Juels, A., Weis, S.A.: Authenticating pervasive devices with human protocols. In: Shoup, V. (ed.) CRYPTO 2005. LNCS, vol. 3621, pp. 293–308. Springer, Heidelberg (2005)
16. Kobara, K., Imai, H.: OAEP++ – another very simple way to fix the bug in OAEP. In: Proc. of 2002 International Symposium on Information Theory and Its Applications: S6-4-5, pp. 563–566 (2002)

17. Kobara, K., Imai, H.: Semantically secure McEliece public-key cryptosystem. IEICE Trans. E85-A(1), 74–83 (2002)
18. Kobara, K., Imai, H.: On the one-wayness against chosen-plaintext attacks on the Loidreau's modified McEliece PKC. IEEE Trans. on IT 49(12) (2003)
19. Kobara, K., Morozov, K., Overbeck, R.: Coding-based oblivious transfer. In: Calmet, J., Geiselmann, W., Müller-Quade, J. (eds.) Mathematical Methods in Computer Science. LNCS, vol. 5393, pp. 142–156. Springer, Heidelberg (2008)
20. Loidreau, P.: Strengthening McEliece cryptosystem. In: Okamoto, T. (ed.) ASIACRYPT 2000. LNCS, vol. 1976, pp. 585–598. Springer, Heidelberg (2000)
21. MacWilliams, F.J., Sloane, N.J.A.: The theory of error-correcting codes, ch. 12, Sec. 3, Pr. 5. North-Holland Mathematical Library, Amsterdam (1977)
22. Misoczki, R., Barreto, P.: Personal communication (2009)
23. Misoczki, R., Barreto, P.: Compact McEliece keys from Goppa codes. In: Rijmen, V. (ed.) SAC 2009. LNCS, vol. 5867. Springer, Heidelberg (2009)
24. Monico, C., Rosenthal, J., Shokrollahi, A.: Using low density parity check codes in the McEliece cryptosystem. In: Proc. of IEEE International Symposium on Information Theory, ISIT 2000, p. 215 (2000)
25. Nojima, R., Imai, H., Kobara, K., Morozov, K.: Semantic security for the McEliece cryptosystem without random oracles. In: Proc. of WCC 2007, pp. 257–268 (2007)
26. Perrig, A., Canetti, R., Tyger, J.D., Song, D.: The TESLA broadcast authentication protocol. CryptoBytes 5(2), 2–13 (Summer/Fall 2002)
27. Shor, P.W.: Polynomial-time algorithms for prime factorization and discrete logarithms on a quantum computer. SIAM Journal on Computing 26(5), 1484–1509 (1997)
28. Shoup, V.: OAEP reconsidered. In: Kilian, J. (ed.) CRYPTO 2001. LNCS, vol. 2139, pp. 239–259. Springer, Heidelberg (2001)
29. Stern, J.: A new identification scheme based on syndrome decoding. In: Stinson, D.R. (ed.) CRYPTO 1993. LNCS, vol. 773, pp. 13–21. Springer, Heidelberg (1994)
30. Suzuki, M., Kobara, K.: Privacy enhancing techniques on RFID systems. In: Development and Implementation of RFID Technology, January 2009, ch. 16, pp. 305–316. IN-TECH (2009) ISBN 978-3-902613-54-7
31. Tzeng, K.K., Zimmermann, K.: On extending Goppa codes to cyclic codes. IEEE Trans. on IT 21(6) (1975)
32. Umana, V.G., Leander, G.: Practical key recovery attacks on two McEliece variants (2009), http://eprint.iacr.org/2009/509
33. Weis, S.A., Sarma, S.E., Rivest, R.L., Engels, D.W.: Security and Privacy Aspects of Low-Cost Radio Frequency Identification Systems. In: 1st Annual Conference on Security in Pervasive Computing (2003)

# On the Security of Pseudorandomized Information-Theoretically Secure Schemes[*]

Koji Nuida and Goichiro Hanaoka

Research Center for Information Security (RCIS), National Institute of Advanced
Industrial Science and Technology (AIST), Akihabara-Daibiru Room 1003,
1-18-13 Sotokanda, Chiyoda-ku, Tokyo 101-0021, Japan
{k.nuida,hanaoka-goichiro}@aist.go.jp

**Abstract.** Dubrov and Ishai (STOC 2006) revealed, by generalizing the
notion of pseudorandom generators (PRGs), that under a computational
assumption, randomness in a protocol can be replaced with pseudoran-
domness in an indistinguishable way for an adversary even if his algorithm has unbounded complexity. However, their argument was applied
only to some special protocols. In this article, we first show that their
argument is not effective for a wide class of more general protocols. Then
we propose a novel evaluation technique for such indistinguishability that
is based on usual PRGs and is effective for those more general protocols.
Examples of such protocols include parallel computation over honest-
but-curious modules, secret sharing, broadcast encryption, traitor tracing, and collusion-secure codes.

**Keywords:** Randomness reduction, derandomization, information-
theoretic security, pseudorandom number generator, security evaluation.

## 1 Introduction

### 1.1 Backgrounds

Randomness is an essential resource for cryptography, and is one of the most important ingredients of applications in information theory, for instance, efficient
computation by probabilistic algorithms. Most of the existing schemes are based
on an (implicit) assumption that perfect random sources are freely available.
However, in practice such sources are either not available, or cost-consuming
even if available by, for instance, applying post-processing techniques [5,16,21]
to imperfect sources. Hence several works have been done on applications of
imperfect random sources, and on randomness reduction or complete derandomization techniques for various information-theoretic and cryptographic schemes.

For the power of imperfect random sources, several results of preceding works
(such as [10,12,19,23,28,29]) are placed on the positive side. Roughly summarizing, these results show that a single entropy source [10,24,29] suffices for *speedup*

[*] A part of this work was supported by 2007 Research Grants of the Science and
Technology Foundation of Japan (JSTF).

of non-cryptographic schemes (i.e., ones concerning no adversaries), and for some cryptographic protocols that assure some kinds of *unpredictability*. However, regarding *privacy* and *indistinguishability*, many negative results have been shown. McInnes and Pinkas [20] showed that a single entropy source alone is not enough for information-theoretically secure encryption of even one bit, unless its min-entropy is extremely high (in latter case one can extract an almost perfectly random bit from the source [24] and then to approximate the one-time pad [26]). Dodis et al. [12] extended the result to many other cryptographic protocols. Moreover, Bosley and Dodis [7] proved that, unless the output length of an imperfect random source is exponential in the bit length $b$ of the plaintext, the possibility of secure encryption with $b$-bit plaintexts implies the extractability of nearly $b$ almost perfectly random bits from the source. They also extended the result to computational primitives which are perfectly-binding.

These negative results seem supporting the importance, particularly in cryptographic situations, of randomness reduction techniques as a way of relaxing the assumption on required randomness. There have been proposed a lot of techniques, such as [1,3,8,17,22], for *information-theoretically indistinguishable* randomness reduction, i.e., ones such that the result of a protocol after the randomness reduction is statistically indistinguishable from the original. However, those techniques are scheme-dependent, and the negative results mentioned in the previous paragraph suggest that information-theoretically indistinguishable *universal* randomness reduction techniques based on a single (imperfect) random source are unlikely to exist. (Here the condition of using just a single source is crucial in some sense, since two independent weak random sources can be used to extract almost perfect random bits [10,24].) On the other hand, there obviously exist *computationally* indistinguishable universal randomness reduction techniques; simply replace the original randomness with outputs of (computationally) secure pseudorandom generators (PRGs).

Dubrov and Ishai [11] studied an intermediate case of randomness reduction that is *information-theoretically indistinguishable under a computational assumption*, as follows. Generalizing a usual notion of PRGs that fool distinguishers with boolean output sets $\{0, 1\}$, they introduced (motivated by Ishai and Kushilevits [15]) a notion of *pseudorandom generators that fool non-boolean distinguishers (nb-PRGs)*. It uses as a measure of indistinguishability the statistical distance between outputs of a distinguisher (with bounded output size) in random and pseudorandom cases, rather than the advantage of a boolean (i.e., usual) distinguisher. They constructed nb-PRGs under some computational assumptions. Then randomness in a protocol is reduced simply by replacing it with outputs of nb-PRGs. Now the *statistical* distance between the random and pseudorandom elements, hence the *statistical* distance between information seen by an adversary in the two cases, is bounded in terms of *computational* hardness of the underlying problem. However, their evaluation technique for indistinguishability was applied only to special kinds of protocols, such as private multi-party computation (see [11, Sect. 6.2]), and as we will show later, their technique is in fact not effective for a wide class of more general protocols.

## 1.2  Our Contributions

In this article, we propose a novel technique to evaluate indistinguishability of randomness reduction based on PRGs. More precisely, when (a part of) randomness used in a protocol is replaced with outputs of a PRG, our technique evaluates the indistinguishability between random and pseudorandom cases for any adversary's attack algorithm with *unbounded computational complexity*, in terms of the amount of information received by the adversary, the computational complexity of the protocol, and the *computational* indistinguishability of the PRG. It sounds good that our technique is based on usual PRGs instead of nb-PRGs as in [11], since PRGs are much more popular than nb-PRGs. Our technique in fact shows that computationally secure PRGs with sufficiently long seed lengths are also nb-PRGs (see [11, Observation 3.1]). Moreover, our technique is effective for a wide class of protocols for which the technique in [11] is not effective. Hence our technique improves the one in [11] significantly.

An outline of the implication of nb-PRGs from PRGs is as follows. Let $\mathsf{G}$ be a computationally secure PRG with output set $O_\mathsf{G}$. Let $\mathsf{D} : O_\mathsf{G} \to X$ be an algorithm that is regarded as a non-boolean distinguisher for $\mathsf{G}$. Then we define the following (boolean) distinguishers $\mathsf{D}_x : O_\mathsf{G} \to \{0,1\}$ parameterized by $x \in X$, where $\delta_{x,\cdot}$ denotes an algorithm $X \to \{0,1\}$ such that the output is 1 if and only if the input is $x$ (i.e., an algorithm computing Kronecker delta):

$$\mathsf{D}_x = \delta_{x,\cdot} \circ \mathsf{D} : O_\mathsf{G} \to \{0,1\} \ (x \in X). \tag{1}$$

This simple trick enables one to express the *statistical* distance of outputs of $\mathsf{D}$ between random and pseudorandom cases in terms of the advantages of the distinguishers $\mathsf{D}_x$. Thus if the PRG $\mathsf{G}$ is sufficiently secure, the advantages of $\mathsf{D}_x$ get sufficiently small, therefore the statistical distance under evaluation gets sufficiently small as well. Although existence of this implication itself has appeared in [11, Observation 3.1] and the implication seems less efficient than constructing nb-PRGs directly as in [11], our idea of introducing such auxiliary distinguishers will also play an important role in our following argument for more general cases.

Before a further explanation of our contributions, here we give a toy example to help intuitive understanding of our result. Let $R_b$ be a source that is either perfectly random (when $b = 0$) or pseudorandom (when $b = 1$). Suppose that $R_1$ is the output distribution of a PRG $\mathsf{G}$. Let an adversary $\mathsf{Eve}$ try to distinguish between random and pseudorandom cases by using an algorithm with *unbounded* complexity, where the $k$-bit information $x_b \in \{0,1\}^k$ on the output of $R_b$ received by her is calculated by a fixed efficient algorithm $\mathsf{H}$ (see Fig. 1). Now it is easily seen that the indistinguishability for $\mathsf{Eve}$ is purely *information-theoretic* (i.e., needing *no additional assumptions*) when $k = 0$ (since $\mathsf{Eve}$ has no information on the output of $R_b$), while it is just *computational* when $k$ is the output length of $R_b$ (i.e., $\mathsf{Eve}$ has full information on the output of $R_b$).

$$\boxed{R_b} \rightsquigarrow w \longrightarrow \boxed{\mathsf{H}} \rightsquigarrow x = x_b \longrightarrow \boxed{\mathsf{Eve}} \rightsquigarrow b' \in \{0,1\}$$

**Fig. 1.** Example of indistinguishability with partial information

The *information-theoretic indistinguishability under a computational assumption* lives in the separation point of these extremal cases, and our technique can evaluate, by regarding H as a non-boolean distinguisher for G, *where the separation point is* (i.e., the corresponding value of $k$) in terms of the computational indistinguishability of G and the efficiency of H. We emphasize that the computational indistinguishability of G used in our argument is evaluated with respect to a *fixed* computational model, hence any hardware speedup for Eve's computer does not affect the evaluation result (see the remark after Definition 1).

Let us come back to our contributions. Recall that Dubrov and Ishai evaluated the indistinguishability of randomness reduction based on nb-PRGs for private multi-party computation protocols [11, Sect. 6.2]. We observe that an essential characteristic of the protocols is that the secret protected by the protocol is *not* derived from the randomness that is the target of the randomness reduction. In fact, when the secret is derived from the target randomness, a naive application of their evaluation technique yields an evaluation result *that depends on the amount of information possessed by the secret* as well as the amount of information received by the adversary. This means that their technique is not effective for such situations, since in general the amount of information possessed by the secret should be significantly large to make the protocol secure. On the other hand, our proposed technique can remove the dependence on the amount of information possessed by the secret, hence is effective for such situations as well. Intuitively, our idea is to "factor out" the adversary's algorithm (with unbounded complexity) from the picture of the situation and to obtain auxiliary efficient distinguishers like $D_x$ in (1). Our technique is also effective for more general kinds of protocols, especially when the information received by the adversary is small. A typical case is that a small piece of the target randomness is distributed to each of a large number of players, including a limited number of adversaries. Such applications include parallel computation over honest-but-curious modules, secret sharing [4,25], broadcast encryption [14], traitor tracing [2,9,18], and collusion-secure codes [6,27].

### 1.3   Organization of the Article

Section 2 presents definitions and notations. In Sect. 3, we briefly summarize the preceding result of Dubrov and Ishai [11] on randomness reduction based on nb-PRGs, and show that their technique is not effective for a wide class of more general protocols. Section 4 explains our contributions mentioned in Sect. 1.2. Finally, in Sect. 5 we give some further remarks and discussion on our results.

## 2   Definitions and Notations

In this article, any algorithm is probabilistic unless otherwise specified. Let $U_X$ denote the uniform probability distribution over a (finite) set $X$. We often identify a probability distribution with the corresponding random variable. We write $x \leftarrow P$ to signify that $x$ is a particular value of a random variable $P$. First, we clarify the meaning of the term "computational model" used in this article:

**Definition 1.** *A computational model* $\mathcal{M} = (\mathcal{A}_{\mathcal{M}}, C_{\mathcal{M}})$ *consists of a set* $\mathcal{A}_{\mathcal{M}}$ *of algorithms described in the model, and a map* $C_{\mathcal{M}} : \mathcal{A}_{\mathcal{M}} \to \mathbb{R}$ *that assigns to each* $\mathsf{A} \in \mathcal{A}_{\mathcal{M}}$ *its "complexity"* $C_{\mathcal{M}}(\mathsf{A}) \in \mathbb{R}$.

Here the "complexity" of an algorithm may take various meanings depending on the context, such as time complexity on a fixed Turing machine, circuit complexity with fixed fundamental gates, average or worst-case running time on a fixed PC, or space complexity. An important point is that computational models based on machines with different performance are distinguished from each other. Then any speedup of an adversary's algorithm induced by hardware development on his computer can be interpreted as a change of the underlying computational model. For instance, a new computer twice as fast as the original corresponds to a new computational model $\mathcal{M}'$ such that $C_{\mathcal{M}'}(\mathsf{A}) = C_{\mathcal{M}}(\mathsf{A})/2$ for any algorithm $\mathsf{A}$. The distinction of classical and quantum adversaries is also regarded as difference of the underlying computational models. Note that in this article, we mainly consider exact (concrete) security rather than asymptotic security.

Let $\mathsf{G} : S_{\mathsf{G}} \to O_{\mathsf{G}}$ be a PRG with seed set $S_{\mathsf{G}}$ and output set $O_{\mathsf{G}}$. Note again that we deal with exact security in this article, therefore $\mathsf{G}$ is a single algorithm rather than a sequence of algorithms with various seed lengths. The following notion of indistinguishability for PRGs (except slight modification mentioned later) is a natural translation of the conventional notion to the case of exact security and has appeared in the literature, for instance, [13, Definition 1]:

**Definition 2.** *An algorithm* $\mathsf{D} : O_{\mathsf{G}} \to \{0,1\}$ *is called a* distinguisher *for a PRG* $\mathsf{G}$. *For any distinguisher* $\mathsf{D}$ *for* $\mathsf{G}$, *its advantage* $\mathsf{adv}_{\mathsf{G}}(\mathsf{D})$ *is defined by*

$$\mathsf{adv}_{\mathsf{G}}(\mathsf{D}) = |Pr[\mathsf{D}(\mathsf{G}(U_{S_{\mathsf{G}}})) = 1] - Pr[\mathsf{D}(U_{O_{\mathsf{G}}}) = 1]|.$$

**Definition 3.** *Let* $\mathcal{M}$ *be a computational model (see Definition 1),* $\mathcal{C} \subset \mathcal{A}_{\mathcal{M}}$, *and* $R(t) \geq 0$ *a non-decreasing function. A PRG* $\mathsf{G}$ *is called* $R(t)$-secure *in* $(\mathcal{M}, \mathcal{C})$ *if for any distinguisher* $\mathsf{D}$ *for* $\mathsf{G}$ *that belongs to* $\mathcal{C}$, *its advantage is bounded by*

$$\mathsf{adv}_{\mathsf{G}}(\mathsf{D}) \leq R(C_{\mathcal{M}}(\mathsf{D})).$$

*For simplicity, we say that* $\mathsf{G}$ *is* $R(t)$-secure *in* $\mathcal{M}$ *if it is* $R(t)$-secure *in* $(\mathcal{M}, \mathcal{A}_{\mathcal{M}})$.

The difference of Definition 3 from the one in the literature is that we restrict the distinguisher to be chosen from a subclass $\mathcal{C}$ of algorithms. The authors hope that this modification can make evaluation of the indistinguishability of a given PRG easier, while this does not decrease practicality of our result if every "ordinary" algorithm is included in $\mathcal{C}$. Nevertheless, for intuitive understanding of our argument, one may ignore the issue of the subclass $\mathcal{C}$ by putting $\mathcal{C} = \mathcal{A}_{\mathcal{M}}$. An instance of $R(t)$-secure PRGs is recently given by Farashahi et al. [13] under DDH assumption, where the function $R(t)$ is estimated in terms of complexity of the best known algorithm in a given computational model to solve the DDH problem. Note that increase of the seed length of the PRG makes the function $R(t)$ smaller, hence makes the PRG more indistinguishable.

We also recall the definition of statistical distances of two distributions:

**Definition 4.** *For two probability distributions* $P_1, P_2$ *over the same finite set* $X$, *their* statistical distance $\mathsf{SD}(P_1, P_2)$ *is defined by*

$$\mathsf{SD}(P_1, P_2) = \frac{1}{2} \sum_{x \in X} |Pr[x \leftarrow P_1] - Pr[x \leftarrow P_2]|$$

$$= \max_{E \subset X} \left( Pr[x \leftarrow P_1 : x \in E] - Pr[x \leftarrow P_2 : x \in E] \right).$$

Note that $\mathsf{SD}(f(P_1), f(P_2)) \leq \mathsf{SD}(P_1, P_2)$ for any (probabilistic) function $f$.

# 3   The Preceding Result

In this section, first we briefly summarize the preceding result by Dubrov and Ishai [11] on randomness reduction based on nb-PRGs. Then we observe that their technique is in fact not effective for a wide class of protocols.

Roughly speaking, $\mathsf{G} : S_\mathsf{G} \rightarrow O_\mathsf{G}$ is called a *PRG that fools non-boolean distinguishers (nb-PRG)* if for any algorithm (a non-boolean distinguisher) $\mathsf{D} : O_\mathsf{G} \rightarrow X$ with bounded complexity and output set $X$ of bounded size, the statistical distance between outputs of $\mathsf{D}$ in random and pseudorandom cases is sufficiently small. See [11, Definition 3.1] for the precise definition. A construction of nb-PRGs based on some computational assumptions is given in [11], where the *statistical* distance between the two cases is bounded in terms of the quantitative hardness of the underlying computational problem.

They also discussed an application of an nb-PRG to randomness reduction of private multi-party computation protocols [11, Sect. 6.2]. The outline is as follows. Let $k$ players $\mathsf{P}_1, \ldots, \mathsf{P}_k$ wish to compute a function $f(x_1, \ldots, x_k)$ from each player's private input $x_i \in X_i$. Let $\pi$ be a multi-party protocol for this purpose that requires an additional random element $r_i \in R_i$ for each $\mathsf{P}_i$. After the protocol, each $\mathsf{P}_i$ obtains the result $y_i \in Y_i$ of computation and the message $m_i \in M_i$ received by $\mathsf{P}_i$ during the protocol. We say that $\pi$ is *t-private* if, for any coalition $T \subset \{1, \ldots, k\}$ of at most $t$ honest-but-curious players, they cannot learn non-negligible information on inputs $(x_i)_{i \notin T}$ of the remaining honest players $\mathsf{P}_i$ $(i \notin T)$ from their messages $(m_i)_{i \in T}$ even if their attack algorithm has unbounded complexity. Now the randomness reduction is done by replacing each $r_i$ with an output of an nb-PRG $\mathsf{G}$. We concern, for each $1 \leq i \leq k$, the statistical distance between information on private inputs $(x_j)_{j \notin T}$ in cases of random $r_i$ and pseudorandom $r_i$, where the distribution of any other $r_{i'}$ is common to the two cases. (Then the "hybrid argument" yields the total statistical distance between random and pseudorandom cases.) Since the information is learned from the coalition's messages $(m_j)_{j \in T}$, the above distance is not larger than the statistical distance between $(m_j)_{j \in T}$ in the two cases. Now a bound of the latter statistical distance is derived by regarding the protocol $\pi$ as a non-boolean distinguisher for $\mathsf{G}$ that computes $(m_j)_{j \in T}$ from $r_i$ by using "internal randomness" $x_j$ $(1 \leq j \leq k)$ and $r_{i'}$ $(i' \neq i)$. This bound depends on the size $|\prod_{j \in T} M_j|$ of the coalition's message space that is closely related to the amount of information possessed by the messages $(m_j)_{j \in T}$ received by the coalition.

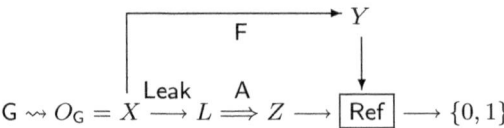

**Fig. 2.** Example of randomness reduction and leakage of random elements (the duplicated arrow means the adversary's algorithm with unbounded complexity)

A characteristic of this successful example is that the secret $(x_j)_{j \notin T}$ protected by the protocol is *not* derived from the random elements $r_i$ that are the target of the randomness reduction. On the other hand, we consider the following another example where the secret protected by the protocol *is* derived from the target randomness. Let a secret element $y$ in a set $Y$ be calculated from a random element $x \in X$ by an algorithm $\mathsf{F} : X \to Y$. During the calculation, certain information on $x$ is leaked to an adversary $\mathsf{Eve}$ according to a leakage function $\mathsf{Leak} : X \to L$. Then she makes a guess $z \in Z$ for the element $y$ from the leaked information $l = \mathsf{Leak}(x)$ by using an algorithm $\mathsf{A} : L \to Z$ with *unbounded* complexity. The "correctness" of her guess is evaluated by an auxiliary referee $\mathsf{Ref} : Y \times Z \to \{0, 1\}$, where $\mathsf{Ref}$ outputs 1 if the guess is "correct" and 0 if it is "incorrect" (see Fig. 2). We assume that the algorithms $\mathsf{F}$, $\mathsf{Leak}$, and $\mathsf{Ref}$ are all efficient. Now the randomness reduction is done by replacing $x \in X$ with an output of an nb-PRG $\mathsf{G}$. We concern the difference of $\mathsf{Eve}$'s success probabilities between random and pseudorandom cases.

To bound the difference by an argument similar to the previous example, we need to regard a certain part of the picture in Fig. 2 as an efficient non-boolean distinguisher $\mathsf{D}$ for $\mathsf{G}$. What are the candidates? Since it is hopeless to bound the statistical distance of the (pseudo)random element $x \in X$ itself, a possible and probably the unique candidate of $\mathsf{D}$ is the product map $\mathsf{Leak} \times \mathsf{F} : X \to L \times Y$. Indeed, we cannot include $\mathsf{A}$ in $\mathsf{D}$ since $\mathsf{A}$ has unbounded complexity, while $\mathsf{Leak}$ alone cannot be regarded as $\mathsf{D}$ since the evaluation result of $\mathsf{Eve}$'s guess depends also on the output of $\mathsf{F}$ that is also derived from the (pseudo)random element $x \in X$. As a result, the bound of the difference derived by a naive application of the argument in [11] *does* depend on the number $|Y|$ of possible choices of the secret element $y$ as well as the size of $L$. This implies that, even if the size of $L$ is small, the obtained bound is not effective in general, since the possibility of the secret should be significantly large in order to make the protocol itself (in random case) secure. Hence a more advanced argument than that in [11] is required to derive an effective bound for such a situation. In the next section, we propose a novel technique to resolve the problem.

## 4   Our Results

In this section, we present the main results of this article. First, we show that any computationally secure PRG (with sufficiently large seed length) is also an nb-PRG in the sense of Sect. 3 or [11, Definition 3.1]. Although existence of the implication itself has appeared in [11, Observation 3.1] and the implication seems less efficient than constructing nb-PRGs directly as in [11], here we mention this fact since the technique used in the proof will also play an important role in our following result. Then we propose a novel technique to derive an effective bound of the difference between random and pseudorandom cases, based on usual PRGs instead of nb-PRGs, for a wide class of situations where the preceding technique by Dubrov and Ishai [11] is not effective (such as in Sect. 3). We emphasize that the derived bound works even against an attack algorithm with *unbounded complexity*, despite of just *computational* security of the PRG. In what follows, let a PRG $\mathsf{G} : S_\mathsf{G} \to O_\mathsf{G}$ be $R(t)$-secure in a fixed $(\mathcal{M}, \mathcal{C})$ (see Definition 3).

## 4.1   The Fundamental Idea

The fundamental idea underlying our results is as follows. Given an algorithm $\mathsf{D} : O_\mathsf{G} \to X$, we introduce the following auxiliary distinguishers $\mathsf{D}_x : O_\mathsf{G} \to \{0, 1\}$ for the PRG $\mathsf{G}$ parameterized by $x \in X$, where $\delta_{x,\cdot}$ denotes an algorithm $X \to \{0, 1\}$ such that the output $\delta_{x,\cdot}(y)$ is 1 if $y = x$ and it is 0 if $y \neq x$:

$$\mathsf{D}_x = \delta_{x,\cdot} \circ \mathsf{D} : O_\mathsf{G} \to \{0, 1\} \ (x \in X). \tag{2}$$

In the following argument, the statistical distance under evaluation will be evaluated in terms of the advantages $\mathsf{adv}_\mathsf{G}(\mathsf{D}_x)$ of efficient distinguishers $\mathsf{D}_x$ that are bounded by the definition of PRGs.

## 4.2   Implication of nb-PRGs from PRGs and Applications

We show the implication of nb-PRGs from PRGs based on the above idea. Recall that $\mathsf{G} : S_\mathsf{G} \to O_\mathsf{G}$ is an nb-PRG if, for any efficient non-boolean distinguisher $\mathsf{D} : O_\mathsf{G} \to X$ with output set $X$ of bounded size, the statistical distance $\mathsf{SD}(\mathsf{D}(U_{O_\mathsf{G}}), \mathsf{D}(\mathsf{G}(U_{S_\mathsf{G}})))$ between outputs of $\mathsf{D}$ in random and pseudorandom cases is sufficiently small, where $U_Y$ denotes the uniform distribution over a set $Y$ (see [11, Definition 3.1] for the precise definition). Now by using the auxiliary distinguishers $\mathsf{D}_x$ defined in (2), we have

$$\mathsf{SD}(\mathsf{D}(\mathsf{G}(U_{S_\mathsf{G}})), \mathsf{D}(U_{O_\mathsf{G}})) = \frac{1}{2} \sum_{x \in X} |Pr[\mathsf{D}(\mathsf{G}(U_{S_\mathsf{G}})) = x] - Pr[\mathsf{D}(U_{O_\mathsf{G}}) = x]|$$

$$= \frac{1}{2} \sum_{x \in X} |Pr[\mathsf{D}_x(\mathsf{G}(U_{S_\mathsf{G}})) = 1] - Pr[\mathsf{D}_x(U_{O_\mathsf{G}}) = 1]| \tag{3}$$

$$= \frac{1}{2} \sum_{x \in X} \mathsf{adv}_\mathsf{G}(\mathsf{D}_x)$$

where the second step follows from the definition of $\mathsf{D}_x$. We emphasize that we did not yet use any computational assumption in the reduction process (3). Owing to this relation, the following result is now almost obvious:

**Theorem 1.** *In the above setting, suppose that for every $x \in X$, the distinguisher $\mathsf{D}_x$ for $\mathsf{G}$ belongs to the given set $\mathcal{C}$ of algorithms and its complexity is bounded by $C_\mathcal{M}(\mathsf{D}_x) \leq T$ for a common constant $T$. Then we have*

$$\mathsf{SD}(\mathsf{D}(\mathsf{G}(U_{S_\mathsf{G}})), \mathsf{D}(U_{O_\mathsf{G}})) \leq (|X|/2) \cdot R(T).$$

*Proof.* Since $\mathsf{G}$ is $R(t)$-secure in $(\mathcal{M}, \mathcal{C})$, the assumption implies that $\mathsf{adv}_\mathsf{G}(\mathsf{D}_x) \leq R(C_\mathcal{M}(\mathsf{D}_x)) \leq R(T)$ (recall that $R(t)$ is non-decreasing) for each $x \in X$, hence the rightmost-hand side of (3) is bounded by $(|X|/2) \cdot R(T)$.

Hence $\mathsf{G}$ is also an nb-PRG if the value of $R(T)$ is sufficiently small relative to the size of $X$, or equivalently, if the seed length of $\mathsf{G}$ is sufficiently long.

Based on this fact, an argument similar to Sect. 3 can derive an effective bound of difference between random and pseudorandom cases in randomness reduction based on usual PRGs for some kinds of schemes. First we consider reduction of internal randomness over a set $R$ for an efficient algorithm $\mathsf{F} : X \to Y$ based on a PRG $\mathsf{G}$ with output set $O_\mathsf{G} = R$. In this case, $F$ can be regarded, by exchanging the roles of $X$ and $R$, as an efficient algorithm $\mathsf{F}' : R \to Y$ with "internal randomness" over $X$. Then the statistical distance between outputs of $\mathsf{F}$ in random and pseudorandom cases is evaluated by using Theorem 1 with $\mathsf{D} = \mathsf{F}'$. Similarly, we consider randomness reduction in a protocol that protects some elements independent of the randomness (such as private multi-party computation discussed in Sect. 3 and [11, Sect. 6.2]). Simplifying the situation, we assume that information $y \in Y$ received by the adversary is calculated from a random element $r \in R$ and a secret $x \in X$ independent of $r$ by an efficient algorithm. For any *fixed* $x$, the independence allows us to regard the algorithm as being in the form $\mathsf{H}_x : R \to Y$. Then for the fixed $x$, any information on $x$ learned by the adversary is calculated from $y$ (and some other elements independent of $y$ and $x$), therefore the statistical distance between the learned information in random and pseudorandom cases is bounded by the statistical distance between the $y$ in the two cases. Now the latter distance is also evaluated by using Theorem 1 with $\mathsf{D} = \mathsf{H}_x$. The resulting bound depends on the size of $Y$ but *not* on the size of $X$. Hence our technique is effective in such a situation.

The bound derived by our technique is a certain function of the amount of information received by the adversary, the quantitative indistinguishability of the PRG in a *fixed* $(\mathcal{M}, \mathcal{C})$, and the computational complexity of the protocol. This characteristic is also common to the more general situations discussed later.

## 4.3 "Factoring-Out" Method: A Finer Evaluation Technique

The argument of Sect. 3 shows that, when the secret element protected by the protocol is derived from the target randomness of the randomness reduction, the estimation result on the difference between random and pseudorandom cases by the arguments in Sect. 4.2 and in [11, Sect. 6.2] depends on the amount of information possessed by the secret element, hence the estimation is not effective in general. From now, we propose a novel technique to overcome the drawback.

We consider the example in the latter part of Sect. 3 (see Fig. 2). In this situation, the success probability $\mathsf{succ}_{\mathsf{rnd},\mathsf{A}}$ in random case for the adversary Eve of guessing the secret $y \in Y$ from the leaked information $\mathsf{Leak}(x) \in L$ is

$$\mathsf{succ}_{\mathsf{rnd},\mathsf{A}} = Pr[x \leftarrow U_{O_G}; y \leftarrow \mathsf{F}(x); l \leftarrow \mathsf{Leak}(x); z \leftarrow \mathsf{A}(l) : \mathsf{Ref}(y, z) = 1]$$

and the success probability $\mathsf{succ}_{\mathsf{prnd},\mathsf{A}}$ in pseudorandom case is given by replacing $U_{O_G}$ in $\mathsf{succ}_{\mathsf{rnd},\mathsf{A}}$ with $\mathsf{G}(U_{S_G})$, namely

$$\mathsf{succ}_{\mathsf{prnd},\mathsf{A}} = Pr[x \leftarrow \mathsf{G}(U_{S_G}); y \leftarrow \mathsf{F}(x); l \leftarrow \mathsf{Leak}(x); z \leftarrow \mathsf{A}(l) : \mathsf{Ref}(y, z) = 1].$$

We give a bound of the difference $\mathsf{diff} = |\mathsf{succ}_{\mathsf{rnd},\mathsf{A}} - \mathsf{succ}_{\mathsf{prnd},\mathsf{A}}|$ of the two success probabilities. An intuitive idea is to obtain an auxiliary efficient distinguisher (like $\mathsf{D}_x$ in (2)) by "factoring out" Eve's algorithm $\mathsf{A}$ from the experiment in the expression of the success probability. For the purpose, we perform the following transformation, where $x$, $y$, $l$, and $z$ in the summations run over the sets $X = O_G$, $Y$, $L$, and $Z$, respectively, and the probabilities are taken over internal randomness of the algorithms specified in the notations:

$\mathsf{succ}_{\mathsf{rnd},\mathsf{A}}$

$$= \sum_{x,y,l,z} Pr[x \leftarrow U_X] \, Pr[\mathsf{F}(x) = y] \, Pr[\mathsf{Leak}(x) = l] \, Pr[\mathsf{A}(l) = z] \, Pr[\mathsf{Ref}(y, z) = 1]$$

$$= \sum_{l,z} Pr[\mathsf{A}(l) = z] \sum_{x,y} Pr[x \leftarrow U_X] \, Pr[\mathsf{F}(x) = y] \, Pr[\mathsf{Leak}(x) = l] \, Pr[\mathsf{Ref}(y, z) = 1]$$

$$= \sum_{l,z} Pr[\mathsf{A}(l) = z] \, Pr[x \leftarrow U_X; y \leftarrow \mathsf{F}(x); l' \leftarrow \mathsf{Leak}(x) : l' = l \wedge \mathsf{Ref}(y, z) = 1].$$

By using the "Kronecker delta algorithm" $\delta_{l,\cdot}$ introduced in Sect. 4.1 and 2-bit AND operation $\{0,1\}^2 \to \{0,1\}$, the second term of the summation in the rightmost-hand side can be written as

$$Pr[x \leftarrow U_X; y \leftarrow \mathsf{F}(x); l' \leftarrow \mathsf{Leak}(x); b_1 \leftarrow \delta_{l,\cdot}(l');$$
$$b_2 \leftarrow \mathsf{Ref}(y, z); b \leftarrow \mathsf{AND}(b_1, b_2) : b = 1]. \tag{4}$$

To visualize the experiment in (4), we perform the following "factoring-out" transformation for the diagram in Fig. 2. First, we remove the arrow corresponding to Eve's algorithm $\mathsf{A}$ with unbounded complexity, and replace the sets $L$ and $Z$ at the origin and the destination of the removed arrow with their arbitrary elements, obtaining a diagram in Fig. 3. Secondly, for the sink of the last diagram denoted by an element $l \in L$, we replace the vertex with the "Kronecker delta algorithm" $\delta_{l,\cdot} : L \to \{0,1\}$, obtaining a diagram in Fig. 4. Finally, we combine the two sinks $\{0,1\}$ in the last diagram by 2-bit AND operation, obtaining a diagram with unique sink $\{0,1\}$ in Fig. 5. We regard this diagram as a flowchart of an algorithm $\mathsf{D}_{l,z} : O_G = X \to \{0,1\}$ parameterized by $l \in L$ and $z \in Z$. This $\mathsf{D}_{l,z}$ corresponds to the experiment in (4), namely (4) is now rewritten as

$$Pr[x \leftarrow U_{O_G} : \mathsf{D}_{l,z}(x) = 1] = Pr[\mathsf{D}_{l,z}(U_{O_G}) = 1].$$

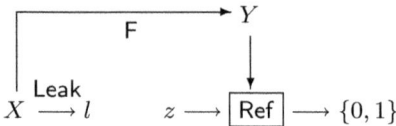

**Fig. 3.** First step of "factoring-out" transformation ($l \in L$, $z \in Z$)

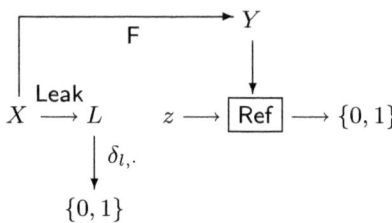

**Fig. 4.** Second step of "factoring-out" transformation ($l \in L$, $z \in Z$)

By the above arguments, we have

$$\mathsf{succ}_{\mathrm{rnd},\mathsf{A}} = \sum_{l \in L, z \in Z} Pr[\mathsf{A}(l) = z]\, Pr[\mathsf{D}_{l,z}(U_{O_G}) = 1]\,,$$

and a similar expression of $\mathsf{succ}_{\mathrm{prnd},\mathsf{A}}$ is also obtained by replacing $U_{O_G}$ with $\mathsf{G}(U_{S_G})$. Then the triangle inequality implies that

$$
\begin{aligned}
\mathsf{diff} &= \left| \sum_{l \in L, z \in Z} Pr[\mathsf{A}(l) = z] \left( Pr[\mathsf{D}_{l,z}(U_{O_G}) = 1] - Pr[\mathsf{D}_{l,z}(\mathsf{G}(U_{S_G})) = 1] \right) \right| \\
&\leq \sum_{l \in L, z \in Z} Pr[\mathsf{A}(l) = z]\, \left| Pr[\mathsf{D}_{l,z}(U_{O_G}) = 1] - Pr[\mathsf{D}_{l,z}(\mathsf{G}(U_{S_G})) = 1] \right| \qquad (5) \\
&= \sum_{l \in L, z \in Z} Pr[\mathsf{A}(l) = z]\, \mathsf{adv}_\mathsf{G}(\mathsf{D}_{l,z}).
\end{aligned}
$$

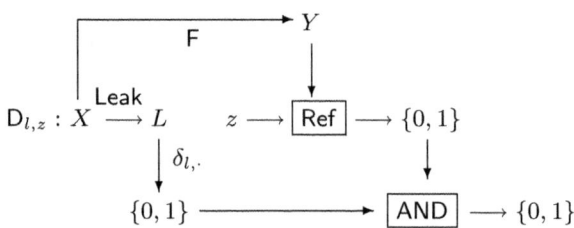

**Fig. 5.** Third step of "factoring-out" transformation ($l \in L$, $z \in Z$)

We emphasize that we used *no* computational assumption to derive the bound (5). Now the following result is easily deduced:

**Theorem 2.** *In the above setting, suppose that for every $l \in L$ and every $z \in Z$, the distinguisher $\mathsf{D}_{l,z}$ for $\mathsf{G}$ belongs to the given set $\mathcal{C}$ of algorithms and its complexity is bounded by $C_{\mathcal{M}}(\mathsf{D}_{l,z}) \leq T$ for a common constant $T$. Then*

$$\mathsf{diff} \leq |L| \cdot R(T).$$

*Proof.* Since $\mathsf{G}$ is $R(t)$-secure in $(\mathcal{M}, \mathcal{C})$, the assumption implies that $\mathsf{adv}_{\mathsf{G}}(\mathsf{D}_{l,z}) \leq R(C_{\mathcal{M}}(\mathsf{D}_{l,z})) \leq R(T)$ for every $l \in L$ and $z \in Z$. Thus the rightmost-hand side of (5) is bounded by

$$\sum_{l \in L} \sum_{z \in Z} Pr[\mathsf{A}(l) = z] \, R(T) = \sum_{l \in L} 1 \cdot R(T) = |L| \cdot R(T).$$

Hence the theorem holds.

We emphasize that the complexity, or even the underlying computational model, of the attack algorithm $\mathsf{A}$ is not relevant to the result of Theorem 2. The bound given by Theorem 2 depends on the amount of information received by the adversary (i.e. $|L|$), the quantitative indistinguishability of the PRG $\mathsf{G}$, and the complexity of the distinguishers $\mathsf{D}_{l,z}$ (that is closely related to the complexity of the protocol), but *not* on the number $|Y|$ of possible choices of the secret element. (We notice for completeness that in a most strict sense, the complexity of $\mathsf{D}_{l,z}$ in fact depends slightly on $|Y|$ since $\mathsf{D}_{l,z}$ needs to compare an element $y$ of $Y$ with $z$, but the dependence will be negligibly small in practical situations.) Hence our evaluation technique indeed improves the one in [11].

### 4.4   Further Examples

To explain our "factoring-out" method further, we discuss a slightly more complicated example. We consider probabilistic parallel computation over modules (players) some of which may be honest but curious. First, the center sends to $k$ players $\mathsf{P}_1, \ldots, \mathsf{P}_k$ their local inputs $x_1, \ldots, x_k$ that are randomly generated. Each player $\mathsf{P}_i$ calculates his local output $y_i \in Y_i$ from his local input $x_i \in X_i$ and sends it back to the center. Then the center calculates his final output $z \in Z$ from the received intermediate elements $y_1, \ldots, y_k$. We assume that some players $\mathsf{P}_i$ ($i \in T \subset \{1, \ldots, k\}$) are honest but curious, and they collude and try to make a guess for the final output $z$ from their local inputs $x_T = (x_i)_{i \in T}$ together with some other auxiliary element $w \in W$ that follows a certain probability distribution $\mathcal{W}$ independent of the local inputs $x_j$. The task of this protocol is to keep the output $z$ secret against such a coalition $T$. In the following explanation, we consider for simplicity a simple case of one adversary $\mathsf{P}_2$ out of two players (see Fig. 6), where $\mathsf{Ref} : Z \times Z' \to \{0, 1\}$ is an auxiliary referee who determines whether the guess $z' \in Z'$ of the coalition is sufficiently correct or not. Now the success probability $\mathsf{succ}_{\mathrm{rnd},\mathsf{A}}$ for the adversary $\mathsf{P}_2$ in random case is given by

$$\mathsf{succ}_{\mathrm{rnd},\mathsf{A}} = Pr[r \leftarrow U_{O_{\mathsf{G}}}; x_1 \leftarrow \mathsf{H}_1(r); x_2 \leftarrow \mathsf{H}_2(r); y_1 \leftarrow \mathsf{F}_1(x_1); y_2 \leftarrow \mathsf{F}_2(x_2);$$
$$z \leftarrow \mathsf{F}(y_1, y_2); w \leftarrow \mathcal{W}; z' \leftarrow \mathsf{A}(x_2, w) : \mathsf{Ref}(z, z') = 1].$$

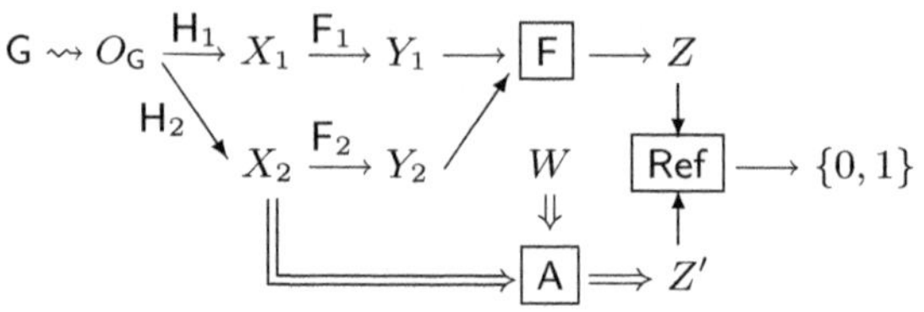

**Fig. 6.** Example of secure parallel computation (the duplicated arrows mean the adversary's algorithm)

This can be rewritten as follows, where $r$, $x_i$, $y_i$, $z$, $z'$, and $w$ in the summation run over the sets $O_G$, $X_i$, $Y_i$, $Z$, $Z'$, and $W$, respectively:

$\mathsf{succ}_{\mathrm{rnd},\mathsf{A}}$

$$= \sum_{x_2,z',w} Pr[w \leftarrow W] \, Pr\big[\mathsf{A}(x_2,w) = z'\big] \sum_{r,x_1,y_1,y_2,z} Pr[r \leftarrow U_{O_G}] \, Pr[\mathsf{H}_1(r) = x_1]$$

$$\cdot Pr[\mathsf{H}_2(r) = x_2] \, Pr[\mathsf{F}_1(x_1) = y_1] \, Pr[\mathsf{F}_2(x_2) = y_2] \, Pr[\mathsf{F}(y_1,y_2) = z] \, Pr\big[\mathsf{Ref}(z,z') = 1\big]$$

$$= \sum_{x_2,z',w} Pr[w \leftarrow W] \, Pr\big[\mathsf{A}(x_2,w) = z'\big] \, Pr\big[r \leftarrow U_{O_G}; x_1 \leftarrow \mathsf{H}_1(r); x_2' \leftarrow \mathsf{H}_2(r);$$

$$y_1 \leftarrow \mathsf{F}_1(x_1); y_2 \leftarrow \mathsf{F}_2(x_2); z \leftarrow \mathsf{F}(y_1,y_2) : x_2' = x_2 \wedge \mathsf{Ref}(z,z') = 1\big] \ .$$

The third term of the summation in the rightmost-hand side is equal to

$$Pr[r \leftarrow U_{O_G}; x_1 \leftarrow \mathsf{H}_1(r); x_2' \leftarrow \mathsf{H}_2(r); y_1 \leftarrow \mathsf{F}_1(x_1); y_2 \leftarrow \mathsf{F}_2(x_2);$$
$$z \leftarrow \mathsf{F}(y_1,y_2); b_1 \leftarrow \delta_{x_2,\cdot}(x_2'); b_2 = \mathsf{Ref}(z,z'); b = \mathsf{AND}(b_1,b_2) : b = 1]. \tag{6}$$

The experiment in (6) is visualized by performing the following "factoring-out" transformation for the diagram in Fig. 6. First, we remove the arrows corresponding to the attack algorithm $\mathsf{A}$, and replace the sets at the origin and the destination of the removed arrows with their arbitrary elements. Now the resulting diagram has two connected components, and we focus on the one containing the output set $O_G$ of the PRG, obtaining a diagram in Fig. 7. This diagram has a vertex that is denoted by a fixed element (namely, $x_2$) rather than a set, and is neither a source nor a sink of the diagram. Secondly, we split this vertex $x_2$ into two copies, to one of which all the incoming arrows are associated and to another of which all the outgoing ones are associated, obtaining a diagram in Fig. 8. Thirdly, for the sink of the last diagram denoted by an $x_2 \in X_2$, we replace the vertex with the corresponding "Kronecker delta algorithm" $\delta_{x_2,\cdot} : X_2 \to \{0,1\}$, obtaining a diagram in Fig. 9. Finally, we combine the two sinks $\{0,1\}$ in the last diagram by 2-bit $\mathsf{AND}$ operation, obtaining a diagram with unique sink $\{0,1\}$ in Fig. 10. We regard this diagram as a flowchart of an algorithm $\mathsf{D}_{x_2,z'} : O_G \to \{0,1\}$ parameterized by $x_2 \in X_2$ and $z' \in Z'$. This $\mathsf{D}_{x_2,z'}$ corresponds to the experiment in the expression (6), and (6) is equal to

$$Pr[r \leftarrow U_{O_G} : \mathsf{D}_{x_2,z'}(r) = 1] = Pr[\mathsf{D}_{x_2,z'}(U_{O_G}) = 1].$$

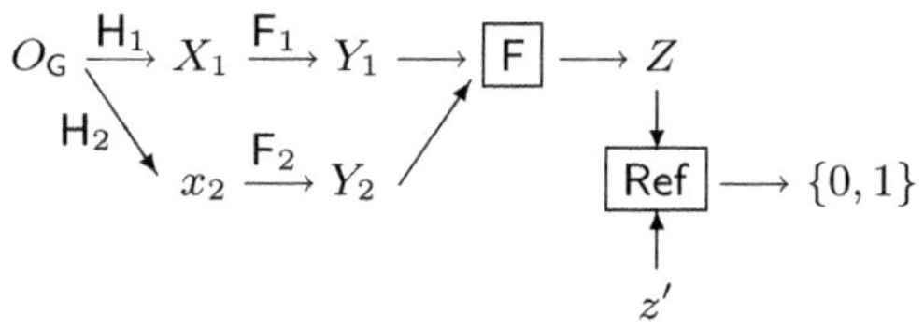

**Fig. 7.** First step of "factoring-out" transformation ($x_2 \in X_2$, $z' \in Z'$)

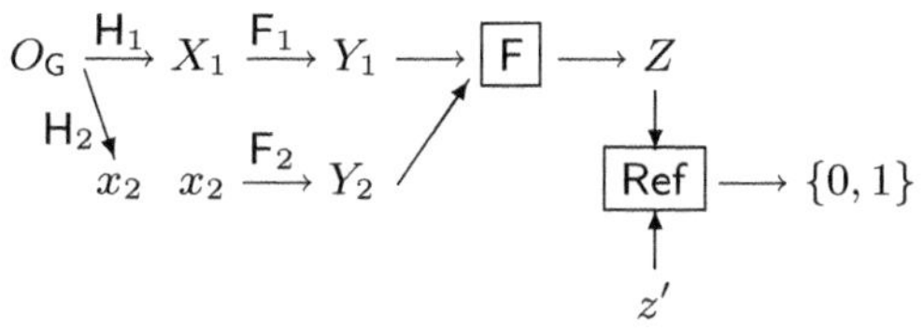

**Fig. 8.** Second step of "factoring-out" transformation ($x_2 \in X_2$, $z' \in Z'$)

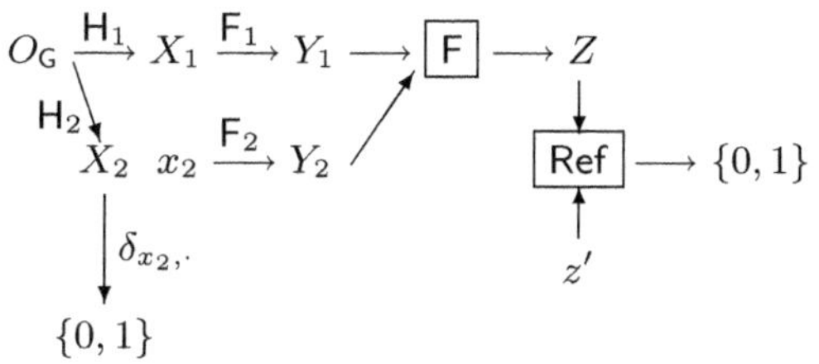

**Fig. 9.** Third step of "factoring-out" transformation ($x_2 \in X_2$, $z' \in Z'$)

By the above arguments, we have

$$\mathsf{succ}_{\mathrm{rnd},A} = \sum_{x_2,z',w} Pr[w \leftarrow \mathcal{W}]\, Pr[\mathsf{A}(x_2, w) = z']\, Pr[\mathsf{D}_{x_2,z'}(U_{O_G}) = 1],$$

and by replacing $U_{O_G}$ with $\mathsf{G}(U_{S_G})$, the success probability $\mathsf{succ}_{\mathrm{prnd},A}$ in pseudo-random case is similarly given by

$$\mathsf{succ}_{\mathrm{prnd},A} = \sum_{x_2,z',w} Pr[w \leftarrow \mathcal{W}]\, Pr[\mathsf{A}(x_2, w) = z']\, Pr[\mathsf{D}_{x_2,z'}(\mathsf{G}(U_{S_G})) = 1].$$

Then the triangle inequality implies that

$$|\mathsf{succ}_{\mathrm{rnd},A} - \mathsf{succ}_{\mathrm{prnd},A}| \le \sum_{x_2,z',w} Pr[w \leftarrow \mathcal{W}]\, Pr[\mathsf{A}(x_2, w) = z']\, \mathsf{adv}_{\mathsf{G}}(\mathsf{D}_{x_2,z'}).$$

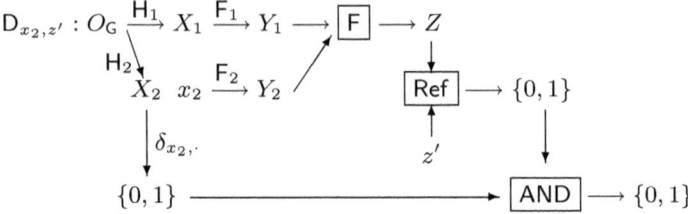

**Fig. 10.** Fourth step of "factoring-out" transformation ($x_2 \in X_2$, $z' \in Z'$)

Now if all the advantages $\mathsf{adv}_\mathsf{G}(\mathsf{D}_{x_2,z'})$ are bounded by $R(T)$ with $T > 0$ a constant, then it follows that

$$|\mathsf{succ}_{\mathrm{rnd,A}} - \mathsf{succ}_{\mathrm{prnd,A}}| \leq \sum_{x_2,w} Pr[w \leftarrow \mathcal{W}] \sum_{z'} Pr[\mathsf{A}(x_2,w) = z']\, R(T)$$

$$= \sum_{x_2,w} Pr[w \leftarrow \mathcal{W}]\, R(T)$$

$$= \sum_{x_2} R(T) = |X_2| \cdot R(T).$$

Thus, under some assumptions similar to Theorem 2, our technique derives a similar bound for the difference of random and pseudorandom cases. We emphasize that the resulting bound depends on the amount of information received by the adversary, but not on the amount of choices for the secret elements.

Note that our proposed technique can be similarly applied to more general situations. (In fact, we can even formalize our "factoring-out" method in a general and abstract way, which is omitted here due to its intricacy.) Since the bound derived by our technique becomes better as the amount of information received by the adversary gets smaller, our technique is effective especially in the following kind of situations: There are a large number of players, including a small number of adversarial ones (like a leaf in a forest), and a small piece of the whole randomness is distributed to each player. Such applications include secret sharing [4,25], broadcast encryption [14], traitor tracing [2,9,18], and collusion-secure codes [6,27].

## 5 Discussion and Miscellaneous Remarks

In this section, we give some further discussion and remarks on our argument and result in this article.

1. A frequently asked question on our result is the following: Why the adversary cannot recover the seed of the just computationally secure PRG, though he is allowed to use algorithms with unbounded complexity? A simple answer is: A common characteristic of our successful examples is that the amount of information received by the adversary is sufficiently small. In such cases, the information is too scanty to recover the seed even for the strong adversary.

2. Although we have focused only on information-theoretically secure (or non-cryptographic) protocols in the above argument, our evaluation technique may give a significant insight in the case of computationally secure protocols as well. For instance, when the protocol under randomness reduction is just computationally secure but *post-quantum*, i.e., when the adversary may be quantum, our technique can show that secure randomness reduction is still possible even by using a PRG whose underlying computational problem is easy for quantum computers. The reason is that the indistinguishability of the PRG is evaluated in a *fixed* $(\mathcal{M}, \mathcal{C})$ that is not relevant to the underlying computational model of the adversary's (quantum) algorithm.

3. In our result, the derived bound of the difference between random and pseudorandom cases depends on computational complexity of the protocol under consideration. This means that the efficiency of the protocol contributes *directly* to the security evaluation result in our argument. On the other hand, in usual situations, efficiency of the protocol contributes *just indirectly* to the security of the scheme (for instance, the more efficient a protocol is, the larger the encryption/decryption keys for the practical implementation can be, hence the more secure the implementation will be).

4. We have mentioned in the last paragraph of Sect. 4.4 that our evaluation technique is effective, for instance, when there are a large number of players, including a small number of adversaries, and a small piece of the whole randomness is distributed to each player. In such a situation, if we could know in advance who are the adversaries among all players, then smaller randomness would suffice for fighting the exposed adversaries directly, since the information on the randomness received by the adversaries is now small. However, actually we have no practical way to know it in advance, and it is inevitable to fight huge possibilities of where the adversaries are hiding, requiring further randomness. The randomness for the latter purpose looks less essential than the former one, and our PRG-based randomness reduction can be intuitively thought of as acting on the latter inessential randomness. The security notion for PRGs (Definition 3) fits the purpose very well; advantages of distinguishers are bounded regardless of the bit positions (corresponding to the place of adversaries) that are picked up from outputs of a PRG.

5. In the above argument, we have carefully avoided to use the term "computationally unbounded adversary"; instead, we used, for instance, "adversary's algorithm with unbounded complexity". Whether or not the term "computationally unbounded adversary" may be used in our argument seems to depend on whether or not a "computationally unbounded adversary" and an assumption on hardness of a problem (*in a fixed computational model*) may be simultaneously considered, or whether or not the ability of a "computationally unbounded adversary" is restricted by innate hardness of a problem *in a fixed computational model*. This would depend on the precise definition of "computationally unbounded adversary". Anyway, our technique can imply that random and pseudorandom cases in the PRG-based randomness reduction are indistinguishable even for an impractically strong adversary who can perform *arbitrary* algorithms based on *arbitrary* (theoretically

consistent) computational models (such an adversary would be able to perform infinitely fast computation in any practical situation, since complexity of an algorithm can be infinitely reduced by choosing a computational model $\mathcal{M}$ with the complexity function $C_{\mathcal{M}}$ taking infinitely small values).

# 6   Conclusion

In this article, we proposed novel ideas and techniques for evaluation of indistinguishability between random and pseudorandom cases in randomness reduction of cryptographic or non-cryptographic protocols based on PRGs. Our technique can prove the indistinguishability even for an adversary who can use algorithms with unbounded computational complexity. Our idea removes the requirement of the generalized notion of nb-PRGs introduced and used in the preceding work of Dubrov and Ishai [11], and our technique is effective in more general situations than the case of their technique. Our technique is effective especially in cases where the amount of information received by the adversary is small.

**Acknowledgments.** The authors would like to thank Hideki Imai, Hajime Watanabe, Kentaro Imafuku, Takayuki Miyadera, Gen Kimura, and the anonymous referees, for their precious comments.

# References

1. Bach, E.: Realistic analysis of some randomized algorithms. Journal of Computer and System Sciences 42, 30–53 (1991)
2. Billet, O., Phan, D.H.: Efficient traitor tracing from collusion secure codes. In: Safavi-Naini, R. (ed.) ICITS 2008. LNCS, vol. 5155, pp. 171–182. Springer, Heidelberg (2008)
3. Binder, I., Braverman, M.: Derandomization of Euclidean random walks. In: Charikar, M., Jansen, K., Reingold, O., Rolim, J.D.P. (eds.) RANDOM 2007 and APPROX 2007. LNCS, vol. 4627, pp. 353–365. Springer, Heidelberg (2007)
4. Blakley, G.R.: Safeguarding cryptographic keys. In: Proceedings of 1979 National Computer Conference. AFIPS Proceedings, vol. 48, pp. 313–317 (1979)
5. Blum, M.: Independent unbiased coin flips from a correlated biased source: A finite state Markov chain. In: Proceedings of 25th FOCS, pp. 425–433. IEEE, Los Alamitos (1984)
6. Boneh, D., Shaw, J.: Collusion-secure fingerprinting for digital data. IEEE Transactions on Information Theory 44, 1897–1905 (1998)
7. Bosley, C., Dodis, Y.: Does privacy require true randomness? In: Vadhan, S.P. (ed.) TCC 2007. LNCS, vol. 4392, pp. 1–20. Springer, Heidelberg (2007)
8. Cheng, Q.: Derandomization of sparse cyclotomic integer zero testing. In: Proceedings of 48th FOCS, pp. 74–80. IEEE, Los Alamitos (2007)
9. Chor, B., Fiat, A., Naor, M.: Tracing traitors. In: Desmedt, Y.G. (ed.) CRYPTO 1994. LNCS, vol. 839, pp. 257–270. Springer, Heidelberg (1994)
10. Chor, B., Goldreich, O.: Unbiased bits from sources of weak randomness and probabilistic communication complexity. SIAM Journal of Computing 17(2), 230–261 (1988)

11. Dubrov, B., Ishai, Y.: On the randomness complexity of efficient sampling. In: Proceedings of STOC 2006, pp. 711–720. ACM, New York (2006)
12. Dodis, Y., Ong, S.J., Prabhakaran, M., Sahai, A.: On the (im)possibility of cryptography with imperfect randomness. In: Proceedings of 45th FOCS, pp. 196–205. IEEE, Los Alamitos (2004)
13. Farashahi, R.R., Schoenmakers, B., Sidorenko, A.: Efficient pseudorandom generators based on the DDH assumption. In: Okamoto, T., Wang, X. (eds.) PKC 2007. LNCS, vol. 4450, pp. 426–441. Springer, Heidelberg (2007)
14. Fiat, A., Naor, M.: Broadcast encryption. In: Stinson, D.R. (ed.) CRYPTO 1993. LNCS, vol. 773, pp. 480–491. Springer, Heidelberg (1994)
15. Ishai, Y., Kushilevits, E.: On the hardness of information-theoretic multiparty computation. In: Cachin, C., Camenisch, J.L. (eds.) EUROCRYPT 2004. LNCS, vol. 3027, pp. 439–455. Springer, Heidelberg (2004)
16. Juels, A., Jakobsson, M., Shriver, E., Hillyer, B.K.: How to turn loaded dice into fair coins. IEEE Transactions on Information Theory 46(3), 911–921 (2000)
17. Kaplan, E., Naor, M., Reingold, O.: Derandomized constructions of $k$-wise (Almost) independent permutations. In: Chekuri, C., Jansen, K., Rolim, J.D.P., Trevisan, L. (eds.) APPROX 2005 and RANDOM 2005. LNCS, vol. 3624, pp. 354–365. Springer, Heidelberg (2005)
18. Kiayias, A., Yung, M.: Traitor tracing with constant transmission rate. In: Knudsen, L.R. (ed.) EUROCRYPT 2002. LNCS, vol. 2332, pp. 450–465. Springer, Heidelberg (2002)
19. Maurer, U., Wolf, S.: Privacy amplification secure against active adversaries. In: Kaliski Jr., B.S. (ed.) CRYPTO 1997. LNCS, vol. 1294, pp. 307–321. Springer, Heidelberg (1997)
20. McInnes, J.L., Pinkas, B.: On the impossibility of private key cryptography with weakly random keys. In: Menezes, A., Vanstone, S.A. (eds.) CRYPTO 1990. LNCS, vol. 537, pp. 421–435. Springer, Heidelberg (1991)
21. Von Neumann, J.: Various techniques for use in connection with random digits. National Bureau of Standards, Applied Mathematics Series 12, 36–38 (1951)
22. Peralta, R., Shoup, V.: Primality testing with fewer random bits. Computational Complexity 3, 355–367 (1993)
23. Renner, R., Wolf, S.: Unconditional authenticity and privacy from an arbitrary weak secret. In: Boneh, D. (ed.) CRYPTO 2003. LNCS, vol. 2729, pp. 78–95. Springer, Heidelberg (2003)
24. Santha, M., Vazirani, U.V.: Generating quasi-random sequences from semi-random sources. Journal of Computer and System Sciences 33, 75–87 (1986)
25. Shamir, A.: How to share a secret. Communications of the ACM 22(11), 612–613 (1980)
26. Shannon, C.: Communication theory of secrecy systems. Bell System Technical Journal 28, 656–715 (1949)
27. Tardos, G.: Optimal probabilistic fingerprint codes. Journal of the ACM 55(2), 1–24 (2008)
28. Vazirani, U.V., Vazirani, V.V.: Random polynomial time is equal to slightly-random polynomial time. In: Proceedings of 26th FOCS, pp. 417–428. IEEE, Los Alamitos (1985)
29. Zuckerman, D.: Simulating BPP using a general weak random source. Algorithmica 16(4/5), 367–391 (1996)

# Efficient Statistical Asynchronous Verifiable Secret Sharing with Optimal Resilience

Arpita Patra*, Ashish Choudhary**, and C. Pandu Rangan***

Dept of Computer Science and Engineering
IIT Madras, Chennai India 600036
arpitapatra10@gmail.com, partho_31@yahoo.co.in, prangan55@gmail.com

**Abstract.** We present a new statistical *asynchronous verifiable secret sharing* (AVSS) protocol with *optimal resilience*; i.e. with $n = 3t + 1$, where $n$ is the total number of participating parties and $t$ is the maximum number of parties that can be under the control of a *computationally unbounded active adversary* $\mathcal{A}_t$. Our protocol privately communicates $\mathcal{O}((\ell n^3 + n^4 \kappa)\kappa)$ bits and A-casts $\mathcal{O}(n^3 \log(n))$ bits to simultaneously share $\ell \geq 1$ elements from a finite field $\mathbb{F}$, where $\kappa$ is the error parameter.

There are only two known statistical AVSS protocols with $n = 3t+1$, reported in [11] and [26]. The AVSS protocol of [11] requires a private communication of $\mathcal{O}(n^9 \kappa^4)$ bits and A-cast of $\mathcal{O}(n^9 \kappa^2 \log(n))$ bits to share a *single* element from $\mathbb{F}$. Thus our AVSS protocol shows a significant improvement in communication complexity over the AVSS of [11]. The AVSS protocol of [26] requires a private communication of $\mathcal{O}((\ell n^3 + n^4)\kappa)$ bits and A-cast of $\mathcal{O}((\ell n^3 + n^4)\kappa)$ bits to share $\ell \geq 1$ elements. However, the shared element(s) may be $NULL \notin \mathbb{F}$. Thus our AVSS is better than the AVSS of [26] due to two reasons: (a) The A-cast communication of our AVSS is *independent* of the number of secrets i.e. $\ell$; (b) Our AVSS makes sure that the shared value(s) always belong to $\mathbb{F}$.

Using our AVSS, we design a new primitive called Asynchronous Complete Secret Sharing (ACSS) which is an essential building block of *asynchronous multiparty computation* (AMPC). Using our ACSS scheme, we can design a statistical AMPC with *optimal resilience*; i.e., with $n = 3t + 1$, that privately communicates $\mathcal{O}(n^5 \kappa)$ bits *per multiplication gate*. This will significantly improve the only known statistical AMPC of [8] with $n = 3t + 1$, which privately communicates $\Omega(n^{11} \kappa^4)$ bits and A-cast $\Omega(n^{11} \kappa^2 \log(n))$ bits per multiplication gate.

## 1 Introduction

A Verifiable Secret Sharing (VSS) [13] protocol is carried out among a set of $n$ parties, say $\mathcal{P} = \{P_1, \ldots, P_n\}$, where every two parties are directly connected by

---

\* Financial support from Microsoft Research India acknowledged.
\*\* Financial support from Infosys Technology India acknowledged.
\*\*\* Work Supported by Project No. CSE/05-06/076/DITX/CPAN on Protocols for Secure Communication and Computation Sponsored by Department of Information Technology, Government of India.

K. Kurosawa (Ed.): ICITS 2009, LNCS 5973, pp. 74–92, 2010.
© Springer-Verlag Berlin Heidelberg 2010

a secure channel and $t$ out of the $n$ parties can be under the influence of a *computationally unbounded Byzantine (active) adversary*, denoted as $\mathcal{A}_t$. The Byzantine adversary $\mathcal{A}_t$ completely dictates the parties under its control and can force them to deviate from a protocol, in any arbitrary manner. Any VSS scheme consists of a pair of protocols (Sh, Rec). Protocol Sh allows a special party in $\mathcal{P}$, called *dealer* (denoted as $D$), to share a secret $s \in \mathbb{F}$ (an element from a finite field $\mathbb{F}$) among all the parties in a way that allow for a unique reconstruction of $s$ by every body using protocol Rec. Moreover, if $D$ is *honest*, then the secrecy of $s$ from $\mathcal{A}_t$ should be preserved till the end of Sh. VSS is one of the fundamental building blocks for many secure distributed computing tasks, such as multiparty computation (MPC) [7,12,28,2,14,21,3,4,5], Byzantine Agreement (BA) [17,11,23,1,22,26], etc. Over the past three decades, the problem has been studied in different settings and computational models (see [20,7,12,16,28,14,15,19,18,22,24]). The VSS problem has been studied extensively over *synchronous* networks, which assumes that there is a global clock and the delay of any message in the network is bounded. However, VSS in asynchronous network has got comparatively less attention, due to its inherent hardness. As asynchronous networks model real life networks like Internet more precisely, it is important to investigate fundamental problem like VSS in asynchronous network.

## 1.1 Definitions

**Asynchronous Networks:** In an asynchronous network, the communication channels have arbitrary, yet finite delay (i.e the messages are guaranteed to reach eventually). To model this, $\mathcal{A}_t$ is given the power to schedule the delivery of *all* messages in the network. However, $\mathcal{A}_t$ can not access the messages communicated between honest parties. Here the inherent difficulty in designing a protocol comes from the fact that when a party does not receive an expected message then he cannot decide whether the sender is corrupted (and did not send the message at all) or the message is just delayed. So it is impossible to consider the values sent by all uncorrupted parties and hence the values of up to $t$ (potentially honest) parties may get ignored, as waiting for them could turn out to be endless. Due to this the protocols in asynchronous network are generally involved in nature and require new set of primitives. For an excellent introduction to asynchronous protocols, see [10].

We now give the definition of primitives which are used in this paper. For all these primitives, we assume that all computations are carried over a finite field $\mathbb{F} = GF(2^\kappa)$, where $\kappa$ is error parameter. So each field element can be represented by $\mathcal{O}(\kappa)$ bits. Also without loss of generality, we assume $n = \text{poly}(\kappa)$.

**Definition 1 (Statistical Asynchronous Weak Secret Sharing (AWSS) [26]).** *Let (Sh, Rec) be a pair of protocols in which a dealer $D \in \mathcal{P}$ shares a secret $s \in \mathbb{F}$ using Sh. We say that (Sh, Rec) is a $t$-resilient statistically secure AWSS scheme if all the following hold:*

- **Termination:** *With probability at least $1 - 2^{-\Omega(\kappa)}$, all the following holds: (1) If $D$ is honest then each honest party will eventually terminate protocol Sh. (2) If some honest party has terminated protocol Sh, then irrespective of* *the behavior of D, each honest party will eventually terminate* Sh. *(3) If all the honest parties have terminated* Sh *and if all the honest parties invoke protocol* Rec, *then each honest party will eventually terminate* Rec.

- **Correctness:** *With probability at least* $1 - 2^{-\Omega(\kappa)}$, *all the following holds: (1) If D is honest then each honest party upon completing* Rec *outputs s. (2) If D is corrupted and some honest party has terminated* Sh, *then there exists a fixed* $\bar{s} \in \mathbb{F} \cup \{NULL\}$, *such that each honest party upon terminating* Rec, *will output either* $\bar{s}$ *or* $NULL$.

- **Secrecy:** *If D is honest and no honest party has begun* Rec, *then* $\mathcal{A}_t$ *has no information about s.*

**Definition 2 (Statistical Asynchronous Verifiable Secret Sharing (AVSS) [6,10]).** *It is same as AWSS except that* **Correctness (2)** *is strengthened:*

- **Correctness (2):** *If D is corrupted and some honest party has terminated* Sh, *then there exists a fixed* $\bar{s} \in \mathbb{F}$, *such that each honest party upon terminating* Rec, *will output only* $\bar{s}$.

**Definition 3 (t-sharing [3,5]).** *A value* $s \in \mathbb{F}$ *is said to be t-shared among the parties in* $\mathcal{P}$ *if there exists a random degree-t polynomial* $f(x)$ *over* $\mathbb{F}$, *with* $f(0) = s$ *such that each (honest) party* $P_i \in \mathcal{P}$ *holds his share* $s_i = f(i)$ *of secret s. The vector of shares of s corresponding to the honest parties is called t-sharing of s and is denoted by* $[s]_t$.

Typically, VSS is used as a tool for generating $t$-sharing of secret. For example, see [7,22]. On the other hand, there do exists VSS scheme which do not generate $t$-sharing of secret. They only ensure that a unique secret is shared (committed) which will be uniquely reconstructed during reconstruction phase. Such schemes are presented in [19,18,24]. So we call a VSS scheme as *Complete Secret Sharing* (CSS) scheme if it generates $t$-sharing of secret.

**Definition 4 (Statistical Asynchronous Complete Secret Sharing (ACSS)).** *The* **termination, correctness** *and* **secrecy** *property of ACSS are same as in AVSS. In addition, ACSS requires the following completeness property to hold at the end of* Sh *with probability at least* $1 - 2^{-\Omega(\kappa)}$:

- **Completeness:** *at the end of* Sh, *there exists a random degree-t polynomial* $f(x)$ *over* $\mathbb{F}$, *with* $f(0) = \bar{s}$ *such that each (honest) party* $P_i \in \mathcal{P}$ *holds his share* $s_i = f(i)$ *of secret* $\bar{s}$. *Moreover, if D is honest, then* $\bar{s} = s$.

*Remark 1* **(AWSS, AVSS and ACSS with Private Reconstruction).** The definitions of AWSS, AVSS and ACSS as given above consider "public reconstruction", where all parties reconstruct the secret in Rec. A common variant of these definitions consider "private reconstruction", where *only* some specific party, say $P_\alpha \in \mathcal{P}$, is allowed to reconstruct the secret in Rec. As per our requirement in this paper, we present our AWSS and AVSS protocols with *only* private reconstruction. However, the public reconstruction for these protocols can be obtained by doing slight modification. For details, see [25].

In our protocols, we also use A-cast primitive, which is formally defined as follows:

**Definition 5 (A-cast [11,10]).** *It is an asynchronous broadcast primitive, which allows a special party in $\mathcal{P}$ (called sender) to identically distribute a message among all parties in $\mathcal{P}$. It was implemented by Bracha [9] with $n = 3t + 1$. Let $\Pi$ be an asynchronous protocol initiated by a special party (called the sender), having input $m$ (the message to be broadcast). We say that $\Pi$ is a t-resilient A-cast protocol if the following hold, for every possible $\mathcal{A}_t$:*

- **Termination**
    1. *If the sender is honest and all the honest parties participate in the protocol, then each honest party will eventually terminate the protocol.*
    2. *Irrespective of the behavior of the sender, if any honest party terminates the protocol then each honest party will eventually terminate the protocol.*
- **Correctness:** *If honest parties terminate the protocol then they do so with a common output $m^*$. Furthermore, if the sender is honest then $m^* = m$.*

*The A-cast protocol of [9] requires a private communication of $\mathcal{O}(n^2 b)$ bits to A-cast a b bit message.*

## 1.2 Existing Results for Statistical AVSS with Optimal Resilience

Statistical AVSS tolerating $\mathcal{A}_t$ is possible iff $n \geq 3t + 1$ [11]. So any statistical AVSS with $n = 3t+1$ is said to have *optimal resilience*. The only known statistical AVSS with optimal resilience are due to [11] and [26], which are used in designing *Asynchronous Byzantine Agreement* (ABA) schemes. These two AVSS schemes are summarized as follows:

1. The authors of [11] have presented a series of protocols for designing their AVSS scheme. They first designed a tool called *Information Checking Protocol* (ICP) which is used as a black box for another primitive *Asynchronous Recoverable Sharing* (A-RS). Subsequently, using A-RS, the authors have designed an AWSS scheme, which is further used to design a variation of AWSS called *Two & Sum AWSS*. Finally using their *Two & Sum AWSS*, an AVSS scheme was presented. Pictorially, the route taken by AVSS scheme of [11] is as follows: $ICP \rightarrow A\text{-}RS \rightarrow AWSS \rightarrow Two \ \& \ Sum \ AWSS \rightarrow AVSS$. Since the AVSS scheme is designed on top of so many sub-protocols, it becomes highly communication intensive as well as very much involved. The scheme requires a private communication of $\mathcal{O}(n^9 \kappa^4)$ bits and A-cast $\mathcal{O}(n^9 \kappa^2 \log(n))$ bits to share a *single* element from $\mathbb{F}$.
2. Pictorially, the authors in [26] used the following simpler route to design their AVSS scheme: $ICP \rightarrow AWSS \rightarrow AVSS$. Moreover, the authors in [26] significantly improved each of the underlying building blocks, namely ICP and AWSS, by employing new design approaches. The AVSS protocol of [26] requires a private communication of $\mathcal{O}((\ell n^3 + n^4)\kappa)$ bits and A-cast of $\mathcal{O}((\ell n^3 + n^4)\kappa)$ bits to share $\ell \geq 1$ elements. However, the AVSS scheme of [26] has the following shortcomings: (a) The AVSS scheme of [26] is not an ACSS scheme and hence is not suitable for AMPC. (b) In AVSS of [26], a *corrupted D* may choose secrets from $\mathbb{F} \cup \{NULL\}$ instead of only $\mathbb{F}$.

## 1.3    Our Contribution

We present a new statistical AVSS with optimal resilience by following the simple
route of [26]. In the following table, we compare the communication complexity
of our AVSS with the AVSS of [11,26]. The table also shows the communication
complexity (CC) after simulating A-cast using the protocol of [9].

| Ref. | CC in bits | CC in bits using A-cast of [9] | # Secrets |
|------|------------|-------------------------------|-----------|
| [11] | Private– $\mathcal{O}(n^9\kappa^4)$ A-cast– $\mathcal{O}(n^9\kappa^2\log(n))$ | private– $\mathcal{O}(n^9\kappa^4 + n^{11}\kappa^2\log n)$ | 1 |
| [26] | Private– $\mathcal{O}((\ell n^3 + n^4)\kappa)$ A-cast– $\mathcal{O}((\ell n^3 + n^4)\kappa)$ | private– $\mathcal{O}((\ell n^5 + n^6)\kappa)$ | $\ell$ |
| This Article | Private– $\mathcal{O}((\ell n^3 + n^4\kappa)\kappa)$ A-cast– $\mathcal{O}(n^3\log(n))$ | private– $\mathcal{O}((\ell n^3 + n^4\kappa)\kappa + n^5\log n)$ | $\ell$ |

As shown in the table, our AVSS attains significantly better communication
complexity than the AVSS of [11] and [26] for any value of $\ell$. As mentioned in
the previous section, the AVSS of [26] has a *weaker* property: *A corrupted D
may choose secrets from* $\mathbb{F} \cup \{NULL\}$. Such an AVSS is sufficient for designing
ABA protocols. However, to be applicable for AMPC, we require that AVSS
should allow to share secret(s) *only* from $\mathbb{F}$ [8]. Our AVSS achieves this crucial
property at a lesser communication cost. Using our AVSS, we design a new ACSS
scheme, which is an essential component of AMPC [8]. Though there exists CSS
in synchronous settings, our ACSS scheme is first of its kind in asynchronous
settings with $n = 3t + 1$. In fact, using our ACSS, we can design an efficient
statistical AMPC with *optimal resilience*; i.e., with $n = 3t + 1$, which privately
communicates $\mathcal{O}(n^5\kappa)$ bits *per multiplication gate*. This will be a significant
improvement over the *only known* statistical AMPC of [8] with $n = 3t + 1$,
which privately communicates $\Omega(n^{11}\kappa^4)$ bits and A-cast $\Omega(n^{11}\kappa^2\log(n))$ bits
per multiplication gate. For details see full version of this paper [25].

In order to design AVSS, we first propose a new ICP which significantly
improves the communication complexity of the ICP of [26]. Using our ICP, we
design an AWSS which is inspired by AWSS of [26]. Using this AWSS, we design
a new AVSS. Finally our new AVSS is used in designing our ACSS scheme. The
design approach of our AVSS and ACSS are novel and first of their kind.

## 2    Information Checking Protocol and IC Signature

Information Checking Protocol (ICP) [28,27] is a tool for authenticating messages in the presence of $\mathcal{A}_t$. Here we present an ICP, called A-ICP$(D, INT, P, S)$
in asynchronous settings. As in [26], A-ICP is executed among three entities: the
dealer $D \in \mathcal{P}$, an intermediary $INT \in \mathcal{P}$ and entire set $\mathcal{P}$ acting as verifiers.
The dealer $D$ hands a secret $s$ to $INT$. At a later stage, $INT$ has to hand over
$s$ to the verifiers in $\mathcal{P}$ and convince them that $s$ is indeed the value which $INT$
received from $D$. We may also run A-ICP to *concurrently* work on *multiple* secrets, denoted by $S$ containing $\ell \geq 1$ secrets. So, instead of repeating multiple
instances of ICP dealing with single secret, we can run a single instance of our
A-ICP dealing with multiple secrets *concurrently*, leading to significant reduction

in communication complexity. We use A-ICP in our AWSS scheme, where it is required to execute instances of A-ICP dealing with multiple secrets concurrently.

For $\ell$ secrets, the A-ICP of [26] incurs a private communication of $\mathcal{O}((\ell+n)\kappa)$ bits and A-cast of $\mathcal{O}((\ell + n)\kappa)$ bits. On the other hand, our A-ICP incurs *only* private communication of $\mathcal{O}((\ell + n\kappa)\kappa)$ bits (and *no* A-cast). As in [11,26], our A-ICP is also structured into sequence of following three phases:

1. **Generation Phase:** It is initiated $D$. Here $D$ hands over the secret $S$, containing $\ell$ elements from $\mathbb{F}$ along with some *authentication information* to $INT$ and some *verification information* to individual *verifiers* in $\mathcal{P}$.
2. **Verification Phase:** is carried out by $INT$ and verifiers in $\mathcal{P}$. Here $INT$ decides whether to continue or abort the protocol depending upon the prediction whether in **Revelation Phase**, $S$ held by $INT$ will be (eventually) accepted/will be considered as valid by the honest verifier(s) in $\mathcal{P}$. $INT$ achieves this by setting a boolean variable $\mathsf{Ver} = 0/1$, where $\mathsf{Ver} = 0$ (resp. 1) implies abortion (resp. continuation) of the protocol. If $\mathsf{Ver} = 1$, then *authentication information*, along with $S$, held by $INT$ at the end of **Verification Phase** is called $D$'s IC *signature* on $S$, denoted as $ICSig(D, INT, \mathcal{P}, S)$.
3. **Revelation Phase:** is carried out by $INT$ and the verifiers in $\mathcal{P}$. **Revelation Phase** can be presented in two flavors: (a) *Public Revelation* of $ICSig(D, INT, \mathcal{P}, S)$ to all the verifiers in $\mathcal{P}$ where all the verifiers can publicly verify whether $INT$ indeed received IC signature on $S$ from $D$; (b) $P_\alpha$-*private-revelation* of $ICSig(D, INT, \mathcal{P}, S)$: Here $INT$ privately reveals $ICSig(D, INT, \mathcal{P}, S)$ to *only* $P_\alpha$. After doing some checking, if $P_\alpha$ believes that $INT$ indeed received IC signature on $S$ from $D$ then $P_\alpha$ sets $\mathsf{Reveal}_\alpha = S$. Otherwise $P_\alpha$ sets $\mathsf{Reveal}_\alpha = NULL$.

Protocol A-ICP satisfies the following properties (assuming *Public Revelation* in **Revelation Phase**):

1. If $D$ and $INT$ are honest, then $S$ will be accepted in **Revelation phase** by each honest verifier.
2. If $INT$ is honest and $\mathsf{Ver} = 1$, then $S$ held by $INT$ will be accepted in **Revelation phase** by each honest verifier, except with probability $2^{-\Omega(\kappa)}$.
3. If $D$ is honest, then during **Revelation phase**, with probability at least $1 - 2^{-\Omega(\kappa)}$, every $S' \neq S$ produced by a corrupted $INT$ will be not be accepted by any honest verifier.
4. If $D$ and $INT$ are honest and $INT$ has not started **Revelation phase**, then $S$ will be information theoretically secure.

For A-ICP with $P_\alpha$-*private-revelation* in **Revelation Phase**, the above properties are modified by replacing "every/any honest verifier" with "honest $P_\alpha$". In the sequel, we present protocol A-ICP. As in reconstruction phase of our of AWSS we require only $P_\alpha$-private-revelation of $ICSig(D, INT, \mathcal{P}, S)$, we present only that (though we have an implementation for public revelation of $ICSig(D, INT, \mathcal{P}, S)$). We now state the properties of protocol A-ICP. The complete proof are given in [25] due to space constraints.

---

## Protocol **A-ICP**$(D, INT, \mathcal{P}, S)$

**Generation Phase: Gen$(D, INT, \mathcal{P}, S)$**

1. The dealer $D$, on having secret $S = (s^1, \ldots, s^\ell)$, selects a random $\ell + t\kappa$ degree polynomial $f(x)$ whose lower order $\ell$ coefficients are elements in $S$. $D$ also picks $n\kappa$ random non-zero elements from $\mathbb{F}$, denoted by $\alpha_1^i, \ldots, \alpha_\kappa^i$, for $i = 1, \ldots, n$.
2. For $i = 1, \ldots, n$, $D$ sends $f(x)$ to $INT$ and the verification tags $z_1^i = (\alpha_1^i, a_1^i), \ldots, z_\kappa^i = (\alpha_\kappa^i, a_\kappa^i)$ to party $P_i$, where $a_j^i = f(\alpha_j^i)$, for $j = 1, \ldots, \kappa$.

**Verification Phase: Ver$(D, INT, \mathcal{P}, S)$**

1. Every verifier $P_i$ *randomly* partitions the index set $\{1, \ldots, \kappa\}$ into two sets $I^i$ and $\overline{I^i}$ of equal size and sends $I^i$ and $z_j^i$ for all $j \in I^i$ to $INT$.
2. For every verifier $P_i$ from whom $INT$ has received values, $INT$ checks whether for *every* $j \in I^i$, $f(\alpha_j^i) \overset{?}{=} a_j^i$.
3. (a) If for at least $2t+1$ verifiers, the above condition is satisfied, then $INT$ sets Ver $= 1$. If Ver $= 1$, then $ICSig(D, INT, \mathcal{P}, S) = f(x)$.
   (b) If for $t+1$ verifiers, the above condition is not satisfied, then $INT$ sets Ver $= 0$.

**Revelation Phase: Reveal-Private$(D, INT, \mathcal{P}, S, P_\alpha)$:** $P_\alpha$-*private-revelation* of $ICSig(D, INT, \mathcal{P}, S)$

1. To party $P_\alpha$, $INT$ sends $f(x)$.
2. To party $P_\alpha$, every verifier $P_i$ sends the index set $\overline{I^i}$ and all $z_j^i$ such that $j \in \overline{I^i}$.
3. On receiving values from verifier $P_i$, party $P_\alpha$ checks whether for *some* $j \in \overline{I^i}$, $f(\alpha_j^i) \overset{?}{=} a_j^i$.
   (a) If for at least $t+1$ verifiers the above condition is satisfied, then $P_\alpha$ sets Reveal$_\alpha = S$, where $S$ is lower order $\ell$ coefficients of $f(x)$. In this case, we say that $INT$ is 'successful' in producing $ICSig(D, INT, \mathcal{P}, S)$ to $P_\alpha$.
   (b) If for at least $2t+1$ verifiers the above condition is not satisfied, then $P_\alpha$ sets Reveal$_\alpha = NULL$. In this case, we say that $INT$ 'fails' in producing $ICSig(D, INT, \mathcal{P}, S)$ to $P_\alpha$.

---

**Lemma 1.** *If $D$, $INT$ and $P_\alpha$ are honest, then $S$ will be accepted by $P_\alpha$.*

**Lemma 2.** *If $INT$ is honest and Ver $=1$, then $S$ held by $INT$ will be accepted in Reveal-Private by honest $P_\alpha$, except with error probability of $2^{-\Omega(\kappa)}$.*

**Lemma 3.** *If $D$ is honest, then in Reveal-Private, with probability $1 - 2^{-\Omega(\kappa)}$, every $S' \neq S$ produced by a corrupted $INT$ will be rejected by honest $P_\alpha$.*

**Lemma 4.** *If $D$ and $INT$ are honest and $INT$ has not started Reveal-Private, then $S$ is information theoretically secure from $\mathcal{A}_t$.*

**Lemma 5.** *Protocol Gen, Ver and Reveal-Private privately communicate $\mathcal{O}((\ell + n\kappa)\kappa)$ bits each.*

**Notation 1 (Notation for Using A-ICP)** . *Recall that $D$ and $INT$ can be any party from $\mathcal{P}$. In the sequel we use the following convention: We say that:*

*(1) "$P_i$ sends $ICSig(P_i, P_j, \mathcal{P}, S)$ to $P_j$" to mean that $P_i$ as a dealer $D$ executes*
*$Gen(P_i, P_j, \mathcal{P}, S)$; (2) "$P_i$ receives $ICSig(P_j, P_i, \mathcal{P}, S)$ from $P_j$" to mean that $P_i$*
*as $INT$ has completed $Ver(P_j, P_i, \mathcal{P}, S)$ with $Ver = 1$ with the help of the verifiers*
*in $\mathcal{P}$; (3) "$P_i$ reveals $ICSig(P_j, P_i, \mathcal{P}, S)$ to $P_\alpha$" to mean $P_i$ as $INT$ executes*
*Reveal-Private$(P_j, P_i, \mathcal{P}, S, P_\alpha)$ along with participation of the verifiers in $\mathcal{P}$; (4)*
*"$P_\alpha$ completes revelation of $ICSig(P_j, P_i, \mathcal{P}, S)$ with $Reveal_\alpha = S$" to mean $P_\alpha$*
*has successfully completed Reveal-Private$(P_j, P_i, \mathcal{P}, S, P_\alpha)$ with $Reveal_\alpha = S$.*

# 3   Our Statistical AWSS Scheme with $n = 3t + 1$

We now present an AWSS scheme called AWSS with $n = 3t + 1$. AWSS consists
of protocols AWSS-Share and AWSS-Rec-Private. While AWSS-Share allows $D$ to
share *a single secret $s$* among $\mathcal{P}$, AWSS-Rec-Private enables private reconstruction
of $s$ or $NULL$ by a specific party, say $P_\alpha \in \mathcal{P}$. We call the private reconstruction
as $P_\alpha$-*weak-private-reconstruction*. In AWSS-Share, a *corrupted $D$* may share $s =$
$NULL \notin \mathbb{F}$ (the meaning of it will be clear in the sequel).

Our AWSS-Share is inspired by the sharing phase of AWSS-Single-Secret given
in [26]. However, instead of using the A-ICP of [26], we use our A-ICP in AWSS-
Share, which leads to better communication complexity.

*Remark 2 (D's Commitment in AWSS-Share). We say that $D$ is committed to*
*$s \in \mathbb{F}$ in AWSS-Share if there is a unique degree-$t$ univariate polynomial $f(x)$ such*
*that $f(0) = s$ and every honest $P_i \in WCORE$ receives $f(i)$ from $D$. Otherwise,*
*we say that $D$ is committed to $NULL$. An honest $D$ is always committed to*
*$s \in \mathbb{F}$, as in this case $f(x) = f_0(x) = F(x, 0)$ and $f(i) = f_0(i) = f_i(0) = F(0, i)$*
*where $F(x, y)$ is the symmetric degree-$(t, t)$ bivariate polynomial chosen by $D$.*
*But AWSS-Share can not ensure that corrupted $D$ also commits to $s \in \mathbb{F}$.*

The proof of the properties of AWSS follows using similar arguments as in AWSS-
Single-Secret [26]. For details, see [25].

**Notation 2 (Notation for Using AWSS-Share).** *In subsequent sections, we*
*will invoke AWSS-Share as AWSS-Share$(D, \mathcal{P}, f(x))$ to mean that $D$ commits to*
*$f(x)$ in AWSS-Share. Essentially here $D$ is asked to choose a symmetric bivari-*
*ate polynomial $F(x, y)$ of degree-$t$ in $x$ and $y$, where $F(x, 0) = f(x)$. $D$ then*
*gives $F(x, i)$ and hence $F(0, i) = f(i)$ to $P_i$. Similarly, AWSS-Rec-Private will be*
*invoked as AWSS-Rec-Private$(D, \mathcal{P}, f(x), P_\alpha)$.*                    □

**Theorem 1.** *Protocols (AWSS-Share, AWSS-Rec-Private) constitutes a valid sta-*
*tistical AWSS scheme with $n = 3t+1$ with private reconstruction. Protocol AWSS-*
*Share incurs a private communication of $\mathcal{O}(n^3 \kappa^2)$ bits and A-cast of $\mathcal{O}(n^2 \log(n))$*
*bits. Protocol AWSS-Rec-Private privately communicates $\mathcal{O}(n^3 \kappa^2)$ bits.*

---

## Protocol $\mathbf{AWSS}(D, \mathcal{P}, s)$

**AWSS-Share$(D, \mathcal{P}, s)$**

DISTRIBUTION: CODE FOR $D$ – Only $D$ executes this code.
1. Select a random, symmetric bivariate polynomial $F(x, y)$ over $\mathbb{F}$ of degree-$t$ in $x$ and $y$, such that $F(0, 0) = s$. For $i = 1, \ldots, n$, let $f_i(x) = F(x, i)$.
2. For $i = 1, \ldots, n$, send $ICSig(D, P_i, \mathcal{P}, f_i(j))$ to $P_i$ for each $j = 1, \ldots, n$.

VERIFICATION: CODE FOR $P_i$ – Every party including $D$ executes this code.
1. Wait to receive $ICSig(D, P_i, \mathcal{P}, f_i(j))$ for each $j = 1, \ldots, n$ from $D$.
2. Check if $(f_i(1), \ldots, f_i(n))$ defines degree-$t$ univariate polynomial. If yes then send $ICSig(P_i, P_j, \mathcal{P}, f_i(j))$ to $P_j$ for all $j = 1, \ldots, n$.
3. If $ICSig(P_j, P_i, \mathcal{P}, f_j(i))$ is received from $P_j$ and if $f_i(j) = f_j(i)$, then A-cast $\mathsf{OK}(P_i, P_j)$.

WCORE CONSTRUCTION : CODE FOR $D$ – Only $D$ executes this code.
1. For each $P_j$, build a set $OKP_j = \{P_i | D \text{ receives } \mathsf{OK}(P_i, P_j) \text{ from the A-cast of } P_i\}$. When $|OKP_j| = 2t + 1$, then $P_j$'s $IC$-Commitment on $f_j(0)$ is over (or we may say that $P_j$ is $IC$-committed to $f_j(0)$) and add $P_j$ in $WCORE$ (which is initially empty).
2. Wait until $|WCORE| = 2t + 1$. Then A-cast $WCORE$ and $OKP_j$ for all $P_j \in WCORE$.

WCORE VERIFICATION & AGREEMENT ON WCORE : CODE FOR $P_i$
1. Wait to obtain $WCORE$ and $OKP_j$ for all $P_j \in WCORE$ from $D$'s A-cast, such that $|WCORE| = 2t + 1$ and $|OKP_j| = 2t + 1$ for each $P_j \in WCORE$.
2. Wait to receive $\mathsf{OK}(P_k, P_j)$ for all $P_k \in OKP_j$ and $P_j \in WCORE$. After receiving all these OKs, accept the $WCORE$ and $OKP_j$'s received from $D$ and terminate **AWSS-Share**.

**AWSS-Rec-Private$(D, \mathcal{P}, s, P_\alpha)$**: $P_\alpha$-weak-private-reconstruction of $s$:

SIGNATURE REVELATION: CODE FOR $P_i$
1. If $P_i$ belongs to $OKP_j$ for some $P_j \in WCORE$, then reveal $ICSig(D, P_i, \mathcal{P}, f_i(j))$ and $ICSig(P_j, P_i, \mathcal{P}, f_j(i))$ to $P_\alpha$.

LOCAL COMPUTATION: CODE FOR $P_\alpha$
1. For every $P_j \in WCORE$, reconstruct $P_j$'s $IC$-Commitment, say $\overline{f_j(0)}$ as follows:
   (a) Construct a set $ValidP_j = \emptyset$.
   (b) Add $P_k \in OKP_j$ to $ValidP_j$ if the following conditions hold:
       i. Revelation of $ICSig(D, P_k, \mathcal{P}, f_k(j))$ and $ICSig(P_j, P_k, \mathcal{P}, f_j(k))$ are completed with $\mathsf{Reveal}_\alpha = \overline{f_k(j)}$ and $\mathsf{Reveal}_\alpha = \overline{f_j(k)}$; and
       ii. $\overline{f_k(j)} = \overline{f_j(k)}$.
   (c) Wait until $|ValidP_j| = t + 1$. Construct a polynomial $\overline{f_j(x)}$ passing through the points $(k, \overline{f_j(k)})$ where $P_k \in ValidP_j$. Associate $\overline{f_j(0)}$ with $P_j \in WCORE$.
2. Wait for every $P_j$ in $WCORE$ to be associated with corresponding $\overline{f_j(0)}$.
3. Check whether the points $(j, \overline{f_j(0)})$ for $P_j \in WCORE$ lie on a unique degree-$t$ univariate polynomial $\overline{f_0(x)}$. If yes, then set $\overline{s} = \overline{f_0(0)}$ and terminate **AWSS-Rec-Private**. Else set $\overline{s} = NULL$ and terminate **AWSS-Rec-Private**.

# 4    Our Statistical AVSS Scheme with $n = 3t + 1$

We now present an AVSS scheme called AVSS, consisting of sub-protocols AVSS-Share and AVSS-Rec-Private. AVSS-Share allows $D$ to share a *single secret* from $\mathbb{F}$. *Notice that unlike AWSS-Share, protocol AVSS-Share ensures that a corrupted $D$ always commits to a secret from $\mathbb{F}$.* Protocol AVSS-Rec-Private allows a specific party, say $P_\alpha$, to *privately* reconstruct $D$'s committed secret. We call the private reconstruction as $P_\alpha$-*private-reconstruction*. While $P_\alpha$-*private-reconstruction* can always ensure that $P_\alpha$ reconstructs $D$'s committed secret with high probability, $P_\alpha$-*weak-private-reconstruction* could only ensure that $P_\alpha$ reconstructs either $D$'s committed secret or $NULL$. Structurally, we divide AVSS-Share into a sequence of following three phases.

1. **Commitment by $D$:** Here $D$ on having a secret $s$, commits to the secret by transferring information to individual parties and by executing several instances of AWSS-Share protocol.
2. **Verification of $D$'s commitment:** Here the parties verify whether indeed $D$ is committed a secret from $\mathbb{F}$.
3. **Re-commitment by Individual Parties:** If the parties are convinced in previous phase, then they together re-commit $D$'s committed secret using instances of AWSS-Share protocol.

While first two phases of AVSS-Share are enough to ensure that $D$ has committed a secret from $\mathbb{F}$, the sole purpose of third phase is to enable robust reconstruction of $D$'s committed secret in AVSS-Rec-Private. That is if protocol AVSS-Share stops after the second phase, then we may only ensure that either $D$'s committed secret or $NULL$ will be reconstructed in AVSS-Rec-Private. This would violate the claim that AVSS is an AVSS scheme. The details are given in the sequel.

## 4.1    Commitment by $D$ Phase

In this phase, $D$ on having a secret $s$, selects a random bivariate polynomial $F(x, y)$ of degree-$(t, t)$ (i.e degree-$t$ in both $x$ and $y$) such that $F(0, 0) = s$. Now to party $P_i$, $D$ passes $f_i(x) = F(x, i)$ and $g_i(y) = F(i, y)$. We refer $f_i(x)$ polynomials as *row polynomials* and $g_i(y)$ polynomials as *column polynomials*. Now $D$ commits to $f_1(x), \ldots, f_n(x)$ using $n$ distinct invocations of AWSS-Share protocol. During the course of executing these $n$ instances of AWSS-Share, a party $P_i$ receives $i^{th}$ point on $f_1(x), \ldots, f_n(x)$, namely $f_1(i), \ldots, f_n(i)$ which should be $n$ distinct points on $g_i(y)$. So $P_i$ checks whether $g_i(j) = f_j(i)$ for all $j = 1, \ldots, n$ and informs this by A-casting a signal. While executing the $n$ instances of AWSS-Share, $D$ employ a trick to guarantee that all the $n$ instances of AWSS-Share terminate with a common $WCORE$. Then $D$ tries to make all the honest parties agree on this common $WCORE$, using similar principle as in AWSS-Share. Once this is done, **Commitment by $D$ Phase** ends. We now state the properties of **Commitment by $D$ Phase**. For details, see [25].

**Lemma 6.** *In the code for* **Commitment by** $D$ **Phase***:*

1. *If $D$ is honest then eventually he will generate a common $WCORE$ of size $2t + 1$ for all the $n$ instances of* **AWSS-Share**. *Moreover, each honest party will eventually accept the common $WCORE$.*
2. *If $D$ is corrupted and some honest party has accepted the $WCORE$ and $OKP_j$s received from the* **A-cast** *of $D$, then every other honest party will also eventually accept the same.*

---

### Code **Commitment**$(D, \mathcal{P}, s)$

i. DISTRIBUTION BY $D$: – Only $D$ executes this code

1. Select a random degree-$(t, t)$ bivariate polynomial $F(x, y)$ such that $F(0, 0) = s$.
2. For $i = 1, \ldots, n$, send *row polynomial* $f_i(x) = F(x, i)$ and *column polynomial* $g_i(y) = F(i, y)$ to $P_i$.
3. For $i = 1, \ldots, n$, initiate **AWSS-Share**$(D, \mathcal{P}, f_i(x))$ for sharing $f_i(x)$.

ii. CODE FOR $P_i$ – Every party in $\mathcal{P}$, including $D$, executes this code

1. Wait to receive $f_i(x)$ and $g_i(y)$ from $D$.
2. Participate in **AWSS-Share**$(D, \mathcal{P}, f_j(x))$ by executing steps in [VERIFICATION: CODE FOR $P_i$] (of **AWSS-Share**) for all $j = 1, \ldots, n$.
3. After the completion of step 1 of [VERIFICATION: CODE FOR $P_i$] for all the $n$ invocations of **AWSS-Share**, check whether $g_i(j) = f_j(i)$ holds for all $j = 1, \ldots, n$. Here $f_j(i)$ is obtained by $P_i$ from $D$ during the execution of first step of [VERIFICATION: CODE FOR $P_i$] of **AWSS-Share**$(D, \mathcal{P}, f_j(x))$. If yes then A-cast Matched-Column and execute the rest of the steps of **AWSS-Share**$(D, \mathcal{P}, f_j(x))$, for all $j = 1, \ldots, n$.

iii. WCORE CONSTRUCTION: CODE FOR $D$ – Only $D$ executes this code.

1. Construct $WCORE$ and corresponding $OKP_j$'s for each **AWSS-Share**$(D, \mathcal{P}, f_i(x))$ following the steps in [WCORE CONSTRUCTION] (of **AWSS-Share**). Denote them by $WCORE^i$ and $OKP_j^i$'s.
2. Keep updating $WCORE^i$'s and corresponding $OKP_j^i$'s.
3. Wait to obtain $WCORE = \cap_{i=1}^n WCORE^i$ of size at least $2t+1$ and for every $P_j \in WCORE$, $OKP_j = \cap_{i=1}^n OKP_j^i$ of size at least $2t + 1$ such that Matched-Column is received from A-cast of every $P_j \in WCORE$.
4. A-cast $WCORE$ and $OKP_j$ for every $P_j \in WCORE$.

iv. WCORE VERIFICATION & AGREEMENT: CODE FOR $P_i$

1. Wait to receive $WCORE$ and $OKP_j$ for every $P_j \in WCORE$ from A-cast of $D$, such that $|WCORE| = 2t + 1$ and each $|OKP_j| = 2t + 1$.
2. Wait to receive $OK(P_k, P_j)$ from the A-cast of $P_k$ for every $P_k \in OKP_j$ and every $P_j \in WCORE$ for all the $n$ executions of **AWSS-Share**.
3. Wait to receive Matched-Column from A-cast of every $P_j \in WCORE$.
4. After receiving all desired OKs and Matched-Column signals, accept $WCORE$ and $OKP_j$ for every $P_j \in WCORE$ received from A-cast of $D$ and proceed to the next phase (**Verification Phase**).

## 4.2   Verification of $D$'s Commitment Phase

After accepting $WCORE$ and corresponding $OKP_j$'s, in this phase, the parties verifies whether indeed $D$ has committed a secret from $\mathbb{F}$. For this, we try to check whether there exists a set of *honest parties* of size at least $t+1$, such that for every two parties $P_i, P_j$ in this set, $f_i(j) = g_j(i)$ holds. If we can ensure the availability of such a set then it implies that the row and column polynomials of the parties in this set define a unique bivariate polynomial of degree-$(t, t)$ and the constant term of the polynomial is $D$'s committed secret. Checking for the availability of such a set is quiet easy in synchronous settings, where the parties can simply pair-wise exchange their common values on their row and column polynomial, as done in several synchronous VSS protocols [7,19,18,22,24]. However, doing the same is not easy in asynchronous settings with $n = 3t + 1$.

To check the availability of the set of parties described above, we proceed as follows: recall that in the **Commitment by $D$ phase**, $D$ is committed to $f_1(x), \ldots, f_n(x)$. So we execute AWSS-Rec-Private$(D, \mathcal{P}, f_j(x), P_j)$ for enabling $P_j$-weak-private-reconstruction of $f_j(x)$. If $P_j$ has reconstructed $\overline{f_j}(x)$ from the execution of AWSS-Rec-Private and $\overline{f_j}(x)$ is same as $f_j(x)$ received from $D$ in the previous phase, then $P_j$ informs this to everyone by A-casting Matched-Row signal. This is a public indication by $P_j$ that $f_j(x)$ which is committed by $D$ to the parties in $WCORE$ is same as the one which $P_j$ has privately received from $D$. Now if at least $2t + 1$ parties, say $\mathcal{R}$, A-cast Matched-Row, then it implies that $D$ is committed to a unique degree-$(t, t)$ bivariate polynomial, say $\overline{F}(x, y)$ (hence a unique secret $\overline{s} = \overline{F}(0, 0)$) such that for every *honest* $P_i \in \mathcal{R}$, the row polynomial $f_i(x)$ held by $P_i$ satisfies $\overline{F}(x, i) = f_i(x)$ and for every *honest* $P_j \in WCORE$, the column polynomial $g_i(y)$ held by $P_j$ satisfies $\overline{F}(j, y) = g_j(y)$ (see Lemma 7). The code for implementing this phase is as follows:

---

### Code Verification$(D, \mathcal{P}, s)$

$P_j$-WEAK-PRIVATE-RECONSTRUCTION OF $f_j(x)$ FOR $j = 1, \ldots, n$:

i. CODE FOR $P_i$ – Every party in $\mathcal{P}$ executes this code.

1. After accepting $WCORE$ and corresponding $OKP_j$'s, participate in AWSS-Rec-Private$(D, \mathcal{P}, f_j(x), P_j)$, for $j = 1, \ldots, n$, to enable $P_j$-weak-private-reconstruction of $f_j(x)$. Notice that the common $WCORE$ acts as $WCORE$ in each AWSS-Rec-Private$(D, \mathcal{P}, f_j(x), P_j)$, for $j = 1, \ldots, n$
2. At the completion of AWSS-Rec-Private$(D, \mathcal{P}, f_i(x), P_i)$, obtain either degree-$t$ polynomial $\overline{f_i}(x)$ or $NULL$.
3. If $f_i(x) = \overline{f_i}(x)$, then A-cast Matched-Row.
4. If Matched-Row is received from A-cast of at least $2t + 1$ parties then proceed to third (**Re-Commitment**) phase.

---

**Lemma 7.** *In code Verification, if Matched-Row is received from the A-cast of at least $2t+1$ parties, say $\mathcal{R}$, then in code Commitment, $D$ is committed to a unique degree-$(t, t)$ bivariate polynomial $\overline{F}(x, y)$ such that the row polynomial $f_i(x)$ held by every honest $P_i \in \mathcal{R}$ satisfies $\overline{F}(x, i) = f_i(x)$ and the column polynomial $g_j(y)$ held by every honest $P_j \in WCORE$ satisfies $\overline{F}(j, y) = g_j(y)$. Moreover if $D$ is honest then $\overline{F}(x, y) = F(x, y)$.*

PROOF: The proof completely follow from the proof of Lemma 4.26 of [10]. For details see [25].                                                                                                      □

**Lemma 8.** *In Verification, if D is honest then all the honest parties will eventually proceed to third phase. Moreover, if D is corrupted and some honest party proceeds to the third phase, then all other honest party will also eventually proceed to the third phase.*

From Lemma 7, if an honest party, say $P_i$, receives A-cast of Matched-Row signal during Verification from at least $2t + 1$ parties, say $\mathcal{R}$, then he is sure that $D$ is committed to a unique bivariate polynomial and thus a unique secret. Now the question is: *If $P_i$ stops protocol AVSS-Share here after finding such a set $\mathcal{R}$, then is there any possible way of robustly reconstructing $D$'s secret in reconstruction phase?* Here we stop a moment and try to find the possibilities for the above question. Our effort in this direction would also motivate the need of the third phase of AVSS-Share which is actually required to enable robust reconstruction of $D$'s committed secret in the reconstruction phase i.e in AVSS-Rec-Private.

One possible way to reconstruct $D$'s committed secret $s$ is to execute AWSS-Rec-Private$(D, \mathcal{P}, f_j(x), *)$ corresponding to every $P_j \in \mathcal{R}$, which may disclose $f_j(x)$ polynomials and using those polynomial the bivariate polynomial and thus the secret $s$ may be reconstructed. But this does not work, because for a *corrupted* $D$, *all* instances of AWSS-Rec-Private may output $NULL$. So it seems that most likely there is no way to robustly reconstruct $D$'s committed secret $s$ in protocol AVSS-Rec-Private, if AVSS-Share stops after current phase. Hence, we require the third phase which is described in the sequel.

### 4.3   Re-commitment by Individual Parties

The outline for this phase is as follows: If $P_i$ A-casts Matched-Row in Verification, then $P_i$ acts as a dealer to re commit his row polynomial $f_i(x)$ by initiating an instance of AWSS-Share. *It is also enforced that if $P_i$ attempts to re-commit $f_i'(x) \neq f_i(x)$, then his re-commitment will not be terminated.* Now AVSS-Share terminates only when all the honest parties in $\mathcal{P}$ accept a common set of at least $2t + 1$ parties, say $VCORE$, who have successfully re-committed their polynomials. Now clearly, if AVSS-Share terminates, then the robust reconstruction of $D's$ committed secret $s$ is guaranteed with very high probability later in reconstruction phase. This is because, the AWSS-Rec-private instance of an *honest* $P_i \in VCORE$ will always reconstruct back $f_i(x)$. On the other hand, AWSS-Rec-private instance of a *corrupted* $P_i \in VCORE$ will output either $f_i(x)$ or $NULL$. This guarantees the reconstruction of at least $t + 1$ $f_i(x)$ polynomials which are enough to reconstruct $D$'s committed bivariate polynomial and hence the $s$. The protocol for this phase is given in next page.

**Lemma 9.** *In code **Re-commitment** if D is honest then D will eventually generate VCORE of size $2t+1$ and each honest party will accept this VCORE. If D is corrupted and some honest party has accepted VCORE received from D, then every other honest party will also eventually do the same.*

PROOF: For details see [25].                                                                                                      □

## Code **Re-commitment**$(D, \mathcal{P}, s)$

i. CODE FOR $P_i$:

1. If you have A-casted `Matched-Row` in Verification then as a dealer, initiate AWSS-Share$(P_i, \mathcal{P}, f_i(x))$ to re commit $f_i(x)$.

2. If $P_j$ has A-casted `Matched-Row` in Verification, then participate in AWSS-Share$(P_j, \mathcal{P}, f_j(x))$ by executing steps in [VERIFICATION: CODE FOR $P_i$] (of AWSS-Share) in the following way:
   After the completion of step 1 of [VERIFICATION: CODE FOR $P_i$], check whether $g_i(j) = f_j(i)$ holds, where $f_j(i)$ is obtained from $P_j$ during the execution of AWSS-Share$(P_j, \mathcal{P}, f_j(x))$ and $g_i(y)$ was obtained from $D$ during **commitment by $D$ phase**. If yes then participate in the remaining steps in [VERIFICATION: CODE FOR $P_i$] corresponding to AWSS-Share$(P_j, \mathcal{P}, f_j(x))$.

3. $WCORE^{P_i}$ CONSTRUCTION FOR AWSS-Share$(P_i, \mathcal{P}, f_i(x))$: If $P_i$ as a dealer initiated AWSS-Share$(P_i, \mathcal{P}, f_i(x))$ to re commit $f_i(x)$, then $P_i$ as a dealer, constructs $WCORE$ and corresponding $OKP_j$s for AWSS-Share$(P_i, \mathcal{P}, f_i(x))$ in a slightly different way than what is described in AWSS-Share *(these steps also ensure that a corrupted $P_i$ will not be able to re-commit $\overline{f_i}(x) \neq f_i(x)$)*.
   (a) Construct a set $ProbCORE^{P_i}$ ( $= \emptyset$ initially). Include $P_j$ in $ProbCORE^{P_i}$ and A-cast $(P_j, ProbCORE^{P_i})$ if at least $2t + 1$ A-casts of the form $OK(., P_j)$ are heard in the instance AWSS-Share$(P_i, \mathcal{P}, f_i(x))$.
   (b) Construct $WCORE^{P_i}$. Add $P_j$ in $WCORE^{P_i}$ if both the following holds:
      (A) $P_j \in ProbCORE^{P_i}$ and
      (B) for at least $2t+1$ $P_k$'s who are re-committing their corresponding $f_k(x)$'s, $(P_j, ProbCORE^{P_k})$ is received from their A-cast.
   (c) A-cast $WCORE^{P_i}$ and $OKP_j$ for every $P_j \in WCORE^{P_i}$ when $|WCORE^{P_i}| = 2t + 1$.

ii. VCORE CONSTRUCTION: CODE FOR $D$

1. If $WCORE^{P_i}$ and $OKP_j$ for every $P_j \in WCORE^{P_i}$ are received from the A-cast of $P_i$, then add $P_i$ to $VCORE$ after performing the following:
   (a) Wait to receive $(P_j, ProbCORE^{P_i})$ for every $P_j \in WCORE^{P_i}$ from the A-cast of $P_i$.
   (b) Wait to receive $(P_j, ProbCORE^{P_k})$ for every $P_j \in WCORE^{P_i}$ from A-cast of at least $2t + 1$ $P_k$'s who are re-committing their corresponding $f_k(x)$'s.
   (c) Wait to receive $OK(P_j, P_k)$ for every $P_k \in OKP_j$ in execution AWSS-Share$(P_i, \mathcal{P}, f_i(x))$.

2. A-cast $VCORE$ when $|VCORE| = 2t + 1$.

iii. VCORE VERIFICATION & AGREEMENT ON VCORE: CODE FOR $P_i$

1. Wait to receive $VCORE$ from the A-cast of $D$.
2. For every $P_i \in VCORE$, wait to receive $WCORE^{P_i}$ and $OKP_j$ for every $P_j \in WCORE^{P_i}$ from the A-cast of $P_i$.
3. Once received, check the validity of received $WCORE^{P_i}$'s and $OKP_j$'s for every $P_j \in WCORE^{P_i}$ by following the same steps as in ii-1(a), ii-1(b) and ii-1(c).
4. After checking the validity, accept (i) $VCORE$; (ii) $WCORE^{P_i}$ and corresponding $OKP_j$'s for every $P_i \in VCORE$ which are received in previous two steps and terminate AVSS-Share.

**Lemma 10.** *If $VCORE$ is generated, then there exists a unique degree-$(t,t)$ bivariate polynomial $\overline{F}(x,y)$ such that every $P_i \in VCORE$ is re-committed to $f_i(x) = \overline{F}(x,i)$. Moreover, if $D$ is honest then $\overline{F}(x,y) = F(x,y)$.*

PROOF: By Lemma 7, there is a unique degree-$(t,t)$ bivariate polynomial $\overline{F}(x,y)$ such that the row polynomial of every *honest* $P_i$ who has A-casted Matched-Row, satisfies $f_i(x) = \overline{F}(x,i)$. Since an honest party $P_i$ who has re-committed his row polynomial $f_i(x)$ in Re-Commitment, has also A-casted Matched-Row in Verification, $f_i(x) = \overline{F}(x,i)$ satisfies for every *honest* $P_i$ in $VCORE$. Now we show that even a *corrupted* $P_i \in VCORE$ has re-committed $f_i(x)$ satisfying $f_i(x) = \overline{F}(x,i)$.

We prove this by showing that every *honest* $P_j \in WCORE^{P_i}$ has received $f_i(j)$ from $P_i$ during AWSS-Share$(P_i, \mathcal{P}, f_i(x))$ (and hence honest $P_j$ is IC-Committed to $f_i(j)$). An honest $P_j$ belongs to $WCORE^{P_i}$ implies that $P_j$ belongs to $ProbCORE$ of at least $2t+1$ parties out of which at least $t+1$ are honest. Let $\mathcal{H}$ be the set of these $(t+1)$ honest parties. So $P_j$'s column polynomial $g_j(y)$ satisfies $g_j(k) = f_k(j)$ for every $P_k \in \mathcal{H}$ (see step i-(2) in Re-Commitment). This implies that $g_j(y) = \overline{F}(j,y)$. Now honest $P_j \in WCORE^{P_i}$ implies that $P_j$ belongs to $ProbCORE$ of $P_i$ as well which means $P_j$ has ensured $g_j(i) = f_i(j)$ (see step i-(2)) in Re-Commitment. The second part of the lemma is trivially true. □

### 4.4   Protocol AVSS

---

**Protocol AVSS$(D, \mathcal{P}, s)$**

**AVSS-Share$(D, \mathcal{P}, S)$:** Replicate Code Commitment$(D, \mathcal{P}, s)$, Code Verification$(D, \mathcal{P}, s)$ and Code Re-commitment$(D, \mathcal{P}, s)$.

**AVSS-Rec-Private$(D, \mathcal{P}, s, P_\alpha)$:** Private reconstruction of $s$ by party $P_\alpha$:

$P_\alpha$-WEAK-PRIVATE-RECONSTRUCTION OF $f_j(x)$ FOR EVERY $P_j \in VCORE$: (CODE
   FOR   $P_i$)   :   Participate   in   AWSS-Rec-Private$(P_j, \mathcal{P}, f_j(x), P_\alpha)$   for   every
   $P_j \in VCORE$.
LOCAL COMPUTATION: CODE FOR $P_\alpha$
   1. For every $P_j \in VCORE$, obtain either $\overline{f_j(x)}$ or $NULL$ from $P_\alpha$-weak-private-reconstruction. Add $P_j \in VCORE$ to $REC$ if $\overline{f_j(x)}$ is obtained.
   2. Wait until $|REC| = t+1$. Construct bivariate polynomial $\overline{F}(x,y)$ such that $\overline{F}(x,j) = \overline{f_j(x)}$ for every $P_j \in REC$. Compute $\overline{s} = \overline{F}(0,0)$ and terminate.

---

Due to space constraints, we give the proof of our AVSS scheme in [25] and state only the following theorem:

**Theorem 2.** *Protocols (AVSS-Share, AVSS-Rec-Private) constitutes a valid statistical AVSS scheme with private reconstruction which incurs a private communication of $\mathcal{O}((n^4\kappa)\kappa)$ bits and A-cast of $\mathcal{O}(n^3 \log(n))$ bits.*

## 5   Our Statistical ACSS Scheme with $n = 3t+1$

Though AVSS is an AVSS scheme, it is not an ACSS scheme because it fails to achieve *completeness* property. This is because in AVSS-Share, only the honest parties in $VCORE$ receive their respective shares of the committed secret. But it may happen that potentially $t$ honest parties are *not* present in $VCORE$. So we now present a statistical ACSS scheme called ACSS, which consists of sub-protocols ACSS-Share and ACSS-Rec-Public. Protocol ACSS-Share allows $D$ to generate $t$-sharing of a secret $s \in \mathbb{F}$. Given $t$-sharing of secret $s$, protocol ACSS-Rec-Public allows every party in $\mathcal{P}$ to reconstruct $D$'s committed secret $s$.

The high level idea of ACSS-Share is similar as that of AVSS-Share with the following difference: in AVSS-Share, we used AWSS-Share as a black-box. So if $D$ is corrupted and even if it is ensured that $D$ is committed to a unique bi-variate polynomial $\overline{F}(x,y)$ during **Verification Phase**, we could only ensure that every honest $P_i$ who A-cast `Matched-Row` signal, holds the corresponding row polynomial $f_i(x) = \overline{F}(x,i)$ and hence his share $f_i(0)$ of the secret $\overline{s} = \overline{F}(0,0)$. It may happen that there are potential $t$ honest $P_i$'s who have not A-cast `Matched-Row` signal and who do not hold their corresponding $\overline{F}(x,i)$'s, as $P_i$-weak-private-reconstruction of $f_i(x)$'s corresponding to these parties would have reconstructed $NULL$ during **Verification Phase**.

On the other hand, we use AVSS-Share as a black-box in ACSS-Share. This avoids the above problem because now $D$ would AVSS-Share each $f_i(x)$, instead of AWSS-Share. So once it is ensured that $D$ is committed to a unique bi-variate polynomial $\overline{F}(x,y)$, by the property of AVSS-Rec-Private, each honest $P_i \in \mathcal{P}$ would successfully reconstruct $f_i(x) = \overline{F}(x,i)$ and hence his share $f_i(0)$ of the secret $\overline{s} = \overline{F}(0,0)$.

Protocol ACSS-Rec-Public uses the properties of *Online Error Correction* (OEC) [10]. Informally, given $t$-sharing of $s$ which is $t$-shared using degree-$t$ polynomial $f(x)$, OEC allows to reconstruct $f(x)$ and hence $s = f(0)$ in an on-line fashion in asynchronous settings by using the properties of Reed-Solomon error correcting codes. Since the technique is quiet familiar, we avoid giving the details of ACSS-Rec-Public. For details, see [25].

We now state the properties of our ACSS scheme. The proof of these properties are available in [25] due to space constraints.

**Lemma 11.** *In protocol ACSS-Share:*

1. *If $D$ is honest then eventually he will generate a common $CCORE$ of size $2t + 1$ for all the $n$ instances of AVSS-Share. Moreover, each honest party will eventually accept this common $CCORE$.*
2. *If $D$ is corrupted and some honest party has accepted the $CCORE$ received from the A-cast of $D$, then every other honest party will also eventually accept the same.*

**Lemma 12.** *In ACSS-Share, if the honest parties accept the common $CCORE$, then it implies that $D$ is committed to a unique degree-$(t,t)$ bivariate polynomial $\overline{F}(x,y)$ such that each row polynomial $f_i(x)$ committed by $D$ in AVSS-Share($D, \mathcal{P}, f_i(x)$) satisfies $\overline{F}(x,i) = f_i(x)$ and the column polynomial $g_j(y)$ held by every honest $P_j \in CCORE$ satisfies $\overline{F}(j,y) = g_j(y)$. Moreover if $D$ is honest then $\overline{F}(x,y) = F(x,y)$.*

**Theorem 3.** *Protocols (ACSS-Share, ACSS-Rec-Public) constitutes a valid statistical ACSS scheme with public reconstruction. ACSS-Share privately communicates $\mathcal{O}(n^5\kappa^2)$ bits and A-casts $\mathcal{O}(n^4 \log n)$ bits. ACSS-Rec-Public, which involves $n$ instances of OEC incurs a private communication of $\mathcal{O}(n^2\kappa)$ bits.*

---

### Protocol ACSS($D, \mathcal{P}, s$)

**ACSS-Share($D, \mathcal{P}, s$)**

i. DISTRIBUTION BY $D$: CODE FOR $D$ – Only $D$ executes this code

  1. Select a random degree-$(t, t)$ bivariate polynomial $F(x, y)$ such that $F(0, 0) = s$.
  2. Send $g_i(y) = F(i, y)$ to party $P_i$. We call $g_i(y)$ as $i^{th}$ column polynomial.
  3. For $i = 1, \ldots, n$, initiate AVSS-Share($D, \mathcal{P}, f_i(x)$) for sharing $f_i(x)$, where $f_i(x) = F(x, i)$. We call $f_i(x)$ as $i^{th}$ row polynomial.

ii. CODE FOR $P_i$ – Every party in $\mathcal{P}$, including $D$, executes this code

  1. Wait to receive $g_i(y)$ from $D$.
  2. Participate in AVSS-Share($D, \mathcal{P}, f_j(x)$) for all $j = 1, \ldots, n$.
  3. If $f_j(i)$ is received from $D$ during AVSS-Share($D, \mathcal{P}, f_j(x)$) then check whether $g_i(j) = f_j(i)$. When the test passes for all $j = 1, \ldots, n$, then A-cast Matched-Column.

iii. CCORE CONSTRUCTION: CODE FOR $D$ – Only $D$ executes this code.

  1. For $i = 1, \ldots, n$, construct $VCORE$ for AVSS-Share($D, \mathcal{P}, f_i(x)$). Denote it by $VCORE^i$.
  2. Keep updating $VCORE^i$. Wait to obtain $CCORE = \cap_{i=1}^n VCORE^i$ of size at least $2t + 1$ such that Matched-Column is received from A-cast of every $P_j \in CCORE$.
  3. A-cast $CCORE$.

iv. CCORE VERIFICATION & AGREEMENT: CODE FOR $P_i$ — Every party including $D$ will execute this code.

  1. Wait to receive $CCORE$ from the A-cast of $D$.
  2. Check whether $CCORE$ is a valid $VCORE$ for AVSS-Share($D, \mathcal{P}, f_j(x)$) for every $j = 1, \ldots, n$ (by following steps 2-4 as specified under [VCORE VERIFICATION & AGREEMENT ON VCORE: CODE FOR $P_i$] in Re-commitment of AVSS-Share).

v. $P_j$-PRIVATE-RECONSTRUCTION OF $f_j(x)$ FOR $j = 1, \ldots, n$: CODE FOR $P_i$ – Every party in $\mathcal{P}$ executes this code.

  1. If CCORE is a valid $VCORE$ for AVSS-Share($D, \mathcal{P}, f_j(x)$) for every $j = 1, \ldots, n$, then participate in AVSS-Rec-Private($D, \mathcal{P}, f_j(x), P_j$), for $j = 1, \ldots, n$, to enable $P_j$-private-reconstruction of $f_j(x)$. Notice that CCORE is used as VCORE in each AVSS-Rec-Private($D, \mathcal{P}, f_j(x), P_j$), for $j = 1, \ldots, n$.
  2. At the completion of AVSS-Rec-Private($D, \mathcal{P}, f_i(x), P_i$), obtain degree-$t$ polynomial $f_i(x)$, output $f_i(0)$ as $i^{th}$ share of $s$ and terminate ACSS-Share.

---

## 6    ACSS Scheme for Sharing Multiple Secrets

We now present an overview of our statistical ACSS scheme ACSS-MS for sharing multiple secrets concurrently. ACSS-MS consists of sub-protocols ACSS-MS-Share and ACSS-MS-Rec-Public. Protocol ACSS-MS-Share allows $D$ to generate $t$-sharing of secret $S = (s^1, \ldots, s^\ell)$, consisting of $\ell > 1$ elements from $\mathbb{F}$. While using $\ell$ executions of ACSS-Share, one for each $s^l \in S$, $D$ can ACSS-share $S$ with a private communication of $\mathcal{O}((\ell n^5 \kappa)\kappa)$ and A-cast of $\mathcal{O}(\ell n^4 \log(n))$ bits, protocol ACSS-MS-Share achieves the same task with a private communication of $\mathcal{O}((\ell n^4 + n^5 \kappa)\kappa)$ and A-cast of $\mathcal{O}(n^4 \log(n))$ (independent of $\ell$) bits. This shows that executing a *single instance* of ACSS-MS dealing with *multiple secrets* concurrently is advantageous over executing *multiple instances* of ACSS dealing with *single secret*. In order to design ACSS-MS, we have to first extend AWSS and AVSS to share $\ell$ secrets concurrently. Then using our AVSS scheme sharing $\ell$ secrets concurrently, we design our ACSS scheme sharing $\ell$ secrets concurrently. Due to space constraints, the complete details are available in [25].

# References

1. Abraham, I., Dolev, D., Halpern, J.Y.: An almost surely terminating polynomial protocol for asynchronous Byzantine Agreement with optimal resilience. In: PODC, pp. 311–322 (2008)
2. Beaver, D.: Efficient multiparty protocols using circuit randomization. In: Feigenbaum, J. (ed.) CRYPTO 1991. LNCS, vol. 576, pp. 420–432. Springer, Heidelberg (1992)
3. Beerliová-Trubíniová, Z., Hirt, M.: Efficient multi-party computation with dispute control. In: Halevi, S., Rabin, T. (eds.) TCC 2006. LNCS, vol. 3876, pp. 305–328. Springer, Heidelberg (2006)
4. Beerliová-Trubíniová, Z., Hirt, M.: Simple and efficient perfectly-secure asynchronous MPC. In: Kurosawa, K. (ed.) ASIACRYPT 2007. LNCS, vol. 4833, pp. 376–392. Springer, Heidelberg (2007)
5. Beerliová-Trubíniová, Z., Hirt, M.: Perfectly-secure MPC with linear communication complexity. In: Canetti, R. (ed.) TCC 2008. LNCS, vol. 4948, pp. 213–230. Springer, Heidelberg (2008)
6. Ben-Or, M., Canetti, R., Goldreich, O.: Asynchronous secure computation. In: STOC, pp. 52–61 (1993)
7. Ben-Or, M., Goldwasser, S., Wigderson, A.: Completeness theorems for non-cryptographic fault-tolerant distributed computation. In: STOC, pp. 1–10 (1988)
8. BenOr, M., Kelmer, B., Rabin, T.: Asynchronous secure computations with optimal resilience. In: PODC, pp. 183–192 (1994)
9. Bracha, G.: An asynchronous $\lfloor (n-1)/3 \rfloor$-resilient consensus protocol. In: PODC, pp. 154–162 (1984)
10. Canetti, R.: Studies in Secure Multiparty Computation and Applications. PhD thesis, Weizmann Institute, Israel (1995)
11. Canetti, R., Rabin, T.: Fast asynchronous Byzantine Agreement with optimal resilience. In: Proc. of STOC 1993, pp. 42–51. ACM, New York (1993)
12. Chaum, D., Crpeau, C., Damgård, I.: Multiparty unconditionally secure protocols (extended abstract). In: STOC, pp. 11–19 (1988)
13. Chor, B., Goldwasser, S., Micali, S., Awerbuch, B.: Verifiable secret sharing and achieving simultaneity in the presence of faults (extended abstract). In: STOC, pp. 383–395 (1985)
14. Cramer, R., Damgård, I., Dziembowski, S., Hirt, M., Rabin, T.: Efficient multiparty computations secure against an adaptive adversary. In: Stern, J. (ed.) EUROCRYPT 1999. LNCS, vol. 1592, pp. 311–326. Springer, Heidelberg (1999)

15. Cramer, R., Damgård, I., Maurer, U.M.: General secure multi-party computation from any linear secret-sharing scheme. In: Preneel, B. (ed.) EUROCRYPT 2000. LNCS, vol. 1807, pp. 316–334. Springer, Heidelberg (2000)
16. Dolev, D., Dwork, C., Waarts, O., Yung, M.: Perfectly secure message transmission. JACM 40(1), 17–47 (1993)
17. Feldman, P., Micali, S.: An optimal algorithm for synchronous Byzantine Agreemet. In: Proc. of STOC 1988, pp. 639–648. ACM, New York (1988)
18. Fitzi, M., Garay, J., Gollakota, S., Pandu Rangan, C., Srinathan, K.: Round-optimal and efficient verifiable secret sharing. In: Halevi, S., Rabin, T. (eds.) TCC 2006. LNCS, vol. 3876, pp. 329–342. Springer, Heidelberg (2006)
19. Gennaro, R., Ishai, Y., Kushilevitz, E., Rabin, T.: The round complexity of verifiable secret sharing and secure multicast. In: STOC, pp. 580–589 (2001)
20. Goldreich, O., Micali, S., Wigderson, A.: How to play any mental game. In: STOC, pp. 218–229 (1987)
21. Hirt, M., Maurer, U., Przydatek, B.: Efficient secure multiparty computation. In: Okamoto, T. (ed.) ASIACRYPT 2000. LNCS, vol. 1976, pp. 143–161. Springer, Heidelberg (2000)
22. Katz, J., Koo, C., Kumaresan, R.: Improving the round complexity of VSS in point-to-point networks. In: Aceto, L., Damgård, I., Goldberg, L.A., Halldórsson, M.M., Ingólfsdóttir, A., Walukiewicz, I. (eds.) ICALP 2008, Part II. LNCS, vol. 5126, pp. 499–510. Springer, Heidelberg (2008)
23. Katz, J., Koo, C.Y.: On expected constant round protocols for Byzantine Agreement. In: Dwork, C. (ed.) CRYPTO 2006. LNCS, vol. 4117, pp. 445–462. Springer, Heidelberg (2006)
24. Patra, A., Choudhary, A., Rabin, T., Pandu Rangan, C.: The round complexity of verifiable secret sharing re-visited. In: Halevi, S. (ed.) Advances in Cryptology - CRYPTO 2009. LNCS, vol. 5677, pp. 487–504. Springer, Heidelberg (2009)
25. Patra, A., Choudhary, A., Pandu Rangan, C.: Efficient statistical asynchronous verifiable secret sharing and multiparty computation with optimal resilience. Cryptology ePrint Archive (2009)
26. Patra, A., Choudhary, A., Pandu Rangan, C.: Simple and efficient asynchronous Byzantine Agreement with optimal resilience. In: PODC, pp. 92–101 (2009)
27. Rabin, T.: Robust sharing of secrets when the dealer is honest or cheating. J. ACM 41(6), 1089–1109 (1994)
28. Rabin, T., Ben-Or, M.: Verifiable secret sharing and multiparty protocols with honest majority (extended abstract). In: STOC, pp. 73–85 (1989)

# On the Optimization of Bipartite Secret Sharing Schemes[*]

Oriol Farràs[1], Jessica Ruth Metcalf-Burton[2], Carles Padró[1],
and Leonor Vázquez[1]

[1] Dep. de Matemàtica Aplicada 4, Universitat Politècnica de Catalunya,
Barcelona, Spain
{ofarras,cpadro,leonor}@ma4.upc.edu
[2] Mathematics Department, University of Michigan, Ann Arbor, U.S.A.
jmetcalf@umich.edu

**Abstract.** Bipartite secret sharing schemes are those having a bipartite access structure, that is, the set of participants is divided into two parts, and all participants in each part play an equivalent role. The bipartite access structures that admit an ideal secret sharing scheme have been characterized, but it is not known which is the optimal complexity of non-ideal bipartite access structures. By using the connection between secret sharing schemes and polymatroids, we find new bounds on the optimal complexity of these acess structures and, for some of them, we find the exact value of this parameter. Some of these bounds are obtained by using a method based on linear programming.

**Keywords:** Cryptography, secret sharing, multipartite secret sharing, polymatroids, linear programming.

## 1 Introduction

A *secret sharing scheme* is a method to protect a secret value by distributing it among a set of participants. In these protocols, each participant receives a share of the secret, and certain *qualified* subsets of participants can recover the secret by pooling their shares, while *unqualified* subsets cannot obtain any information about the secret. The family $\Gamma$ of qualified subsets is called the *access structure* of the scheme. It is *monotone*, which means that any superset of a qualified subset is qualified, and so any access structure $\Gamma$ is determined by the family $\min \Gamma$ of its minimal qualified subsets. Only *unconditionally secure, perfect* secret sharing schemes are considered in this work. In particular, a subset is unqualified if and only if it is not qualified.

Secret sharing schemes have important applications in cryptography as a building block of many different protocols. The efficiency of such schemes is commonly measured by the relation between the size of the secret and the size

---

[*] The authors' work was partially supported by the Spanish Ministry of Education and Science under project TSI2006-02731.

K. Kurosawa (Ed.): ICITS 2009, LNCS 5973, pp. 93–109, 2010.
© Springer-Verlag Berlin Heidelberg 2010

of the shares. The *complexity* is the result of dividing the size of the biggest share by the size of the secret. Ito, Saito, Nishizeki [20] proved that there is a secret sharing scheme for every access structure, and so it is natural to consider the *optimal complexity* $\sigma(\Gamma)$ of an access structure $\Gamma$, which is the infimum of the complexities of all secret sharing schemes with access structure $\Gamma$. A secret sharing scheme is *optimal* if its complexity attain this infimum. In particular, if its complexity is equal to 1, which is the best possible situation, then both the scheme and its access structure are called *ideal*.

The first secret sharing schemes were presented by Shamir [28] and Blakley [8], and are ideal. Brickell [10] generalized these schemes and presented a construction of ideal secret sharing schemes based on linear algebra. These schemes are called *linear*, and can be generalized to the non-ideal case. The best known constructions provide linear secret sharing schemes, and their homomorphic properties are very useful in some applications of secret sharing. Hence it is worth to know, for each access structure $\Gamma$, which is the infimum of the complexity of all the linear schemes with access structure $\Gamma$. This value is denoted by $\lambda(\Gamma)$, and it is an upper bound on $\sigma(\Gamma)$. The best known general upper bound on $\lambda$ is exponential on the number of participants [20].

A way to obtain lower bounds on $\sigma$ is to use inequalities on the entropy of the random variables determined by the shares. For every access structure $\Gamma$, $\kappa(\Gamma)$ is the bound on $\sigma(\Gamma)$ derived from the Shannon inequalities that the entropy of the shares of the participants must satisfy, and from the fact that the shares of subsets in $\Gamma$ determine the secret but the shares of the other subsets do not provide any information about the secret.

The study of the separation between $\sigma$, $\kappa$ and $\lambda$, as well as the search of ideal and optimal schemes have posed several deep and challenging mathematical problems. The techniques used to find partial solutions to these problems involve different mathematical objects as matroids, polymatroids and graphs, and results in different areas as combinatorics, coding theory or algebra.

Fujishige [17] showed that the entropies of any set of random variables determine a polymatroid. Hence, for each secret sharing scheme we obtain a polymatroid by considering the random variables associated to the shares of the participants. Namely, for every subset of participants we define the rank of the subset as the joint entropy of the random variables of the shares of the participants in the subset divided by the entropy of the secret. In fact, $\kappa(\Gamma)$ can be obtained by analyzing the polymatroids that are related to $\Gamma$. Csirmaz [12] proved that for any set of $n$ participants, any access structure $\Gamma$ satisfies $\kappa(\Gamma) \leq n$, and that there exists an access structure whose optimal complexity is at least about $n/\log n$.

Brickell and Davenport [11] proved that ideal access structures are *matroid ports*, which means that for each ideal access structure there exists a matroid in which the circuits containing a fixed point are in one to one relation with the minimal authorized subsets. Moreover, if this matroid is representable, then the access structure is ideal. This result was improved by Martí-Farré and Padró [22] by applying results on matroid ports. The applications of matroids to secret sharing schemes have been widely studied, for instance in [2,3,23].

Recently, the discovering of new inequalities on the entropy of random variables that are not derived from the Shannon inequalities, and the study of the polymatroids related to secret sharing schemes have provided new interesting results as [3,4,24,25].

The problem of determining the optimal complexity has been studied for several particular classes of access structures. For instance, a great achievement has been obtained recently by Csirmaz and Tardos [13] by determining the optimal complexity of all access structures defined by trees. Many of these studied families are formed by *multipartite access structures*, in which the set of participants is divided into several parts and all participants in the same part play an equivalent role in the structure. The first ideal schemes for multipartite access structures were constructed by Brickell [10]. Padró and Sáez [27] studied the bipartite access structures, characterized the ideal ones, and gave bounds on the optimal complexity of those that are not ideal. There are other families of access structures for which the ideal ones have been characterized, as the the family of tripartite [14] and the family of hierarchical access structures [15], which were characterized by means of the connection with integer polymatroids [14], and the family of weighted threshold access structures [5]. However, the characterization of ideal access structures and the construction of optimal schemes are still open problems.

In this article we present new results on the parameters $\kappa$, $\lambda$ and $\sigma$ for bipartite access structures that improve our knowledge on them. We show new bounds on the optimal complexity by using polymatroids, we determine the value of this parameter for some non-ideal bipartite access structures, and we present some results on the polymatroids related to bipartite access structures.

In Section 6 we present a method to find the value of $\kappa$ for bipartite access structures. This method is based on the fact that the verification of Shannon-type inequalities can be formulated as a linear programming problem [34]. A general lower bound on $\kappa$ for bipartite access structures is presented in Section 5. This lower bound is derived from the independent sequence method and improves the existing bounds for these access structures [27]. In addition, we present new optimal linear constructions for non-ideal bipartite access structures. Some of these access structures were previously considered by Mecalf-Burton [25]. By taking into account the bounds obtained on $\kappa$, we show that for these access structures, $\sigma$, $\lambda$ and $\kappa$ coincide.

The polymatroids related to bipartite access structures are studied in Section 8. In particular, we show that there exist bipartite polymatroids that are non-entropic, and linearly representable bipartite polymatriods that are not a sum of matroids.

## 2 Preliminaries

Several definitions and basic facts as well as the main known results about the optimization of secret sharing schemes for general access structures are surveyed in this section. The reader is referred to the full version of [22] for a more detailed exposition.

Let $Q$ be a finite set of *participants*, and consider a finite set $E$ with a probability distribution on it. For every $i \in Q$, consider a finite set $E_i$ and a surjective map map $\pi_i \colon E \to E_i$. Those maps induce random variables on the sets $E_i$. Let $H(E_i)$ denote the Shannon entropy of one of these random variables. For a subset $A = \{i_1, \ldots, i_r\} \subseteq Q$, we write $H(E_A)$ for the joint entropy $H(E_{i_1} \ldots E_{i_r})$, and a similar convention is used for conditional entropies as, for instance, in $H(E_j|E_A) = H(E_j|E_{i_1} \ldots E_{i_r})$.

Consider a distinguished participant $p_0 \in Q$, which is usually called *dealer*, and an access structure $\Gamma$ on the set $P = Q - \{p_0\}$. The maps $\pi_i$ define an *unconditionally secure perfect secret sharing scheme* $\Sigma$ with access structure $\Gamma$ if the following properties are satisfied.

1. $H(E_{p_0}|E_A) = 0$ if $A \in \Gamma$.
2. $H(E_{p_0}|E_A) = H(E_{p_0})$ if $A \notin \Gamma$.

In this situation, every random choice of an element $\mathbf{x} \in E$, according to the given probability distribution, results in a *distribution of shares* $((s_i)_{i \in P}, s)$, where $s_i = \pi_i(\mathbf{x}) \in E_i$ is the *share* of the participant $i \in P$ and $s = \pi_{p_0}(\mathbf{x}) \in E_{p_0}$ is the *shared secret value*. Observe that the first requirement in the definition implies that the qualified subsets can recover the secret value from their shares and, by the second one, the shares of the participants in an unqualified subset do not provide any information at all about the secret value.

We define the *complexity* $\sigma(\Sigma)$ of a secret sharing scheme $\Sigma$ as the ratio between the maximum length of the shares and the length of the secret, that is, $\sigma(\Sigma) = \max_{i \in P} H(E_i)/H(E_{p_0})$. For each participant $i \in P$, $H(E_i) \geq H(E_{p_0})$ and so $\sigma(\Sigma) \geq 1$. A secret sharing scheme $\Sigma$ with $\sigma(\Sigma) = 1$ is said to be *ideal*, and its access structure is called *ideal* as well. The *optimal complexity* $\sigma(\Gamma)$ of an access structure $\Gamma$ is defined as the infimum of the complexities $\sigma(\Sigma)$ of the secret sharing schemes for $\Gamma$.

A secret sharing scheme is said to be *linear* if $E$ and $E_i$ are vector spaces over a finite field $\mathbb{K}$, the mappings $\pi_i$ are linear, and the uniform probability distribution is taken on $E$. The security of these schemes, which are also called geometric schemes or monotone span programs, is based on linear algebra. If $E_i = \mathbb{K}$ for every $i \in Q$, then it is a $\mathbb{K}$-*vector space secret sharing scheme*. Every access structure admits a linear construction [20], so we notate $\lambda(\Gamma)$ for the infimum of the complexities of the linear secret sharing schemes with access structure $\Gamma$.

**Proposition 1.** *For every access structure $\Gamma$ it follows $\sigma(\Gamma) \leq \lambda(\Gamma)$.*

Therefore, the construction of efficient linear schemes is interesting both for practical applications and for finding upper bounds on the optimal complexity of general access structures.

**Definition 2.** *Let $Q$ be a set, $\mathcal{P}(Q)$ the power set of $Q$, and $h : \mathcal{P}(Q) \to \mathbb{R}$ a function. The pair $\mathcal{S} = (Q, h)$ is a* polymatroid *if it satisfies the following properties.*

1. $h(\emptyset) = 0$, and
2. $h$ is monotone increasing: if $X \subseteq Y \subseteq Q$, then $h(X) \leq h(Y)$, and
3. $h$ is submodular: if $X, Y \subseteq Q$, then $h(X \cup Y) + h(X \cap Y) \leq h(X) + h(Y)$.

Let $\mathcal{S}_1 = (Q, h_1)$ and $\mathcal{S}_2 = (Q, h_2)$ be two polymatroids on the same ground set. Clearly, $h = h_1 + h_2$ is the rank function of a polymatroid on $Q$, which is called the *sum* of $\mathcal{S}_1$ and $\mathcal{S}_2$ and is denoted by $\mathcal{S}_1 + \mathcal{S}_2 = (Q, h)$. For every polymatroid $(Q, h)$, the pair $(Q, ah)$ is also a polymatroid for any $a \in \mathbb{R}$ with $a > 0$. A polymatroid is said to be *integer* if its rank function is integer-valued. A *matroid* is an integer polymatroid $\mathcal{S} = (Q, h)$ such that $h(A) \leq |A|$ for all $A \subseteq Q$.

A polymatroid $\mathcal{S} = (Q, h)$ is *entropic* if there exist some random variables $\{E_i\}_{i \in Q}$ and a real number $a > 0$ such that $h(A) = aH(A)$ for every $A \subseteq Q$. And it is *linearly representable* if there exist a vector space $E$ with finite dimension over a finite field $\mathbb{K}$, and a subspace $V_i \subseteq E$ for every $i \in Q$ such that $h(A) = \dim(\sum_{i \in A} V_i)$ for every $A \subseteq Q$.

We say that $p_0 \in Q$ is an *atomic point* of the polymatroid $\mathcal{S} = (Q, h)$ if, for every $X \subseteq Q$, either $h(X \cup \{p_0\}) = h(X)$ or $h(X \cup \{p_0\}) = h(X) + 1$. In this case, we define on the set $P = Q \setminus \{p_0\}$ the access structure

$$\Gamma_{p_0}(\mathcal{S}) = \{A \subseteq P : h(A \cup \{p_0\}) = h(A)\}.$$

For an access structure $\Gamma$ on $P = Q \setminus \{p_0\}$, a polymatroid $\mathcal{S} = (Q, h)$ is said to be a $\Gamma$-polymatroid if $p_0$ is an atomic point of $\mathcal{S}$ and $\Gamma = \Gamma_{p_0}(\mathcal{S})$.

Let $\Sigma$ be a secret sharing scheme with access structure $\Gamma$ on the set of participants $P = Q \setminus \{p_0\}$, and $\{E_i\}_{i \in Q}$ the random variables associated to the shares of the participants in $Q$. Consider the mapping $h : \mathcal{P}(Q) \to \mathbb{R}$ defined by

$$h : X \to H(X)/H(E_{p_0}).$$

Observe that the pair $\mathcal{S}(\Sigma) = (Q, h)$ is a $\Gamma$-polymatroid. In this way, $\Gamma$-polymatroids are studied in order to obtain properties of secret sharing schemes. Actually, these properties are exactly those that derive from the Shannon inequalities satisfied by the random variables $\{E_i\}_{i \in Q}$. Nevertheless, not all $\Gamma$-polymatroids are associated to secret sharing schemes.

For a polymatroid $\mathcal{S} = (q, h)$ and an atomic point $p_0 \in Q$, we define $\sigma_{p_0}(\mathcal{S}) = \max\{h(\{x\}) : x \in P\}$, where $P = Q \setminus \{p_0\}$. Observe that $\sigma_{p_0}(\mathcal{S}) = \sigma(\Sigma)$ if $\mathcal{S}$ is the polymatroid associated to a secret sharing $\Sigma$. For every access structure $\Gamma$ on $P$, we consider the value

$$\kappa(\Gamma) = \inf\{\sigma_{p_0}(\mathcal{S}) : \mathcal{S} \text{ is a } \Gamma\text{-polymatroid}\}.$$

**Proposition 3.** *For every access structure $\Gamma$, it follows $\sigma(\Gamma) \geq \kappa(\Gamma)$.*

Since $\kappa(\Gamma) \leq \sigma(\Gamma) \leq \lambda(\Gamma)$, upper and lower bounds on $\sigma(\Gamma)$ are obtained, respectively, from the parameters $\lambda$ and $\kappa$. Bounds on the first one can be obtained by using linear algebra, while combinatorics is the tool to derive bounds on the second one.

An access structure $\Gamma$ is a *matroid port* if there exists a matroid $\mathcal{S} = (Q, h)$ with $p_0 \in Q$ such that $\Gamma = \Gamma_{p_0}(\mathcal{S})$. In this case $\kappa(\Gamma) = 1$, and if $\mathcal{S}$ is $\mathbb{K}$-linearly representable, then $\Gamma$ admits a vector space secret sharing scheme, and so $\lambda(\Gamma) = 1$. Brickell and Davenport [11] proved that ideal access structures are matroid ports, and Martí-Farré and Padró [22] generalized this result.

**Theorem 4 ([22]).** *There is no access structure $\Gamma$ with $1 < \kappa(\Gamma) < 3/2$. In addition, an access structure $\Gamma$ is a matroid port if and only if $\kappa(\Gamma) = 1$.*

The *independent sequence method* was introduced in [9] and subsequently improved in [27]. We use the description of this method presented in [22], which is in terms of polymatroids, to obtain bounds on the information rate of bipartite access structures. We present these bounds in Section 5.

Consider $A \subseteq P$ and an increasing sequence of subsets $B_1 \subseteq \cdots \subseteq B_m \subseteq P$. We say that $(B_1, \ldots, B_m \mid A)$ is an *independent sequence* in $\Gamma$ with *length* $m$ and *size* $s$ if $|A| = s$ and, for every $i = 1, \ldots, m$ there exists $X_i \subseteq A$ such that $B_i \cup X_i \in \Gamma$, while $B_m \notin \Gamma$ and $B_{i-1} \cup X_i \notin \Gamma$ if $i \geq 2$. The independent sequence method is based on the following result.

**Theorem 5.** *Let $\Gamma$ be an access structure on the set $P$ and let $\mathcal{S} = (Q, h)$ be a $\Gamma$-polymatroid on $Q = P \smallsetminus \{p_0\}$. If there exists in $\Gamma$ an independent sequence $(B_1, \ldots, B_m \mid A)$ with length $m$ and size $s$, then $h(A) \geq m$. As a consequence, $\kappa(\Gamma) \geq m/s$.*

## 3    Multipartite Access Structures and Multipartite Polymatroids

We describe in this section the geometric representation of multipartite access structures that was introduced in [14,27]. In addition, we prove that the parameter $\kappa$ for multipartite access structures can be determined by considering only a special class of polymatroids that is introduced here, the so-called *multipartite polymatroids*.

An *m-partition* $\Pi = (X_1, \ldots, X_m)$ of a set $X$ is a disjoint family of $m$ subsets of $X$ with $X = X_1 \cup \cdots \cup X_m$. A permutation $\tau$ on $X$ is said to be a *$\Pi$-permutation* if $\tau(X_i) = X_i$ for every $i = 1, \ldots, m$. Roughly speaking, a combinatorial object defined on $X$ is said to be *$\Pi$-partite* if every $\Pi$-permutation on $X$ is an automorphism of it. We will use as well the term *m-partite* to refer to $\Pi$-partite objects in which $\Pi$ is an $m$-partition of $X$.

In particular, a family of subsets $\Lambda \subseteq \mathcal{P}(X)$ is *$\Pi$-partite* if if $\tau(\Lambda) = \{\tau(A) : A \in \Lambda\} = \Lambda$ for every $\Pi$-permutation $\tau$ on $X$. Analogously, a polymatroid $\mathcal{S} = (X, h)$ with ground set $X$ is *$\Pi$-partite* if $h(A) = h(\tau(A))$ for every $A \subseteq X$ and for every $\Pi$-permutation $\tau$ on $X$.

We describe in the following the geometric representation of multipartite access structures that was introduced in [14,27]. We notate $\mathbb{Z}_+$ for the set of the non-negative integers, and we consider in $\mathbb{Z}_+^m$ the order relation defined as follows. For a pair of points $\mathbf{x}, \mathbf{y} \in \mathbb{Z}_+^m$ with $\mathbf{x} = (x_1, \ldots, x_m)$ and

$\mathbf{y} = (y_1, \ldots, y_m)$, we say that $\mathbf{x} \leq \mathbf{y}$ if $x_i \leq y_i$ for every $i = 1, \ldots, m$. For a partition $\Pi = (X_1, \ldots, X_m)$ of a set $X$, consider the mapping $\Pi \colon \mathcal{P}(X) \to \mathbb{Z}_+^m$ defined by

$$\Pi(A) = (|A \cap X_1|, \ldots, |A \cap X_m|).$$

For a $\Pi$-partite family of subsets $\Lambda \subseteq \mathcal{P}(X)$, we consider the set of integer points $\Pi(\Lambda) = \{\Pi(A) : A \subseteq X, A \in \Lambda\} \subseteq \mathbb{Z}_+^m$. We notate

$$\mathbf{X} = \Pi(\mathcal{P}(X)) = \{\mathbf{x} \in \mathbb{Z}_+^m : \mathbf{x} \leq \Pi(X)\}.$$

Obviously, $\Pi(\Lambda) \subseteq \mathbf{X}$. Observe that $A \subseteq X$ is in $\Lambda$ if and only if $\Pi(A) \in \Pi(\Lambda)$. Then $\Lambda$ is completely determined by the set of points $\Pi(\Lambda)$. If $\Lambda$ is monotone increasing, that is, if $\Lambda$ is a $\Pi$-partite access structure on $X$, then $\Pi(\Lambda)$ is monotone increasing as well. That is, if $\mathbf{x}, \mathbf{y} \in \mathbf{X}$ are such that $\mathbf{x} \in \Pi(\Lambda)$ and $\mathbf{x} \leq \mathbf{y}$, then $\mathbf{y} \in \Pi(\Lambda)$. Therefore, $\Lambda$ is determined by $\Pi(\min \Lambda)$, which is the family of minimal points of $\Pi(\Lambda)$.

This geometric representation can be also applied to multipartite polymatroids. If $\mathcal{S} = (X, h)$ is a $\Pi$-partite polymatroid, then $h(A) = h(B)$ if $\Pi(A) = \Pi(B)$. Therefore, the polymatroid $\mathcal{S}$ is univocally determined by the mapping $\widehat{h} \colon \mathbf{X} \to \mathbb{R}$ defined by $\widehat{h}(\mathbf{x}) = h(A)$, where $A \subseteq X$ is such that $\Pi(A) = \mathbf{x}$.

For every $m$-partition $\Pi = (X_1, \ldots, X_m)$ of $P$, we consider the $(m+1)$-partition $\Pi_0 = (X_1, \ldots, X_m, \{p_0\})$ of $Q = P \cup \{p_0\}$. We prove in the following that, for every $\Pi$-partite access structure $\Gamma \subseteq \mathcal{P}(P)$, the value of $\kappa(\Gamma)$ can be determined by considering only the $\Gamma$-polymatroids that are $\Pi_0$-partite.

**Proposition 6.** *Let $\Pi = (X_1, \ldots, X_m)$ be an $m$-partition of a set $P$ and let $\Pi_0$ be the corresponding $(m+1)$-partition of $Q = P \cup \{p_0\}$. Let $\Gamma$ be a $\Pi$-partite access structure on $P$. Then*

$$\kappa(\Gamma) = \inf\{\sigma_{p_0}(\mathcal{S}) : \mathcal{S} \text{ is a } \Pi_0\text{-partite } \Gamma\text{-polymatroid}\}.$$

*Proof.* Consider $\omega(\Gamma) = \inf\{\sigma_{p_0}(\mathcal{S}) : \mathcal{S} \text{ is a } \Pi_0\text{-partite } \Gamma\text{-polymatroid}\}$. Clearly, $\kappa(\Gamma) \leq \omega(\Gamma)$. Let $\Psi$ be the set of the $\Pi_0$-permutations on $Q$. For every $\Gamma$-polymatroid $\mathcal{S} = (Q, h)$, consider the mapping $\widetilde{h} \colon \mathcal{P}(Q) \to \mathbb{R}$ defined by

$$\widetilde{h}(A) = \frac{1}{|\Psi|} \sum_{\tau \in \Psi} h(\tau(A)).$$

It is not difficult to check that $\widetilde{\mathcal{S}} = (Q, \widetilde{h})$ is a $\Pi_0$-partite $\Gamma$-polymatroid with $\sigma_{p_0}(\widetilde{\mathcal{S}}) \leq \sigma_{p_0}(\mathcal{S})$. Therefore, $\omega(\Gamma) = \kappa(\Gamma)$. $\qquad\square$

## 4   Duality and Minors

Duality and minors are operations on access structures, and also on matroids and polymatroids, that are important in secret sharing. This is mainly due to the fact of the parameters that are considered here have a good behavior with respect to those operations. In addition, minors of access structures correspond to a natural scenario in secret sharing. Namely, if several participants leave the scheme and maybe some of them reveal their shares, then the new access structure will be a minor of the original one.

Let $\Gamma$ be an access structure on a set $P$. For any $B \subseteq P$, we consider on the set $P \smallsetminus B$ the access structures $\Gamma \setminus B$ and $\Gamma/B$ defined by $\Gamma \setminus B = \{A \subseteq P \smallsetminus B : A \in \Gamma\}$ and $\Gamma/B = \{A \subseteq P \smallsetminus B : A \cup B \in \Gamma\}$. These operations are called *deletion* and *contraction*, respectively. Any access structure obtained by a sequence of deletions and contractions of subsets of $P$ is a *minor* of $\Gamma$. For a polymatroid $\mathcal{S} = (Q, h)$ and a subset $B \subseteq Q$, we consider the polymatroids $\mathcal{S} \setminus B = (Q \smallsetminus B, h_{\setminus B})$ and $\mathcal{S}/B = (Q \smallsetminus B, h_{/B})$ with $h_{\setminus B}(X) = h(X)$ and $h_{/B}(X) = h(X \cup B) - h(B)$ for every $X \subseteq Q \smallsetminus B$. Every polymatroid that is obtaind from $\mathcal{S}$ by a sequence of such operations is a *minor* of $\mathcal{S}$.

If $\mathcal{S}$ is a $\Gamma$-polymatroid, then $\mathcal{S} \setminus B$ is a $(\Gamma \setminus B)$-polymatroid and $\mathcal{S}/B$ is a $(\Gamma/B)$-polymatroid. Because of that, $\kappa(\Gamma') \leq \kappa(\Gamma)$ if $\Gamma'$ is a minor of $\Gamma$. In addition, the aforementioned connection between minors and secret sharing implies that $\sigma(\Gamma') \leq \sigma(\Gamma)$ and $\lambda(\Gamma') \leq \lambda(\Gamma)$.

The *dual* $\Gamma^*$ of an access structure $\Gamma$ on $P$ is the access structure on the same set defined by $\Gamma^* = \{A \subseteq P : P \smallsetminus A \in \Gamma\}$. From every linear secret sharing scheme $\Sigma$ for $\Gamma$, a linear secret sharing scheme $\Sigma^*$ for the dual access structure $\Gamma^*$ with $\sigma(\Sigma^*) = \sigma(\Sigma)$ can be constructed [16,21]. In addition, it was proved in [22] that $\kappa(\Gamma) = \kappa(\Gamma^*)$. The relation between $\sigma(\Gamma)$ and $\sigma(\Gamma^*)$ is an open problem.

If $\Gamma$ is $\Pi$-partite for some partition $\Pi = (P_1, \ldots, P_m)$ of the set $P$, then the dual access structure $\Gamma^*$ is $\Pi$-partite as well. If $B \subseteq P$, the minors $\Gamma \setminus B$ and $\Gamma/B$ are $(\Pi \setminus B)$-partite access structures, where $\Pi \setminus B = (P_1 \smallsetminus B, \ldots, P_m \smallsetminus B)$.

We prove in the next theorem that the value of $\kappa(\Gamma)$ for a multipartite access structure depends only on the minimal points, and it does not depend on the number of participants in every part.

**Theorem 7.** *Let $\Gamma$ be a $\Pi$-partite access structure on $P$ and let $B \subseteq P$ be such that the access structure $\Gamma \setminus B$ has the same minimal points as $\Gamma$, that is, $\Pi(\min \Gamma) = \Pi'(\min(\Gamma \setminus B))$, where $\Pi' = \Pi \setminus B$. Then $\kappa(\Gamma) = \kappa(\Gamma \setminus B)$.*

*Proof.* Clearly, $\kappa(\Gamma \setminus B) \leq \kappa(\Gamma)$. Take $\Pi = (P_1, \ldots, P_m)$ and consider the sets $Q = P \cup \{p_0\}$ and $Q' = (P \smallsetminus B) \cup \{p_0\} = Q \smallsetminus B$. We prove the other inequality by constructing, for every $\Pi_0'$-partite $(\Gamma \setminus B)$-polymatroid $\mathcal{S}' = (Q', h')$, a $\Pi_0$-partite $\Gamma$-polymatroid $\mathcal{S} = (Q, h)$ with $\sigma_{p_0}(\mathcal{S}) = \sigma_{p_0}(\mathcal{S}')$. Consider $\mathbf{Q}' = \Pi_0'(\mathcal{P}(Q')) \subseteq \mathbb{Z}_+^{m+1}$ and the mapping $\widehat{h}' \colon \mathbf{Q}' \to \mathbb{R}$ that determines the $\Pi_0'$-partite $(\Gamma \setminus B)$-polymatroid $\mathcal{S}' = (Q', h')$. For every vector $\mathbf{x} = (x_1, \ldots, x_m, x_{m+1}) \in \mathbf{Q} = \Pi_0(\mathcal{P}(Q))$, take $\mathbf{x}' = (\min\{x_1, |P_1 \smallsetminus B|\}, \ldots, \min\{x_m, |P_m \smallsetminus B|\}, x_{m+1}) \in \mathbf{Q}'$ and consider the mapping $\widehat{h} \colon \mathbf{Q} \to \mathbb{R}$ defined by $\widehat{h}(\mathbf{x}) = \widehat{h}'(\mathbf{x}')$. It is not difficult to prove that this mapping defines a $\Pi_0$-partite $\Gamma$-polymatroid $\mathcal{S} = (Q, h)$ with $\sigma_{p_0}(\mathcal{S}) = \sigma_{p_0}(\mathcal{S}')$. $\square$

To determine whether the analogous result holds for the parameters $\kappa$ and $\lambda$ is an open problem. Nevertheless, as a consequence of the results in [14], in the conditions of Theorem 7, if $\Gamma \setminus B$ admits a vector space secret sharing scheme, then the same applies for $\Gamma$. In the particular families of bipartite, tripartite and hierarchical access structures, the ideal access structures coincide with the vector space access structures [14,15,27]. Then, for the access structures in these families, $\Gamma \setminus B$ is ideal if and only if $\Gamma$ is so.

## 5  The Optimal Complexity of Bipartite Access Structures

In this section we present bounds on the optimal complexity of bipartite access structures, and we present an optimal construction for some non-ideal bipartite access structures. Padró and Sáez [27] characterized the ideal bipartite access structures. We rewrite the result as follows.

**Theorem 8 ([27]).** *Let $\Pi = (P_1, P_2)$ be a partition of $P$. A $\Pi$-partite access structure $\Gamma$ is ideal if and only if $\Pi(\min \Gamma) = \mathcal{B}_1 \cup \mathcal{B}_2$, where*

- $\Pi(\mathcal{B}_1) \subseteq \{(0, y), (x, 0)\}$ *for some $x, y > 0$ and*
- $\mathcal{B}_2 = \emptyset$ *or $\Pi(\mathcal{B}_2) = \{(x - m, y - 1), \ldots, (x - 1, y - m)\}$ for $0 < m < x, y$.*

*In addition, every ideal bipartite access structure admits a vector space secret sharing scheme. Moreover, $\sigma(\Gamma) \geq 3/2$ for every non-ideal bipartite access structure $\Gamma$.*

Differently to the general case, the asymptotic behavior of the parameter $\sigma$ is known for bipartite access structures. Actually,, if $\Gamma$ is $\Pi = (P_1, P_2)$-partite, then $\lambda(\Gamma) \leq \min\{|P_1|, |P_2|\}$. This is due to the fact that the bipartite access structures with one minimal point admit a vector space secret sharing scheme and $\Pi(\min \Gamma)$ consists of at most $\min\{|P_1|, |P_2|\}$ points. It can be proved by using well known basic decomposition techniques (see [31], for instance) that $\Gamma$ admits a linear secret sharing scheme $\Sigma$ with $\sigma(\Sigma) = |\Pi(\min \Gamma)|$.

We present next a new lower bound on $\kappa$ for bipartite access structures. Our result generalize and improve the one presented by Padró and Sáez in [27], and for many access structures, some of them presented in this section, our bound is tight. First, we present a lemma that is needed in the proof of the result. For a polymatroid $\mathcal{S} = (Q, h)$ and subsets $X, Y, Z \subseteq Q$, we notate

- $h(X \mid Y) = h(X \cup Y) - h(Y) \geq 0$,
- $i(X; Y) = h(X) - h(X \mid Y) = h(X) + h(Y) - h(X \cup Y) \geq 0$, and
- $i(X; Y \mid Z) = h(X \mid Z) - h(X \mid Y \cup Z) \geq 0$.

**Lemma 9.** *Let $\mathcal{S} = (Q, h)$ be a $\Gamma$-polymatroid and $X, Y, Z$ subsets of $P = Q \setminus \{p_0\}$. If $X \cup Z$ and $Y \cup Z$ are in $\Gamma$ but $Z$ is not in $\Gamma$, then $i(X; Y|Z) \geq 1$.*

**Theorem 10.** *Let $\{(x_0, y_0), \ldots, (x_m, y_m)\}$ be the set of minimal points of a bipartite access structure, ordered in such a way that $x_i < x_{i+1}$ for every $i = 1, \ldots, m - 1$. Set $\delta = 0$ if $x_0 > 0$ and $\delta = 1$ if $x_0 = 0$. Take*

$$k = \max_{\delta \leq i \leq m-1} \{x_{i+1} - x_i\},$$

$r = x_m - x_\delta$, *and* $s = y_\delta - y_{m-1}$. *Then*

$$\kappa(\Gamma) \geq \frac{k+r-1}{k+s}.$$

*Proof.* Let $A \subseteq P$ be a subset with $\Pi(A) = (k-1, s+1)$ and let $B_1 \subseteq \ldots \subseteq B_{r+1}$ be a sequence of subsets with $\Pi(B_i) = (x_\delta + i - 2, y_{m-1} - 1)$ and $A \cap B_{r+1} = \emptyset$. For every $i = 1, \ldots, r+1$ we define $\gamma(i)$ as the smallest integer for which $x_{\gamma(i)} \geq x_\delta + i - 2$. Then for each $i = 1, \ldots, r+1$ with $\gamma(i) \neq m$, consider a subset $X_i \subseteq A$ with $\Pi(X_i) = (x_{\gamma(i)}, y_{\gamma(i)}) - \Pi(B_i)$. If $\gamma(i) = m$, consider a subset $X_i \subseteq A$ with $\Pi(X_i) = (x_m, y_{m-1} - 1) - \Pi(B_i)$. Since $(B_1, \ldots, B_{r+1} \mid A)$ is an independent sequence, $h(A) \geq r+1$ by Theorem 5.

Define $A \cap P_1 = \{p_1, \ldots, p_{k-1}\}$ and $A \cap P_2 = \{q_1, \ldots, q_{s+1}\}$. By Lemma 9 we obtain that

$$h(A) = h(q_1) + \sum_{i=2}^{s+1} h(q_i \mid q_{i-1} \ldots q_1) +$$
$$+ h(p_1 \mid q_{s+1} \ldots q_1) + \sum_{i=2}^{k-1} h(p_i \mid p_{i-1} \ldots p_1 q_{s+1} \ldots q_1) \leq$$
$$\leq \sum_{i=1}^{s+1} h(q_i) + h(p_1) + \sum_{i=2}^{k-1} h(p_i \mid p_1 q_{s+1} \ldots q_1) =$$
$$= \sum_{i=1}^{s+1} h(q_i) + h(p_1) + \sum_{i=2}^{k-1} h(p_i \mid q_{s+1} \ldots q_1) - i(p_i; p_1 \mid q_{s+1} \ldots q_1) \leq$$
$$\leq \sum_{i=1}^{s+1} h(q_i) + h(p_1) + \sum_{i=2}^{k-1} h(p_i \mid q_{s+1} \ldots q_1) - (k-2) \leq$$
$$\leq \sum_{i=1}^{s+1} h(q_i) + \sum_{i=1}^{k-1} h(p_i) - (k-2).$$

Hence, taking into account the previous inequality it follows that $k + r - 1 \leq \sum_{i=1}^{s+1} h(q_i) + \sum_{i=1}^{k-1} h(p_i)$. Therefore, there is some $p \in A$ that satisfies $h(p) \geq (k+r-1)/(k+s)$ and so $\kappa(\Gamma) \geq \kappa(\Gamma') \geq (k+r-1)/(k+s)$.    □

In particular, we find a lower bound on $\kappa(\Gamma)$ for the case of bipartite access structures having exactly two minimal points.

**Corollary 11.** *Let* $\{(x_1, y_1), (x_2, y_2)\}$ *be the set of minimal points of a bipartite access structure. If* $x_1 > 0$, *then*

$$\kappa(\Gamma) \geq \frac{2(x_2 - x_1) - 1}{x_2 - x_1}.$$

We present next a construction of optimal secret sharing schemes for a family of non-ideal bipartite access structures. This family includes the access structures studied by Metcalf-Burton in [25]. It consists of all the access structures $\Gamma$ that are $\Pi$-partite for some partition $\Pi = (P_1, P_2)$ such that $\Pi(\min \Gamma) = \{(x_1, y_1), (x_2, 0)\}$ with $0 < x_1 < x_2$ and $y_1 > 0$. For these access structures, $\kappa(\Gamma) \geq (2(x_2 - x_1) - 1)/(x_2 - x_1)$ by Corollary 11. For every one of them, we construct a linear secret sharing scheme with complexity equal to this lower bound on $\kappa(\Gamma)$, and hence

$$\lambda(\Gamma) \leq \frac{2(x_2 - x_1) - 1}{x_2 - x_1} \leq \kappa(\Gamma),$$

which implies that

$$\kappa(\Gamma) = \sigma(\Gamma) = \lambda(\Gamma) = \frac{2(x_2 - x_1) - 1}{x_2 - x_1}.$$

for every one of those access structures.

Define $P_1 = \{p_1, \ldots, p_{N_1}\}$ and $P_2 = \{q_1, \ldots, q_{N_2}\}$, with $N_1 = |P_1|$ and $N_2 = |P_2|$. Suppose that $N_1 \geq x_2$ and $N_2 \geq y_1$. Let $\mathbb{K}$ be a finite field larger than $N_1 + x_2 - x_1$ and $N_2$. Define $r = x_1$, $t = x_2 - x_1$ and $u = y_1$. Let $E_{p_0}$ be a $\mathbb{K}$-vector space of dimension $t$. Every $(s_1, \ldots, s_t) \in E_{p_0}$ is shared among the participants in $P$ by using two schemes, $\Sigma_1$ and $\Sigma_2$. The coordinate $s_1$ is shared by means of $\Sigma_1$ and each one of the coordinates $s_2, \ldots, s_t$ by means of $\Sigma_2$.

Let $k \in \mathbb{K}$ be the secret of $\Sigma_1$, and $k_1, k_2 \in \mathbb{K}$ elements that satisfy $k = k_1 + k_2$. Choose uniformly at random the polynomials

- $g$ of degree $t + u - 1$ such that $g(0) = k$.
- $f$ and $h$ of degree $r - 1$ such that $f(0) = k_2$ and $h(0) = k_1$.

Choose $x_1, \ldots, x_{N_1}$ and $y_1, \ldots, y_{N_2}$ in $\mathbb{K} \setminus \{0\}$ such that $x_i \neq x_j$ and $y_i \neq y_j$ for $i \neq j$. For every $i = 1, \ldots, N_1$, the share of the participant $p_i$ in the scheme $\Sigma_1$ is $(h(x_i), g(x_i)) \in \mathbb{K}^2$, while for every $i = 1, \ldots, N_2$ the share of $q_i$ is $f(y_i) \in \mathbb{K}$.

Now let $k \in \mathbb{K}$ be the secret of the scheme $\Sigma_2$. Choose $x_1, \ldots, x_{N_1+t}$ and $y_1, \ldots, y_{N_2}$ in $\mathbb{K} \setminus \{0\}$ such that $x_i \neq x_j$ and $y_i \neq y_j$ for $i \neq j$. Choose uniformly at random the polynomials

- $g$ of degree $t + u - 1$ such that $g(0) = k$.
- $f_1 \ldots f_t$ of degree $r - 1$ such that $f_i(0) = g(x_i)$ for all $1 \leq i \leq t$.

For every $i = 1, \ldots, N_1$, the share of the participant $p_i$ in the scheme $\Sigma_2$ is $g(x_{s+i})$, while for all $i = 1, \ldots, N_2$ the share of $q_i$ is $(f_1(y_i), \ldots, f_s(y_t))$.

Both $\Sigma_1$ and $\Sigma_2$ are linear and their access structure is $\Gamma$. Combining $\Sigma_1$ and $\Sigma_2$ as detailed, we obtain a linear scheme with access structure $\Gamma$ in which both the participants in $P_1$ and in $P_2$ receive a sequence of $2t - 1$ elements of $\mathbb{K}$. Since $\dim(E_{p_0}) = t$, $\sigma(\Sigma) = (2t - 1)/t$.

**Theorem 12.** *The bipartite access structure $\Gamma$ defined by the minimal points $\{(x_1, y_1), (x_2, 0)\}$ with $x_1, x_2, y_1 > 0$ satisfy:*

$$\kappa(\Gamma) = \sigma(\Gamma) = \lambda(\Gamma) = \frac{2(x_2 - x_1) - 1}{x_2 - x_1}.$$

## 6    A Linear Programming Approach

In this section we present a procedure to compute the value of $\kappa$ for bipartite access structures. We search the minimum of $h(\{p\})$ for all $p \in Q \setminus \{p_0\}$ among all bipartite polymatroids $\mathcal{S} = (Q, h)$ that satisfy $\Gamma = \Gamma_{p_0}(\mathcal{S})$. Yeung [34] showed that this kind of problems, which are determined by the Shannon inequalities, can be formulated as a linear programming problem. We improve this technique by considering results by Matúš on polymatroids [24], and by using the results on bipartite polymatroids presented in previous sections. The use of the pair $(\mathbf{Q}, \widehat{h})$ instead of $(Q, h)$ in the linear programming problem reduces dramatically the size of the linear programming problem, because the size of the vector to consider changes from $2^{|P_1|+|P_2|+1}$ to $2(|P_1|+1)(|P_2|+1)$. This procedure can be extended to $m$-partite access structures with $m > 2$, so it can be used to compute $\kappa$ for any access structure. Nevertheless, our method only makes sense if the number of parts is much smaller than the number of participants. Linear programming was previously used in secret sharing by Stinson [32] in order to find efficient constructions of secret sharing schemes by using decomposition techniques.

Let $\Pi = (P_1, P_2)$ be a partition of $P$ and define $N_1 = |P_1|$ and $N_2 = |P_2|$. A $\Pi_0$-partite polymatroid $\mathcal{S}$ is completely determined by a vector $\mathbf{s} = (\widehat{h}(x, y, z))_{(x,y,z) \in \mathbf{Q}} \in \mathbb{R}^{|\mathbf{Q}|}$, where $(\mathbf{Q}, \widehat{h})$ is the pair associated to $\mathcal{S}$ and every entry of $\mathbf{s}$ is indexed by $(x, y, z) \in \mathbf{Q}$. For every $(x, y, z) \in \mathbf{Q}$, define the vector $\mathbf{e}_{(x,y,z)} \in \mathbb{R}^{|\mathbf{Q}|}$ as the vector with entry 1 in the position $(x, y, z)$ and 0 elsewhere.

For a bipartite access structure, we construct the matrices $\mathbf{A}$ and $\mathbf{B}$, and the vector $\mathbf{b}$ for which a vector $\mathbf{s} \in \mathbb{R}^{|\mathbf{Q}|}$ corresponds to a $\Pi_0$-partite $\Gamma$-polymatroid $\mathcal{S}$ if and only if $\mathbf{A} \cdot \mathbf{s}^T \leq 0$, $\mathbf{B} \cdot \mathbf{s}^T = \mathbf{b}$, and $\mathbf{s} \geq \mathbf{e}_{(0,0,1)}$. Then $\kappa(\Gamma)$ is obtained by minimizing $\mathbf{e}_{(1,0,0)} \cdot \mathbf{s}^T$ and $\mathbf{e}_{(0,1,0)} \cdot \mathbf{s}^T$ for these vectors.

Let $\Gamma$ be an access structure on $P$. A pair $\mathcal{S} = (Q, h)$ with $Q = P \cup \{p_0\}$ is a $\Gamma$-polymatroid if and only if the following conditions are satisfied:

1. $h(\emptyset) = 0$, and
2. $h(Q \smallsetminus \{p\}) \leq h(Q)$, for all $p \in Q$, and
3. $h(X) + h(X \cup \{p, q\}) \leq h(X \cup \{p\}) + h(X \cup \{q\})$ for all $p, q \in Q \smallsetminus X$, and
4. $h(X \cup \{p_0\}) = h(X)$ for every $X \subseteq P$ in $\Gamma$, and $h(X \cup \{p_0\}) = h(X) + 1$ for every $X \subseteq P$ not in $\Gamma$.

The first three conditions are an alternative characterization of polymatroids due to Matúš [24], and the fourth condition characterizes the $\Gamma$-polymatroids. The matrices $\mathbf{A}$ and $\mathbf{B}$ and the vector $\mathbf{b}$ are constructed according to the conditions 1 to 4 as follows.

1. Add the row $\mathbf{e}_{(0,0,0)}$ to $\mathbf{B}$ and the element 0 in $\mathbf{b}$ in the corresponding position.
2. Add the following rows to the matrix $\mathbf{A}$: $\mathbf{e}_{(N_1-1,N_2,1)} - \mathbf{e}_{(N_1,N_2,1)}$, $\mathbf{e}_{(N_1,N_2-1,1)} - \mathbf{e}_{(N_1,N_2,1)}$, and $\mathbf{e}_{(N_1,N_2,0)} - \mathbf{e}_{(N_1,N_2,1)}$.
3. Add the following rows to $\mathbf{A}$ for all $(x, y, z) \in \mathbf{Q}$ satisfying the following conditions:

    (a) $\mathbf{e}_{(x,y,z)} + \mathbf{e}_{(x+2,y,z)} - \mathbf{e}_{(x+1,y,z)} - \mathbf{e}_{(x+1,y,z)}$ if $x < N_1 - 1$.
    (b) $\mathbf{e}_{(x,y,z)} + \mathbf{e}_{(x,y+2,z)} - \mathbf{e}_{(x,y+1,z)} - \mathbf{e}_{(x,y+1,z)}$ if $y < N_2 - 1$.
    (c) $\mathbf{e}_{(x,y,z)} + \mathbf{e}_{(x+1,y+1,z)} - \mathbf{e}_{(x+1,y,z)} - \mathbf{e}_{(x,y+1,z)}$ if $x < N_1 - 1$ and $y < N_2$.
    (d) $\mathbf{e}_{(x,y,0)} + \mathbf{e}_{(x+1,y,1)} - \mathbf{e}_{(x+1,y,0)} - \mathbf{e}_{(x,y,1)}$ if $x < N_1$.
    (e) $\mathbf{e}_{(x,y,0)} + \mathbf{e}_{(x,y+1,z)} - \mathbf{e}_{(x,y+1,0)} - \mathbf{e}_{(x,y,1)}$ if $y < N_2$.

4. Add the row $\mathbf{e}_{(x,y,1)} - \mathbf{e}_{(x,y,0)}$ to the matrix $\mathbf{B}$ for every $(x, y) \in \Pi(P)$ and add the entry 0 to $\mathbf{b}$ if $(x, y) \geq (x', y')$ for some $(x', y') \in \Pi(\min \Gamma)$ or 1 otherwise.

Since $\sigma_{p_0}(\mathcal{S}) = \max\{\widehat{h}(1, 0, 0), \widehat{h}(0, 1, 0)\}$, we have to split the computation of $\kappa(\mathcal{S})$ into two different linear programming problems. In the first case, we suppose that $\widehat{h}(0, 1, 0) \leq \widehat{h}(1, 0, 0)$, and so we add the row $\mathbf{e}_{(0,1,0)} - \mathbf{e}_{(1,0,0)}$ to the matrix $\mathbf{A}$. Then we solve the following linear programming problem:

$$\min \quad \mathbf{e}_{(1,0,0)} \cdot \mathbf{s}^T \tag{1}$$
$$\text{subject to:} \quad \mathbf{A} \cdot \mathbf{s}^T \leq \mathbf{0} \tag{2}$$
$$\mathbf{B} \cdot \mathbf{s}^T \leq \mathbf{b} \tag{3}$$
$$\mathbf{s} \in \mathbb{R}^{|\mathbf{Q}|}$$

where (1) is the *objective function*, (2) and (3) are the linear constraints and linear equalities, respectively. The smallest value of the objective function is called the *optimal value*, and a vector $\mathbf{s}^*$ that gives the optimal value is an *optimal solution*.

In the second case, we solve the linear programming problem assuming that $\widehat{h}(1,0,0) \leq \widehat{h}(0,1,0)$ instead of $\widehat{h}(0,1,0) \leq \widehat{h}(1,0,0)$.

In both problems, we observe that $\mathbf{A}$, $\mathbf{B}$ and $\mathbf{b}$ determine a convex region $\mathbf{U} \subseteq \mathbb{R}^{|\mathbf{Q}|}$. Moreover, since the number of linear constraints and linear equalities involved is finite, $\mathbf{U}$ is a polytope. The set $\mathbf{U}$ is commonly called the *feasible region* and a vector $\mathbf{s} \in \mathbf{U}$ is called a *feasible solution*. Notice that polymatroids from secret sharing schemes must be in at least one of the two possible feasible regions. Thus, at least one of the two linear programming problems have solution because the feasible region cannot be empty in both cases and all entries in every feasible solution are lower bounded. If $\mathbf{s}_1$ is an optimal solution of the first linear programming problem (when $\widehat{h}(0,1,0) \leq \widehat{h}(1,0,0)$) and $\mathbf{s}_2$ is an optimal solution of the second one, then $\kappa(\Gamma) = \min\{\mathbf{e}_{(1,0,0)} \cdot \mathbf{s}_1^T, \mathbf{e}_{(0,1,0)} \cdot \mathbf{s}_2^T\}$.

# 7   Some Experimental Results

We use MATLAB® and the optimization software MOZEK® to implement the linear programming approach described in the previous section. The program receives as input, the minimal points in the access structure, namely, $\{(x_1, y_1), \ldots, (x_m, y_m)\}$ with $x_i < x_{i+1}$ for every $i = 1, \ldots, m-1$. As a consequence of Theorem 7, we can consider that the number of elements in $P_1$ and $P_2$ are $N_1 = x_m$ and $N_2 = y_1$, respectively. For some structures $\kappa$ coincides with the bound given in Theorem 10. For instance, bipartite access structures with two minimal points (Corollary 11), and bipartite access structures whose set of minimal points are $\{(x, y), (x+r, y-1), \ldots, (x+mr, y-m)\}$ (where $x, r, m > 0$ and $y - m \geq 0$).

However, in general $\kappa$ does not attain the bound given in Theorem 10. We present some examples. First we consider the structures $\Gamma_{r,s,t}^1$ and $\Gamma_{r,s,t}^2$ (over the set of participants $P = P_1 \cup P_2$) whose minimal points are $\{(r, 2), (s, 1), (t, 0)\}$ (where $0 \leq r < s < t$, $N_1 = t$ and $N_2 = 2$) and $\{(r, 4), (s, 3), (t, 1)\}$ (where $0 \leq r < s < t$, $N_1 = t$ and $N_2 = 4$), respectively.

In the Tables **1**, **2** and **3**, we present some outputs for the access structures $\Gamma_{r,s,t}^1$ and $\Gamma_{r,s,t}^2$. The first row of each table shows the values of $r, s, t$, while the second one shows the value of $\kappa$.

Table 1.

| $r,s,t$ | 1,3,7 | 1,5,7 | 1,4,8 | 1,5,8 | 1,3,8 | 1,6,8 | 1,4,9 | 1,6,9 | 1,5,10 | 1,6,10 |
|---|---|---|---|---|---|---|---|---|---|---|
| $\kappa(\Gamma^1_{r,s,t})$ | 13/7 | 13/7 | 23/11 | 23/11 | 17/9 | 17/9 | 30/14 | 30/14 | 43/19 | 43/19 |

Table 2.

| $r,s,t$ | 1,2,4 | 1,3,4 | 1,2,5 | 1,4,5 | 1,2,6 | 1,5,6 | 1,2,7 | 1,6,7 | 1,2,8 | 1,7,8 |
|---|---|---|---|---|---|---|---|---|---|---|
| $\kappa(\Gamma^1_{r,s,t})$ | 3/2 | 3/2 | 5/3 | 5/3 | 7/4 | 7/4 | 9/5 | 9/5 | 11/6 | 11/6 |

Table 3.

| $r,s,t$ | 1,3,5 | 1,3,6 | 1,4,6 | 1,3,7 | 1,5,7 | 1,4,8 | 1,5,8 | 1,3,8 | 1,6,8 | 1,4,9 |
|---|---|---|---|---|---|---|---|---|---|---|
| $\kappa(\Gamma^2_{r,s,t})$ | 22/13 | 9/5 | 99/53 | 43/22 | 13/7 | 23/11 | 23/11 | 17/9 | 263/121 | 15/7 |

Notice that for each access structure $\Gamma$ in Table **2**, there is a minor $\Gamma'$ for which $\kappa(\Gamma)$ attains the lower bound of $\kappa(\Gamma')$ given in Theorem 10. The minimal points of $\Gamma'$ are of the kind $\{(r,2),(s,1)\}$ or $\{(s,1),(t,0)\}$.

# 8    Results on Bipartite Polymatroids

In this section we study the separation between $\sigma$, $\kappa$ and $\lambda$ by analyzing the tripartite polymatroids associated to bipartite access structure. If for a certain access structure $\Gamma$ all $\Gamma$-polymatroids are entropic, then $\sigma(\Gamma) = \kappa(\Gamma)$, and if each entropic $\Gamma$-polymatroid is the sum of $\mathbb{K}$-linearly representable matroids for a finite field $\mathbb{K}$, then $\sigma(\Gamma) = \lambda(\Gamma)$. We show that all unipartite polymatroids satisfy these properties, but this is not the case for $m$-partite polymatroids with $m \geq 2$. First we show a technical lemma.

**Proposition 13.** *The sum of two integer polymatroids that are linearly representable over $\mathbb{K}$ is linearly representable over $\mathbb{K}$.*

*Proof.* For $i = 1,2$, let $\mathcal{S}_i = (Q, h_i)$ be two integer polymatroids that are linearly representable over $\mathbb{K}$, and consider vector spaces $E^i$ over $\mathbb{K}$ and subspaces $V^i_1, \ldots, V^i_n \subseteq E^i$ that provide a linear representation of $\mathcal{S}_i$. Consider $E = E^1 \oplus E^2$ and $V_j = V^1_j \oplus V^2_j \subseteq E$ for $j = 1, \ldots, n$. Clearly, these subspaces linearly represent $\mathcal{S}_1 + \mathcal{S}_2$.    $\square$

## 8.1    Unipartite Polymatroids

Let $\mathcal{S} = (Q, h)$ be a unipartite polymatroid and $(\mathbf{Q}, \widehat{h})$ the pair associated to it. Define $h_0 = 0$, and for every $i = 1, \ldots, n$ define the integers $h_i = \widehat{h}(i)$ and $\delta_i = h_i - h_{i-1}$. A sequence of integers $h_0, \ldots, h_n$ with $h_0 = 0$ defines a unipartite polymatroid if and only if $\delta_1 \geq \cdots \geq \delta_n \geq 0$. The vector $(\delta_1, \ldots, \delta_n)$ is called the *increment vector* of the unipartite polymatroid $\mathcal{S}$. Obviously, a unipartite polymatroid is determined by its increment vector, and it is an integer polymatroid if and only if its increment vector has integer components. If $\mathcal{S} = (Q, h)$ is a unipartite matroid, then there exists an integer $r$ with $0 \leq r \leq |Q|$ such that the increment vector of $\mathcal{S}$ satisfies $\delta_i = 1$ if $i \leq r$ and $\delta_i = 0$ otherwise. We notate $U_{r,n}$ for such a unipartite matroid. It is well known that the unipartite matroid $U_{r,n}$ is linearly representable over every finite field $\mathbb{K}$ with $|\mathbb{K}| \geq n$.

**Proposition 14.** *Every unipartite integer polymatroid is a sum of unipartite matroids.*

*Proof.* Given a unipartite integer polymatorid $\mathcal{S} = (Q, h)$, consider the integer values $\delta_1 \geq \cdots \geq \delta_n \geq 0$. Then there exists a sequence of integers $n = r_0 \geq r_1 \geq \cdots \geq r_{\delta_1} \geq r_{\delta_1+1} = 0$ such that $r_{\delta_i} \geq i > r_{\delta_i+1}$ for every $i = 1, \ldots, n$. We claim that $\mathcal{S} = U_{r_1,n} + \cdots + U_{r_{\delta_1},n}$. We have to check that $\delta_i = \delta_i^1 + \cdots + \delta_i^{\delta_1}$ for every $i = 1, \ldots, n$, where $\delta^k$ is the increment vector of the uniform matroid $U_{r_k,n}$. Recall that $\delta_i^k = 1$ if $r_k \geq i$ and $\delta_i^k = 0$ otherwise. $\square$

**Theorem 15.** *Every unipartite integer polymatroid is linearly representable, and hence entropic.*

*Proof.* Straightforward from Propositions 14 and 13 and the fact that the uniform matroid $U_{r,n}$ is linearly representable over every finite field with at least $n$ elements. $\square$

All bipartite matroids are linearly representable [14] and so entropic. However, next we show that not all bipartite polymatroids are entropic. The Vamos matroid $V$ is the matroid of dimension four on the set $\{1, \ldots, 8\}$ with rank function $r$ such that $r(A) = 4$ for every $A \subseteq \{1, \ldots, 8\}$ of size 4 except $\{1, 2, 3, 4\}, \{1, 2, 5, 6\}, \{3, 4, 5, 6\}$ $\{3, 4, 7, 8\}$ and $\{5, 6, 7, 8\}$. Define $a = \{1, 2\}$, $b = \{3, 4\}$, $c = \{5, 6\}$, $d = \{7, 8\}$, the set $P = \{a, b, c, d\}$, and the partition $\Pi = (\{a, b\}, \{c, d\})$. Consider $\mathcal{S}$ the $\Pi$-partite polymatroid whose rank function is derived from the rank function of $V$. Since $\mathcal{S}$ is non-entropic, we have the following result.

**Proposition 16.** *There exist bipartite integral polymatroids that are non-entropic.*

Let $\mathbb{K}$ be a finite field with $|\mathbb{K}| \geq 10$ and $x_1, \ldots, x_{10}$ different elements in $\mathbb{K}$. Consider the function $v : \mathbb{K} \to \mathbb{K}^7$ defined by $v(x) = (1, x, \ldots, x^6)$. Consider $P = \{a, b, c, d\}$ and the vector subspaces $V_a = \langle v(x_1), v(x_2), v(x_3) \rangle$, $V_b = \langle v(x_4), v(x_5), v(x_6) \rangle$, $V_c = \langle v(x_4), v(x_7), v(x_8) \rangle$, and $V_d = \langle v(x_4), v(x_9), v(x_{10}) \rangle$. Consider the partition $\Pi = (\{a\}, \{b, c, d\})$, and $\mathcal{S}$ the $\Pi$-partite polymatroid whose rank function is the dimension of these subspaces. Let $(\mathbf{Q}, \widehat{h})$ be the pair associated to $\mathcal{S}$. After some computation, we see that this polymatroid is not a sum of matroids. The details will appear in the full version of the paper.

**Proposition 17.** *There exist bipartite integral entropic polymatroids that are not the sum of bipartite matroids.*

## 9   Conclusions and Open Problems

In general it is not known how far is $\sigma$ from $\kappa$ and $\lambda$. In this article we study this problem restricted to multipartite access structures and we obtain better bounds on these parameters. We present a method to compute $\kappa$ for any multipartite access structure, bounds on $\kappa$ and $\lambda$, and optimal schemes for non-ideal bipartite access structures. These non-ideal access structures have the property that $\kappa$ coincides with $\sigma$ and $\lambda$. It is also satisfied by bipartite matroid ports, but it is not known if it is true for all bipartite access structures. We study the entropic polymatroids and the linearly representable ones in order to solve this problem, but we just obtain negative results. The characterization of the bipartite polymatroids that are entropic and the ones that are linearly representable could be an interesting approximation to this open problem.

It has been proved in [3] that, for 4-partite access structures, the non-Shannon inequalities give better bounds on $\sigma$ for matroid ports. All bipartite matroid ports are ideal, but maybe these inequalities could give better bounds on $\sigma$ for non-ideal access structures.

In Theorem 7, we prove that if two access structures have the same minimal points, then $\kappa$ is the same. However, it is not known if in general $\lambda$ is also the same. A positive answer would simplify a lot the search of optimal linear constructions and the study of this parameter.

## References

1. Beimel, A., Ishai, Y.: On the power of nonlinear secret sharing schemes. SIAM J. Discrete Math. 19, 258–280 (2005)
2. Beimel, A., Livne, N.: On Matroids and Non-ideal Secret Sharing. In: Halevi, S., Rabin, T. (eds.) TCC 2006. LNCS, vol. 3876, pp. 482–501. Springer, Heidelberg (2006)
3. Beimel, A., Livne, N., Padró, C.: Matroids Can Be Far From Ideal Secret Sharing. In: Canetti, R. (ed.) TCC 2008. LNCS, vol. 4948, pp. 194–212. Springer, Heidelberg (2008)
4. Beimel, A., Orlov, I.: Secret Sharing and Non-Shannon Information Inequalities. In: Reingold, O. (ed.) TCC 2009. LNCS, vol. 5444, pp. 539–557. Springer, Heidelberg (2009)
5. Beimel, A., Tassa, T., Weinreb, E.: Characterizing Ideal Weighted Threshold Secret Sharing. SIAM J. Discrete Math. 22, 360–397 (2008)
6. Beimel, A., Weinreb, E.: Separating the power of monotone span programs over different fields. SIAM J. Comput. 34, 1196–1215 (2005)
7. Beimel, A., Weinreb, E.: Monotone Circuits for Monotone Weighted Threshold Functions. Information Processing Letters 97, 12–18 (2006)
8. Blakley, G.R.: Safeguarding cryptographic keys. In: AFIPS Conference Proceedings, vol. 48, pp. 313–317 (1979)
9. Blundo, C., De Santis, A., Gargano, L., Vaccaro, U.: Tight Bounds on the Information Rate of Secret Sharing Schemes. Des. Codes Cryptogr. 11, 107–122 (1997)
10. Brickell, E.F.: Some ideal secret sharing schemes. J. Combin. Math. and Combin. Comput. 9, 105–113 (1989)

11. Brickell, E.F., Davenport, D.M.: On the classification of ideal secret sharing schemes. J. Cryptology 4, 123–134 (1991)
12. Csirmaz, L.: The size of a share must be large. J. Cryptology 10, 223–231 (1997)
13. L. Csirmaz, G. Tardos. Secret sharing on trees: problem solved (preprint) (2009), Cryptology ePrint Archive, http://eprint.iacr.org/2009/071
14. Farràs, O., Martí–Farré, J., Padró, C.: Ideal Multipartite Secret Sharing Schemes. In: Naor, M. (ed.) EUROCRYPT 2007. LNCS, vol. 4515, pp. 448–465. Springer, Heidelberg (2007); The full version of this paper is available at the Cryptology ePrint Archive, http://eprint.iacr.org/2006/292
15. Farràs, O., Padró, C.: Ideal Hierarchical Secret Sharing Schemes. Cryptology ePrint Archive, Report 2009/141, http://eprint.iacr.org/2009/141
16. Fehr, S.: Efficient Construction of the Dual Span Program (manuscript)
17. Fujishige, S.: Polymatroidal Dependence Structure of a Set of Random Variables. Information and Control 39, 55–72 (1978)
18. Herranz, J., Sáez, G.: New Results on Multipartite Access Structures. IEEE Proceedings on Information Security 153, 153–162 (2006)
19. Herzog, J., Hibi, T.: Discrete polymatroids. J. Algebraic Combin. 16, 239–268 (2002)
20. Ito, M., Saito, A., Nishizeki, T.: Secret sharing scheme realizing any access structure. In: Proc. IEEE Globecom 1987, pp. 99–102 (1987)
21. Jackson, W.-A., Martin, K.M.: Geometric secret sharing schemes and their duals. Des. Codes Cryptogr. 4, 83–95 (1994)
22. Martí-Farré, J., Padró, C.: On Secret Sharing Schemes, Matroids and Polymatroids. In: Vadhan, S.P. (ed.) TCC 2007. LNCS, vol. 4392, pp. 273–290. Springer, Heidelberg (2007); The full version of this paper is available at the Cryptology ePrint Archive, http://eprint.iacr.org/2006/077
23. Matúš, F.: Matroid representations by partitions. Discrete Math. 203, 169–194 (1999)
24. Matúš, F.: Adhesivity of polymatroids. Discrete Math. 307, 2464–2477 (2007)
25. Metcalf-Burton, J.R.: Information Rates of Minimal Non-Matroid-Related Access Structures. arxiv.org/pdf/0801.3642
26. Morillo, P., Padró, C., Sáez, G., Villar, J.L.: Weighted Threshold Secret Sharing Schemes. Inf. Process. Lett. 70, 211–216 (1999)
27. Padró, C., Sáez, G.: Secret sharing schemes with bipartite access structure. IEEE Trans. Inform. Theory 46, 2596–2604 (2000)
28. Shamir, A.: How to share a secret. Commun. of the ACM 22, 612–613 (1979)
29. Shannon, C.E.: A Mathematical Theory of Communication. Bell. Sys. Tech. Journal 27 (1948)
30. Simmons, G.J.: How to (Really) Share a Secret. In: Goldwasser, S. (ed.) CRYPTO 1988. LNCS, vol. 403, pp. 390–448. Springer, Heidelberg (1990)
31. Stinson, D.R.: An explication of secret sharing schemes. Des. Codes Cryptogr. 2, 357–390 (1992)
32. Stinson, D.R.: Decomposition constructions for secret-sharing schemes. IEEE Transactions on Information Theory 40, 118–125 (1994)
33. Welsh, D.J.A.: Matroid Theory. Academic Press, London (1976)
34. Yeung, R.W.: A framework for linear information inequalities. IEEE Trans. Inform. Theory IT-41, 412–422 (1995)
35. Yeung, R.W.: A First Course in Information Theory. Springer, Heidelberg (2002)

# Linear Threshold Multisecret Sharing Schemes*

Oriol Farràs, Ignacio Gracia, Sebastià Martín and Carles Padró

Dept. Matemàtica Aplicada IV, Universitat Politècnica de Catalunya (UPC),
Barcelona, Spain
{ofarras,ignacio,sebasm,cpadro}@ma4.upc.edu

**Abstract.** In a multisecret sharing scheme, several secret values are
distributed among a set of $n$ users, and each secret may have a different associated access structure. We consider here unconditionally secure
schemes with multithreshold access structures. Namely, for every subset
$P$ of $k$ users there is a secret key that can only be computed when at
least $t$ of them put together their secret information. Coalitions with at
most $w$ users with less than $t$ of them in $P$ cannot obtain any information
about the secret associated to $P$. The main parameters to optimize are
the length of the shares and the amount of random bits that are needed
to set up the distribution of shares, both in relation to the length of
the secret. In this paper, we provide lower bounds on this parameters.
Moreover, we present an optimal construction for $t = 2$ and $k = 3$, and
a construction that is valid for all $w$, $t$, $k$ and $n$. The models presented
use linear algebraic techniques.

**Keywords:** Unconditional security, multisecret sharing schemes, threshold access structures.

## 1 Introduction

### 1.1 Multisecret Sharing Schemes

In a secret sharing scheme some secret information is distributed into shares
among a set of users in such a way that only authorized coalitions of users can
reconstruct the secret from their shares. Such a scheme is said to be perfect if
unauthorized subsets of users do not obtain any information about the secret.

Multisecret sharing schemes are a generalization of such schemes. In a multisecret sharing scheme a number of secret values are distributed; we use $\mathcal{J}$ as the
set of indices for this secret values. For each one of these secrets there will be
some coalitions authorized to know it, and some other coalitions that will not
be able to obtain any information about it.

For every $j \in \mathcal{J}$, we call $\Gamma_j$ the access structure associated with the secret
corresponding to the index $j$, that is the collection of subsets authorized to
know that particular secret. We also call $\Delta_j$ the forbidden structure associated
with the secret corresponding to the index $j$, that is the collection of subsets

---

* This work was partially supported by the Spanish Ministry of Science and Technology under project TSI2006-02731.

unauthorized to know it. Naturally, the collection of subsets $\Gamma_j$ is monotone increasing, while $\Delta_j$ is monotone decreasing. Obviously, $\Gamma_j \cap \Delta_j = \emptyset$ for every $j \in \mathcal{J}$.

In a multisecret sharing scheme we define the *specification structure* $\Gamma$ as the collection of pairs of access and forbidden structures associated with the secret indexed by the elements in $\mathcal{J}$,

$$\Gamma = \{(\Gamma_j, \Delta_j) : j \in \mathcal{J}\}.$$

Multisecret sharing schemes are defined as a collection of random variables satisfying certain properties in terms of Shannon entropy. We denote by $S_i$ the random variable associated with the share of user $i \in \mathcal{U}$. Likewise, if $A = \{i_1, \ldots, i_r\}$ is a set of users, then $S_A$ is the random variable associated with the shares of users in $A$, that is $S_A = S_{i_1} \times \cdots \times S_{i_r}$.

A *perfect multisecret sharing scheme with specification structure* $\Gamma = \{(\Gamma_j, \Delta_j) : j \in \mathcal{J}\}$ is formed by two collections, $\{S_i\}_{i \in \mathcal{U}}$ and $\{K_j\}_{j \in \mathcal{J}}$, of random variables satisfying:

1. If $A \in \Gamma_j$ then $H(K_j|S_A) = 0$.
2. If $B \in \Delta_j$ then $H(K_j|S_B) = H(K_j)$.

The random variables $\{S_i\}_{i \in \mathcal{U}}$ correspond to the secret information distributed among the users, while the random variables $\{K_j\}_{j \in \mathcal{J}}$ correspond to the shared secret keys. Observe that, with this definition, we require the schemes to be unconditionally secure, namely the forbidden subsets cannot obtain any information on the secrets, independently of the computational power of the adversary.

The efficiency of a multisecret sharing scheme is measured by means of the complexity $\sigma$ and the randomness $\sigma_T$. The complexity $\sigma$ is the ratio between the amount of information received by every user and the amount of information corresponding to the key. The randomness $\sigma_T$ is the ratio between the amount of information distributed to the set of users $\mathcal{U}$ and the amount of information corresponding to the key. Namely,

$$\sigma = \frac{\max_{i \in \mathcal{U}} H(S_i)}{\min_{j \in \mathcal{J}} H(K_j)} \qquad \sigma_T = \frac{H(S_{\mathcal{U}})}{\min_{j \in \mathcal{J}} H(K_j)}$$

We observe that both complexity and randomness are greater or equal than 1. These parameters are a generalization of the ones used to measure the efficiency of secret sharing schemes. As for the easier case of secret sharing schemes, the optimization of these parameters for general specification structures is a very difficult open problem. Nevertheless, in the seminal paper on secret sharing by Shamir [10], optimal schemes are presented for threshold access structures. In contrast, no general optimal constructions of multisecret sharing schemes are known for this simple case of threshold specification structures. The optimality of such a construction is proved by comparing its complexity to some lower bound. General lower bounds for the complexity of multisecret sharing schemes with threshold structure were given in [7]. We present here general lower bounds for the randomness of such schemes. Optimal constructions are only known for very particular values of the thresholds [1,3,8]. Shamir's polynomial construction of secret sharing schemes was generalized by Brickell [5] and Simmons [11], by using linear algebra technics; specifically they introduced linear secret sharing schemes. The same development took place in key predistribution schemes. The polynomial construction by Blundo et al. [3] was generalized by Padró et al. [9] to a linear construction. This linear framework is the starting point in our new approach to multithreshold schemes.

## 1.2 Multithreshold Sharing Schemes

This paper presents constructions of multisecret sharing schemes for some type of specification structures defined by thresholds. These kind of schemes are called multisecret threshold sharing schemes, or multithreshold schemes for short, and were introduced by Jackson, Martin and O'Keefe [7].

In these schemes, every secret is associated with a subset $P \subset \mathcal{U}$ of $k$ users. Shares distributed among users must be created in such a way that every subset with at least $t$ users in $P$ is authorized to know $P$'s secret, and every subset with at most $w$ users, having less than $t$ users in $P$, is unauthorized.

The specification structure of a multithreshold schemes depends on four positive integers $w$, $t$, $k$ and $n$ satisfying:

- $1 \leq t \leq k \leq n$
- $t - 1 \leq w \leq n - k + t - 1$

On a set $\mathcal{U}$ of $n$ users, the specification structure of a $w$-secure $(t, k, n)$ multithreshold sharing scheme is defined as follows:

- $\mathcal{J} = \{P \subseteq \mathcal{U} : |P| = k\}$
- For every $P \in \mathcal{J}$,
  - $\Gamma_P = \{A \subseteq \mathcal{U} : |A \cap P| \geq t\}$
  - $\Delta_P = \{B \subseteq \mathcal{U} : |B| \leq w, |B \cap P| \leq t - 1\}$

When $k = n$, then a single secret is shared. In this case, we have a threshold access structure, and the threshold sharing scheme by Shamir [10] provides an optimal solution. If $t = 1$, then we have a Key Predistribution Scheme (KPS). Optimal constructions were given in [3].

Complete $w$-secure $(t, k, n)$ multithreshold schemes are those with $w = n - k + t - 1$. If a multithreshold scheme is complete, for any $P \in \mathcal{J}$ and $B \subseteq \mathcal{U}$, a subset $B$ such that $|B \cap P| < t$ is $P$-unauthorized.

## 1.3 Known Results

The first multisecret schemes were multithreshold schemes with $t = 1$, and they were called Key Predistribution Schemes (KPS) [3]. In these schemes, any user in $P \in \mathcal{J}$ can calculate $P$'s secret by itself without any additional information. There are some interesting constructions of KPSs: the model presented in [3], based on symmetric polynomials, and the model in [9], called Linear KPS, designed using linear maps. Linear KPS unify the previous proposals of KPS. On the other hand, when $k = n$ and $w = t - 1$, then we have a threshold secret sharing scheme [10].

In the rest of constructions of multithreshold schemes, $t = 2$. Namely, Jackson, Martin and O'Keefe found a geometric construction of an $(n - k + 1)$-secure $(2, k, n)$ multithreshold scheme [8]. Moreover, Barwick and Jackson [1] gave another geometric construction for $w$-secure $(2, 3, n)$ multithreshold schemes.

Jackson, Martin and O'Keefe studied in [7] some bounds on the size of shares, and gave a lower bound on the complexity of a $w$-secure $(2, 3, n)$.

## 1.4   Our Results

We present here a new framework to study multisecret sharing schemes. We introduce the concept of linear multisecret sharing scheme that extends the corresponding notion in secret sharing and key predistribution schemes. This formal setting simplifies the security proofs in the constructions of multisecret sharing schemes.

By using our approach, we present a new construction of a $w$-secure $(2, 3, n)$ multithreshold scheme with optimal complexity and randomness that is simpler than the scheme with the same properties given by Barwick and Jackson [1].

We find a new lower bound on the randomness of a multithreshold scheme. Furthermore, by using entropies we present a new proof for the lower bound on the complexity given in [7].

Finally, in Section 5, we present a general construction of $w$-$(t, k, n)$ multithreshold scheme for general values of the parameters. In general, this is not an optimal scheme, but it is the best known construction that applies to all possible values of the parameters $w, t, k, n$.

## 2   Lower Bounds on the Complexity and Randomness

The complexity and the randomness of a scheme, defined in Section 1.2, are ratios that indicate the amount of information the trusted authority sends to users. This section is devoted to study the information rates of multithreshold schemes, namely to proof the next theorem, a result that provides bounds for the complexity and the randomness of multithreshold schemes.

**Theorem 1.** *Let $\mathcal{U} = \{1, \ldots, n\}$ be the set of users of a $w$-secure $(t, k, n)$ multithreshold scheme, such that $H(K_Q)$ is the same for every $Q \in \mathcal{J}$ and $H(S_i)$ is the same for every $i \in \mathcal{U}$. Then, we have following lower bounds on the complexity $\sigma$ and the randomness $\sigma_T$:*

$$\sigma \geq \binom{w+k-2t+1}{k-t} \qquad \sigma_T \geq \left( \binom{w+k-2t+2}{k-t+1} + (t-1)\binom{w+k-2t+1}{k-t} \right)$$

The following technical lemmas show properties of the entropy of keys in a multithreshold scheme. They will be used to prove Theorem 1.

**Lemma 1.** *Let $X$, $Y$, $Z$ be three random variables, $H(X)$ the entropy of the variable $X$ and $H(Y|Z)$ the entropy of $Y$ conditional on $Z$. If $H(Y|Z) = 0$, then $H(X|Y) \geq H(X|Z)$ and $H(Z) \geq H(Y)$.*

**Lemma 2.** *Let* $\mathcal{U} = \{1, \ldots, n\}$ *be the set of participants of a w-secure* $(t, k, n)$ *multithreshold scheme. Let* $A \subseteq \mathcal{U}' \subseteq \mathcal{U}$ *such that* $|\mathcal{U}'| = w + k - (t - 1)$ *and* $|A| = t - 1$. *Let* $\mathcal{A}$ *be the following collection of subsets:* $\mathcal{A} = \{Q \in \mathcal{J} \mid A \subseteq Q \subseteq \mathcal{U}'\} = \{Q_1, \ldots, Q_\mu\}$, *where* $\mu = \binom{w+k-2(t-1)}{k-(t-1)}$.

*Then,* $H(K_{Q_i} \mid K_{Q_1}, \ldots, K_{Q_{i-1}}, K_{Q_{i+1}}, \ldots K_{Q_\mu}) = H(K_{Q_i})$ *for every* $Q_i \in \mathcal{A}$. *That is, the random variables* $K_{Q_1}, \ldots, K_{Q_\mu}$ *are independent.*

*Proof.* Let $Q_i \in \mathcal{A}$ and $C = (\mathcal{U}' \smallsetminus Q_i) \cup A$. Observe that $C$ consists of $w$ users. Since $C \cap Q_i = A$, then $|C \cap Q_i| = t - 1$, and therefore $C$ is an unauthorized subset related to the key associated with $Q_i$. That is, $H(K_{Q_i} \mid S_C) = H(K_{Q_i})$.

On the other hand, $C \cap Q_j \supsetneq A$ for every $j \neq i$, hence $|C \cap Q_j| \geq t$. Then, $C$ is an authorized subset related to the key associated with $Q_j$, that is $H(K_{Q_j} \mid S_C) = 0$, for every $j \neq i$. Moreover, $H(K_{Q_1}, \ldots, K_{Q_{i-1}}, K_{Q_{i+1}}, \ldots, K_{Q_\mu} \mid S_C) = 0$.

Now, using Lemma 1, it follows that $H(K_{Q_i} \mid K_{Q_1}, \ldots, K_{Q_{i-1}}, K_{Q_{i+1}}, \ldots, K_{Q_\mu}) \geq H(K_{Q_i} \mid S_C)$. Consequently, $H(K_{Q_i} \mid K_{Q_1}, \ldots, K_{Q_{i-1}}, K_{Q_{i+1}}, \ldots, K_{Q_\mu}) = H(K_{Q_i})$, and therefore the random variables associated with the keys of subsets in $\mathcal{A}$ are independent.

**Lemma 3.** *Let* $\mathcal{U} = \{1, \ldots, n\}$ *be the set of participants of a w-secure* $(t, k, n)$ *multithreshold scheme. Let* $B \subseteq \mathcal{U}' \subseteq \mathcal{U}$ *such that* $|\mathcal{U}'| = w + k - (t - 1)$ *and* $|B| = t$. *Consider the following collection of subsets of* $\mathcal{U}$: $\mathcal{B} = \{Q \in \mathcal{J} \mid B \subseteq Q \subseteq \mathcal{U}'\} = \{Q_1, \ldots, Q_\nu\}$, *where* $\nu = \binom{w+k-(t-1)-t}{k-t} = \binom{w+k-2t+1}{k-t}$.

*Then,* $H(K_{Q_i} \mid K_{Q_1} \ldots K_{Q_{i-1}}, K_{Q_{i+1}}, \ldots, K_{Q_\nu}) = H(K_{Q_i})$ *for every* $Q_i \in \mathcal{B}$, *that is, the random variables* $K_{Q_1}, \ldots, K_{Q_\nu}$ *are independent.*

*Proof.* Let $A$ be a subset of $B$ such with $t - 1$ elements. If we define $\mathcal{A}$ as in Lemma 2, observe that $\mathcal{B} \subseteq \mathcal{A}$, thus the random variables $K_{Q_1}, \ldots, K_{Q_\nu}$ are independent.

**Lemma 4.** *Under the conditions and notation of the preceding two lemmas,* $H(K_\mathcal{B} \mid S_A) = H(K_\mathcal{B})$ *and* $H(K_A \mid S_B) = H(K_{A \smallsetminus B})$, *for any subset* $A \subseteq B$.

*Proof.* Suppose, without loss of generality, that $A = \{1, \ldots, t - 1\}$ and $B = \{1, \ldots, t\}$. For every $Q_i \in \mathcal{A}$ we define $C_i = (\mathcal{U}' \smallsetminus Q_i) \cup A$. Observe that, as seen during the proof of Lemma 2,

$$H(K_{Q_i} \mid S_{C_i}) = H(K_{Q_i}) \text{ and } H(K_{Q_j} \mid S_{C_i}) = 0 \text{ for every } j \neq i.$$

On the other hand, due to entropy properties,

$$H(K_\mathcal{B} \mid S_A) = \sum_{i=1}^{\nu} H(K_{Q_i} \mid S_A K_{Q_1} \ldots K_{Q_{i-1}}).$$

Since $A \subseteq C_i$, it follows that $H(K_{Q_i} \mid S_A K_{Q_1} \ldots K_{Q_{i-1}}) \geq H(K_{Q_i} \mid S_{C_i} K_{Q_1} \ldots K_{Q_{i-1}})$. Furthermore, since $H(K_{Q_1} \ldots K_{Q_{i-1}} \mid S_{C_i}) = 0$, it follows that

$$H(K_{Q_i} \mid S_{C_i} K_{Q_1} \ldots K_{Q_{i-1}}) = H(K_{Q_i} \mid S_{C_i}) = H(K_{Q_i}).$$

Hence,

$$H(K_{\mathcal{B}}) \geq H(K_{\mathcal{B}} \mid S_A) \geq \sum_{i=1}^{\nu} H(K_{Q_i}) = H(K_{\mathcal{B}}),$$

which leads to $H(K_{\mathcal{B}} \mid S_A) = H(K_{\mathcal{B}})$.

Using again entropy properties, we obtain

$$H(K_{\mathcal{A}} \mid S_B) = \sum_{i=1}^{\mu} H(K_{Q_i} \mid S_B K_{Q_1} \dots K_{Q_{i-1}}).$$

For every $Q_i$ in $\mathcal{B}$ we have $H(K_{Q_i} \mid S_B K_{Q_1} \dots K_{Q_{i-1}}) = 0$, because $|Q_i \cap B| = t$. For every $Q_i$ in $\mathcal{A} \setminus \mathcal{B}$, we have that $B \subseteq C_i$, thus

$$H(K_{Q_i} \mid S_B K_{Q_1} \dots K_{Q_{i-1}}) \geq H(K_{Q_i} \mid S_{C_i} K_{Q_1} \dots K_{Q_{i-1}}) =$$

$$= H(K_{Q_i} \mid S_{C_i}) = H(K_{Q_i}).$$

Hence,

$$H(K_{\mathcal{A}} \mid S_B) = \sum_{i \in \mathcal{A} \setminus \mathcal{B}} H(K_{Q_i} \mid S_B K_{Q_1} \dots K_{Q_{i-1}}) = \sum_{i \in \mathcal{A} \setminus \mathcal{B}} H(K_{Q_i}) = H(K_{\mathcal{A} \setminus \mathcal{B}}).$$

Finally, we provide the proof of Theorem 1.

*Proof.* First, we prove the upper bound on $\sigma$. Let $B = \{1, \dots, t\}$, $A = \{1, \dots, t-1\}$ and $\mathcal{U}' \subset \mathcal{U}$ such that $B \subset \mathcal{U}'$ and $|\mathcal{U}'| = w + k - t + 1$, and consider the collection of subsets $\mathcal{B} = \{Q \in \mathcal{J} \mid B \subseteq Q \subset \mathcal{U}'\} = \{Q_1, \dots, Q_\nu\}$, where $\nu = \binom{w+k-(t-1)-t}{k-t}$.

Lemma 3 ensures that the variables $K_{Q_1}, \dots, K_{Q_\nu}$ are independent, thus $H(K_{\mathcal{B}}) = \nu H(K)$. Now, for every $Q \in \mathcal{B}$ we know $|B \cap Q| = t$ and $|A \cap Q| = t - 1$, hence $H(K_Q \mid S_t S_A) = 0$ and $H(K_Q \mid S_A) = H(K_Q)$. Consequently, $H(K_{\mathcal{B}} \mid S_t S_A) = 0$ and, by Lemma 4, $H(K_{\mathcal{B}} \mid S_A) = H(K_{\mathcal{B}})$. Lemma 1 leads to $H(S) = H(S_t) \geq H(K_{\mathcal{B}}) = \nu H(K)$, and the desired upper bound on $\sigma$ is obtained.

Let $\mathcal{A}$ be the structure associated with $A$, defined in Lemma 2. In order to find an upper bound on $\sigma_T$ we use $H(S_{\mathcal{U}}) = H(S_B) + H(S_{\mathcal{U}} \mid S_B)$. First, we are going to bound $H(S_B)$. Since $H(S_B) = \sum_{i=1}^{t} H(S_i \mid S_1 \dots S_{i-1})$, $H(K_{\mathcal{B}} \mid S_t S_A) = 0$ and $H(K_{\mathcal{B}} \mid S_A) = H(K_{\mathcal{B}})$, then it follows that $H(S_t \mid S_A) \geq H(K_{\mathcal{B}})$. Now, since $H(S_i) = H(S)$ for every $i$, then $H(S_i \mid S_1, \dots S_{i-1}) \geq H(S_t \mid S_A)$, and therefore $H(S_B) \geq t \cdot \nu H(K)$.

Now, we are going to bound $H(S_{\mathcal{U}} \mid S_B)$. Since $H(K_{\mathcal{A}} \mid S_{\mathcal{U}}) = 0$, we have $H(S_{\mathcal{U}} \mid S_B) \geq H(K_{\mathcal{A}} \mid S_B)$. Applying Lemma 4, it follows that $H(K_{\mathcal{A}} \mid S_B) = (\mu - \nu)H(K)$, thus $H(S_{\mathcal{U}}) \geq (\mu + (t-1)\nu)H(K)$, and the desired upper bound on $\sigma_T$ is obtained.

## 3   Linear Multisecret Sharing Schemes

A useful method to define secret sharing schemes is to consider some linear maps to define the share of each user and the keys in the scheme. Using this kind of maps, it will be easy to check whether a coalition can obtain a key through a linear combination of their shares. Furthermore, the use of linear techniques can simplify the construction of the scheme.

In linear multisecret schemes, there are some vector spaces over a finite field $\mathbb{K}$ called $E$, $E_i$ and $V_P$ for every $i \in \mathcal{U}$ and $P \in \mathcal{J}$. There is a surjective linear map $\phi_i : E \to E_i$ for every $i \in \mathcal{U}$ that generates the secret information (the share) of each user, and there is a surjective linear map $\pi_P : E \to V_P$ for every $P \in \mathcal{J}$. Choosing $x \in E$ uniformly at random, $\pi_P(x)$ is $P$'s secret and $\phi_i(x)$ is the secret information of the user $i$.

Next result shows a property of linear maps widely used within the security proofs for most of the schemes presented in this paper. This result is Lemma 3.1 in [9].

**Lemma 5.** *Let $E, E_0$ and $E_1$ be vector spaces over a finite field $\mathbb{K}$. Consider two linear mappings, $\phi_0 : E \to E_0$ and $\phi_1 : E \to E_1$, where $\phi_0$ and $\phi_1$ are surjective. Suppose that a vector $x \in E$ is chosen uniformly at random. Then,*

1. *the value of $x_0 = \phi_0(x)$ can be uniquely determined from $x_1 = \phi_1(x)$ if and only if $\ker \phi_1 \subset \ker \phi_0$.*
2. *the value of $x_1$ provides no information about the value of $x_0$ if and only if $\ker \phi_1 + \ker \phi_0 = E$.*

A Key Predistribution Scheme (KPS) is a method by which a trusted authority distributes secret information among a set of users in such a way that every user belonging to a set in a family of privileged subsets is able to compute a common key associated with that set. This kind of schemes can be seen as multisecret schemes where the minimal authorized sets are single users.

C. Padró, I. Gracia, S. Martín and P. Morillo present in [9] some KPSs defined trough linear maps, that they call Linear KPS (LKPS). That paper presents a method to generate schemes that base their security on linear algebra properties. Next theorem is a generalization of Theorem 3.2 in [9] for multisecret sharing schemes with a given specification structure $\Gamma$.

**Theorem 2.** *Let $\Gamma$ be a specification structure on the set of $n$ users $\mathcal{U} = \{1, \ldots, n\}$. Let $E$ and $E_i \neq \{0\}$, for every $i \in \{0, 1, \ldots, n\}$, be vector spaces over a finite field $\mathbb{K}$. Suppose there exist a surjective linear mapping $\phi_i : E \to E_i$ for every user $i \in \mathcal{U}$ and a surjective linear mapping $\pi_P : E \to E_0$ for every subset $P \in \mathcal{J}$ satisfying:*

1. *$\bigcap_{i \in A} \ker \phi_i \subset \ker \pi_P$ for any $A \in \Gamma_P$.*
2. *$\bigcap_{j \in F} \ker \phi_j + \ker \pi_P = E$ for any $F \in \Delta_P$.*

*Then there exists a linear multisecret sharing scheme with specification structure $\Gamma$ whose complexity and randomness are:*

$$\sigma = \frac{\max_{i \in \mathcal{U}} \dim E_i}{\dim E_0} \qquad \sigma_T = \frac{\dim E}{\dim E_0}$$

*Proof.* The theorem is proven analogously to theorem 3.2 in [9]. We construct a scheme where we assume that $E$, $E_i$, $E_0$, $\pi_P$ and $\phi_i$ are publicly known, for all $i \in \mathcal{U}$ and $P \in \mathcal{J}$. Given an element $x \in E$ randomly chosen, the secret of $P \in \mathcal{J}$ is $\pi_P(x)$ and the share of user $i$ is $\phi_i(x)$.

Let $A = \{i_1, \ldots, i_r\}$ be a subset of users. We consider $\phi_A$ a map from $E$ to $E_{i_1} \times \cdots \times E_{i_r}$ defined as $\phi_A = \phi_{i_1} \times \ldots \times \phi_{i_r}$. Observe that $\phi_A(x)$ is the secret information known by the users of $A$ and, as $\phi_i$ is surjective for all $i \in \mathcal{U}$, $\phi_A$ is surjective for all $A \subset \mathcal{U}$.

Let $\Gamma_P$ and $\Delta_P$ be the collection of authorized and unauthorized subsets for a given $P$ in $\mathcal{J}$. If $A$ is in $\Gamma_P$, Lemma 5 says that $\pi_P(x)$ can be obtained from $\phi_A(x)$ if and only if $\ker \phi_A \subset \ker \pi_P$. But $\ker \phi_A = \bigcap_{i \in A} \ker \phi_i$, so by hypothesis this property holds. But if $F \in \Delta_P$, by hypothesis $\bigcap_{i \in F} \ker \phi_i + \ker \pi_P = E$, so it implies that $\ker \phi_F + \ker \pi_P = E$. By Lemma 5, users in $F$ cannot obtain any information about $\pi_P$, and the proof is concluded.

Observe that condition 1 in Theorem 2 guarantees $H(K_P \mid S_A) = 0$, so subsets in $\Gamma_P$ can calculate $P$'s secret. Besides, if the scheme satisfies condition 2, then we can ensure that $H(K_P \mid S_F) = H(K_P)$ for all subset in $\Delta_P$, so the scheme is perfect.

We will use Theorem 2 to construct our schemes, so we will use the same kind of operators and notation used in [9]. For all schemes presented in this paper, the keys are in $\mathbb{K}$, $E_0 = V_P = \mathbb{K}$ for all $P \in \mathcal{J}$.

# 4   An Optimal $w$-Secure $(2, 3, n)$ Multithreshold Scheme

In this section we present an optimal $w$-secure $(2, 3, n)$ multithreshold scheme constructed using linear techniques, according to the model discussed in section 3. In section 1.2 we have seen that $w$ must be an integer between 0 and $n - k + t - 1$, so in our case $0 \leq w \leq n - 2$. When $w = n - 2$, this scheme is complete and allows a simpler model, which is presented in subsection 4.3.

In a $w$-secure $(2, 3, n)$ multithreshold scheme every subset of three users has a common secret, that will only be revealed if at least two of them share their secret information. If a subset $P \in \mathcal{J}$ has a secret, coalitions of $w$ users or less will have zero knowledge about $P$'s secret if such coalitions have at most one user in $P$. Considering the notation in 1.2, our case leads to:

- $|\mathcal{U}| = n$
- $\mathcal{J} = \{P \subseteq \mathcal{U} : |P| = 3\}$
- For all $P \in \mathcal{J}$,
    - $\Gamma_P = \{A \subseteq \mathcal{U} : |A \cap P| \geq 2\}$
    - $\Delta_P = \{B \subseteq \mathcal{U} : |B| \leq w, |B \cap P| \leq 1\}$

## 4.1   Optimal $w$-Secure $(2, 3, n)$ Multithreshold Scheme Construction

To design a linear multithreshold scheme, some vector spaces $E, E_0, E_1, \ldots, E_n$, defined over a finite field $\mathbb{K}$ are required. There is no restriction on the characteristic of $\mathbb{K}$ but, as we will see in subsection 4.2, the field must be large enough.

The understanding of the scheme requires familiarity with linear algebra concepts such as dual vector space and tensor product. The appendix provides some notions on these subjects.

The trusted authority creates an identifier $x_i \in \mathbb{K} - \{0\}$ for each user $i \in \mathcal{U}$, that is public; let $X = \{x_i\}_{i \in \mathcal{U}}$. Then, the trusted authority privately sends to each user a linear map that depends on its identifier.

In the scheme presented in this section,

- $E = S_2(\mathbb{K}^w) \times (\mathbb{K}^w)^*$
- $E_i = (\mathbb{K}^w)^*$   for all $i \in \mathcal{U}$
- $E_0 = \mathbb{K}$
- For every $i \in \mathcal{U}$, the map $\phi_i : S_2(\mathbb{K}^w) \times (\mathbb{K}^w)^* \longrightarrow (\mathbb{K}^w)^*$ is defined as follows:

$$\phi_i(T, S) = T(v_i, \cdot) + \lambda_i S$$

- For every $P = \{i, j, k\} \in \mathcal{J}$, the map $\pi_P : S_2(\mathbb{K}^w) \times (\mathbb{K}^w)^* \longrightarrow \mathbb{K}$ is defined as follows:
$$\pi_P(T, S) =$$

$$= x_i \cdot \phi_i(T, S)(\lambda_k v_j - \lambda_j v_k) + x_j \cdot \phi_j(T, S)(\lambda_i v_k - \lambda_k v_i) + x_k \cdot \phi_k(T, S)(\lambda_j v_i - \lambda_i v_j)$$

where

- $\lambda_i = -x_i^w$ for all $i \in \mathcal{U}$
- $v_i = (1, x_i, x_i^2, \ldots, x_i^{w-1})$ for all $i \in \mathcal{U}$

The trusted authority chooses some $(T, S) \in S_2(\mathbb{K}^w) \times (\mathbb{K}^w)^*$ and distributes privately the linear forms $\phi_i(T, S)$ to every user in $\mathcal{U}$. This linear form is the secret information of each user. Given $P = \{i, j, k\}$ a subset in $\mathcal{J}$, if two users $i$ and $j$ share their secrets, using linearity of $S$ together with the symmetry and bilinearity of $T$, they can calculate $\pi_P(T, S)$. Namely, since for any $\{i, j, k\} \subset \mathcal{U}$ we have

$$[\phi_i(T, S)](\lambda_k v_j - \lambda_j v_k) + [\phi_j(T, S)](\lambda_i v_k - \lambda_k v_i) + [\phi_k(T, S)](\lambda_j v_i - \lambda_i v_j) = 0 \quad (1)$$

then,

$$\pi_P(T, S) = x_i \phi_i(T, S)(\lambda_k v_j - \lambda_j v_k) + x_j \phi_j(T, S)(\lambda_i v_k - \lambda_k v_i) +$$
$$+ x_k(-\phi_i(T, S)(\lambda_k v_j - \lambda_j v_k) - \phi_j(T, S)(\lambda_i v_k - \lambda_k v_i)).$$

For the sake of security in our constructions, in some cases $X$ needs to fulfill a condition. For a clearer formulation of this condition, we are going to introduce the following rational functions:

- $f(\mathbf{z}, y) = \sum_{i=1}^{w} z_i^w \cdot \prod_{j=1, j \neq i}^{w} \dfrac{y - z_j}{z_i - z_j}$,

where $y \in \mathbb{K}$, $\mathbf{z} = (z_1, \cdots, z_w) \in \mathbb{K}^w$, such that $z_i \neq z_j$ if $i \neq j$.

Observe that $f(\mathbf{z}, z_i) = z_i^w$, for every $i \in \{1, \cdots, w\}$.

• $g(\mathbf{z}, z_{w+1}, z_{w+2}, z_{w+3}) =$
$= (z_{w+1} - z_{w+2})[z_{w+3}^w f(\mathbf{z}, z_{w+1}) f(\mathbf{z}, z_{w+2}) + z_{w+1}^w z_{w+2}^w f(\mathbf{z}, z_{w+3})] +$
$+ (z_{w+2} - z_{w+3})[z_{w+1}^w f(\mathbf{z}, z_{w+2}) f(\mathbf{z}, z_{w+3}) + z_{w+2}^w z_{w+3}^w f(\mathbf{z}, z_{w+1})] +$
$+ (z_{w+3} - z_{w+1})[z_{w+2}^w f(\mathbf{z}, z_{w+3}) f(\mathbf{z}, z_{w+1}) + z_{w+3}^w z_{w+1}^w f(\mathbf{z}, z_{w+2})],$

where $z_{w+1}, z_{w+2}, z_{w+3} \in \mathbb{K}$, $\mathbf{z} = (z_1, \cdots, z_w) \in \mathbb{K}^w$, such that $z_i \neq z_j$ if $i \neq j$.

Observe that $g(x_{i_1}, \ldots, x_{i_{w+3}})$ is well defined for every $(x_{i_1}, \ldots, x_{i_{w+3}}) \in X^{w+3}$. The condition on $X$ is:

**Condition 1.** $g(x_{i_1}, \ldots, x_{i_{w+3}}) \neq 0$ for every $(x_{i_1}, \ldots, x_{i_{w+3}}) \in X^{w+3}$.

Since the least common multiple of the denominators involved in the expression of $g$ is

$$m(\mathbf{z}) = \prod_{1 \leq i < j \leq w}^{w} (z_i - z_j)^2$$

then we will require that the polynomial

$$p(\mathbf{z}, z_{w+1}, z_{w+2}, z_{w+3}) = g(\mathbf{z}, z_{w+1}, z_{w+2}, z_{w+3}) \cdot m(\mathbf{z})$$

does not vanish for every $(x_{i_1}, \ldots, x_{i_{w+3}}) \in X^{w+3}$, for $x_{i_j} \neq x_{i_k}$ for $j \neq k$, and this implies a restriction on the size of the field $\mathbb{K}$. Namely, observe that the degree of every numerator in $f$ is $2w - 1$, and so the degree of every numerator in $g$ is at most $w + 1 + 2(2w - 1) = 5w - 1$. Consequently, $\deg(p) \leq (5w - 1) + 2[w(w - 1)]$.

Due to the symmetries in the definition of $f$ and $g$, it suffices to check that $p(\mathbf{z}, z_{w+1}, z_{w+2}, z_{w+3}) \neq 0$ only for $\binom{n}{3}\binom{n-3}{w}$ points in $X^{w+3}$. Therefore, applying Schwartz's Lemma (Theorem 6 in the appendix), the restriction on the size of the field is $|\mathbb{K}| > \binom{n}{3}\binom{n-3}{w}[2(5w - 1)w(w - 1)] + 1$.

Eventually, Condition 1 must be checked only once, at the beginning of the protocol. As we will see in 4.3, this condition will not be necessary when the scheme is complete.

## 4.2 Security Proof

**Theorem 3.** *Under Condition 1, the scheme just defined is an optimal $w$-secure $(2, 3, n)$ multithreshold scheme.*

*Proof.* In order to prove that this construction defines a $w$-secure $(2, 3, n)$ multithreshold scheme we will use Theorem 2. Taking into account that the structure $\Delta_P$ is monotone decreasing and the structure $\Gamma_P$ is monotone increasing for all $P \in \mathcal{J}$, it is enough to prove the conditions in Theorem 2 for minimal subsets in $\Gamma_P$ and maximal subsets in $\Delta_P$. So we have to show that for any

$P = \{i, j, k\} \in \mathcal{J}$ and for any subset of $P$ with two elements, e.g. $\{i, j\}$, then $\ker \phi_i \cap \ker \phi_j$ is included in $\ker \pi_P$, and for any $B \in \Delta_P$, with $|B| = w$, then $E = \bigcap_{i \in B} \ker \phi_i + \ker \pi_P$.

Suppose $(T, S)$ belongs to $\ker \phi_i \cap \ker \phi_j$ for some $i, j \in B$. Then, for every $\{i, j, k\} \in \mathcal{J}$, it follows from (1) that $[\phi_k(T, S)](\lambda_j v_i - \lambda_i v_j) = 0$. Now, if we calculate $\pi_P(T, S)$ for any $(T, S) \in \ker \phi_i \cap \ker \phi_j$ we see that $\pi_P(T, S) = 0$, so the first part is proved.

Now we have to prove the second part. Since $\pi_P$ is a linear map and the image of $\pi_P$ is $\mathbb{K}$, then $\dim \ker \pi_P = \dim E - 1$. Therefore it suffices to show that, for every $B \in \Delta_P$, there exists an element belonging to $\bigcap_{i \in B} \ker \phi_i$ that does not belong to $\ker \pi_P$.

As previously mentioned, it suffices to prove the second part for maximal subsets in $\Delta_P$, namely the subsets $B \in \Delta_P$ such that $|B| = w$. Observe that, given $P \in \mathcal{J}$ from a $w$-secure $(2, 3, n)$ multithreshold scheme, $0 \le |B \cap P| \le 1$ for any $B \in \Delta_P$. Thus, given $P \in \mathcal{J}$ we will separately prove the condition for the cases $|B \cap P| = 0$ and $|B \cap P| = 1$.

First, we consider maximal subsets in $\Delta_P$ with one element in $P$. In order to simplify notation, we can assume, without loss of generality, that $P = \{1, 2, 3\}$ and $B = \{3, 4, \ldots, w + 2\}$. Clearly, $\{v_3, v_4, \ldots, v_{w+2}\}$ is a basis of $\mathbb{K}^w$, since $x_i \ne x_j$ for $i \ne j$.

Consider the operator $S \in (\mathbb{K}^w)^*$ such that $S(v_i) = -\lambda_i$ for all $i \in B$ and the operator $T = S \otimes S$. Observe that $T$ is a bilinear symmetrical operator, $T \in S_2(\mathbb{K}^w)$ (see Appendix A for more details). For any $i \in B$, $\phi_i(T, S) = (S \otimes S)(v_i, \cdot) + \lambda_i S = (S(v_i) + \lambda_i)S = 0$, thus $(T, S)$ belongs to $\bigcap_{i \in B} \ker \phi_i$. In particular, since $\{3\} = P \cap B$, the chosen operator satisfies $\phi_3(T, S) = 0$ and $S(v_3) = -\lambda_3$. Thus, it is straightforward to check that $\pi_P(T, S) = (x_1 - x_2)\lambda_3(S(v_1) + \lambda_1)(S(v_2) + \lambda_2)$.

Now, we check that $\pi_P(T, S) \ne 0$ showing that each factor is nonzero. By definition of $x_i$ and $\lambda_i$, $(x_1 - x_2)$ and $\lambda_3$ are different from zero. Let $p(x)$ be the polynomial of degree $w - 1$ defined by $p(x) = S(1, x, \ldots, x^{w-1})$. Observe that $p(x_i) = x_i^w$ for all $i \in B = \{3, \ldots, w + 2\}$. Suppose that $p(x)$ satisfies $p(x_2) = x_2^w$ (analogously for $p(x_1) = x_1^w$). Then $x^w - p(x)$ is a polynomial of degree $w$ with $w + 1$ zeroes, which is a contradiction. Therefore, the result is proved for the maximal subsets in $\Delta_P$ having one element in common with $P$.

Now suppose $B$ and $P$ are disjoint and, without loss of generality, that $P = \{1, 2, 3\}$ and $B = \{4, \ldots, w + 3\}$. Let $S$ be the operator defined by $S(v_i) = -\lambda_i$ for all $i \in B$ and $T = S \otimes S \in S_2(\mathbb{K}^w)$. Analogously to the other case, $(T, S)$ belongs to $\bigcap_{i \in B} \ker \phi_i$.

Let $p(x)$ be a polynomial defined, as above, by $p(x) = S(1, x, \ldots, x^{w-1})$. Since $p(x_i) = x_i^w$ for all $i \in B = \{4, \ldots, w + 3\}$, by Lagrange interpolation, the expression of this polynomial is

$$p(x) = \sum_{i=4}^{w+3} x_i^w \cdot \prod_{j=4, j \ne i}^{w+3} \frac{x - x_j}{x_i - x_j} = f(x, x_4, \ldots, x_{w+3})$$

If we express $\pi_P(T, S)$ replacing $S(v_i)$ by $p(x_i)$, we have

$$
\begin{aligned}
\pi_P(T, S) = & (x_1 - x_2)(\lambda_3 p(x_1)p(x_2) - \lambda_1\lambda_2 p(x_3)) \\
& +(x_2 - x_3)(\lambda_1 p(x_2)p(x_3) - \lambda_2\lambda_3 p(x_1)) \\
& +(x_3 - x_1)(\lambda_2 p(x_3)p(x_1) - \lambda_1\lambda_3 p(x_2)) = g(x_1, \ldots, x_{w+3})
\end{aligned}
$$

Taking into account condition 1, we can conclude that $\pi_P(T, S) \neq 0$. Hence, for all $B \in \Delta_P$, $\bigcap_{i \in B} \ker \phi_i + \ker \pi_P = E$, and the security proof is completed.

This scheme is optimal, so complexity and randomness obtained are minimum for a $w$-secure $(2, 3, n)$ multithreshold scheme.

Since $\dim(E_i) = \dim(\mathbb{K}^w)^* = w$ for all $i \in \mathcal{U}$ and $\dim E = \dim S_2(\mathbb{K}^w) + \dim(\mathbb{K}^w)^* = \binom{w+1}{2} + w$, then

$$
\sigma = w \qquad \sigma_T = \frac{w(w+1)}{2} + w
$$

According to Theorem 1, our scheme is optimal.

## 4.3   Optimal $(n - 2)$- Secure $(2, 3, n)$ Multithreshold Scheme Construction

If the above scheme is complete, then $w = n - 2$, and Condition 1 is not needed to obtain an $(n - 2)$- secure $(2, 3, n)$ multithreshold scheme. The field $\mathbb{K}$ needs only to satisfy $|\mathbb{K}| > n$.

**Theorem 4.** *The scheme defined in subsection 4.1 is an optimal $(n-2)$- secure $(2, 3, n)$ multithreshold scheme.*

*Proof.* Observe that, in a $(n - 2)$- secure $(2, 3, n)$ multithreshold scheme, given $P \in \mathcal{J}$, if $B$ is a maximal subset in $\Delta_P$, since $|B| = n - 2$ then necessarily $|B \cap P| = 1$. For this reason, in this case, Condition 1 is not needed in the proof of Theorem 3.

## 5   $w$-Secure $(t, k, n)$ Multithreshold Scheme

In this section, we will design a family of $w$-secure $(t, k, n)$ multithreshold schemes for any possible values of $w$, $t$, $k$, $n$. Namely, $1 \leq t \leq k \leq n$ and $0 \leq w \leq n - k + t - 1$, as seen in section 1.2. Unfortunately, these schemes are not optimal in general.

We also show how to design linear $w$-secure $(t, k', n)$ multithreshold schemes, for any $k'$ such that $t \leq k' < k$, from a given linear $w$-secure $(t, k, n)$ multithreshold.

Observe that for $t = 1$ this is an optimal linear KPS, and when $k = n$ and $w = t - 1$ the scheme presented is also optimal, since it is an ideal secret sharing scheme.

## 5.1  $w$-Secure $(t, k, n)$ Multithreshold Scheme Construction

Taking into account the definition of linear multithreshold schemes, we are going to define the vector spaces $E$ and $E_i$, for $i \in \{0, \ldots, n\}$, over a finite field $\mathbb{K}$. There is no restriction on the characteristic of $\mathbb{K}$, but the size of this field must be greater than $n$. Again, the understanding of the scheme requires some linear algebra concepts as dual vector space and tensor product (see Appendix A).

During the setup phase, the trusted authority chooses $X = \{x_i\}_{i \in \mathcal{U}} \subseteq \mathbb{K} \setminus \{0\}$, such that $x_i \neq x_j$ if $i \neq j$, which will be the identifiers of users in $\mathcal{U}$.

Let $m = w - t + 2$. For the scheme presented in this section,

- $E = (S_k(\mathbb{K}^m))^t = S_k(\mathbb{K}^m) \times \overset{t)}{\cdots} \times S_k(\mathbb{K}^m)$
- $E_i = S_{k-1}(\mathbb{K}^m)$    for all $i \in \mathcal{U}$
- $E_0 = \mathbb{K}$

- For every $i \in \mathcal{U}$, the map $\phi_i : (S_k(\mathbb{K}^m))^t \longrightarrow S_{k-1}(\mathbb{K}^m)$ is defined as follows:

$$\phi_i(T_1, \ldots, T_t) = \lambda_{i,1} T_1(v_i, \ldots) + \cdots + \lambda_{i,t} T_t(v_i, \ldots)$$

  where
  - $v_i = (1, x_i, x_i^2, \ldots, x_i^{m-1}) \in \mathbb{K}^m$ for all $i \in \mathcal{U}$.
  - $\lambda_{i,j} = x_i^{j-1}$ for all $i \in \mathcal{U}$, $1 \leq j \leq t$.

- For every $P = \{i_1, \ldots, i_k\} \in \mathcal{J}$, the map $\pi_P : (S_k(\mathbb{K}^m))^t \longrightarrow \mathbb{K}$ is defined as follows:

$$\pi_P(T_1, \ldots, T_t) = T_1(v_{i_1}, \ldots, v_{i_k})$$

Let $P$ be a set in $\mathcal{J}$, and $A$ a subset of $t$ users in $P$. Without loss of generality, we can suppose that $P = \{1, \ldots, k\}$ and $A = \{1, \ldots, t\}$. Since $T_j$ is symmetrical, $T_j(v_i, v_1, \ldots, v_{i-1}, v_{i+1}, \ldots, v_k) = T_j(v_1, \ldots, v_k)$, then user $i$ can calculate

$$s_{i,P} = \lambda_{i,1} T_1(v_1, \ldots, v_k) + \cdots + \lambda_{i,t} T_t(v_1, \ldots, v_k)$$

By sharing the values $s_{i,P}$, for $i = 1, \ldots, t$, the users in $A$ can solve the linear system

$$\begin{pmatrix} 1 & x_1 & \cdots & x_1^{t-1} \\ \vdots & \vdots & \ddots & \vdots \\ 1 & x_t & \cdots & x_t^{t-1} \end{pmatrix} \begin{pmatrix} T_1(v_1, \ldots, v_k) \\ \vdots \\ T_t(v_1, \ldots, v_k) \end{pmatrix} = \begin{pmatrix} s_{1,P} \\ \vdots \\ s_{t,P} \end{pmatrix}$$

and they obtain the secret $T_1(v_1, \ldots, v_k)$.

The complexity and randomness of this scheme are:

$$\sigma = \binom{w+k-t}{k-1} \qquad \sigma_T = \frac{1}{t} \cdot \binom{w+k-t+1}{k}$$

Now we prove the validity of the scheme.

**Theorem 5.** *The scheme above defined is a $w$-secure $(t, k, n)$ multithreshold scheme.*

*Proof.* We follow the same steps as in the proof of Theorem 3. That is, it suffices to show that for any $P \in \mathcal{J}$, then every $A \subseteq P$ such that $|A| = t$ satisfies $\bigcap_{i \in A} \ker \phi_i \subseteq \ker \pi_P$, and every $B \in \Delta_P$ such that $|B| = w$, satisfies $\bigcap_{i \in B} \ker \phi_i + \ker \pi_P = E$.

Let $P = \{1, \ldots, k\} \in \mathcal{J}$ and $A = \{1, \ldots, t\} \subset P$. If we take $(T_1, \ldots, T_t)$ in $\bigcap_{i=1}^{t} \ker \phi_i$, then $\lambda_{i,1} T_1(v_i, \ldots) + \cdots + \lambda_{i,t} T_t(v_i, \ldots) = 0 \in S_{k-1}(\mathbb{K}^m)$ for every $i \in A$, and consequently $\lambda_{i,1} T_1(v_1, \ldots, v_k) + \cdots + \lambda_{i,t} T_t(v_1, \ldots, v_k) = 0$ for every $i \in A$.

Since $\lambda_{i,j} = x_i^{j-1}$, the above equations can be expressed as follows:

$$
\begin{pmatrix}
1 & x_1 & \cdots & x_1^{t-1} \\
\vdots & \vdots & \ddots & \vdots \\
1 & x_t & \cdots & x_t^{t-1}
\end{pmatrix}
\begin{pmatrix}
T_1(v_1, \ldots, v_k) \\
\vdots \\
T_t(v_1, \ldots, v_k)
\end{pmatrix}
=
\begin{pmatrix}
0 \\
\vdots \\
0
\end{pmatrix}
$$

Since $\left( x_i^{j-1} \right)_{i,j}$ is an invertible matrix, then $T_i(v_1, \ldots, v_k) = 0$, for every $i = 1, \ldots, t$. In particular, $T_1(v_1, \ldots, v_k) = 0$, and so $(T_1, \ldots, T_t) \in \ker \pi_P$.

Since $\pi_P$ is a non-zero linear form, then $\dim \ker \pi_P = \dim E - \dim \mathrm{Im}(\pi_P) = \dim E - 1$. Thus, to prove that for any $B \in \Delta_P$ we have $\bigcap_{i \in B} \ker \phi_i + \ker \pi_P = E$, it suffices to show that there exists an element belonging to $\bigcap_{i \in B} \ker \phi_i$ that does not belong to $\ker \pi_P$.

Let $B$ a maximal subset in $\Delta_P$, $F \subseteq B \setminus P$ such that $|F| = w - t + 1 = m - 1$, and $G$ the vector subspace of $\mathbb{K}^m$ with dimension $m - 1$ spanned by $\langle v_i \rangle_{i \in F}$. Observe that, if $i \notin F$, then $v_i \notin G$. Let $\{e_1, \ldots, e_{m-1}\}$ be an orthogonal basis of $G$. Then, there exists a vector $e_m \in \mathbb{K}^m$ such that $\{e_1, \ldots, e_m\}$ is an orthogonal basis of $\mathbb{K}^m$. Let $(\mathbb{K}^m)^*$ be the dual space of $\mathbb{K}^m$ and $\{e^1, \ldots, e^m\}$ its dual basis. Now, consider the symmetric operator $\widehat{T} = e^m \otimes \overset{k)}{\cdots} \otimes e^m \in S_k(\mathbb{K}^m)$. It is straightforward to check that $\widehat{T}(v_i, \ldots) = 0$ for every $i \in F$, and $\widehat{T}(v_1, \ldots, v_k) \neq 0$, for $P = \{1, \ldots, k\}$.

Let $T = (\mu_1 \widehat{T}, \ldots, \mu_t \widehat{T}) \in (S_k(\mathbb{K}^m))^t$. We want to determine the coefficients $\mu_1, \ldots, \mu_t \in \mathbb{K}$ such that $T \in \bigcap_{i \in B} \ker \phi_i$, but $T \notin \ker \pi_P$. By definition of $\widehat{T}$, $\phi_i(T) = 0$ for every $i \in F$. On the other hand, $\phi_i(T) = \phi_i(\mu_1 \widehat{T}, \ldots, \mu_t \widehat{T}) = (\lambda_{i,1}\mu_1 + \cdots + \lambda_{i,t}\mu_t) \widehat{T}(v_i, \ldots)$, for every $i \in B \setminus F$. The homogeneous $(t-1) \times t$ linear system $\lambda_{i,1}\mu_1 + \cdots + \lambda_{i,t}\mu_t = 0$, where $i \in B \setminus F$ has non-trivial solution, and $\mu_i \neq 0$ for every $i \in B$ (if any $\mu_i$ were 0, then the resulting homogeneous $(t-1) \times (t-1)$ linear system would have only the trivial solution, $\mu_j = 0$ for every $j$).

Hence, we have found an operator $T$ in $\bigcap_{i \in B} \ker \phi_i$ such that $\pi_P(T) = \mu_1 \widehat{T}(v_1, \ldots, v_k)$ is different from zero, so $T$ does not belong to $\ker \pi_P$. Therefore, the proof is completed.

## 5.2  A Family of $w$-Secure $(t, k', n)$ Multithreshold Schemes, from a Given $w$-Secure $(t, k, n)$ Multithreshold Scheme

As a final observation, we show how to construct, from a given $w$-secure $(t, k, n)$ multithreshold scheme, a $w$-secure $(t, k', n)$ multithreshold scheme for any $k'$ satisfying $t \leq k' < k$.

The new scheme is like the one in subsection 5.1, except for the following differences:

- The collection of subsets of users that have a key is $\mathcal{J}' = \{P' \subseteq \mathcal{U} : |P'| = k'\}$.
- To implement this scheme the set of users must be ordered, and this order must be known by every user.
- For every ordered set $P' = \{i_1, \ldots, i_{k'}\} \in \mathcal{J}'$, the map $\pi_P : (S_k(\mathbb{K}^m))^t \longrightarrow \mathbb{K}$ is defined as follows:

$$\pi_{P'}(T_1, \ldots, T_t) = T_1(v_{i_1}, \ldots, v_{i_{k'-1}}, v_{i_{k'}}, \ldots, v_{i_{k'}})$$

Let $P'$ be a set in $\mathcal{J}'$, and $A$ a subset of $t$ users in $P'$. Without loss of generality, we can suppose that $P' = \{1, \ldots, k'\}$ and $A = \{1, \ldots, t\}$. Since $T_j$ is symmetrical, then user $i$ can calculate

$$s_{i,P'} = \lambda_{i,1} T_1(v_1, \ldots, v_{k'-1}, v_{k'}, \ldots, v_{k'}) + \cdots + \lambda_{i,t} T_t(v_1, \ldots, v_{k'-1}, v_{k'}, \ldots, v_{k'})$$

Users from $A$ can share $s_{i,P'}$, $i = 1, \ldots, t$, and consequently they obtain the secret $T_1(v_1, \ldots, v_{k'-1}, v_{k'}, \ldots, v_{k'})$ associated with $P'$, by solving the following linear system:

$$\begin{pmatrix} 1 & x_1 & \cdots & x_1^{t-1} \\ \vdots & \vdots & \ddots & \vdots \\ 1 & x_t & \cdots & x_t^{t-1} \end{pmatrix} \begin{pmatrix} T_1(v_1, \ldots, v_{k'-1}, v_{k'}, \ldots, v_{k'}) \\ \vdots \\ T_t(v_1, \ldots, v_{k'-1}, v_{k'}, \ldots, v_{k'}) \end{pmatrix} = \begin{pmatrix} s_{1,P'} \\ \vdots \\ s_{t,P'} \end{pmatrix}$$

# References

1. Barwick, S.G., Jackson, W.-A.: An Optimal Multisecret Threshold Scheme Construction. Designs, Codes and Cryptography 37, 367–389 (2005)
2. Blakley, G.R.: Safeguarding cryptographic keys. In: AFIPS Conference Proceedings, vol. 48, pp. 313–317 (1979)
3. Blundo, C., DeSantis, A., Herzberg, A., Kutten, S., Vaccaro, U., Yung, M.: Perfectly secure key distribution for dynamic conferences. In: Brickell, E.F. (ed.) CRYPTO 1992. LNCS, vol. 740, pp. 471–486. Springer, Heidelberg (1993)
4. Blundo, C., D'Arco, P., Daza, V., Padró, C.: Bounds and constructions for unconditionally secure distributed key distribution schemes for general access structures. Theoretical Computer Science 320, 269–291 (2004)
5. Brickell, E.F.: Some ideal secret sharing schemes. J. Combin. Math. and Combin. Comput. 9, 105–113 (1989)

6. Cover, T.M., Thomas, J.A.: Elements of Information Theory. John Wiley & Sons, Chichester (1991)
7. Jackson, W.-A., Martin, K.M., O'Keefe, C.M.: Multisecret threshold schemes. In: Stinson, D.R. (ed.) CRYPTO 1993. LNCS, vol. 773, pp. 126–135. Springer, Heidelberg (1994)
8. Jackson, W.-A., Martin, K.M., O'Keefe, C.M.: A Construction for Multisecret Threshold Schemes. Designs Codes Cryptography 9, 287–303 (1996)
9. Padró, C., Gracia, I., Martín Molleví, S., Morillo, P.: Linear Key Predistribution Schemes. Designs, Codes and Cryptography 25, 281–298 (2002)
10. Shamir, A.: How to share a secret. Commun. of the ACM 22, 612–613 (1979)
11. Simmons, G.J.: How to (Really) Share a Secret. In: Goldwasser, S. (ed.) CRYPTO 1988. LNCS, vol. 403, pp. 390–448. Springer, Heidelberg (1990)
12. Stinson, D.R.: On some methods for unconditionally secure key distribution and broadcast encryption. Designs, Codes and Cryptography 12, 215–243 (1997)

# A  Appendix

For the sake of completeness, this appendix contains some additional definitions and results. Since the schemes presented in this paper are based on linear maps and multilinear forms, we present here a brief introduction to the notions of dual space and multilinear forms over a vector space.

Given a vector space $E$ over a field $\mathbb{K}$, we define the *dual space* $E^*$ as the set of linear applications from $E$ to $\mathbb{K}$. The spaces $E$ and $E^*$ have the same dimension.

If $\{e_1, \ldots, e_n\}$ is a basis of $E$, then the *dual basis* $\{e^1, \ldots, e^n\}$ of $E^*$ is defined as follows:

$$e^i(e_j) = \begin{cases} 1 & \text{if } i = j \\ 0 & \text{otherwise} \end{cases}$$

Let $v = \sum_{i=1}^{n} \lambda_i e_i \in E$ and $w = \sum_{j=1}^{n} \mu_j e^j \in E^*$, then

$$w(v) = \sum_{j=1}^{n} \mu_j e^j \left( \sum_{i=1}^{n} \lambda_i e_i \right) = \sum_{i=1}^{n} \lambda_i \mu_i$$

Let $F$ be a subspace of $E$, then the *orthogonal subspace* of $F$ is the following subspace of $E^*$:

$$F^{\perp} = \{w \in E^* : w(v) = 0 \text{ for every } v \in F\}$$

A *multilinear form* in $E^n$ is a map from $E^n$ to $\mathbb{K}$ that is separately linear in each variable. If $w$ is a multilinear form in $E^n$, then $w = (w_1, \ldots, w_n) \in (E^*)^n$, and for every $v = (v_1, \ldots, v_n) \in E^n$ we have

$$\begin{aligned} w : E^n &\to \mathbb{K} \\ v &\mapsto w(v) = w_1(v_1) w_2(v_2) \cdots w_n(v_n) \end{aligned}$$

Multilinear forms that are invariant under permutation of its variables are called *symmetric multilinear forms*, and the subspace of symmetric multilinear forms in $E^n$ is $S_n(E)$. Observe that, given $w \in S_n(E)$, for every permutation $\sigma$ of $\{1, \ldots, n\}$ and for every $(v_1, \ldots, v_n) \in E^n$ we have:

$$w(v_1, \ldots, v_n) = w(v_{\sigma(1)}, \ldots, v_{\sigma(n)})$$

If $\dim E = m$, then $\dim S_n(E) = \binom{n+m-1}{n}$.

Finally, we provide Schwartz's Lemma.

**Theorem 6.** *(Schwartz's Lemma) Let $p \in \mathbb{K}[X_1, \ldots, X_N]$ be a nonzero polynomial on $N$ variables of degree $d < |\mathbb{K}|$. Then, there exists a point $(x_1, \ldots, x_N)$ in $\mathbb{K}^N$ such that $p(x_1, \ldots, x_N) \neq 0$.*

# Multiterminal Secrecy Generation and Tree Packing

Prakash Narayan

Dept. of Electrical and Computer Engineering
and Institute for Systems Research
University of Maryland
College Park, MD. 20742, USA

This talk addresses connections between the information theoretic notions of common randomness and multiterminal secrecy and the combinatorial notion of tree packing in a multigraph.

Consider a situation in which multiple terminals observe separate but correlated signals. In a multiterminal data compression problem, a la the classic work of Slepian and Wolf, a subset of these terminals seek to acquire the signals observed by all the terminals by means of efficiently compressed interterminal communication. This problem of generating common randomness does not involve any secrecy constraints. On the other hand, in a secret key generation problem, the same subset of terminals seek to devise "secret" common randomness or a secret key, through public communication that is observed by an eavesdropper, in such a way that the key is concealed from the eavesdropper. Such a secret key can be used for subsequent encryption. We show how these two problems are intertwined, and illustrate the connection with a simple key construction. Next, for a special "pairwise independent network" model, of relevance to wireless communication, in which every pair of terminals observe correlated signals that are independent of the signals observed by all other pairs of terminals, we show a natural connection between secrecy generation and a (separate) combinatorial problem of maximal packing of Steiner trees in an associated multigraph. Such a tree packing serves to form a groupwide secret key out of pairwise keys, which is rate-optimal when all the terminals seek to share a secret key.

This talk is based on joint works with Imre Csiszár, Sirin Nitinawarat, Chunxuan Ye, Alexander Barg and Alex Reznik.

K. Kurosawa (Ed.): ICITS 2009, LNCS 5973, p. 127, 2010.

# Information Theoretic Security Based on Bounded Observability

Jun Muramatsu, Kazuyuki Yoshimura, and Peter Davis

NTT Communication Science Laboratories, NTT Corporation
Hikaridai 2-4, Soraku-gun, Seika-cho, Kyoto 619-0237, Japan
{pure,kazuyuki,davis}@cslab.kecl.ntt.co.jp

**Abstract.** Under the condition that all users can observe a common object, each using an observation function independently chosen from the same limited set of observation functions, we show necessary and sufficient conditions for users to be able to generate secret keys by public discussion.

**Keywords:** Bounded observability, bounded storage model, information theoretic security, satellite scenario, secret key agreement by public discussion.

## 1 Introduction

As proven by Maurer [1], when two users have access to correlated random variables, it is possible for them to create a shared secret key, which is information theoretically secure, by exchanging messages over a public channel. A scenario known as the Satellite Scenario has been presented as an example of how in principle such a scheme could be implemented. In the satellite scenario, a common random signal is received by all users, but the signal received by each user is corrupted by independent noise. On the other hand, a model known as the Bounded Storage Model [2][3] has been used to show that secret key agreement is possible if the memory space of the attacker is bounded. In this model, all users have noise-free access to a huge common data source before the public discussion for secret key agreement.

In this paper, we study the problem where there is a common source as in the satellite scenario, but instead of considering limitation on user information due to noise error or bounded memory, we consider limitation on observation. We show necessary and sufficient conditions for creating secret keys in this case. Specifically, we suppose that the object of observation is an unpredictable information source, prepared by a separate legitimate entity, or by a legitimate user. Also, we suppose that there exist multiple observation functions which map states of the object to various different observation values, and each user must independently choose just one of these multiple observation functions to observe the object, before revealing his choice of function in a public discussion. Furthermore, we assume that knowledge of the whole state cannot be obtained using any single observation function, and different observation values may be

K. Kurosawa (Ed.): ICITS 2009, LNCS 5973, pp. 128–139, 2010.

obtained using different observation functions, but users observe the same result if they use the same observation function.

Intuitively, it is easy to understand that secret key agreement is impossible if a user can obtain complete knowledge of the state of the object from the observation. In the Bounded Storage Model, it was shown that secure key agreement is possible when the attacker's memory is bounded so that they cannot store all the information from the source. In this paper, we generalize this by considering limitations on the observation functions, and show necessary and sufficient conditions for creating secret keys.

We consider this scenario to be physically plausible. Imagine that some physical instrument, corresponding to an observation function, is used to observe a random physical phenomenon. It is physically plausible that knowledge of the whole physical state cannot be obtained by using any single physical observation method available to the users, but users can observe the same result if they use the same observation method. The results of this paper show that it is possible to create secret keys in this scenario.

## 2    Formal Description of Problem

In this section, we provide a formal description of the problem. We assume that two legitimate users Alice and Bob and an eavesdropper Eve can observe an object prepared by a legitimate entity. Formally, we define the following terminology.

**Definition 1.** *We call a member of a set $\mathcal{S}$ the state of an object and assume that the state of an object is decided at random according to a probability distribution $\mu_S$, where $S$ represents a random variable on $\mathcal{S}$.*

**Definition 2.** *Let $\overline{\mathcal{M}}$ be the set of all functions with the domain $\mathcal{S}$, and let $\mathcal{V}_f$ be the range of a function $f \in \overline{\mathcal{M}}$. We call a member of $\overline{\mathcal{M}}$ an observation function, and we call $f(s) \in \mathcal{V}_f$ the observed value of a state $s \in \mathcal{S}$.*

Note that an observed value $f(s)$ is determined uniquely depending on the state $s \in \mathcal{S}$ of the observed object.

Now, to specify the situation described in the introduction, we assume that the following conditions hold.

1. **Unknown State:** The state $s \in \mathcal{S}$ of an object is completely unknown before observation and can be observed only through an observation function. The probability distribution $\mu_S$ can be set only by a legitimate entity.
2. **Passive Observation:** Every user observes the same state $s \in \mathcal{S}$ and the state cannot be changed by observation.
3. **Limited Observation:** For each observation, each user independently selects *a single* observation function $f$, where the selection is restricted to a subset $\mathcal{M}$ of $\overline{\mathcal{M}}$, i.e., $\mathcal{M} \subset \overline{\mathcal{M}}$. The observation is completed before the public discussion, and the same state cannot be observed after the public discussion.

4. **Public Discussion:** Alice and Bob can use a public authenticated error-free channel, which may be monitored by Eve.

The restriction on the observation functions is the key idea behind our problem. Let us comment briefly on these assumed conditions. First, the assumption of passive observation is different from the conditions of quantum cryptography [4], where the effect of observation on the state is a key aspect of the scheme. Next, let us consider the physical meaning of a limited observation. We rely on the limit of observation technology. We could consider the fundamental physical limit of observability of quantum states, but we have excluded this with our passive observation assumption. So we assume a technological limit rather than an absolute physical limit. We assume the existence of physical phenomena that are too fast, or too large, or too noisy or too complex to be completely observed with current technology. We also note that the addition of noise during the observation is not an essential part of the scheme. Of course, in actual implementations this may affect the performance e.g. the key generation rate. Finally, we note that Alice and Bob are free to adopt an arbitrary key agreement protocol using the knowledge of the probability distribution $\mu_S$ and the set $\mathcal{M}$ of observation functions. Also, Eve is free to adopt an optimal strategy using the public knowledge of $\mu_S$, $\mathcal{M}$ and the protocol designed by Alice and Bob.

Next, we define a protocol for public discussion, which is used in Section 5, and then define the secret key capacity introduced by Maurer [1].

**Definition 3.** *Let $X$ and $Y$ be two sources available to Alice and Bob, respectively. A protocol $(C, \widehat{X}, \widehat{Y})$ for $(X^n, Y^n)$ with step $t$ is composed of a sequence of random variables $C = (C_1, \ldots, C_t)$, which represents communication between a sender and a receiver, and random variables $\widehat{X}$ and $\widehat{Y}$, which are generated by the computations of the sender and the receiver, respectively, such that*

- *When $1 \leq i \leq t$ is odd, Alice sends $C_i$ which is calculated deterministically from $X^n$ and $(C_1, \ldots, C_{t-1})$, where $(C_1, \ldots, C_{i-1})$ is a null sequence when $i = 1$.*
- *When $2 \leq i \leq t$ is even, Bob sends $C_i$ which is calculated deterministically from $Y^n$ and $(C_1, \ldots, C_{i-1})$.*
- *After the public discussion, Alice obtains $\widehat{X}$, which is calculated deterministically from $X^n$ and $(C_1, \ldots, C_t)$. Bob obtains $\widehat{Y}$, which is calculated deterministically from $Y^n$ and $(C_1, \ldots, C_t)$.*

**Definition 4.** *Let $X$, $Y$, and $Z$ be three sources available to Alice, Bob, and Eve, respectively. A secret key agreement protocol $(C, K, K')$ for $(X, Y, Z)$ with a rate $R \geq 0$ is composed of two-way communication $C^t = (C_1, \ldots, C_t)$ and computations of secret keys $K, K' \in \mathcal{K}$ such that for all $\varepsilon > 0$ and all sufficiently large $n$*

$$\frac{H(K)}{n} \geq R - \varepsilon$$
$$\Pr[K \neq K'] \leq \varepsilon$$

$$I(K; Z^n C^t) \leq \varepsilon$$
$$H(K) \geq \log |\mathcal{K}| - \varepsilon,$$

*where $| \cdot |$ denotes the cardinality of a set. The secret key capacity $\mathsf{S}(X; Y \| Z)$ of the sources is defined as the least upper bound of such $R$ for all possible key agreement protocols.*

## 3   Relationship with Maurer's Secret Key Agreement from Correlated Source Outputs

Our problem setting is motivated by the satellite scenario introduced by Maurer [1], where a satellite broadcasts a signal, and all users are allowed to access the signal through respective noisy receivers. In this setting, the satellite signal corresponds to the state of an object, and the noisy receivers correspond to the observations. When the channels between the satellite and the receivers are binary symmetric, we can let $\mathcal{S} \equiv \{0, 1\}$ and the following two deterministic maps

$$f_0(s) \equiv s$$
$$f_1(s) \equiv \bar{s}$$

are selected randomly depending on the random noise, where $\bar{s}$ denotes the reverse symbol of $s \in \{0, 1\}$. Let $F_A, F_B, G \in \{f_0, f_1\}$ be random variables that represent noise between the satellite signal and Alice, Bob, and Eve, respectively. Then the random variable corresponding to the correlated sources is represented by $(F_A(S), F_B(S), G(S))$. The possibility of a secret key agreement corresponds to the fact that $(F_A(S), F_B(S), G(S))$ has the positive secret key capacity defined above. The necessary and sufficient condition for the possibility of a secret key agreement has been clarified by [5] when $\mathcal{S}$ is binary. However, it is still an open problem for a general case. It should be noted that our setting is different from the setting in Maurer's satellite scenario because we assume that Alice, Bob, and Eve can each choose their respective observation functions *freely*. We do not discuss the case where Alice, Bob, and Eve are forced to select observation functions.

## 4   Necessary and Sufficient Conditions for Possibility of Secret Key Agreement Based on Limited Observation

In this section, we present the necessary and sufficient conditions for the possibility of a secret key agreement based on limited observation.

We describe the strategy of Alice and Bob. Alice and Bob determine a finite set $\mathcal{M}_{AB} \subset \mathcal{M}$. We can consider the set $\mathcal{M}_{AB}$ as the specification of a physical sensing device and $f \in \mathcal{M}_{AB}$ as a parameter that represents the input of this device. First, Alice and Bob choose one of the observation functions independently. Next they observe the state of an object by using their respective observation functions. Finally, they agree on a secret key by using public discussion. On the other hand, we assume that Eve can choose one of the observation functions in the superset $\mathcal{M}$ of $\mathcal{M}_{AB}$, where Eve may know the set $\mathcal{M}_{AB}$ and the secret key agreement protocol. Furthermore, we assume that all users are allowed to choose their respective observation functions independently at random. This implies that the possible strategies of Alice, Bob, and Eve can be represented by their respective probability distributions. Let $F_A, F_B \in \mathcal{M}_{AB}$ and $G \in \mathcal{M}$ be random variables corresponding to the random choice of the respective observation functions. Then the respective observation values form correlated sources $((F_A, F_A(S)), (F_B, F_B(S)), (G, G(S)))$ and the secret key capacity of these sources is described by $\mathsf{S}(F_A, F_A(S); F_B, F_B(S)\|G, G(S))$.

We consider the following two situations, which differ with respect to the identity of the legitimate entity who prepares the state of the observed object.

1. The probability distribution $\mu_S$ of the state of an object is set *a priori* by a legitimate entity other than Alice, Bob or Eve. Alice, Bob, and Eve choose observation functions $F_A$, $F_B$, and $G$, respectively, so that the random variables $\{S, F_A, F_B, G\}$ are mutually independent. Then the secret key capacity can be represented by the equilibrium point of a game (see [6])

$$\sup_{F_A, F_B} \inf_G \mathsf{S}(F_A, F_A(S); F_B, F_B(S)\|G, G(S)).$$

2. Alice sets the probability distribution $\mu_S$, including the possibility that $F_A$ is correlated with $S$. Bob, and Eve choose observation functions $F_B$ and $G$, respectively, so that the random variables $\{(S, F_A), F_B, G\}$ are mutually independent. Then the secret key capacity can be represented by the equilibrium point of a game (see [6])

$$\sup_{S, F_A, F_B} \inf_G \mathsf{S}(F_A, F_A(S); F_B, F_B(S)\|G, G(S)).$$

In the following, we assume that the observation functions are measurable. Also, for simplicity, we assume throughout the paper that $\mathcal{S}$, $\mathcal{V}_f$ ($f \in \mathcal{M}$) are discrete sets. We believe the results can be extended to continuous sets under suitable technical assumptions.

In the above two situations, the condition for the existence of the possibility of a secret key agreement is equivalent to the condition whereby the equilibrium point of the game has a positive value. We have the following theorem which provides the necessary and sufficient condition for the possibility of a secret key agreement based on bounded observability. The proof is presented in the Appendix.

**Theorem 1.** *When a probability distribution $\mu_S$ is given a priori and random variables $\{S, F_A, F_B, G\}$ are mutually independent, the following conditions are equivalent.*

*(C1) The secret key agreement is possible for Alice and Bob, that is,*

$$\sup_{F_A, F_B} \inf_G S(F_A, F_A(S); F_B, F_B(S) \| G, G(S)) > 0.$$

*(C2) The triplet $(\mu_S, \mathcal{M}_{AB}, \mathcal{M})$ satisfies*

$$\inf_{g \in \mathcal{M}} \max_{f \in \mathcal{M}_{AB}} H(f(S)|g(S)) > 0. \tag{1}$$

*(C3) For any $g \in \mathcal{M}$, there are $f \in \mathcal{M}_{AB}$ and $u, u', v \in \mathcal{V}$ such that*

$$u \neq u' \tag{2}$$
$$\mathrm{Prob}(f(S) = u, g(S) = v) > 0 \tag{3}$$
$$\mathrm{Prob}(f(S) = u', g(S) = v) > 0, \tag{4}$$

*where* Prob *denotes the probability with respect to the random variable $S$.*

*When a probability distribution $\mu_S$ is given by Alice and random variables $\{(S, F_A), F_B, G\}$ are mutually independent, the following conditions are equivalent.*

*(C'1) The secret key agreement is possible for Alice and Bob, that is,*

$$\sup_{S, F_A, F_B} \inf_G S(F_A, F_A(S); F_B, F_B(S) \| G, G(S)) > 0.$$

*(C'2) There is a probability distribution $\mu_S$ such that $(\mu_S, \mathcal{M}_{AB}, \mathcal{M})$ satisfies (1).*
*(C'3) For any $g \in \mathcal{M}$, there are $f \in \mathcal{M}_{AB}$ and $s, s' \in \mathcal{S}$ such that*

$$g(s) = g(s') \tag{5}$$
$$f(s) \neq f(s'). \tag{6}$$

*Remark 1.* In the first situation, we could also assume, as in the second situation, that Alice chooses an observation function $F_A$ correlated with $S$, and Bob and Eve choose observation functions $F_B$ and $G$, respectively, so that the random variables $\{(S, F_A), F_B, G\}$ are mutually independent. This is a more general but less realistic situation.

We note that condition (1) is equivalent to

$$\sup_{g \in \mathcal{M}} \min_{f \in \mathcal{M}_{AB}} I(f(S); g(S)) < H(f(S)). \tag{7}$$

We propose that conditions (1) and (7) can be called "bounded observability."

Let us remark on the intuitive meaning of these conditions. Condition (1) corresponds to the fact that there is no universal observation function $g \in \mathcal{M}$ that allows the determination of the observation value for all functions $f \in \mathcal{M}_{AB}$. Conditions (2)–(4) correspond to the fact that Alice and Bob can choose $f$ such that there are two or more possibilities for Eve with respect to the observation value even by the best choice of $g$. Conditions (5) and (6) correspond to the fact that Eve cannot distinguish two states $s$ and $s'$, which can be distinguished by using the observation function $f$, by using the observation function $g$. It should be noted that the existence of $s, s' \in \mathcal{S}$ satisfying (5) and (6) is equivalent to the existence of $v \in \text{Im } g$ such that

$$|f(g^{-1}(v))| \geq 2,$$

where $|\cdot|$ denotes the cardinality of a set.

From the above theorem, we have the following corollary, which is intuitively trivial.

**Corollary 1.** *If the invertible function (e.g. identity) $g : \mathcal{S} \to \mathcal{V}_g$ is included in $\mathcal{M}$, then a secret key agreement is impossible using any $\mu_S$ and $\mathcal{M}_{AB}$.*

*Proof.* For any $f \in \mathcal{M}$, we have

$$H(f(S)|g(S)) \leq H(f(S)|g^{-1}(g(S))) = H(f(S)|S) = 0.$$

This implies that

$$\inf_{g \in \mathcal{M}} \max_{f \in \mathcal{M}_{AB}} H(f(S)|g(S)) = 0$$

for any $S$ and $\mathcal{M}_{AB} \subset \mathcal{M}$. From the theorem, we have the fact that a secret key agreement is impossible by using any $\mu_S$ and $\mathcal{M}_{AB}$.   □

## 5   Advantage Distillation and Information Reconciliation Protocol

In this section, we introduce an advantage distillation and information reconciliation protocol (cf. [7]) for a secret key agreement based on bounded observability. This protocol is used to prove Theorem 1. We assume that there is a finite set $\mathcal{M}_{AB}$ satisfying (1).

1. Alice and Bob choose $f_A, f_B \in \mathcal{M}_{AB}$ independently and uniformly at random, and observe the state $S$ by using their respective observation functions. Let $F_A$ and $F_B$ be random variables corresponding to their respective choices of functions. Then Alice and Bob obtain the observed values $F_A(S)$ and $F_B(S)$, respectively.
2. After Eve obtains a value $g(S)$ using an observation function $g$, Alice and Bob exchange the information $F_A$ and $F_B$ via a public channel.
3. Alice and Bob calculate $X$ and $Y$, respectively, defined as

$$X \equiv \begin{cases} F_A(S), & \text{if } F_A = F_B \\ \phi, & \text{if } F_A \neq F_B \end{cases}$$

$$Y \equiv \begin{cases} F_B(S), & \text{if } F_B = F_A \\ \phi, & \text{if } F_B \neq F_A, \end{cases}$$

where $\phi$ denotes the erasure symbol.

It should be noted that $X = Y$ holds and the secret key generation rate is given by

$$
\begin{aligned}
&I(X;Y) - I(X; F_A, F_B, G, G(S)) \\
&= H(X|F_A, F_B, G, G(S)) \\
&= \mathrm{Prob}(F_A = F_B) H(F_A(S)|F_A, G, G(S)) + \mathrm{Prob}(F_A \neq F_B) \cdot 0 \\
&= \frac{H(F_A(S)|F_A, G, G(S))}{|\mathcal{M}_{AB}|}.
\end{aligned}
$$

## 6  Bounded Storage Model

In this section, we investigate the bounded storage model introduced in [2][3] from the viewpoint of bounded observability. Let $n$ be a sufficiently large number and let $\mathcal{S} \equiv \{0,1\}^n$. We define the set of observation functions $\mathcal{M}$ as the following.

$$
\mathcal{M} \equiv \left\{ f_{\mathcal{I}} : \begin{array}{l} \mathcal{I} \subset \{1,2,\ldots,n\} \\ |\mathcal{I}| \leq m < n \\ f_{\mathcal{I}}(s) \equiv (v_1, v_2, \ldots, v_n), \\ \text{where } v_i \equiv \begin{cases} s_i & \text{if } i \in \mathcal{I} \\ v_i = \phi & \text{if } i \notin \mathcal{I} \end{cases} \end{array} \right\}
$$

It should be noted that $f_{\mathcal{I}} \in \mathcal{M}$ is characterized by a set $\mathcal{I} \subset \{1,2,\ldots,n\}$. By using an observation function $f \in \mathcal{M}$, all users can observe at most $m(< n)$ bits of $s \in \mathcal{S}$. The parameter $m$ corresponds to the bound of storage space for Eve in the context of the bounded storage model.

Assume that Alice and Bob define the set $\mathcal{M}_{AB} \subset \mathcal{M}$ as

$$
\mathcal{M}_{AB} \equiv \left\{ f_i : \begin{array}{l} i \in \{1,2,\ldots,n\} \\ f_i(s) \equiv (v_1, v_2, \ldots, v_n), \\ \text{where } v_i' \equiv \begin{cases} s_i' & \text{if } i' = i \\ \phi & \text{if } i' \neq i \end{cases} \end{array} \right\}.
$$

This set corresponds to a situation where Alice and Bob observe only one bit of $s \in \mathcal{S}$. Let $(v_1, v_2, \ldots, v_n)$ and $(v_1', v_2', \ldots, v_n')$ be sequences of $f_i(s)$ and $f_{\mathcal{I}'}(s)$, respectively. Then we have

$$
v_i = v_i' = s_i \text{ if } i \in \mathcal{I}'
$$
$$
v_i = s_i \text{ and } v_i' = \phi \text{ if } i \notin \mathcal{I}'
$$

for all $f_i \in \mathcal{M}_{AB}$ and $f_{\mathcal{I}'} \in \mathcal{M}$. By letting $\mu_S(s^n) \equiv 1/2^n$, we have the fact that for any $f_{\mathcal{I}'} \in \mathcal{M}$ there is $i \notin \mathcal{I}'$ such that

$$
H(f_i(S)|f_{\mathcal{I}'}(S)) = 1.
$$

This implies that

$$\min_{f_{\mathcal{I}'}\in\mathcal{M}} \max_{f_i\in\mathcal{M}_{AB}} H(f_i(S)|f_{\mathcal{I}'}(S)) = 1 > 0.$$

Then, from the theorem, we have the fact that Alice and Bob can agree on a secret key. On the other hand, the corollary implies that it is impossible for Alice and Bob to agree on any secret key when $f_{\{1,2,\ldots,n\}} \in \mathcal{M}$ because this function is the identity function.

# 7   Conclusion

We introduced the information theoretically secure key generation based on bounded observability and derived the necessary and sufficient conditions for the secret key agreement. We also show that the Bounded Storage Model can be formulated within the framework of the bounded observability model.

# Acknowledgements

Authors wishes to thank Dr. Harayama for constructive comments.

# References

1. Maurer, U.M.: Secret key agreement by public discussion from common information. IEEE Transactions on Information Theory IT-39(3), 733–742 (1993)
2. Chachin, C., Maurer, U.M.: Unconditional security against memory-bounded adversaries. In: Kaliski Jr., B.S. (ed.) CRYPTO 1997. LNCS, vol. 1294, pp. 292–306. Springer, Heidelberg (1997)
3. Aumann, Y., Ding, Y.Z., Rabin, M.O.: Everlasting security in the bounded storage model. IEEE Transactions on Information Theory IT-48(6), 1668–1680 (2002)
4. Bennett, C.H., Brassard, G.: Quantum cryptography: Public key distribution and coin tossing. In: Proceedings of IEEE International Conference on Computers Systems and Signal Processing, Bangalore, India, pp. 175–179 (1984)
5. Maurer, U.M., Wolf, S.: Unconditionally secure key agreement and the intrinsic conditional information. IEEE Transactions on Information Theory IT-45(2), 499–514 (1999)
6. von Neumann, J., Morgenstern, O.: Theory of Games and Economic Behavior. Princeton University Press, Princeton (1944)
7. Bennett, C.H., Brassard, G., Crepeau, C., Maurer, U.M.: Generalized privacy amplification. IEEE Transactions on Information Theory IT-41(6), 1915–1923 (1995)
8. Muramatsu, J., Yoshimura, K., Davis, P.: Secret key capacity and advantage distillation capacity. IEICE Transactions on Fundamentals E89-A(10), 2589–2596 (2006)

## Appendix: Proof of Theorem

First, we prepare the following lemma.

**Lemma 1.** *If $(S, F_A, G)$ and $F_B$ are independent and $H(F_B(S)|F_B, G, G(S)) = 0$, then*

$$\mathsf{S}(F_A, F_A(S); F_B, F_B(S)\|G, G(S)) = 0.$$

*Proof.* It is enough to show $\mathsf{S}(F_A, F_A(S); F_B, F_B(S)\|G, G(S)) \leq 0$, because $\mathsf{S}(F_A, F_A(S); F_B, F_B(S)\|G, G(S)) \geq 0$ is trivial. Since $(S, F_A, G)$ and $F_B$ are independent, we have

$$
\begin{aligned}
H(F_B, F_B(S)|G, G(S)) &= H(F_B|G, G(S)) + H(F_B(S)|G, G(S), F_B) \\
&= H(F_B|G, G(S)) \\
&= H(F_B)
\end{aligned}
$$

and

$$
\begin{aligned}
&H(F_B, F_B(S)|F_A, F_A(S), G, G(S)) \\
&= H(F_B|F_A, F_A(S), G, G(S)) + H(F_B(S)|F_A, F_A(S), G, G(S), F_B) \\
&= H(F_B|F_A, F_A(S), G, G(S)) \\
&= H(F_B).
\end{aligned}
$$

Then we have

$$
\begin{aligned}
&\mathsf{S}(F_A, F_A(S); F_B, F_B(S)\|G, G(S)) \\
&\leq I(F_A, F_A(S); F_B, F_B(S)|G, G(S)) \\
&= H(F_B, F_B(S)|G, G(S)) - H(F_B, F_B(S)|F_A, F_A(S), G, G(S)) \\
&= 0,
\end{aligned}
$$

where the first inequality comes from [1, Theorem 2]. □

Now, we prove the main theorem by showing

$$(C1) \Leftrightarrow (C2) \Leftrightarrow (C3)$$
$$(C'2) \Rightarrow (C'1) \Rightarrow (C'3) \Rightarrow (C'2).$$

First, we show the fact that (C1) does not hold for a given $\mu_S$ if (C2) does not hold; that is, a secret key agreement is impossible if $(\mu_S, \mathcal{M}_{AB}, \mathcal{M})$ does not satisfy (1). This fact implies (C1) $\Rightarrow$ (C2). When (C2) does not hold, we have

$$\inf_{g \in \mathcal{M}} \max_{f \in \mathcal{M}_{AB}} H(f(S)|g(S)) = 0.$$

This implies that Eve can use $g \in \mathcal{M}$, which satisfies $H(f(S)|g(S)) = 0$ for any $f \in \mathcal{M}_{AB}$. By letting $G$ be a random variable taking value $g$ with probability one, $G$ satisfies $H(F_B(S)|F_B, G, G(S)) = 0$ for any $(F_A, F_B)$. From Lemma 1, we have

$$\sup_{F_A, F_B} \inf_G S(F_A, F_A(S); F_B, F_B(S)\|G, G(S)) = 0.$$

Next, we show (C2)$\Rightarrow$(C1) for a given $\mu_S$; that is, a secret key agreement is possible when $(\mu_S, \mathcal{M}_{AB}, \mathcal{M})$ satisfies (1). The proof of (C'2)$\Rightarrow$(C'1) is the same as the following. Assume that the function $g$ satisfies $P_G(g) > 0$. From the assumption, there is $f_g \in \mathcal{M}_{AB}$ such that $H(f_g(S)|g(S)) > 0$. Let $(X, Y, (F_A, F_B, G, G(S)))$ be the correlated random variables obtained after the advantage distillation protocol introduced in Section 5. We have

$$\begin{aligned}
& S(F_A, F_A(S); F_B, F_B(S)\|G, G(S)) \\
& \geq S(X, Y\|F_A, F_B, G, G(S)) \\
& \geq I(X; Y) - I(X; F_A, F_B, G, G(S)) \\
& = H(X|F_A, F_B, G, G(S)) \\
& = \mathrm{Prob}(F_A = F_B) H(F_A(S)|F_A, G, G(S)) + \mathrm{Prob}(F_A \neq F_B) \cdot 0 \\
& \geq P_{F_A}(f_g) P_{F_B}(f_g) P_G(g) H(f_g(S)|g(S)) \\
& > 0,
\end{aligned}$$

where the first inequality comes from [8, Theorem 1] and the second inequality comes from [1, Theorem 3]. Since this inequality holds for any $g$ satisfying $P_G(g) > 0$, we have the fact that a secret key agreement is possible from $(\mu_S, \mathcal{M}_{AB}, \mathcal{M})$ satisfying (1).

Next, we show the fact that (C2) does not hold if (C3) does not hold; that is, if there is $g \in \mathcal{M}$ such that at least one of (2)–(4) does not hold for $f \in \mathcal{M}_{AB}$ and $u, u', v \in \mathcal{V}$, then $g$ satisfies

$$\max_{f \in \mathcal{M}_{AB}} H(f(S)|g(S)) = 0. \tag{8}$$

This implies (C2)$\Rightarrow$(C3). Assume that (3) holds for $u, v \in \mathcal{V}$ satisfying $\mathrm{Prob}(g(S) = v) > 0$. Then, we have the fact that

$$\mathrm{Prob}(f(S) = u', g(S) = v) = 0$$

for any $u' \neq u$ because (C3) does not hold. This implies that

$$\mathrm{Prob}(f(S) = u|g(S) = v) = \frac{\sum_u \mathrm{Prob}(f(S) = u, g(S) = v)}{\mathrm{Prob}(g(S) = v)}$$

$$= 1$$

for any $u, v \in \mathcal{V}$ satisfying $\mathrm{Prob}(g(S) = v) > 0$. Then we have

$$H(f(S)|g(S)) = 0$$

for any $f \in \mathcal{M}_{AB}$ and

$$0 \leq \max_{f \in \mathcal{M}_{AB}} H(f(S)|g(S)) = 0,$$

which implies (8).

Next, we show (C'3)⇒(C'2); that is, $\mu_S$ satisfying (1) exists if for any $g \in \mathcal{M}$ there are $f_g \in \mathcal{M}_{AB}$ and $s_g, s'_g \in \mathcal{S}$ satisfying (5) and (6). Let $\mu_S$ be a probability distribution that assigns a positive probability for every $s \in \mathcal{S}$. Since

$$\text{Prob}(f_g(S) = u_g, g(S) = v_g) \geq \text{Prob}(S = s_g) > 0$$
$$\text{Prob}(f_g(S) = u'_g, g(S) = v_g) \geq \text{Prob}(S = s'_g) > 0$$

by letting

$$u_g \equiv f_g(s_g)$$
$$u'_g \equiv f_g(s'_g)$$
$$v_g \equiv g(s_g) = g(s'_g),$$

we have

$$\text{Prob}(g(S) = v_g) > 0 \tag{9}$$
$$0 < \text{Prob}(f_g(S) = u_g | g(S) = v_g) < 1 \tag{10}$$
$$0 < \text{Prob}(f_g(S) = u'_g | g(S) = v_g) < 1 \tag{11}$$

where (10) and (11) come from the fact that $u_g \neq u'_g$. Then we have

$$H(f_g(S)|g(S)) = \sum_{u,v} \text{Prob}(f_g(S) = u, g(S) = v) \log \frac{1}{\text{Prob}(f_g(S) = u|g(S) = v)}$$
$$\geq \text{Prob}(f_g(S) = u_g, g(S) = v_g) \log \frac{1}{\text{Prob}(f_g(S) = u_g|g(S) = v_g)}$$
$$+ \text{Prob}(f_g(S) = u'_g, g(S) = v_g) \log \frac{1}{\text{Prob}(f_g(S) = u'_g|g(S) = v_g)}$$
$$> 0,$$

where the last inequality comes from (9)—(11). Then we have the fact that

$$\max_{f \in \mathcal{M}_{AB}} H(f(S)|g(S)) \geq H(f_g(S)|g(S)) > 0$$

for any $g \in \mathcal{M}$. This implies (1). Similarly, we can show (C3)⇒(C2) because (9)–(11) can be shown immediately from (2)–(4).

Finally, we show that if (C'3) does not hold then (C'1) does not hold; that is,

$$\mathsf{S}(F_A, F_A(S); F_B, F_B(S)\|G, G(S)) = 0 \tag{12}$$

for any independent random variables $(S, F_A)$ and $F_B$ if there is a random variable $G \in \mathcal{M}$ such that at least one of (5) and (6) does not hold for any $f \in \mathcal{M}_{AB}$ and $s, s' \in \mathcal{S}$. This fact implies (C'1)⇒(C'3). Since $g(s) = g(s') = v$ for any $v \in \text{Im} \, g$ and $s, s' \in g^{-1}(v)$, we have $f(s) = f(s')$ for any $f \in \mathcal{M}_{AB}$ from the assumption. This implies that $|f(g^{-1}(v))| = 1$ for any $v \in \text{Im} \, g$ and $f \in \mathcal{M}_{AB}$. Let $u(f,v)$ be the unique element of $f(g^{-1}(v))$. Then we have the fact that $F_B(S) = u(F_B, g(S))$, which implies $H(F_B(S)|F_B, G, G(S)) = 0$, for any $S$ and $F_B$. From Lemma 1, we have (12). □

# Group Testing and Batch Verification

Gregory M. Zaverucha and Douglas R. Stinson

David R. Cheriton School of Computer Science
University of Waterloo
Waterloo ON, N2L 3G1, Canada
{gzaveruc,dstinson}@uwaterloo.ca

**Abstract.** We observe that finding invalid signatures in batches of signatures that fail batch verification is an instance of the classical group testing problem. We survey relevant group testing techniques, and present and compare new sequential and parallel algorithms for finding invalid signatures based on group testing algorithms. Of the five new algorithms, three show improved performance for many parameter choices, and the performance gains are especially notable when multiple processors are available.

## 1 Introduction

A *batch verification algorithm* for a digital signature scheme verifies a list of $n$ (message, signature) pairs as a group. It outputs 1 if all $n$ signatures are valid, and it outputs 0 if one or more are invalid. In the most general case, the messages and signers may be different. Batch verification algorithms may provide large gains in efficiency, as verification of the $n$ signatures is significantly faster than $n$ individual verifications. In this paper, we address the problem of handling batches which fail verification, i.e., finding the invalid signatures which caused the batch to fail.

It has not been previously observed that finding invalid signatures in bad batches is an instance of the *group testing problem*, which in brief, is as follows. Given a set $B$, of $n$ items, $d$ of which are defective, determine which items are defective by asking queries of the form "Does $B' \subseteq B$ contain a defective item?". Group testing is an old, well-studied problem, for which many algorithms exist. We re-cast some solutions to the group testing problem as solutions to the invalid signature finding problem, which are then compared for efficiency, parallelizability and accuracy. The group testing algorithms are well-known, but have not been considered in the context of batch verification by previous work that has studied methods to find invalid signatures [18,25,26,30,29]. Performance will be measured by the number of subset tests required to find $d$ invalid signatures.

In total, five new algorithms for finding invalid signatures are presented and included in our comparison. Of these, three give performance improvements. With a single processor, generalized binary splitting [16] gives a modest improvement over the well-known binary splitting algorithm. In the case of two or more processors, large improvements are possible using one of two new group testing-based algorithms: Li's *s*-stage algorithm [16] and the Karp, Upfal and Wigderson

K. Kurosawa (Ed.): ICITS 2009, LNCS 5973, pp. 140–157, 2010.
© Springer-Verlag Berlin Heidelberg 2010

algorithm [23]. The other two algorithms also have interesting properties. The algorithm based on cover-free families is fully parallelizable, and is an improved instance of a known algorithm for batch verification, the id-code algorithm [30] (for some parameter choices). The random matrices algorithm is probabilistic, fully parallelizable and enjoys a simple implementation. Some algorithms require an *a priori* bound on $d$ (this will be addressed in our comparison).

We also give some general results on the limits of group testing that are also interesting in the context of finding invalid signatures in batches, such as the conditions when the naïve testing strategy is optimal.

*Contributions and Outline.* The first contribution of this work is describing the link between finding invalid signatures in bad batches and group testing (§1.1, 1.2), a connection previously overlooked. We then provide a survey of algorithms from the group testing literature, and describe how they correspond to new algorithms for finding invalid signatures (§2). These are classified according to the adaptive (i.e. sequential §2.2) or nonadaptive (i.e. parallel §2.3) nature of the algorithm. We then compare the performance of the new invalid signature finding algorithms (and some previously known algorithms) and determine the best one under various parameter choices (§3). For many parameter choices, especially with multiple processors, the new methods outperform previously known methods.

## 1.1  Batch Verification

Let the algorithms (Gen, Sign, Verify) specify a signature scheme. Gen takes as input a security parameter $k$, and outputs a signing and verification keypair $(sk, pk)$. Sign$(sk, m)$ outputs a signature $\sigma$ on the message $m$ using the secret key $sk$, and Verify$(pk, \sigma, m)$ outputs 1 if $\sigma$ is a valid signature of $m$ under the secret key $sk$ which corresponds to $pk$, and 0 otherwise.

Here is the most general definition of batch verification.

**Definition 1 ([8]).** *Let $P_1, \ldots, P_n$ be $n$ signers, with corresponding keypairs $K = \{(sk_1, pk_1), \ldots, (sk_n, pk_n)\}$ output by Gen$(k)$ for some security parameter $k$. Let $B$ be a list containing $K$, and $n$ tuples of the form $(P_{t_i}, \sigma_i, m_i)$ called the batch (note that the $t_i$ and $m_i$ values may be repeated.) The algorithm Batch$(B)$ is a batch verification algorithm provided Batch$(B) = 1$ if and only if Verify$(pk_{t_i}, \sigma, m_i) = 1$ for all $i$.*

A few variations appear in the literature, including the case with a single signer or the case of multiple signers with a single message. We also mention the related concept of *aggregate signatures*. Suppose $\sigma_1, \ldots, \sigma_n$ are signatures on messages $m_1, \ldots, m_n$ with corresponding verification keys $pk_1, \ldots, pk_n$. An aggregation algorithm is a public algorithm, which given the $\sigma_i$, $m_i$ and $pk_i$ $(i = 1, \ldots, n)$ outputs a compressed signature $\sigma$. An associated verification algorithm verifies if $\sigma$ is a valid compressed signature, given $pk_i$ and $m_i$ (for $i = 1, \ldots n$).

A number of signature schemes in the literature support batch verification. Batch cryptography was introduced by Fiat [19,20] to improve efficiency of an

RSA-like scheme, where large numbers of operations are performed at a central site. History shows that secure batch verification algorithms are tricky to construct; a number of schemes were presented and subsequently broken or shown to be otherwise flawed. One example is the scheme of Al-Ibrahim et al. [1], which was broken by Stinson in [40]. Camenisch et al. list and reference ten proposed schemes which were later broken [8, §1.2]. Despite this poor track record, a number of signature schemes have batch verification, many of them based on the general techniques described in Bellare et al. [4].

We list a few examples, but omit details since the techniques in this work will apply to any scheme with batch verification. RSA* is an RSA-variant with batch verification presented by Boyd and Pavlovski [6]. DSA** is a signature scheme based on DSA, given by Naccache et al. [28], which uses the small exponents test from [4]. Camenisch et al. [8] give a variant of the Camenisch-Lysyanskaya signature scheme [7] which supports batch verification, present a batch verifier for the $\Pi$-IBS scheme of Chatterjee and Sarkar [11], and discuss batch verification of BLS signatures [5]. Practical considerations and implementation timings of batch verification are given in Ferrara et al. [18].

## 1.2   Finding Invalid Signatures in Bad Batches

Suppose we are given a batch $B$ such that $\mathsf{Batch}(B) = 0$. We know that $B$ contains at least one invalid signature, but what is the best way to determine *which* of the signatures do not verify? Verifying each signature individually is certainly an option, but can $\mathsf{Batch}$ be applied to subsets of $B$ to perform less work overall? This problem can be considered the computational version of the batch verification problem (which is a decision problem). We name it the *invalid signature finding* (ISF) problem. This does not apply to aggregate signatures, where, since the batch is compressed, we do not have enough information to determine which of the original signatures were invalid.

We will treat the algorithm $\mathsf{Batch}$ as a generic test for invalid signatures, and present solutions which work for *any signature scheme* equipped with a $\mathsf{Batch}$ function as described in Definition 1. There are several advantages of generic ISFs.

1. *Applicability.* A generic ISF algorithm may be used with any signature scheme which provides batch verification. This includes future schemes.
2. *Implementation.* A single implementation may be used to locate bad signatures of multiple signature schemes, reducing the need to maintain multiple ISF algorithm implementations. The single generic ISF algorithm may be optimized, verified and otherwise improved since the effort is amortized over a larger number of applications.
3. *Ability to handle variations of the ISF problem.* The group testing literature has considered many variations of the problem, many of which are applicable to variations of the ISF problem. As examples, group testing with competitive algorithms [16, Ch. 4], or when the size of each test group is restricted [17,32], or with unreliable tests [16, Ch. 5], all correspond to interesting variations of the ISF problem.

The performance of an ISF algorithm will be evaluated based on the number of calls to Batch and the parallel performance of the algorithm (this is discussed further in Sections 2 and 3).

**Related Work.** There have been five papers addressing the ISF problem. The first two are by Pastuszak et al. [30,29]. They consider a generic Batch function for a signature scheme and study the *divide-and-conquer* method of finding bad signatures in [29]. The divide-and-conquer verifier was originally described in [28] under the name *cut and choose*, and is referred to *binary splitting* in the group testing literature. In brief, a batch $B$ is divided in half, then Batch is recursively called on each sub-batch, until 1 is output (this sub-batch contains only valid signatures) or until the sub-batch has size one, which identifies the bad signatures. This method was implemented in the work of Ferrara et al. [18], and we discuss their findings in §2.2 when we relate the divide-and-conquer verifier to well-known techniques from group testing.

The second paper [30] approaches the problem using identification codes (id-codes), a code which encodes an ISF algorithm, by specifying subsets of $B$ to test with Batch in such a way that all bad signatures may be identified. This approach is an instance of well-known non-adaptive group testing algorithms based on cover-free, separable and disjunct matrices, discussed in §2.3. A limitation of [30,29] is that either the number of bad signatures in a batch, or a bound on the number of bad signatures is required *a priori*. This is common to most group testing algorithms as well.

The work of Law and Matt [25] improves the divide-and-conquer method by considering the details of the signature scheme. The second part of [25] gives an improved invalid signature finder using a special version of Batch. The batch verification and invalid signature finding tasks are combined, to allow information and intermediate computations from the verification step to be used in the ISF step. This trades off general applicability for improved computational efficiency. Along similar lines, Matt improves the performance of these methods when the number of invalid signatures is large [26]. This addresses a limitation of [25]. The improved techniques of [26] are applicable to the Cha-Cheon signature scheme [10] and the pairing-based schemes discussed in Ferrara et al. [18].

## 2   Group Testing-Based ISF Algorithms

We begin with a general description of the group testing problem called the $(d, n)$-*problem*. Consider a set of $n$ items which contains exactly $d$ defective items, called the *defective set*. Identification of a defective item requires the application of an error-free test, and we may test an arbitrary subset of the items. The test outcome may be *positive* if the subset of items contains at least one defective item, or *negative* if no defective items are present in the subset. An algorithm $A$ which finds all $d$ defective items is a solution to the problem. An algorithm where the tests are applied sequentially, and subsequent tests depend on the results of previous tests is called an *adaptive algorithm*. *Nonadaptive algorithms* require all tests to be specified at the outset; hence they may be executed in parallel.

Group testing has a long history, originating in World War II, motivated by the task of testing blood samples of draftees to detect syphilis [14,16]. In this application, a single test on a combination of blood samples will return positive if any of the samples would test positive for syphilis. Since there were only a few thousand cases of the disease in millions of draftees, large subsets would come back negative, saving many individual tests. Group testing later found many industrial applications, a line of research initiated by Sobel and Groll [41]. In the past 50 years or so, a large literature has grown around the problem, and many variants have been considered. The book of Du and Hwang [15,16] is a comprehensive reference.

It should now be clear that the ISF problem is a group testing problem: the items are signatures, the test applied to subsets is the batch verification algorithm, and the defectives are invalid signatures. This basic model makes the following assumptions:

– The subset tests all have the same cost, regardless of the number of items being tested.
– The number of defectives $d$, or a bound on $d$, is known *a priori*.

The first assumption, which is standard in the group testing literature, is a simplifying assumption for the ISF problem, since the cost of $\mathsf{Batch}(B)$ is typically composed of a fixed overhead cost independent of $|B|$, plus a variable cost which grows with $|B|$. The fixed cost is typically high (e.g. an exponentiation) while the variable cost consists of $|B|$ cheaper operations (e.g. multiplications). This assumption does however, allow us to keep our analysis general, and ignore the details of $\mathsf{Batch}$. The second assumption allows some group testing algorithms to be more efficient. We will discuss the importance of the bound on $d$ for each algorithm, and the behaviour of the algorithm when $d$ is initially bounded incorrectly.

Probabilistic group testing (PGT) assumes a probability distribution on the defective set, while combinatorial group testing (CGT) does not. The only information CGT assumes about the defective set is that it is a $d$-subset of the $n$ items. Some applications of batch verification may benefit from PGT if it is reasonable to make an assumption about the distribution of invalid signatures; however, we do not consider PGT algorithms in this paper.

Denote the minimal number of calls to $\mathsf{Batch}$ required to find $d$ invalid signatures in a batch of size $n$ by $M(d,n)$. First note that $M(d,n) \leq n-1$, by verifying $n-1$ signatures individually and inferring the validity of the last signature from knowledge of $d$ and the other $n-1$ signatures. The following general lower bound is proven in [16, Cor. 2.1.11].

**Theorem 1.** $M(d,n) \geq \min \left\{ n-1, 2\ell + \left\lceil \log \binom{n-\ell}{d-\ell} \right\rceil \right\}$ *for* $0 < \ell \leq d < n$.

Unless stated otherwise, $\log x$ is the base two logarithm of $x$, $\ln x$ is the natural logarithm of $x$, and $e$ is the natural base.

## 2.1   Individual Testing

The simplest way of identifying all invalid signatures in a bad batch is to individually verify each signature. The question is, when is this naïve testing strategy optimal? Recall that $M(d,n)$ is the smallest possible number of tests for any $(d,n)$ algorithm. Combining [16, Th. 3.5.1] and [16, Th. 3.5.3], we have the following result.

**Theorem 2.** *Let $d$ be the number of invalid signatures in a batch of size $n$, and let $M(d,n)$ be as defined above. Then*

$$M(d,n) < n - 1 \text{ for } n > 3d, \text{ and}$$
$$M(d,n) = n - 1 \text{ for } n \leq 2.625d.$$

Therefore, when the number of bad signatures is at most $n/3$ it is possible to do better than individual testing, and when there are more than $n/2.625$ bad signatures the naïve strategy is optimal. What is best when $n < 3d$ and $n \geq 2.625d$ remains unknown; however, Hu, Hwang and Wang [22] conjectured that individual testing is optimal whenever $n \leq 3d$.

We note that individual testing is trivially parallelizable.

## 2.2   Adaptive ISF Algorithms

In this section we will present some adaptive ISF algorithms, based on group testing algorithms. In adaptive (or sequential) algorithms, the results of each test determines the items to be tested in subsequent tests. We will use the notation $(d,n)$, where $d$ is an upper bound on the number of bad signatures in the batch of size $n$.

**Binary Splitting.** An adaptive group testing algorithm is naturally represented as a binary tree. Nodes of the tree contain elements to be tested, starting at the root, which contains all $n$ items. In binary splitting, at each level of the tree, we halve (i.e. divide as evenly as possible) the set of items in the parent node, to create two child nodes. When a test returns negative, this node becomes a leaf, since we know the set of items at this node is valid. Repeating this process recursively, we ultimately end up with nodes containing a single item, thus identifying the invalid items of the batch. By using depth first search from the root of the tree we may locate an invalid item using at most $\lceil \log(n) \rceil$ tests. We may remove the invalid item, and repeatedly apply the binary splitting algorithm to find $d$ invalid items using at most $d \lceil \log(n) \rceil$ tests.

An implementation of binary splitting for the BLS signature scheme [5] is discussed in the work of Ferrara et al. [18]. They performed experiments with $n = 1024$ and they found binary splitting was faster than individual verification when $d < 0.15n$. In these experiments, a random fraction of the batch was corrupted, however Ferrara et al. note that in practice if corrupted signatures occur in bursts, the binary splitting algorithm will have better performance.

Ordering of the batch may be an important consideration for applications using binary splitting.

A variant of binary splitting is Hwang's *generalized binary splitting*. The intuition of the algorithm is that there is roughly one defective item in every $n/d$ items, and therefore a group smaller than $n/2$ could be tested and a defective found with fewer tests. When $d = 1$ the number of tests required by generalized binary splitting is $\lfloor \log(n) \rfloor + 1$, and when $d \geq 2$, the number of tests is not more than $d - 1 + \lceil \log \binom{n}{d} \rceil$, which gives a noticeable saving as $d$ gets larger [16, Cor. 2.2.4].

Karp, Upfal and Wigderson describe an algorithm to identify a single invalid item using $p$ processors in at most $\lceil \log_{p+1} n \rceil$ parallel tests [23]. The algorithm is identical to binary splitting when $p = 1$, since it uses a $(p + 1)$-ary tree in the same way that binary splitting does. At each level, $p$ of the child sets are tested in parallel, and (if necessary) the validity of the $(p + 1)$-th set is inferred. We may repeatedly apply this algorithm to identify $d$ invalid items in at most $d \lceil \log_{p+1} n \rceil$ parallel tests. We will refer to this algorithm as the *KUW algorithm*.

**Li's $s$-Stage Algorithm.** This algorithm has $s$ rounds of testing, identifying good items at each round, until the last round when the algorithm corresponds to individual testing. Li's algorithm begins by grouping the batch into $g_1$ groups of size $k_1$ (some groups might have $k_1 - 1$ items). The groups are tested, and items in valid groups are set aside. The $i$-th stage divides the remaining elements into $g_i$ groups of size $k_i$, tests them, and then removes items in valid groups. The final stage has $k_s = 1$, and remaining items are identified as valid or invalid.

When optimal choices are made for $g_i, k_i$ and $s$ (see [16, §2.3]), the number of tests is not more than

$$\frac{e}{\log e} d \log \left( \frac{n}{d} \right) .$$

When $p$ processors are available, Li's algorithm may be parallelized (see [15, p. 33]), and the number of parallel tests is not more than

$$\frac{e}{\log e} \frac{d}{p} \log \left( \frac{n}{dp} \right) + \ln \left( \frac{n}{dp} \right) + d .$$

## 2.3   Nonadaptive Algorithms

As we have seen, some adaptive algorithms are somewhat parallelizable. All nonadaptive algorithms are completely parallelizable. Recall that nonadaptive tests may be completely specified without information from previous tests. This can be especially useful for online batch verification in a system with time constraints where a batch of $n$ signatures arrive every time interval and must be processed before the next batch arrives, with a known number of tests. This might be applicable in the example of public key authentication in vehicular networks (this example is discussed in [8,18]) or authentication of data reported periodically from sensors (as discussed in [9]). We continue to use the $(d, n)$ notation defined at the beginning of Section 2.

**Nonadaptive Group Testing with Cover-Free Families.** A useful combinatorial structure for designing nonadaptive CGT (NACGT) algorithms is a cover-free family. Cover-free families are also studied under the terms *disjunct matrices* [16], *binary superimposed codes* [24], and *strongly selective families* [12]. Stinson et al. [38] discusses relations between these structures. We choose the language of cover-free families since they have found multiple applications in cryptography (see [21,27,37] for examples).

**Definition 2.** *A d-cover-free family is a* $t \times n$ *binary matrix, with* $n \geq d + 1$, *such that for any set of columns C and single column c such that* $|C| = d$ *and* $c \notin C$ *the following property holds. Let* $U(C)$ *be the binary OR of the columns in C. The cover-free property ensures that* $c \notin U(C)$, *that is, c is 1 in at least one position where* $U(C)$ *is 0. We will use the notation d-CFF$(t, n)$ for cover-free families.*

The cover-free property ensures that no $d$-set of columns "covers" any other column. A $d$-*separable* matrix satisfies a weaker property, namely, the OR of any two sets of $d$ columns are distinct. While any $d$-separable matrix yields a NACGT algorithm, it is not efficient [16, Ch. 7]. We now describe how a $d$-CFF$(t, n)$ defines an efficient $(d, n)$ NACGT algorithm.

**Input:** Signatures $\sigma_1, \ldots, \sigma_n$, batch verification function Batch.
**Output:** Up to $d$ invalid signatures.

1. Construct a matrix $A$ which is a $d$-CFF$(t, n)$ .
2. Associate $\sigma_i$ to column $i$ of $A$. Each row of $A$ will define a sub-batch to test; if $\sigma_i$ has a 1 in row $j$ then $\sigma_i$ is included in sub-batch $j$.
3. Compute Batch$(B_1), \ldots,$ Batch$(B_t)$ where $B_i = \{\sigma_j : A_{i,j} = 1\}$.
4. For each row $i$ such that Batch$(B_i) = 1$ mark all $\sigma_j \in B_i$ as valid.
5. Output all the remaining signatures as invalid, i.e., signatures which do not belong to a valid batch.

We now explain how the algorithm correctly identifies valid signatures (and thus correctly outputs invalid signatures in step 5). Suppose $\sigma_i$ is a valid signature. Let $C$ be the set of columns corresponding to the invalid signatures. We are assuming that $|C| \leq d$. Let $C'$ be any set of $d$ columns that contains $C$ as a subset and does not contain $i$ ($C'$ exists because $n \geq d + 1$). Since $A$ is the matrix of a $d$-CFF$(t, n)$, there exists a row $j$ such that $A_{j,i} = 1$ and $A_{j,c} = 0$ for all $c$ in $C'$. Therefore Batch$(B_j) = 1$ and $\sigma_i$ is recognized as a valid signature in step 4 of the algorithm.

*Remark 1.* Shultz makes the following observation for batches containing $d' > d$ invalid signatures [34]. Let $B'$ be the resulting set of signatures after removing all the signatures belonging to valid sub-batches, in step 4. If $|B'| > d$, the number of invalid signatures in the input batch exceeds $d$. In this case some valid signatures may be covered by $U(D)$, but are not present in a valid test. Thus $B'$ contains all $d'$ invalid signatures, but may contain some valid signatures as well.

A recent paper of Porat and Rothschild [31] explicitly constructs $(n, d)$-*strongly selective families* from error correcting codes. This structure is equivalent to a $(d-1)$-CFF$(t, n)$ (see [12]), and hence it gives a nonadaptive ISF.

**Theorem 3 ([31], Th. 1).** *It is possible to construct a $d$-CFF$(t, n)$ with $t = \Theta((d+1)^2 \log n)$ in $\Theta((d+1)n \log n)$ time.*

In light of the bounds on $t$ given in Appendix B, this construction is asymptotically optimal. We choose to ignore the constant hidden by the $\Theta$-notation, as even with this assumption the CFF algorithm is outperformed by other methods.

**Nonadaptive Group Testing with id-codes.** The definition of identification codes is very general: any binary matrix which specifies a group testing algorithm is an id-code. Thus CFF are id-codes, and the $d$-separable property defined in 2.3 is both necessary and sufficient for an id-code. The construction of id-codes put forward in Pastuszak et al. [30] is a cover-free family with some additional constraints on the number of nonzero row and column entries. Using their construction gives the following ISF.

**Theorem 4 ([30], Cor. 4).** *The number $t$ of tests necessary to identify $d$ bad signatures in a batch of size $n$ satisfies $t \le (d+1)\sqrt{n}$.*

Clearly, as $n \to \infty$ for fixed $d$, this method will require a much larger number of tests than CFF-based methods, since $\sqrt{n}$ dominates $\log n$. However, the CFF constructions presented have a quadratic dependence on $d$, while $d$ is linear in Theorem 4. Therefore, for fixed $n$ and increasing $d$, there will be a crossover point after which the id-code ISF outperforms the CFF ISF. Comparing the formulas,

$$(d+1)^2 \log(n) < (d+1)\sqrt{n}$$

$$d < \frac{\sqrt{n}}{\log n} - 1.$$

This gives the value of $d$ in terms of $n$ before which the CFF ISF outperforms the id-code ISF. For example, when $n = 10^3, 10^4, 10^5, 10^6$, $d$ must be greater than $2, 6, 18, 49$ (resp.) for the id-code ISF to be more efficient.

**Random Matrices.** In this section we describe a probabilistic nonadaptive ISF which is based on a random matrix, and fails with a given probability. Du and Hwang give the probability that a random matrix is a $d$-CFF.

**Theorem 5.** *Let $C$ be a random $t \times n$ binary matrix where $C_{i,j} = 1$ with probability $q = 1/(d+1)$. Then $C$ is a $d$-CFF$(t, n)$ with probability at least*

$$(d+1)\binom{n}{d+1}\left[1 - q(1-q)^d\right]^t.$$

*Proof.* Let $D$ be a set of $d$ columns of $C$, and let $c$ a single column. In a single row, the probability that $c = 1$ and $D = 0, \ldots, 0$ is $q(1 - q)^d$. (Note that $q = 1/(d+1)$ maximizes this probability.) The probability that this pattern does not occur in any of the $t$ rows is $\left[1 - q(1 - q)^d\right]^t$. Since the $d + 1$ columns of $D$ and $c$ may be chosen in $(d + 1)\binom{n}{d+1}$ ways, this gives the bound on the probability that $C$ is a CFF stated in the theorem.

Now we consider constructing an ISF as described at the beginning of Section 2.3 using random matrices. Certainly, this approach would succeed with probability at least that given by Theorem 5. However, the ISF will have significantly better performance, since the only case that affects our result is when the $d$ columns corresponding to the bad signatures cover another column. If this occurs, then the covered column may be valid, but it will not appear in a valid test. Columns corresponding to valid signatures which cover each other will have no effect on the ISF. Therefore, we need only consider the probability that a *fixed set of $d$ columns covers another column*. Since the $d$ columns corresponding to defectives are fixed with respect to a batch, the remaining column may be chosen in $n - d$ ways, which gives the following result. The same improvement may be used in DNA library screening (see [16, Th. 9.3.3] and [2]).

**Theorem 6.** *There exists an ISF which identifies $d$ defectives in a batch of size $n$ using $t$ tests with failure probability $P_{d,n} \leq (n - d)\left[1 - q(1 - q)^d\right]^t$, where $q = 1/(d + 1)$.*

*Remark 2.* The error of this ISF is one-sided. It may output a valid signature as invalid. To detect this, we must individually test the output signatures, to confirm that they are invalid.

## 3  Comparison of Algorithms

In this section we compare the ISF algorithms given in Section 2. We compare them based on the number of tests, and their behaviour when $d$ (the number of defectives) is unknown, or estimated incorrectly. Finally we discuss how the ISFs given by Law and Matt [25,26] for a specific class of signature schemes compare to the generic ISF algorithms given in this paper.

### 3.1  Number of Tests

First, for each of the ISF algorithms in Section 2, we give the bound on the worst case number of calls to Batch (Table 1). Table 1 gives the bound for the trivial parallelization of (generalized) binary splitting: divide the original batch into $p$ equal-sized sub-batches. The KUW algorithm is a better parallelization of binary splitting. For generalized binary splitting, the bounds given hold for $d \geq 2$, while for $d = 1$ the number of required tests is $\lfloor \log n \rfloor + 1$.

Next we compare the number of tests required by each method for various choices of $n$, $d$, and $p$ (the number of processors available). In Ferrara et al. [18],

**Table 1.** Summary of the number of tests required for the ISF algorithms presented in §2. The number of tests required by the random matrices ISF must be computed using Theorem 6. "PR CFF" is the ISF based on Theorem 3, and "PPS id-codes" is the ISF in Theorem 4. The algorithms marked with an asterisk ($^*$) require an *a priori* bound on $d$.

| Method | Sec. | Tests (worst case) | Tests with $p$ processors |
|---|---|---|---|
| Individual Testing | 2.1 | $n-1$ | $\lceil n/p \rceil - p$ |
| Binary Splitting (B.S.) | 2.2 | $d \lceil \log n \rceil$ | $d \left\lceil \log \left( \frac{n}{p} \right) \right\rceil$ |
| Gen. Bin. Splitting (G.B.S)$^*$ | 2.2 | $d - 1 + \lceil \log \binom{n}{d} \rceil$ | $d - 1 + \left\lceil \log \binom{n/p}{d} \right\rceil$ |
| Li's $s$-stage$^*$ | 2.2 | $\frac{e}{\log e} d \log \frac{n}{d}$ | $\frac{e}{\log e} \frac{d}{p} \log \frac{n}{dp} + \ln \frac{n}{dp} + d$ |
| PR CFF$^*$ | 2.3 | $(d+1)^2 \log n$ | $((d+1)^2 \log n)/p$ |
| PPS id-codes$^*$ [30] | 2.3 | $(d+1)\sqrt{n}$ | $((d+1)\sqrt{n})/p$ |
| KUW | 2.2 | $d \lceil \log_2 n \rceil$ | $d \lceil \log_{p+1} n \rceil$ |

the choices $n = 1024$, $d = 1, \ldots, 153$ were used when investigating the practical performance of the binary splitting method. In Pastuszak et al. [29], choices of $n \in [16, 1024]$ are used to give the average number of tests for the binary splitting method when $d = 1, \ldots, 16$. In Law and Matt [25], tables are given with $n = 2^4, 2^6, 2^8, 2^{10}, 2^{12}$ and $d = 1, \ldots, 4$. In Matt [26], the parameters chosen for comparison are $n = 2^4, 2^6, 2^8, 2^{10}$ and $d = 1, \ldots, n$ (here the goal was to show better performance with large $d$). All previous work considered $p = 1$, i.e., a single processor. We will compare the ISF algorithms with $n = 10^3, 10^4, 10^5, 10^6$, $d = 1, 2, 3, 4, 10$ and $p = 2, 4, 8, 16$. When $p = 1$ the algorithm requiring the fewest tests is always generalized binary splitting, and for smaller values of $d$, binary splitting performs equally well. Table 2 lists the algorithm requiring the fewest number of tests when $p \geq 2$ (according to the bounds in Table 1). A finer grained comparison is given in Appendix A, where Tables 4, 5 and 6 give the actual number of tests required under various combinations of parameters.

*Discussion.* In the case of a single processor (Table 4) we find that the adaptive algorithms have the best performance. In particular, generalized binary splitting slightly outperforms binary splitting, especially as $d$ grows. With a single processor the KUW algorithm has the same performance as binary splitting, hence we have omitted it from the table.

When two or more processors are available to the ISF (Tables 2, 5 and 6), Li's $s$-stage algorithm and the KUW algorithm begin to show the best performance. The performance gap is most pronounced as the number of processors grows for any of the choices of $(n, d)$ presented. In general, the nonadaptive algorithms improve when more processors are available, as they provide a speedup linear in the number of processors. Regarding the nonadaptive algorithms, the PR CFF

**Table 2.** Algorithm requiring the fewest number of tests with $p$ processors. The number of tests required by all algorithms listed in Table 1 is given in Tables 5 and 6. Here, LI stands for Li's Algorithm (§2.2).

| $n$ | $d$ | Fewest Tests when $p =$ | | | |
|-----|-----|-----|-----|-----|-----|
|  |  | 2 | 4 | 8 | 16 |
| $10^3$ | 4 | KUW | LI | LI | LI |
| $10^4$ | 4 | KUW | KUW | LI | LI |
| $10^5$ | 4 | KUW | KUW | LI | LI |
| $10^6$ | 4 | KUW | KUW | KUW | LI |
| $10^3$ | 10 | LI | LI | LI | LI |
| $10^4$ | 10 | KUW | LI | LI | LI |
| $10^5$ | 10 | KUW | LI | LI | LI |
| $10^6$ | 10 | KUW | LI | LI | LI |

algorithm (Th. 3) requires fewer tests than the PPS id-code algorithm (Th. 4) when $d < \sqrt{n}/\log n - 1$. If a failure probability of 0.001 is tolerable (see Remark 2), the random matrix ISF (RM ISF) outperforms the CFF and id-codes methods since it requires a weaker property from the matrix, as discussed following Theorem 5. The RM ISF with failure probability 0.001 is best overall when $p = 16$, $d = 4$ and $n = 10^4, 10^5, 10^6$ (see Appendix A). However, determining whether the RM ISF has failed requires $d$ individual verifications.

In the detailed tables of Appendix A, there are many parameter combinations where multiple ISFs require a nearly equal number of tests. In these cases, implementation factors, average case performance, and the size of subset tests may influence the best choice.

## 3.2 Unknown Number of Invalid Signatures

Table 3 lists the behaviour of each of the algorithms when the true number of signatures, is $d'$, a value different from our estimate $d$.

The binary splitting algorithm has a certain grace with respect to handling arbitrary $d$, in that the algorithm's behaviour is unchanged, and the bound on the number of tests holds as $d$ changes. On the other hand, Li's $s$-stage algorithm, and generalized binary splitting begin by computing some parameters based on $n$ and $d$ in order to meet the performance bound stated in Table 1. If a batch contains $d' \neq d$ invalid signatures these parameters will not be chosen optimally, and it is unclear to what extent this will hurt the performance of the algorithm. It is also unclear whether better performance is obtained by underestimating or overestimating $d'$. Therefore, if no *a priori* information about $d$ is available, the best choice is binary splitting when $p = 1$, and KUW when $p > 1$.

When a batch contains $d' > d$ invalid signatures, the CFF and id-code algorithms output a set $B'$ of $\ell$ signatures, where $d < \ell \leq n$. All $d'$ defectives are in $B'$; however, it may contain valid signatures as well. As $d'$ increases, $\ell$ will increase as well, and less information is gained. The case $d' > d$ is easily recognized (if $|B'| > d$), and we may restart the ISF with a larger estimate of $d$.

**Table 3.** Behaviour of ISFs when the true number of invalid signatures $d'$ differs from the estimated number $d$. Here, $M_A(d, n)$ represents the number of tests required by algorithm $A$ for a batch of size $n$ with $d$ defectives.

| Algorithm | When $d' < d$ | When $d' > d$ |
|---|---|---|
| B.S. | Outputs $d'$ invalid signatures in time $M_{\text{B.S.}}(d', n)$. | |
| G.B.S., Li | Outputs $d'$ invalid signatures but using suboptimal parameter choices thus requiring extra work. | |
| KUW | Outputs $d'$ invalid signatures in time $M_{\text{KUW}}(d', n)$. | |
| CFF, id-codes | returns $d'$ invalid signatures | returns a set of $d \leq \ell \leq n$ potentially invalid signatures |
| RM | Outputs $d'$ signatures in $M_{\text{RM}}(d, n)$ tests | Outputs $d$ bad signatures with probability $P_{d,n}$ and $d'$ bad signatures with probability $P_{d',n}$ (see Th. 6) |

The random matrix ISF outputs each $d' > d$ with probability $P_{d',n}$, given in Theorem 6. For these algorithms we may run $t$ tests to identify some valid signatures, remove them from the batch, re-estimate $d$, and re-run the ISF.

Another option when $d$ is unknown is to use a *competitive algorithm*, i.e., one which assumes no *a priori* information about $d$, yet completes in a bounded number of tests (see [16, Ch. 4]). For example, the "jumping algorithm" of Bar-Noy et al. [3], identifies $d$ invalid signatures in at most $1.65d(\log \frac{n}{d} + 1.031) + 6$ tests, for $0 \leq d \leq n$. Note that this flexibility comes at a cost because the performance of a competitive algorithm when $d$ is known to be small is poorer than the other ISFs presented.

### 3.3   Comparison to Non-generic ISF Algorithms

Recall from Section 1.2 that a non-generic ISF is an ISF which is customized to a particular signature scheme, integrated into the Batch algorithm. In the single processor setting, the ISFs requiring the fewest number of tests were binary splitting and generalized binary splitting. Since the non-generic ISF given by Law and Matt [25,26] outperforms binary splitting, their ISF will outperform the generic ISF algorithms presented here (for the pairing-based signature schemes to which it applies).

The faster choice in the parallel case would depend on how well the specialized ISFs described by Law and Matt parallelize. If their improved version of binary splitting yields an improved version of the KUW test (which is similar to binary splitting) then the parameter combinations where KUW is the best may be improved upon.

A general comparison is beyond the scope of this work since the units are different: number of calls to Batch() (this work) vs. number of multiplications in a finite field (Law and Matt).

# 4   Conclusion

We have introduced algorithms based on group testing for finding invalid signatures in bad batches. For many parameter choices, and especially with multiple processors, the new methods outperform known methods. Our comparison shows that the best algorithm depends strongly on the choice of parameters, and no single algorithm is best in all cases. One way to more precisely compare these algorithms, while still maintaining some generality, would be to count the number of calls to Batch() and the size the input to each, then assign values to the fixed and variable cost, depending on the underlying Batch() function, to arrive at a final performance number. Other topics for future work include: i) comparison of implementations to compensate for not considering the sizes of sub-batches, and ii) specializing the given ISFs to specific signature schemes, perhaps by using techniques from Law and Matt's specialized ISFs for pairing-based signature schemes.

*Acknowledgements.* Thanks are due to Urs Hengartner, Artur Jackson, and Aniket Kate for providing feedback on an earlier draft of this paper. This research was supported by an NSERC discovery grant, and PGS scholarship.

# References

1. Al-Ibrahim, M., Ghodosi, H., Pieprzyk, J.: Authentication of concast communication. In: Menezes, A., Sarkar, P. (eds.) INDOCRYPT 2002. LNCS, vol. 2551, pp. 185–198. Springer, Heidelberg (2002)
2. Balding, D.J., Bruno, W.J., Knill, E., Torney, D.C.: A comparative survey of non-adaptive probing designs. In: Genetic Mapping and DNA Sequencing, IMA. Math. and Its Applications, pp. 133–154. Springer, Heidelberg (1996)
3. Bar-Noy, A., Hwang, F.K., Kessler, I., Kutten, S.: Competitive group testing in high speed networks. Discrete Applied Math. 52, 29–38 (1994)
4. Bellare, M., Garay, J., Rabin, T.: Fast batch verification for modular exponentiation and digital signatures. In: Nyberg, K. (ed.) EUROCRYPT 1998. LNCS, vol. 1403, pp. 236–250. Springer, Heidelberg (1998)
5. Boneh, D., Lynn, B., Shacham, H.: Short signatures from the Weil pairing. Journal of Cryptology 17, 297–319 (2004)
6. Boyd, C., Pavlovski, C.: Attacking and repairing batch verification schemes. In: Okamoto, T. (ed.) ASIACRYPT 2000. LNCS, vol. 1976, pp. 58–71. Springer, Heidelberg (2000)
7. Camenisch, J., Lysyanskaya, A.: A signature scheme with efficient protocols. In: Cimato, S., Galdi, C., Persiano, G. (eds.) SCN 2002. LNCS, vol. 2576, pp. 268–289. Springer, Heidelberg (2003)
8. Camenisch, J., Hohenberger, S., Østergaard Pedersen, M.: Batch verification of short signatures. In: Naor, M. (ed.) EUROCRYPT 2007. LNCS, vol. 4515, pp. 246–263. Springer, Heidelberg (2007)
9. Camenisch, J., Hohenberger, S., Kohlweiss, M., Lysyanskaya, A., Meyerovich, M.: How to win the clonewars: efficient periodic $n$-times anonymous authentication. In: Proceedings of the 13th ACM Conference on Computer and Communications Security (CCS), pp. 201–210 (2006)
10. Cha, J., Cheon, J.: An identity-based signature scheme from gap Diffie-Hellman groups. In: Desmedt, Y.G. (ed.) PKC 2003. LNCS, vol. 2567, pp. 18–30. Springer, Heidelberg (2002)

11. Chatterjee, S., Sarkar, P.: Trading time for space: Towards an efficient IBE scheme with short(er) public parameters in the standard model. In: Won, D.H., Kim, S. (eds.) ICISC 2005. LNCS, vol. 3935, pp. 424–440. Springer, Heidelberg (2006)
12. Clementi, A.E.F., Monti, A., Silvestri, R.: Distributed broadcast in radio networks of unknown topology. Th. Comp. Sci. 302, 337–364 (2003)
13. De Bonis, A., Vaccaro, U.: Constructions of generalized superimposed codes with applications to group testing and conflict resolution in multiple access channels. Th. Comp. Sci. 306, 223–243 (2003)
14. Dorfman, R.: The detection of defective members of large populations. Ann. Math. Statist. 14, 436–440 (1943)
15. Du, D., Hwang, F.K.: Combinatorial Group Testing and its Applications. World Scientific, Singapore (1993)
16. Du, D., Hwang, F.K.: Combinatorial Group Testing and its Applications, 2nd edn. World Scientific, Singapore (2000)
17. D'yachkov, A.G., Rykov, V.V.: Optimal superimposed codes and designs for Renyi's search model. J. Statist. Plann. Inference 100, 281–302 (2002)
18. Ferrara, A.L., Green, M., Hohenberger, S., Østergaard Pedersen, M.: Practical Short Signature Batch Verification. In: Fischlin, M. (ed.) RSA Conference 2009. LNCS, vol. 5473, pp. 309–324. Springer, Heidelberg (2009)
19. Fiat, A.: Batch RSA. In: Brassard, G. (ed.) CRYPTO 1989. LNCS, vol. 435, pp. 175–185. Springer, Heidelberg (1990)
20. Fiat, A.: Batch RSA. Journal of Cryptology 10, 75–88 (1997)
21. Garay, J.A., Staddon, J.N., Wool, A.: Long-lived broadcast encryption. In: Bellare, M. (ed.) CRYPTO 2000. LNCS, vol. 1880, pp. 333–352. Springer, Heidelberg (2000)
22. Hu, M.C., Hwang, F.K., Wang, J.K.: A boundary problem for group testing. SIAM J. Alg. Disc. Methods 2, 81–87 (1981)
23. Karp, R.M., Upfal, E., Wigderson, A.: The complexity of parallel search. J. Comput. Syst. Sci. 36, 225–253 (1988)
24. Kautz, W.H., Singleton, R.G.: Nonrandom binary superimposed codes. IEEE Transactions on Information Theory 10, 363–373 (1964)
25. Law, L., Matt, B.J.: Finding invalid signatures in pairing-based batches. In: Galbraith, S.D. (ed.) Cryptography and Coding 2007. LNCS, vol. 4887, pp. 34–53. Springer, Heidelberg (2007)
26. Matt, B.J.: Identification of multiple invalid signatures in pairing-based batched signatures. In: PKC 2009. LNCS, vol. 5443, pp. 337–356 (2009)
27. Mitchell, C.J., Piper, F.C.: Key storage in secure networks. Discrete applied mathematics 21, 215–228 (1988)
28. Naccache, D., M'raihi, D., Vaudenay, S., Raphaeli, D.: Can DSA be improved? Complexity trade-offs with the digital signature standard. In: De Santis, A. (ed.) EUROCRYPT 1994. LNCS, vol. 950, pp. 77–85. Springer, Heidelberg (1995)
29. Pastuszak, J., Michalek, D., Pieprzyk, J., Seberry, J.: Identification of bad signatures in batches. In: Imai, H., Zheng, Y. (eds.) PKC 2000. LNCS, vol. 1751, pp. 28–45. Springer, Heidelberg (2000)
30. Pastuszak, J., Pieprzyk, J., Seberry, J.: Codes identifying bad signatures in batches. In: Roy, B., Okamoto, E. (eds.) INDOCRYPT 2000. LNCS, vol. 1977, pp. 143–154. Springer, Heidelberg (2000)
31. Porat, E., Rothschild, A.: Explicit non-adaptive combinatorial group testing schemes. In: Aceto, L., Damgård, I., Goldberg, L.A., Halldórsson, M.M., Ingólfsdóttir, A., Walukiewicz, I. (eds.) ICALP 2008, Part I. LNCS, vol. 5125, pp. 748–759. Springer, Heidelberg (2008)

32. Reyni, A.: On the theory of random search. Bull. Amer. Math Soc. 71, 809–828 (1965)
33. Ruszinkó, M.: On the upper bound of the size of the $r$-cover-free families. Journal of Combinatorial Theory Series A 66, 302–310 (1994)
34. Shultz, D.J.: Topics in nonadaptive group testing. Ph.D. Dissertation, Temple University (1992)
35. Spencer, J.: Minimal completely separating systems. Journal of Combinatorial Theory 8, 446–447 (1970)
36. Sperner, E.: Ein Satz Uber Untermengen einer endliche Menge. Math. Zeit. 27, 544–548 (1928)
37. Staddon, J.N., Stinson, D.R., Wei, R.: Combinatorial properties of frameproof and traceability codes. IEEE Trans. Inf. Theory 47, 1042–1049 (2001)
38. Stinson, D.R., van Trung, T., Wei, R.: Secure frameproof codes, key distribution patterns, group testing algorithms and related structures. Journal of Statistical Planning and Inference 86, 595–617 (2000)
39. Stinson, D.R., Wei, R., Zhu, L.: Some new bounds for cover-free families. Journal of Combinatorial Theory Series A 90, 224–234 (2000)
40. Stinson, D.R.: Attack on a concast signature scheme. Information Processing Letters 91, 39–41 (2004)
41. Sobel, M., Groll, P.A.: Group testing to eliminate efficiently all defectives in a binomial sample. Bell System Tech. J. 28, 1179–1252 (1959)

# A   Comparison Details

Table 4 gives the number of tests required by each algorithm when $p = 1$, with varying $n$ and $d$, while Tables 5 and 6 fix $d = 4$ and $d = 10$ respectively, with varying $n$ and $p$.

**Table 4.** Table showing the number of tests required by each group testing algorithm from Table 1 when $n = 10^3, 10^4, 10^5, 10^6$ and $d = 1, 2, 3, 4, 10$. For random matrices a success probability of 99.9% is required.

| Method | $n = 10^3, d =$ | | | | | $n = 10^4, d =$ | | | | |
|---|---|---|---|---|---|---|---|---|---|---|
| | 1 | 2 | 3 | 4 | 10 | 1 | 2 | 3 | 4 | 10 |
| Binary Splitting | 10 | 20 | 30 | 40 | 100 | 14 | 28 | 42 | 56 | 140 |
| Gen. Bin. Splitting | 10 | 20 | 30 | 39 | 87 | 14 | 27 | 40 | 52 | 121 |
| Li's $s$-stage | 18 | 33 | 47 | 60 | 125 | 25 | 46 | 66 | 85 | 187 |
| PR CFF | 13 | 89 | 159 | 249 | 1205 | 16 | 119 | 212 | 332 | 1607 |
| PPS id-codes | 63 | 94 | 126 | 158 | 347 | 200 | 300 | 400 | 500 | 1100 |
| Random Matrices | 49 | 87 | 124 | 162 | 387 | 57 | 101 | 145 | 189 | 452 |
| | $n = 10^5$ | | | | | $n = 10^6$ | | | | |
| Binary Splitting | 17 | 34 | 51 | 68 | 170 | 20 | 40 | 60 | 80 | 200 |
| Gen. Bin. Splitting | 17 | 34 | 50 | 65 | 154 | 20 | 40 | 60 | 79 | 187 |
| Li's $s$-stage | 31 | 58 | 84 | 110 | 250 | 37 | 71 | 103 | 135 | 312 |
| PR CFF | 20 | 149 | 265 | 415 | 2009 | 23 | 179 | 318 | 498 | 2411 |
| PPS id-codes | 632 | 948 | 1264 | 1581 | 3478 | 2K | 3K | 4K | 5K | 11K |
| Random Matrices | 65 | 115 | 166 | 216 | 517 | 73 | 130 | 186 | 243 | 581 |

**Table 5.** Table showing the number of tests required by each group testing algorithm from Table 1 when $n = 10^3, 10^4$, $d = 4$ and the number of processors available is $p = 2, 4, 8, 16$. For random matrices a success probability of 99.9% is required.

| Method | $d = 4$ | | | | | | | |
|---|---|---|---|---|---|---|---|---|
| | $n = 10^3$, $p =$ | | | | $n = 10^4$, $p =$ | | | |
| | 2 | 4 | 8 | 16 | 2 | 4 | 8 | 16 |
| Binary Splitting | 36 | 32 | 28 | 24 | 52 | 48 | 44 | 40 |
| Gen. Bin. Splitting | 35 | 31 | 27 | 23 | 48 | 44 | 40 | 36 |
| KUW | 28 | 20 | 16 | 12 | 36 | 24 | 20 | 16 |
| Li's $s$-stage | 35 | 19 | 12 | 8 | 49 | 27 | 17 | 12 |
| PR CFF | 125 | 63 | 32 | 16 | 166 | 83 | 42 | 21 |
| PPS id-codes | 79 | 40 | 20 | 10 | 250 | 125 | 63 | 32 |
| Random Matrices | 81 | 41 | 21 | 11 | 95 | 48 | 24 | 12 |
| | $n = 10^5$ | | | | $n = 10^6$ | | | |
| Binary Splitting | 64 | 60 | 56 | 52 | 76 | 72 | 68 | 64 |
| Gen. Bin. Splitting | 61 | 57 | 53 | 49 | 75 | 71 | 67 | 63 |
| KUW | 44 | 32 | 24 | 20 | 52 | 36 | 28 | 20 |
| Li's $s$-stage | 64 | 36 | 22 | 16 | 79 | 45 | 28 | 20 |
| PR CFF | 208 | 104 | 52 | 26 | 249 | 125 | 63 | 32 |
| PPS id-codes | 719 | 396 | 198 | 99 | 2.5K | 1250 | 625 | 313 |
| Random Matrices | 108 | 54 | 27 | 14 | 122 | 61 | 31 | 16 |

**Table 6.** Table showing the number of tests required by each group testing algorithm from Table 1 when $n = 10^3, 10^4$, $d = 10$ and the number of processors available is $p = 2, 4, 8, 16$. For random matrices a success probability of 99.9% is required.

| Method | $d = 10$ | | | | | | | |
|---|---|---|---|---|---|---|---|---|
| | $n = 10^3$, $p =$ | | | | $n = 10^4$, $p =$ | | | |
| | 2 | 4 | 8 | 16 | 2 | 4 | 8 | 16 |
| Binary Splitting | 90 | 80 | 70 | 60 | 130 | 120 | 110 | 100 |
| Gen. Bin. Splitting | 77 | 67 | 57 | 47 | 111 | 101 | 91 | 80 |
| KUW | 70 | 50 | 40 | 30 | 90 | 60 | 50 | 40 |
| Li's $s$-stage | 67 | 35 | 21 | 14 | 100 | 53 | 31 | 21 |
| PR CFF | 603 | 302 | 151 | 76 | 804 | 402 | 201 | 101 |
| PPS id-codes | 174 | 87 | 44 | 22 | 550 | 275 | 138 | 69 |
| Random Matrices | 194 | 97 | 49 | 25 | 226 | 113 | 57 | 29 |
| | $n = 10^5$, $p =$ | | | | $n = 10^6$, $p =$ | | | |
| | 2 | 4 | 8 | 16 | 2 | 4 | 8 | 16 |
| Binary Splitting | 160 | 150 | 140 | 130 | 190 | 180 | 170 | 160 |
| Gen. Bin. Splitting | 144 | 134 | 124 | 114 | 177 | 167 | 157 | 147 |
| KUW | 110 | 80 | 60 | 50 | 130 | 90 | 70 | 50 |
| Li's $s$-stage | 134 | 70 | 41 | 27 | 167 | 88 | 51 | 33 |
| PR CFF | 1005 | 503 | 252 | 126 | 1206 | 603 | 302 | 151 |
| PPS id-codes | 1739 | 870 | 435 | 218 | 5500 | 2750 | 1375 | 688 |
| Random Matrices | 259 | 130 | 65 | 33 | 291 | 146 | 73 | 37 |

# B    Bounds on Cover-Free Families

The number of rows, $t$, in the matrix representation of a $d$-CFF$(t, n)$ gives the number of tests required using the method of §2.3. In this section we present bounds for $t$ since this indicates how well (at best) we can expect CFF-based nonadaptive group tests to perform. First we present a necessary condition for the existence of CFF, a lower bound on the number of rows.

**Theorem 7 (see [39], Th. 1.1).** *For any $d \geq 1$, in a $d$-CFF$(t, n)$*

$$t \geq c \left( \frac{d^2}{\log d} \right) \log n .$$

*The constant $c$ is approximately $1/8$ (shown in [33]).*

It is immediately clear that the nonadaptive feature comes at a cost, since the number of tests will always be larger than $d \lceil \log(n) \rceil$, the number of tests required by binary splitting (c.f. 2.2).

De Bonis and Vaccaro bound $t$ from the other direction.

**Theorem 8 ([13], Cor. 1).** *There exists a $d$-CFF$(t, n)$ with*

$$t < 24d^2 \log(n + 2) .$$

Their proof method is constructive, based on a greedy algorithm, and it is efficient for small CFF.

# What Can Cryptography Do for Coding Theory?

Adam Smith

Computer Science and Engineering Department
Pennsylvania State University, University Park, PA, USA*

By Shannon's seminal work, we know that for the binary symmetric channel $\mathrm{BSC}_p$ which flips each transmitted bit independently with probability $p$, there exist binary codes of rate $1 - H(p) - \epsilon$ that enable reliable information transmission with exponentially small probability of miscommunication. Here $\epsilon > 0$ is arbitrary and $H(\cdot)$ is the binary entropy function. The quantity $1 - H(p)$ is called the (Shannon) capacity of the $\mathrm{BSC}_p$ channel. But what if the errors are *adversarial* and not randomly distributed? For the adversarial channel $\mathrm{ADV}_p$ where the channel can corrupt up to a fraction $p$ of symbols in an arbitrary manner *after* seeing the codeword, it is known that for error-free communication to be possible, the rate has to be much smaller than the Shannon capacity $1 - H(p)$.

In this talk, we survey a line of work which considers relaxations of the model that enable achieving capacity even against adversarial errors. The talk will focus on models which limit the channel to *computationally simple behavior* and use ideas from cryptography to reason about the channel. Such settings were considered in several previous works, notably those of Lipton (STACS 1994) and Micali *et al.* (TCC 2005); both of those works showed how to achieve the Shannon capacity in the presence of arbitrary polynomial-time channels, at the cost of additional setup assumptions (either shared randomness or a public-key infrastructure). Both works also assume the existence of one-way functions.

We also describe some new results which use similar techniques to correct against weaker channel adversaries without the need for extra setup or assumptions (joint work with V. Guruswami). Some of the results discussed are available as preprint arXiv:0912.0965.

Slides of the talk are available from `http://www.cse.psu.edu/~asmith`.

---

* Supported in part by US National Science Foundation (NSF) TF award #0747294 and NSF CAREER/PECASE award #0729171.

K. Kurosawa (Ed.): ICITS 2009, LNCS 5973, p. 158, 2010.

# Cryptanalysis of Secure Message Transmission Protocols with Feedback

Qiushi Yang[1,*] and Yvo Desmedt[1,2,**]

[1] Department of Computer Science, University College London, UK
{q.yang,y.desmedt}@cs.ucl.ac.uk
[2] RCIS, AIST, Japan

**Abstract.** In the context of secure point-to-point message transmission in networks with minimal connectivity, previous studies showed that feedbacks from the receiver to the sender can be used to reduce the requirements of network connectivity. We observe that the way how feedbacks were used in previous work does not guarantee perfect privacy to the transmitted message, when the adversary performs a *Guessing Attack*. In this paper, we shall describe our new Guessing Attack to some existing protocols (in fact, we are the first to point out a flaw in the protocols of Desmedt-Wang's Eurocrypt'02 paper and of Patra-Shankar-Choudhary-Srinathan-Rangan's CANS'07 paper), and propose a scheme defending against a general adversary structure. In addition, we also show how to achieve almost perfectly secure message transmission with feedbacks when perfect reliability or perfect privacy is not strictly required.

**Keywords:** secure message transmission, privacy and reliability, Guessing Attack, adversary structure, feedback.

## 1 Introduction

Secure point-to-point communication requires both private and reliable message transmission from a sender $A$ to a receiver $B$, despite the possibility that some parties on the channels between them are corrupted. Dolev et al. [8] initialized the problem of secure message transmission by showing that secure communication is possible in a network graph that is not complete. The interplay of the network connectivity and secure communication has been studied extensively [7, 2, 4, 8, 9, 5, 13, 6, 25, 14].

The general setting of this problem assumes an active *Byzantine* adversary, who has unlimited computational power (not only a passive listener). An adversary $X$ can be characterized as *threshold* ($k$-bounded) or *non-threshold* (general adversary structure). In the initial studies, Dolev [7] and Dolev et al. [8] showed that $2k + 1$ connectivity is required for reliable message transmission, and if all

---

* Funded by a UCL PhD studentship.
** This work was done while funded by EPSRC EP/C538285/1 and by BT, as BT Chair of Information Security.

communication links are one-way, then the system's network needs to be $3k+1$ connected. Some further studies on threshold adversaries have been done by Franklin and Wright [9], Desmedt and Wang [5], and Kurozawa and Suzuki [14]. Furthermore, in the presence of a *general adversary structure* [11], Kumar et al. [13] gave the necessary and sufficient conditions for perfectly secure message transmission in bi-direction networks (all links are two-way), and later, Desmedt et al. [6] extended the research and provided some results on all-one-way linked networks.

Although the concerning problem may seem trivial, it is far from straightforward. Many solutions on the topic of secure message transmission require careful examination. For instance, in Crypto 04, Srinathan et al. [24] proposed an optimal (in transmission rate) protocol for all-two-way communication. However, that protocol was later proved not perfectly reliable as originally claimed, by Agarwal et al. [1]. Similarly, in this work, we show that perfect privacy can be breached in many schemes that use the so-called *feedback channels* (e.g. some protocols of Desmedt and Wang [5] in Eurocrypt'02).

Given a sender $A$ and a receiver $B$ in a network. The channel that $A$ uses to transmit a message to $B$ is called the *forward channel*, and the channel that $B$ transmits feedbacks to $A$ is called the *feedback channel*. In an all-two-way linked network, the forward channels and the feedback channels have the same connectivity (symmetric). That is, if $B$ can reliably receive message from $A$, then $A$ can reliably receive feedbacks from $B$. However, in general, the feedbacks that $A$ receives may not be reliable. That is, the feedback channels may have less connectivity than the forward channels do. Desmedt and Wang [5] motivated this with the following scenarios: a channel from $A$ to $B$ is cheap, but a channel from $B$ to $A$ is expensive; in another scenario, $A$ has access to more resources than $B$ does.

Some studies have been done concerning this network setting (with unreliable feedback channels). This problem was initialized by Desmedt and Wang [5] in Eurocrypt'02. In their paper they showed that if there are $u$ directed node-disjoint paths from $B$ to $A$, then it is sufficient to have $3k + 1 - u > 2k + 1$ directed node-disjoint paths from $A$ to $B$ against a $k$-active adversary. Another study has been done by Patra et al. [19], in which they extended the previous results and considered a general adversary structure.[1] However, we observe that *all* the protocols in these papers are not so *perfectly* secure as they claimed, as those protocols actually leak some information about the message to the adversary $X$, when $X$ corrupts the feedback channel and acts on it. Thus we shall show how $X$ can attack those protocols in this paper.

*Our contributions.* In our work we study the use of the feedback channels in depth. Particularly, we observe that the major functionality of the feedback channels is to be used by the receiver $B$ for reliable message transmission purpose when faulty messages are received, but this may undermine perfect privacy of the transmitted messages. We will describe a new *Guessing Attack* that the

---

[1] We noticed that some recent studies have been done considering this network setting (see [17, 18]). However, those results are less relative to our concern.

adversary may perform on many existing protocols that work in networks with feedback channels.

Next we show how to construct a perfectly secure message transmission protocol that withstands the Guessing Attack and any other attack. In this paper we consider a general adversary structure, thus our results can be applied in more general cases. In addition, we study *almost* perfectly secure message transmission. First we show that the network connectivity required for achieving almost perfectly private message transmission is *exactly the same* as that for achieving perfect privacy. Next, we study almost perfectly reliable message transmission tolerating a general adversary structure, and propose a protocol, which is a generalization of the result in [5].

*Organization of this paper.* We describe our model in Section 2. In Section 3 we propose our Guessing Attack that breaches perfect privacy of some existing protocols. Section 4 is devoted to present the necessary and sufficient conditions for perfectly secure message transmission, and we shall give our main protocol that tolerates the Guessing Attack in this section. In Section 5, we show our result on almost perfectly private message transmission, and in Section 6, we discuss almost perfectly reliable message transmission.

## 2   Model and Background

*Basic definitions.* We abstract away the concrete network structure and model a network by a directed graph $G(V, E)$, whose nodes are the parties in the network and edges are point-to-point secure communication links, where all the edges in $E$ have directions. We also denote $\mathbb{F}$ as the finite field that both $A$ and $B$ agree on, and $\mathcal{M} \subseteq \mathbb{F}$ as the message space that $A$ chooses message from. Let $S$ be a set, we write $|S|$ to denote the number of elements in $S$, and $a \in_R S$ to indicate that $a$ is chosen from $S$ with respect to the uniform distribution. Let $a \in \mathbb{R}$. We write $\lfloor a \rfloor \in \mathbb{Z}$ to denote the integer part of $a$. Let $a, b, M \in \mathbb{F}$. We employ an authentication function $auth(M; a, b) := aM + b$, by which each authentication key $key = (a, b)$ can be used to authenticate one message $M$ without revealing any information about the authentication key (see [10, 21, 20, 9]).

Throughout the paper, we assume that $A, B \in V$, and use $\mathcal{P}$ as the set of all the directed paths from $A$ to $B$ and $\mathcal{Q}$ as the set of all the directed paths from $B$ to $A$ (the directed paths are not necessarily node-disjoint). Let $Z \subseteq V$, we write $\mathcal{P}_Z$ to denote the set of all paths in $\mathcal{P}$ that pass through nodes in $Z$, and write $\bar{\mathcal{P}}_Z$ to denote the set of all paths in $\mathcal{P}$ that are free of nodes in $Z$. Similarly, we denote $\mathcal{Q}_Z$ and $\bar{\mathcal{Q}}_Z$.

*Secret sharing.* We define a $(k+1)$-out-of-$n$ $\epsilon$-private secret sharing scheme $((k+1, n, \epsilon)$-SSS).

**Definition 1.** *Let $\epsilon < 1$. A $(k+1, n, \epsilon)$-SSS is a probabilistic function $S : \mathbb{F} \to \mathbb{F}^n$ such that for any $m \in \mathbb{F}$ and $(v_1, ..., v_n) = S(m)$,*
*property-1 m can be recovered from any $k + 1$ entries of $(v_1, ..., v_n)$ with probability 1, and*

*property-2 m can also be recovered (without random guessing) from any $r \leq k$ entries with probability at most $\epsilon$.*

Therefore, the classic Shamir's scheme [22] is a $(k+1, n, 0)$-SSS, and Blakely's scheme [3] is a $(k+1, n, \epsilon)$-SSS (almost perfectly private). The set of all possible $(v_1, ..., v_n)$ can be viewed as a code and its elements codewords. When there is no ambuiguity, we view $S(m)$ as a subset of this code. We say a $(k+1, n, \epsilon)$-SSS can detect $d$ errors if given any codeword $(v_1, ..., v_n)$ and any tuple $(u_1, ..., u_n)$ such that $0 < |i : u_i \neq v_i, 1 \leq i \leq n| \leq d$, one can detect that $(u_1, ..., u_n)$ is not a codeword; a $(k+1, n, \epsilon)$-SSS can correct $c$ errors if given $(v_1, ..., v_n) \in S(m)$, from any tuple $(u_1, ..., u_n)$ such that $|i : u_i \neq v_i, 1 \leq i \leq n| \leq c$, one can recover the secret $m$. It has been proved that a $(k+1, n, 0)$-SSS can detect $n-k-1$ errors and correct (not simultaneously) $\lfloor (n - k - 1)/2 \rfloor$ errors using error-correcting code [15, 16].

*Adversary model.* We consider an adversary $X$ who is characterized by an adversary structure $\mathcal{Z}$ that consists of all sets of parties that $X$ can corrupt. A definition of an adversary structure was given by Hirt and Maurer [11] (see also [12]): Given a party set $P$, an adversary structure $\mathcal{Z}$ on $P$ is a family of subsets $\mathcal{Z} \subset 2^P$ such that: $Z \in \mathcal{Z}, Z' \subseteq Z \subseteq P \Rightarrow Z' \in \mathcal{Z}$. A set $Z \in \mathcal{Z}$ is called *maximal* if $Z' \supset Z \Rightarrow Z' \notin \mathcal{Z}$, and we use $\tilde{\mathcal{Z}}$ as the set of all maximal sets in $\mathcal{Z}$.

Throughout the paper we use $Z_x \in \mathcal{Z}$ to denote the set of parties that the adversary $X$ chooses to control. We allow an *active*, or *Byzantine*, adversary, who has unlimited computational power and resources. The adversary $X$ can read the traffic of $Z_x$ and perform any local computation on $Z_x$. In this paper we only consider a static adversary, whose choice of $Z_x$ does not change throughout the protocol.

*Message transmission protocol.* Let $\Pi$ be a message transmission protocol. $A$ starts with a message $M^A$ drawn from a message space $\mathcal{M}$ with respect to a certain probability distribution. At the end of the protocol $\Pi$, $B$ outputs a message $M^B \in \mathcal{M}$. For any execution of the protocol $\Pi$, let $adv$ be the adversary $X$'s view of the entire protocol. We write $adv(M, r)$ to denote $X$'s view when $M^A = M$ and when the sequence of coin flips used by $X$ is $r$ (follows [9, 6]).

**Privacy:** $\Pi$ is $\epsilon$-*private* if, for any two messages $M_0, M_1 \in \mathcal{M}$ and every $r$,
    $\sum_c |Pr[adv(M_0, r) = c] - Pr[adv(M_1, r) = c]| \leq 2\epsilon$.
**Reliability:** $\Pi$ is $\delta$-*reliable* if, with probability at least $1 - \delta$ $(0 \leq \delta < \frac{1}{2})$, $B$ terminates $M^B = M^A$.
**Security:** $\Pi$ is $(\epsilon, \delta)$-*secure* if it is $\epsilon$-private and $\delta$-reliable.

We say $\Pi$ is a perfectly secure message transmission protocol if it is $(0, 0)$-secure. In this paper, we also discuss $(0, \delta)$-secure and $(\epsilon, 0)$-secure message transmissions, which are almost perfectly secure.

In the presence of an adversary structure $\mathcal{Z}$, Kumar et al. [13] showed that in a bi-direction network, the necessary and sufficient condition for $(0, 0)$-secure message transmission from $A$ to $B$ is that $\mathcal{P}_{Z_a \cup Z_b} \subsetneq \mathcal{P}$ for any $Z_a, Z_b \in \mathcal{Z}$. In the case that all communication links are one-way without feedback, Desmedt et al. [6]

proved that 0-reliable message transmission from $A$ to $B$ can be achieved if and only if $\mathcal{P}_{Z_a \cup Z_b} \subsetneq \mathcal{P}$ for any $Z_a, Z_b \in \mathcal{Z}$, and $(0,0)$-secure message transmission is possible if and only if $\mathcal{P}_{Z_a \cup Z_b \cup Z_c} \subsetneq \mathcal{P}$ for any $Z_a, Z_b, Z_c \in \mathcal{Z}$. Furthermore, we will discuss the case, in which the feedback channels exist, in Section 4.

## 3    Attack on Feedback Channels

In this section we propose a *Guessing Attack* that takes advantage of how the feedback channels are normally used. In most protocols that work on networks with feedback channels, the feedbacks are used by the receiver $B$ to seek for help from $A$ when $B$ does not have enough information to recover the message (i.e., for reliability purpose). In our attack, we propose the following. Since the adversary $X$ can choose to corrupt some feedback paths, it can simulate how $B$ uses the feedback channels and learn from $A$ the information it needs to recover the message with better probability than guessing. This allows $X$ to breach perfect privacy, as we describe now in more detail.

Here we give an example of how Guessing Attack breaches perfect privacy of one of Desmedt and Wang's protocols in [5]. This DW protocol (the protocol corresponding to [5, Theorem 5]) is for $(0,0)$-secure message transmission against a threshold adversary. First we shall sketch the DW protocol before we show that it is not 0-private.

**Condition for the DW protocol.** There are $3k \geq 2k+1$ directed node-disjoint paths from $A$ to $B$ and one directed node-disjoint path from $B$ to $A$.[2]

**Sketch of the DW protocol.** Let $p_1, ..., p_{3k}$ be the directed paths from $A$ to $B$ and $q$ be the directed path from $B$ to $A$.

   Step 1 ...

   Step 2 $A$ chooses a $key^A \in_R \mathbb{F}$ and constructs $(k+1, 3k, 0)$-secret-shares $v = (s_1, ..., s_{3k})$ of $key^A$. For each $1 \leq i \leq 3k$, $A$ sends $s_i$ to $B$ via path $p_i$.

   Step 3 Let $v^B = (s_1^B, ..., s_{3k}^B)$ be the shares $B$ receives. If $B$ finds that there are at most $k-1$ errors (using error-correcting code), $B$ recovers $key^B$ from the shares, sends 'stop' to $A$ via path $q$; otherwise, $B$ sends $v^B$ to $A$ via path $q$.

   Step 4 If $A$ receives $v^A = (s_1^A, ..., s_{3k}^A)$ from path $q$, $A$ broadcasts $P = \{i : s_i^A \neq s_i\}$ ($|P| = k$) via all paths $p_1, ..., p_{3k}$; otherwise, $A$ broadcasts 'stop'.

   Step 5 ...

   Step 6 $A$ broadcasts $key^A + M^A$ via all paths $p_1, ..., p_{3k}$, where $M^A$ is the actual message.

   Step 7 ...

---

[2] This condition is sufficient for $(0,0)$-secure message transmission from $A$ to $B$, but is stronger than the necessary condition. See [5] for more detail.

The $k$-active adversary $X$ chooses to control paths $p_1, ..., p_{k-1}$ and path $q$. Thus $X$ is able to get shares $(s_1, ..., s_{k-1})$ in Step 2. With these $k-1$ shares, $X$ performs the following:

$X$ chooses a share $s_k^X \in_R \mathbb{F}$ and two keys $key_1^X, key_2^X \in_R \mathbb{F}$ ($key_1^X \neq key_2^X$). Corresponding to $key_1^X$, $X$ assumes that $(s_1, ..., s_{k-1}, s_k^X)$ are $k$ shares of $key_1^X$, thus using Lagrange interpolation, $X$ gets another $k$ shares $(s_{k+1}^X, ..., s_{2k}^X)$ of $key_1^X$. Similarly, corresponding to $key_2^X$, $X$ assumes that $(s_1, ..., s_{k-1}, s_k^X)$ are $k$ shares of $key_2^X$, and gets another $k$ shares $(s_{2k+1}^X, ..., s_{3k}^X)$ of $key_2^X$. $X$ sets $v^X = (s_1, ..., s_{k-1}, s_k^X, ..., s_{3k}^X)$.

In each execution step of the DW protocol, $X$ acts passive on paths $p_1, ..., p_{k-1}$. Thus $B$ sends 'stop' to $A$ in Step 3. On the feedback path $q$ that $X$ corrupts, $X$ ignores what $B$ sends and forwards $v^X$ to $A$. Then in Step 4, if $A$ finds exactly $k$ errors in $v^A = v^X$, $A$ broadcasts $P = \{i : s_i^X \neq s_i\}$, according to which $X$ recovers $key^A = key_j^X$ ($j \in \{1, 2\}$); otherwise, $A$ broadcasts 'stop', and $X$ randomly guesses a $key^X$.

Fig. 1. Guessing Attack to the DW protocol

This single feedback channel protocol is the basis of the main protocols in [5]. We observe that this DW protocol is 0-reliable, so in the above sketch we did not describe how $B$ recovers the message (see [5] for the entire protocol). Now we show that using our Guessing Attack, the adversary $X$ can learn the message $M^A$ with probability better than guessing.

**Theorem 1.** *This DW protocol is not a 0-private message transmission protocol from $A$ to $B$.*

*Proof.* Due to the fact that $key^A \in_R \mathbb{F}$, if this DW protocol is 0-private, then the probability that the adversary $X$ guesses $key^A$ is $\frac{1}{|\mathbb{F}|}$. That is, $X$ learns nothing from the shares it gets, and can only guess a uniformly random number $key^X \in \mathbb{F}$, and with probability $\frac{1}{|\mathbb{F}|}$, $key^X = key^A$. We call this a *random guess*. Now we show a Guessing Attack by which $X$ can learn $key^A$ with a probability better than $\frac{1}{|\mathbb{F}|}$ (see Fig.1).

In this Guessing Attack, $X$ guesses a share $s_k^X$ and two keys $key_1^X$ and $key_2^X$. It is straightforward that $A$ will broadcast $P$ if and only if $A$ finds exactly $k$ errors in $v^X$, and the $k$ errors can only be either $(s_{k+1}^X, ..., s_{2k}^X)$ or $(s_{2k+1}^X, ..., s_{3k}^X)$. That is, the guess is successful if $s_k^X = s_k$ and one of the two keys is correct (i.e., $key_i^X = key^A, i \in \{1, 2\}$). Thus the probability $T$ that the guess is successful is

$$T = \frac{1}{|\mathbb{F}|} \times \left( 2 \times \frac{1}{|\mathbb{F}|} \right) = \frac{2}{|\mathbb{F}|^2}.$$

If the guess fails, then $X$ will use a random guess with probability $\frac{1}{|\mathbb{F}|}$ to get $key^X = key^A$. Thus, the total probability $G$ that $X$ learns $key^A$ by performing Guessing Attack is

$$G = T + (1 - T) \times \frac{1}{|\mathbb{F}|} > \frac{1}{|\mathbb{F}|}.$$

Therefore, $X$ can learn $key^A$ with a probability better than $\frac{1}{|\mathbb{F}|}$ and simultaneously recover $M^A$ with probability better than guessing.[3] Hence we proved that the DW protocol is not 0-private.    □

Note that in journal paper [26], Wang and Desmedt provided a new protocol that uses induction when $A$ receives tuples of shares in feedbacks (the case that Guessing Attack may happen). When $A$ notices that Guessing Attack may happen according to the feedbacks it receives, it uses an induction and re-sends the message without revealing the message to the adversary (0-private). The property of the threshold adversray, $t$-bounded, allows the induction to be continued until the message is transmitted 0-reliably. Thus the protocol in [26] enables perfect security. For details of the $(0,0)$-secure message transmission protocol tolerating a threshold adversary, we refer to [26, Theorem 4.2].

As we showed in the above example, the basic idea of Guessing Attack is to replace the feedbacks from $B$ to $A$ on the feedback channel with something that may reveal the message. There is some probability associated with this guessing of being successful.

Besides the Desmedt-Wang protocols, we observe that all protocols given by Patra et al. in [19] that tolerate either threshold or non-threshold adversaries do not guarantee perfect privacy when the Guessing Attack takes place, and hence they are not $(0,0)$-secure. We show our Guessing Attacks to the protocols from [19] in Appendix A and the full version of this paper [27].

# 4    $(0,0)$-Secure Message Transmission

In this section, we address the question of perfectly secure message transmission, for which both 0-private and 0-reliable message transmissions are required. That is, we shall provide a new protocol that tolerates the Guessing Attack. We focus on a $(0,0)$-secure message transmission against a general adversary structure (as Wang and Desmedt [26] recently provided a $(0,0)$-secure protocol for the threshold case), hence our protocol can be used in more general cases. Before we show our protocol, we generalize the following theorem based on the result by Patra et al. [19].

**Theorem 2.** *Let $G(V,E)$ be a directed graph, $\mathcal{Z}$ be an adversary structure on $V \setminus \{A,B\}$, and $\mathcal{Q} \neq \emptyset$. The necessary and sufficient conditions (CONs) for $(0,0)$-secure message transmission from $A$ to $B$ are:*

*CON-1 for any two sets $Z_a, Z_b \in \mathcal{Z}$: $\mathcal{P}_{Z_a \cup Z_b} \subsetneq \mathcal{P}$, and*
*CON-2 for any three sets $Z_a, Z_b, Z_c \in \mathcal{Z}$, if $\mathcal{P}_{Z_a \cup Z_b \cup Z_c} = \mathcal{P}$, then out of the three sets, there is at most one $Z_i$ ($i \in \{a,b,c\}$) such that $\mathcal{Q}_{Z_i} = \mathcal{Q}$.*

---

[3] Although $M^A$ can be chosen with respect to any probability distribution (not necessarily uniform), more knowledge of the key $key^A$ gives better probability of getting $M^A$.

We also employ a lemma from [19] for a simpler protocol, as using this lemma, we only need to consider a set $\tilde{\mathcal{Y}}$ of size 3 that contains the set $Z_x \in \tilde{\mathcal{Z}}$ that the adversary $X$ chooses to control.

**Lemma 1.** (see [19]) *Let $\mathcal{Z}$ be an adversary structure on $V \setminus \{A, B\}$. $(0,0)$-secure message transmission from $A$ to $B$ tolerating $\mathcal{Z}$ is possible if: for any monotone subset $\mathcal{Y} \subseteq \mathcal{Z}$ such that $|\tilde{\mathcal{Y}}| = 3$ and $Z_x \in \tilde{\mathcal{Y}}$, there is a $(0,0)$-secure message transmission protocol from $A$ to $B$ tolerating $\tilde{\mathcal{Y}}$.*

In [19], Patra et al. proposed a *Secure Protocol* tolerating $\tilde{\mathcal{Y}}$. However, the Secure Protocol is vulnerable to Guessing Attack, and hence is not 0-private (see Appendix A for the proof).

Now we show a $(0,0)$-secure message transmission protocol (PSP) under CONs tolerating such a sub-structure $\tilde{\mathcal{Y}}$ and defending Guessing Attack. First we let $\tilde{\mathcal{Y}} = \{Z_1, Z_2, Z_3\}$. The case that $\mathcal{P}_{Z_1 \cup Z_2 \cup Z_3} \subsetneq \mathcal{P}$ has been proved in [6]. Now we consider the case that $\mathcal{P}_{Z_1 \cup Z_2 \cup Z_3} = \mathcal{P}$. Here we employ the similar settings to the proof to [19, Theorem 10]; that is, due to CON-1, three forward paths $p_1 \in \bar{\mathcal{P}}_{Z_2 \cup Z_3}$, $p_2 \in \bar{\mathcal{P}}_{Z_1 \cup Z_3}$ and $p_3 \in \bar{\mathcal{P}}_{Z_1 \cup Z_2}$ exist to transmit messages from $A$ to $B$. This implies that, since $Z_x \in \tilde{\mathcal{Y}}$, the adversary $X$ can corrupt at most one $p_i$ ($1 \leq i \leq 3$). Thus if $A$ sends a value via all three paths $p_1, p_2, p_3$, then $B$ can recover this value using a majority vote. In our protocol we say that $A$ *reliably sends* a value to $B$ to indicate this kind of transmission.

Based on CON-2, we assume that $\mathcal{Q}_{Z_1} \subsetneq \mathcal{Q}$, $\mathcal{Q}_{Z_2} \subsetneq \mathcal{Q}$ and $\mathcal{Q}_{Z_3} \subseteq \mathcal{Q}$. Moreover, due to CON-2, two feedback paths $q_1 \in \bar{\mathcal{Q}}_{Z_1}$ and $q_2 \in \bar{\mathcal{Q}}_{Z_2}$ exist to transmit feedbacks from $B$ to $A$.

In our protocol, we use 0 as default received value. That is, when $A$ is sending to $B$, if $B$ receives nothing on path $p \in \mathcal{P}$, then $B$ assumes that 0 is received on path $p$. Similarly if $A$ receives nothing on path $q \in \mathcal{Q}$ from $B$, then $A$ assumes that 0 is received on path $q$.

*Underlying idea.* Our protocol runs a loop. In each round of the loop, the feedback paths $q_1$ and $q_2$ are used to transmit only one bit: either 0 or 1. This prevents the Guessing Attack from happening at the first place. If in a round of the loop, $B$ found that one of the forward paths $p_1$, $p_2$ or $p_3$ transmits a faulty message, then $B$ will send 0 via the feedback paths. If $A$ receives 0 on $q_j$ ($j \in \{1, 2\}$), then $A$ will reliably send the message to $B$ again, so $B$ will then know which path $p_f$ ($1 \leq f \leq 3$) is faulty. In the rest of the protocol, $B$ will only recover the message on $p_i$ and $p_j$ ($i, j \in \{1, 2, 3\} \setminus \{f\}$), and will not send 0 as feedback again. Therefore, if $A$ receive 0 on $q_j$ ($j \in \{1, 2\}$) more than once, then $A$ knows that $q_j$ is faulty, and will not consider the feedbacks received on $q_j$ again in the rest of the protocol. In our protocol, we let $A$ use $err_1$ and $err_2$ to count the numbers of 0's received on paths $q_1$ and $q_2$ respectively. Furthermore, if in a round of the loop, $A$ does not receive 0 on the feedback path(s) that $A$ considers not faulty, then $A$ will not send any information about the message again, and $A$ knows that the message has been transmitted 0-privately. $A$ sets a variable $pri = 1$ in this case. We let the loop halt when $A$ finds both $q_1$ and $q_2$ are faulty (i.e., $err_1 > 1$ and $err_2 > 1$), or when $A$ concludes that the message has been

---

$A$ sets $err_1 := 0$, $err_2 := 0$, $pri := 0$;
$B$ sets $f := 0$, $flag := 0$;[a]
**while** $(err_1 \leq 1$ **or** $err_2 \leq 1)$ **and** $pri = 0$ **loop**
$\quad$ $A$ chooses an $m_1^A \in_R \mathbb{F}$ and constructs $(2,3,0)$-secret-shares $(s_1^A, s_2^A, s_3^A)$ of $m_1^A$;
$\quad$ Step 1 For each $1 \leq i \leq 3$, $A$ sends $s_i^A$ to $B$ via path $p_i$;
$\quad$ Step 2 $B$ receives three shares $(s_1^B, s_2^B, s_3^B)$;
$\quad\quad$ **if** $f \neq 0$ **then**
$\quad\quad\quad$ $B$ recovers $m_1^A$ from shares $s_i^B$ and $s_j^B$ where $i, j \in \{1, 2, 3\} \setminus \{f\}$;
$\quad\quad\quad$ $B$ sends 1 to $A$ via path $q_1$ and path $q_2$;
$\quad\quad$ **else if** $B$ detects[b] 1 error in $(s_1^B, s_2^B, s_3^B)$ **then**
$\quad\quad\quad$ $B$ sends 0 to $A$ via path $q_1$ and path $q_2$, and sets $flag := 1$;
$\quad\quad$ **else if** $B$ detects 0 error in $(s_1^B, s_2^B, s_3^B)$ **then**
$\quad\quad\quad$ $B$ recovers $m_1^A$ from $(s_1^B, s_2^B, s_3^B)$, and sends 1 to $A$ via path $q_1$ and $q_2$;
$\quad\quad$ **end if**;
$\quad$ Step 3 $A$ receives $fdb_1 \in \{0, 1\}$ on path $q_1$ and $fdb_2 \in \{0, 1\}$ on path $q_2$;
$\quad\quad$ **if** $err_1 > 1$ **or** $err_2 > 1$ **then**
$\quad\quad\quad$ $A$ only considers $fdb_h$ where $h \in \{1, 2\}$ and $err_h \leq 1$;
$\quad\quad\quad$ **if** $fdb_h = 0$ **then**
$\quad\quad\quad\quad$ $A$ sets $err_h := err_h + 1$, and reliably sends $m_1^A$ to $B$;
$\quad\quad\quad$ **else if** $fdb_h = 1$ **then**
$\quad\quad\quad\quad$ $A$ sets $pri := 1$, and reliably sends 'OK' to $B$;
$\quad\quad\quad$ **end if**;
$\quad\quad$ **else if** $err_1 \leq 1$ **and** $err_2 \leq 1$ **then**
$\quad\quad\quad$ **if** $fdb_1 = fdb_2 = 1$ **then**
$\quad\quad\quad\quad$ $A$ sets $pri := 1$, and reliably sends 'OK' to $B$;
$\quad\quad\quad$ **else then**
$\quad\quad\quad\quad$ $A$ sets $err_h := err_h + 1$ for each $1 \leq h \leq 2$ such that $fdb_h = 0$;
$\quad\quad\quad\quad$ $A$ reliably sends $m_1^A$ to $B$;
$\quad\quad\quad$ **end if**;
$\quad\quad$ **end if**;
$\quad$ Step[c] 4 **if** $flag = 1$ **then**
$\quad\quad$ **if** $B$ reliably receives $m_1^B := m_1^A$ **then**
$\quad\quad\quad$ $B$ sets $f := l$ such that $s_l^B$ is not a correct share of $m_1^B$;
$\quad\quad$ **else if** $B$ reliably receives 'OK' **then**
$\quad\quad\quad$ $B$ sets $f = 3$,[d] and recovers $m_1^B$ from $s_1^B$ and $s_2^B$;
$\quad\quad$ **end if**;
$\quad$ **end if**;
**end loop**; - while

---

[a] Later in PSP, if $B$ concludes that a path $p_i$ $(1 \leq i \leq 3)$ is faulty, then $B$ sets $f := i$ to mark the faulty path $p_f$.
[b] As we mentioned in Section 2, a $(k+1, n, 0)$-SSS can detect $n - k - 1$ errors using error-detecting code. Thus $B$ can detect 1 error with the $(2, 3, 0)$-secret-shares.
[c] $B$ does not come to Step 4 unless $B$ sent 0 as feedback in Step 2.
[d] In this case, $B$ knows that $A$ did not receive 0, so $B$ concludes that both paths $q_1 \in \bar{\mathcal{Q}}_{Z_1}$ and $q_2 \in \bar{\mathcal{Q}}_{Z_2}$ are faulty. Thus $B$ knows that $Z_3$, and hence $p_3$, are faulty.

**Fig. 2.** Perfectly Secure Protocol (PSP)

---

$A$ reliably sends '$err_1 > 1$ and $err_2 > 1$' or '$pri = 1$' to $B$;
$B$ then halts the loop and keeps the last $m_1^B$;
$A$ sets $m_2^A := m^A - m_1^A$;
**if** $err_1 > 1$ **and** $err_2 > 1$ **then**
    $A$ sends $m_2^A$ to $B$ via paths $p_1$;[e]
    $B$ receives $m_2^B$ on path $p_1$, and recovers $m^B = m_1^B + m_2^B$;
**else if** $pri = 1$ **then**
    $A$ reliably sends $m_2^A$ to $B$;
    $B$ reliably receives $m_2^B = m_2^A$, and recovers $m^B = m_1^B + m_2^B$;
**end if; - end PSP**

---

[e] In this case, $A$ concludes that both paths $q_1 \in \bar{\mathcal{Q}}_{Z_1}$ and $q_2 \in \bar{\mathcal{Q}}_{Z_2}$ are faulty. Thus $A$ knows that $Z_3$ is faulty, so $p_1 \in \bar{\mathcal{P}}_{Z_2 \cup Z_3}$ is honest.

**Fig. 2.** (*continued*)

transmitted 0-privately (i.e., $pri = 1$). Based on this idea, we give a $(0,0)$-secure message transmission protocol (PSP) that tolerates Guessing Attack to transmit a message $m^A$ (see Fig.2).

**Lemma 2.** *PSP is a $(0,0)$-secure message transmission protocol from $A$ to $B$.*

*Proof.* First we show that PSP is 0-private. That is, the adversary $X$ cannot learn $m^A$ throughout the protocol. We consider the following two cases:

1. When **while loop** halts, $err_1 > 1$ and $err_2 > 1$. As we discussed before, this case means that both paths $q_1$ and $q_2$ are faulty, and $X$ can corrupt both paths only if $X$ chooses $Z_3$ to control. Thus $A$ knows that $p_3$ is faulty and only transmits $m_2^A$ via path $p_1$. It is straightforward that $X$ is not able to learn $m^A$ without knowing $m_2^A$.
2. When **while loop** halts, $pri = 1$. This case only happens when $A$ receives 1 on each path $q_j$ where $j \in \{1,2\}$ and $err_j \leq 1$, and $A$ will then reliably send 'OK' to $B$. Thus the adversary $X$ who chooses $Z_x$ and corrupts $p_x$ can get only one share $s_x^A$, and hence cannot recover $m_1^A$, and simultaneously cannot learn $m^A$.

Thus, we showed that in both cases, $m^A$ is transmitted 0-privately.

Next, we prove that PSP is 0-reliable. That is, $B$ is guaranteed to recover $m^B = m^A$. It is straightforward that if $X$ keeps passive on path $p_x$ ($1 \leq x \leq 3$) that it corrupts, then $B$ can reliably recover $m_1^B = m_1^A$. Now we show that if $X$ forwards faulty shares on $p_x$, then $B$ can get $f = x$ (i.e., $p_f = p_x$). When $f = 0$ and $B$ finds error in the received shares in Step 2, $B$ sends 0 to $A$ via paths $q_1$ and $q_2$. Then in Step 4, if $B$ reliably receives $m_1^A$, then $B$ can work out which path transmitted the faulty share in the previous Step 2, thus $B$ gets $f = x$; else if $B$ reliably receives 'OK', then it is straightforward that $f = x = 3$. Thus, $B$ can always identify which path $p_f = p_x$ is faulty, and recover $m_1^B = m_1^A$ with the shares received on the other two paths. Since it is straightforward that $B$ can reliable receive $m_2^B = m_2^A$, $B$ can recover $m^B = m^A$. Thus PSP is 0-reliable.   □

## 5    $(\epsilon, 0)$-Secure Message Transmission

In this section, we show that the necessary and sufficient conditions for achieving $(\epsilon, 0)$-secure message transmission are the same to those for achieving $(0, 0)$-secure message transmission. That is, lowering privacy level does not reduce the requirement of network connectivity. Before we prove this, we first show some results on $(k + 1, n, \epsilon)$-SSS where $0 \leq \epsilon < 1$.[4] It has been discussed that a $(k + 1, n, 0)$-SSS can detect $n - k - 1$ errors and correct $\lfloor (n - k - 1)/2 \rfloor$ errors (see [15, 16, 5]). In the following we show that a $(k + 1, n, \epsilon)$-SSS can do just the same.

**Lemma 3.** *Let $m$ be a secret, $S$ be a $(k + 1, n, \epsilon)$-SSS and $(v_1, ..., v_n) \in S(m)$, then any $k + 1$ entries of $(v_1, ..., v_n)$ are unique to the codeword of $S(m)$.*

*Proof.* Assume there are some $k + 1$ entries that also belong to the codeword of $S(m')$, where $m' \neq m$. Then with these $k + 1$ entries, one cannot distinguish whether $m$ or $m'$ is shared, so $m$ cannot be recovered with probability 1. This contradicts to property-1 of the $(k + 1, n, \epsilon)$-SSS.                    □

**Lemma 4.** *Let $m$ be a secret, $S$ be a $(k + 1, n, \epsilon)$-SSS and $(v_1, ..., v_n) \in S(m)$. For any $k$ such entries $v_{l_1}, ..., v_{l_k}$ $(1 \leq l_1 < ... < l_k \leq n)$, there exists a secret $m' \neq m$ such that $(v'_1, ..., v'_n) \in S(m')$ and for each $1 \leq i \leq k : v'_{l_i} = v_{l_i}$.*

*Proof.* Assume that there are $k$ entries $v_{l_1}, ..., v_{l_k}$ that belong to a codeword in $S(m)$, but not to any in $S(m')$, where $m' \neq m$. That is, these $k$ entries are unique to the codeword of $S(m)$, so $m$ can be recovered from these $k$ entries with probability 1. This contradicts to property-2 of the $(k + 1, n, \epsilon)$-SSS.                    □

**Theorem 3.** *A $(k + 1, n, \epsilon)$-SSS can detect $n - k - 1$ errors, but not more.*

*Proof.* Let $S$ be a $(k + 1, n, \epsilon)$-SSS and $(v_1, ..., v_n) \in S(m)$ be a codeword. First we show that if there is a tuple $T = (u_1, ..., u_n)$ such that $|\{i : u_i \neq v_i, 1 \leq i \leq n\}| = d$ and $0 < d \leq n - k - 1$, then one can detect that $T$ is not a codeword. Since $n - d \geq n - (n - k - 1) = k + 1$, there are at least $k + 1$ entries $u_{l_1}, ..., u_{l_{k+1}}$ $(1 \leq l_1 < ... < l_{k+1} \leq n)$ such that for each $1 \leq i \leq k + 1 : u_{l_i} = v_{l_i}$. Thus according to Lemma 3, $u_{l_1}, ..., u_{l_{k+1}}$ are unique to the codeword of $S(m)$. Since the $d$ errors are not in the codeword of $S(m)$, it is easy to show that $T$ is not a codeword.

Next we show that if $d \geq n - k$, then the tuple $T$ can also be a codeword of a secret $m' \neq m$. Since $n - d \leq n - (n - k) = k$, there are at most $k$ entries $u_{l_1}, ..., u_{l_k}$ $(1 \leq l_1 < ... < l_k \leq n)$ such that for each $1 \leq i \leq k : u_{l_i} = v_{l_i}$. According to Lemma 4, there exists a secret $m'$ such that the $n - d$ entries belong to the codeword of $S(m')$, and it is possible that the $d$ errors are also in the codeword of $S(m')$. Thus $T$ can be codeword, and hence one cannot detect $d \geq n - k$ errors.                    □

---

[4] See Definition 1 in Section 2 for the definition of $(k + 1, n, \epsilon)$-SSS.

**Theorem 4.** *A $(k+1, n, \epsilon)$-SSS can correct $\lfloor (n-k-1)/2 \rfloor$ errors, but not more.*

*Proof.* Let $S$ be a $(k+1, n, \epsilon)$-SSS and $(v_1, ..., v_n) \in S(m)$ be a codeword. First we show that if there is a tuple $T = (u_1, ..., u_n)$ such that $|\{i : u_i \neq v_i, 1 \leq i \leq n\}| = c$ and $c \leq \lfloor (n-k-1)/2 \rfloor$, then one can recover the secret $m$ from $T$. To correct $c$ errors, one selects $n - c$ entries from $T$ and put them into a new tuple $T'$ of length $n - c$. Since $n - c \geq k + 1$, $T'$ is a corrupted codeword of a $(k+1, n-c, \epsilon)$-SSS that shares $m$, with at most $c$ errors. According to Theorem 3, a $(k+1, n-c, \epsilon)$-SSS can detect

$$n - c - k - 1 \geq n - \lfloor (n-k-1)/2 \rfloor - k - 1 \geq \lfloor (n-k-1)/2 \rfloor \geq c$$

errors. With at most $c$ errors in $T'$, one can detect if $T'$ is a codeword. If one finds that $T'$ is not a codeword, it uses exhaustive search until it finds a $T'$ that is a codeword (i.e., the $c$ errors are not entries in $T'$), and finally recovers the secret $m$ from $T'$.

Next we show that if $c > \lfloor (n-k-1)/2 \rfloor$, then one cannot correct $c$ errors and recover $m$ from $T$. We will construct the tuple $T$, in a way we explain further. Assume that $c = \lfloor (n-k-1)/2 \rfloor + 1$. Since $|\{i : u_i = v_i, 1 \leq i \leq n\}| = n - c \geq k$, according to Lemma 4, there exists a secret $m' \neq m$ such that some $k$ error-free entries in $T$ not only belong to a codeword $(v_1, \ldots, v_n) \in S(m)$, but also belong to a codeword of $(v'_1, \ldots, v'_n) \in S(m')$. Let us analyze the remaining $n - k$ entries of $T$. They consist of $c$ errors and $c' = n - k - c$ error-free entries, i.e., $c'$ entries identical to the corresponding ones in $(v_1, \ldots, v_n)$. We now observe that:

$$\begin{aligned} c' = n - k - c &= n - k - (\lfloor (n-k-1)/2 \rfloor + 1) \\ &\leq 2 \times \lfloor (n-k-1)/2 \rfloor + 2 - (\lfloor (n-k-1)/2 \rfloor + 1) \\ &= \lfloor (n-k-1)/2 \rfloor + 1 \\ &= c. \end{aligned}$$

We are now in a position to prove our claim. We first explain how we construct the $c$ entries $u_i$ in $T$ that differ from $(v_1, \ldots, v_n)$. We let these correspond to the corresponding $c$ entries in $(v'_1, \ldots, v'_n)$. Now since $c' \leq c$, observe that given the tuple $T$, one cannot distinguish whether the secret $m$ is shared and the $c$ entries are errors, or the secret $m'$ is shared and the $c'$ entries are errors. Thus cannot recover $m$ with probability 1.    $\square$

Now we show that the conditions for achieving $(\epsilon, 0)$-secure message transmission are the same to those for achieving $(0, 0)$-security.

**Theorem 5.** *The CONs of Theorem 2 are also necessary and sufficient for $(\epsilon, 0)$-secure message transmission.*

*Proof.* The sufficiency of CONs is straightforward, and Patra et al.'s *Secure Protocol* in [19] is actually an $(\epsilon, 0)$-secure protocol. Now we prove the necessity of CONs, using a method similar to [5,6].

It is straightforward that CON-1 is necessary for 0-reliable message transmission from $A$ to $B$. Now we show that CON-2 is also necessary. For a contradiction, we assume that there are three sets $Z_1, Z_2, Z_3 \in \mathcal{Z}$ such that $\mathcal{Q}_{Z_1} \subsetneq \mathcal{Q}$,

$Q_{Z_2} = Q_{Z_3} = Q$ and $P_{Z_1 \cup Z_2 \cup Z_3} = P$. We assume an $(\epsilon, 0)$-secure message transmission protocol $\Pi$, and show how a non-threshold adversary $X$ can defeat this protocol $\Pi$.

Let $m^A$ be the message that $A$ wants to send to $B$. $X$ will simulate the possible behaviors of $A$ and $B$ by executing $\Pi$ to transmit another message $\hat{m}^A \in \mathcal{M}$. The strategy of $X$ is to flip two coins $c \in \{00, 01, 10, 11\}$:

- $c = 00$. $X$ re-flips.
- $c = 01$. $X$ chooses $Z_1$ to control, and acts passive on all paths in $P_{Z_1}$ and $Q_{Z_1}$.
- $c = 10$ (or $c = 11$). $X$ chooses $Z_2$ (or $Z_3$) to control. On all paths in $P_{Z_2}$ (or $P_{Z_3}$), $X$ ignores what $A$ sends in each step of $\Pi$ and simulates what $A$ would send to $B$ if $A$ was sending $\hat{m}^A$. On all paths in $Q_{Z_2} = Q$ (or $Q_{Z_3} = Q$), $X$ ignores what $B$ sends in each step of $\Pi$ and simulates what $B$ would send to $A$ if $c = 01$.

Note that the simulation of $X$ on the feedback channel $Q$ when $c = 10$ or $c = 11$ may not succeed, since $B$ may send something that $X$ fails to catch. However, there is a non-zero probability that the simulation succeeds, given $X$ knows the protocol and can always guess. This non-zero probability can breach the 0-reliability, as we show next. It is straightforward that, when the simulation succeeds, despite what the outcome of $c$ is, the feedbacks that $A$ receives are the same. That is, according to the feedbacks, $A$ will always learn that $B$ has reliably received $m^A$ without an error happening on the forward channel. At the end of the protocol, the view $view^B$ of $B$ could be divided into three parts $view_{Z_1}$, $view_{Z_2}$ and $view_{Z_3}$, where $view_{Z_i}$ $(i = 1, 2, 3)$ consists of all information that paths in $P_{Z_i}$ have learned (see [6]). Since the view $view^A$ of $A$ is the same despite which set of $Z_1$, $Z_2$ or $Z_3$ that $X$ chooses, and $\Pi$ is $\epsilon$-private, $m^A$ can be recovered from any single $view_{Z_i}$ with probability at most $\epsilon$ ($\epsilon < 1$). Thus we regard $(view_{Z_1}, view_{Z_2}, view_{Z_3})$ as shares of $m^A$ in a $(2, 3, \epsilon)$-SSS. Next, since $\Pi$ is a 0-reliable, $B$ should be able to recover the message $m^A$ from two of the views $(view_{Z_1}, view_{Z_2}, view_{Z_3})$ with probability 1. That is, when $c = 10$ or $c = 11$, $B$ should be able to distinguish which view of $view_{Z_2}$ or $view_{Z_3}$ contains faulty information. To sum up, $(view_{Z_1}, view_{Z_2}, view_{Z_3})$ is a $(2, 3, \epsilon)$-SSS that can correct 1 error (either $view_{Z_2}$ or $view_{Z_3}$). According to Theorem 4, a $(2, 3, \epsilon)$-SSS can only correct $\lfloor (3 - 1 - 1)/2 \rfloor = 0$ error. We have a contradiction, which concludes the proof. $\qquad \square$

Straightforwardly, using the result of Theorem 4 and similar proof to Theorem 5, we give the following corollary:

**Corollary 1.** *Let $0 \le \delta < \frac{1}{2}$ and $0 \le \epsilon_1 < \epsilon_2 < 1$. In any network model and any adversary model, the network connectivity required for $(\epsilon_1, \delta)$-secure message transmission is the same as that for $(\epsilon_2, \delta)$-secure message transmission.*

## 6   $(0, \delta)$-Secure Message Transmission

In this section we discuss $(0, \delta)$-secure message transmission. Achieving probabilistic reliability has been studied extensively in the presence of a threshold adversary (see [5, 25, 23]). We use the same network model to that in [5]. Thus our result is a generalization of the results in [5], only that we consider a more general adversary structure.

**Theorem 6.** *Let $G(V, E)$ be a directed graph, $\mathcal{Z}$ be an adversary structure on $V \setminus \{A, B\}$, and $\mathcal{Q} \neq \emptyset$. The necessary and sufficient conditions for $(0, \delta)$-secure $(0 < \delta < \frac{1}{2})$ message transmission from $A$ to $B$ are:*

*(i) for any set $Z_a \in \mathcal{Z}$: $\mathcal{P}_{Z_a} \subsetneq \mathcal{P}$, and*
*(ii) for any two sets $Z_a, Z_b \in \mathcal{Z}$: $\mathcal{P}_{Z_a \cup Z_b} \cup \mathcal{Q}_{Z_a \cup Z_b} \subsetneq \mathcal{P} \cup \mathcal{Q}$.*

*Proof.* First we show that the conditions are necessary. It is straightforward that condition (i) must be satisfied, since it must be ensured that at least one path can transmit the correct message from $A$ to $B$. To prove condition (ii) is also necessary, we assume that there are two sets $Z_1, Z_2 \in \mathcal{Z}$ such that $\mathcal{P}_{Z_1 \cup Z_2} = \mathcal{P}$ and $\mathcal{Q}_{Z_1 \cup Z_2} = \mathcal{Q}$, and there is a $(0, \delta)$-secure $(0 < \delta < \frac{1}{2})$ message transmission protocol $\Pi$. Let $M^A$ be the message $A$ transmits, and the adversary $X$ chooses a faulty message $\hat{M}^A$. The strategy of $X$ is to flip a coin and decide which set of $Z_x$ $(x \in \{1, 2\})$ to control. In each execution step of $\Pi$, $X$ causes each path in $\mathcal{P}_{Z_x}$ to follow the protocol as if the transmitted message is $\hat{M}^A$; if $x = 1$, then on each path in $\mathcal{Q}_{Z_1}$ (if such path exists), $X$ simulates what $B$ will send if $B$ had received the faulty message $\hat{M}^A$ from paths in $\mathcal{P}_{Z_2}$ and received the actual message $M^A$ from the other paths; else if $x = 2$, then on each path in $\bar{\mathcal{Q}}_{Z_1}$ (if such path exists), $X$ simulates what $B$ will send if $B$ had received $\hat{M}^A$ from paths in $\mathcal{P}_{Z_1}$ and received $M^A$ from the other paths.

Therefore, at the end of the protocol, $A$ receives the same feedbacks despite whether $x = 1$ or $x = 2$. The view $view^B$ of $B$ could divided into two parts $view_{Z_1}$ and $view_{Z_2}$, where $view_{Z_r}$ $(r \in \{1, 2\})$ consists of all information that the nodes in $Z_r$ have learned (see similar proof in [6]). Due to the fact that the forward channel is not reliable for message transmission, $B$ cannot distinguish whether $x = 1$ or $x = 2$, neither. Since $\Pi$ is 0-private, $M^A$ must not be recovered from any single $view_{Z_r}$. Since $\Pi$ is $\delta$-reliable, $B$ should be able to recover the $M^A$ from one of the two views $view_{Z_1}$ or $view_{Z_2}$ with high probability. Thus we have a contradiction.

Next we show that the conditions are sufficient. Let $\tilde{\mathcal{Z}} = \{Z_1, ..., Z_t\}$, and $M^A \in \mathcal{M}$ be the message $A$ wants to transmit to $B$. We shall construct a $(0, \delta)$-secure message transmission protocol (APRP), which is similar to that in [5, Theorem 3] (see Fig.3).

Due to condition (ii), $X$ cannot corrupt all paths in $\bar{\mathcal{P}}_{Z_i} \cup \bar{\mathcal{Q}}_{Z_i}$ for any $Z_i \in \tilde{\mathcal{Z}}$. Thus it is obvious that $X$ cannot learn $C^A$, $D^A$ and $E^A$ in any round $i$ of **for loop**, and hence cannot recover the message $M^A$. Thus APRP is 0-private.

It is straightforward that in round $x$, all values are transmitted via paths in $\bar{\mathcal{P}}_{Z_x} \cup \bar{\mathcal{Q}}_{Z_x}$. It is clear that in this round, $B$ can recover $M^B = M^A$, since $X$ who chooses $Z_x$ can do nothing with the message transmission. The reliability is breached only if in a round $i$ of APRP, $X$ corrupts all paths in $\bar{\mathcal{P}}_{Z_i}$ (then $X$ cannot corrupt all paths in $\bar{\mathcal{Q}}_{Z_i}$, due to condition (ii)), and $X$ correctly guesses the key $(C^A, D^A)$ with small probability. This makes APRP $\delta$-reliable.    □

---

**for** $1 \le i \le t$ **loop**

Step 1 For each $p_j \in \bar{\mathcal{P}}_{Z_i}$, $A$ chooses $(a_{i,j}^A, b_{i,j}^A, c_{i,j}^A) \in_R \mathbb{F}^3$ and sends the 3-tuple $(a_{i,j}^A, b_{i,j}^A, c_{i,j}^A)$ to $B$ via path $p_j$;

Step 2 For each $p_j \in \bar{\mathcal{P}}_{Z_i}$, $B$ receives $(a_{i,j}^B, b_{i,j}^B, c_{i,j}^B)$ on path $p_j$;

For each $q_j \in \bar{\mathcal{Q}}_{Z_i}$, $B$ chooses $(d_{i,j}^B, e_{i,j}^B, f_{i,j}^B) \in_R \mathbb{F}^3$ and sends the 3-tuple $(d_{i,j}^B, e_{i,j}^B, f_{i,j}^B)$ to $A$ via path $q_j$;

Step 3 For each $q_j \in \bar{\mathcal{Q}}_{Z_i}$, $A$ receives $(d_{i,j}^A, e_{i,j}^A, f_{i,j}^A)$ on path $q_j$;

$A$ computes $C^A := \sum_{p_j \in \bar{\mathcal{P}}_{Z_i}} a_{i,j}^A + \sum_{q_j \in \bar{\mathcal{Q}}_{Z_i}} d_{i,j}^A$,

$$D^A := \sum_{p_j \in \bar{\mathcal{P}}_{Z_i}} b_{i,j}^A + \sum_{q_j \in \bar{\mathcal{Q}}_{Z_i}} e_{i,j}^A,$$

$$E^A := \sum_{p_j \in \bar{\mathcal{P}}_{Z_i}} c_{i,j}^A + \sum_{q_j \in \bar{\mathcal{Q}}_{Z_i}} f_{i,j}^A;$$

$A$ sends the 2-tuple $(M^A + E^A, auth(M^A + E^A; C^A, D^A))$ to $B$ via $\bar{\mathcal{P}}_{Z_i}$;

Step 4 For each $p_j \in \bar{\mathcal{P}}_{Z_i}$, $B$ receives $(g_{i,j}^B, h_{i,j}^B)$ on path $p_j$;

**if** $(g_{i,j}^B, h_{i,j}^B) = (g_{i,k}^B, h_{i,k}^B)$ for all $p_j, p_k \in \bar{\mathcal{P}}_{Z_i}$ **then**

$B$ computes $C^B := \sum_{p_j \in \bar{\mathcal{P}}_{Z_i}} a_{i,j}^B + \sum_{q_j \in \bar{\mathcal{Q}}_{Z_i}} d_{i,j}^B$,

$$D^B := \sum_{p_j \in \bar{\mathcal{P}}_{Z_i}} b_{i,j}^B + \sum_{q_j \in \bar{\mathcal{Q}}_{Z_i}} e_{i,j}^B,$$

$$E^B := \sum_{p_j \in \bar{\mathcal{P}}_{Z_i}} c_{i,j}^B + \sum_{q_j \in \bar{\mathcal{Q}}_{Z_i}} f_{i,j}^B;$$

**if** $h_{i,j}^B = auth(g_{i,j}^B; C^B, D^B)$ **then**

$B$ recovers $M^B := g_{i,j}^B - E^B$, and terminates the protocol;

**end if;**

**end if;**

**end loop; - end APRP**

---

Fig. 3. Almost Perfectly Reliable Protocol (APRP)

**Acknowledgement.** The authors of this paper would like to thank the anonymous referees for their helpful comments on the earlier version of the paper.

# References

1. Agarwal, S., Cramer, R., de Hann, R.: Asymptotically optimal two-round perfectly secure message transmission. In: Dwork, C. (ed.) CRYPTO 2006. LNCS, vol. 4117, pp. 394–408. Springer, Heidelberg (2006)

2. Ben-Or, M., Goldwasser, S., Wigderson, A.: Completeness theorems for non-cryptographic fault-tolerant distributed computing. In: Proc. ACM STOC 1988, pp. 1–10. ACM Press, New York (1988)

3. Blakley, G.: Safeguarding cryptographic keys. In: Proc. AFIPS 1979 National Computer Conference, New York, June 1979, vol. 48, pp. 313–317 (1979)

4. Chaum, D., Crépeau, C., Damgård, I.: Multiparty unconditional secure protocols. In: Proc. ACM STOC 1988, pp. 11–19. ACM Press, New York (1988)

5. Desmedt, Y., Wang, Y.: Perfectly secure message transmission revisited. In: Knudsen, L.R. (ed.) EUROCRYPT 2002. LNCS, vol. 2332, pp. 502–517. Springer, Heidelberg (2002)

6. Desmedt, Y., Wang, Y., Burmester, M.: A complete characterization of tolerable adversary structures for secure point-to-point transmissions without feedback. In: Deng, X., Du, D.-Z. (eds.) ISAAC 2005. LNCS, vol. 3827, pp. 277–287. Springer, Heidelberg (2005)

7. Dolev, D.: The Byzantine generals strike again. J. of Algorithms 3, 14–30 (1982)

8. Dolev, D., Dwork, C., Waarts, O., Yung, M.: Perfectly secure message transmission. Journal of the ACM 40(1), 17–47 (1993)
9. Franklin, M., Wright, R.: Secure communication in minimal connectivity models. Journal of Cryptology 13(1), 9–30 (2000)
10. Gilbert, E., MacWilliams, F., Sloane, N.: Codes which detect deception. The BELL System Technical Journal 53(3), 405–424 (1974)
11. Hirt, M., Maurer, U.: Player simulation and general adversary structures in perfect multiparty computation. Journal of Cryptology 13(1), 31–60 (2000)
12. Ito, M., Saito, A., Nishizeki, T.: Secret sharing schemes realizing general access structures. In: Proc. IEEE Global Telecommunications Conf., Globecom 1987, pp. 99–102. IEEE Communications Soc. Press, Los Alamitos (1987)
13. Kumar, M., Goundan, P., Srinathan, K., Rangan, C.P.: On perfectly secure communication over arbitrary networks. In: Proc. ACM PODC 2002, pp. 293–202 (2002)
14. Kurosawa, K., Suzuki, K.: Truly efficient 2-round perfectly secure message transmission scheme. In: Smart, N.P. (ed.) EUROCRYPT 2008. LNCS, vol. 4965, pp. 324–340. Springer, Heidelberg (2008)
15. MacWilliams, F.J., Sloane, N.J.A.: The theory of error-correcting codes. North-Holland Publishing Company, Amsterdam (1978)
16. McEliece, R.J., Sarwate, D.V.: On sharing secrets and Reed-Solomon codes. Communications of ACM 24(9), 583–584 (1981)
17. Patra, A., Cloudhary, A., Rangan, C.P.: Unconditionally reliable and secure message transmission in directed networks revisited. In: Ostrovsky, R., De Prisco, R., Visconti, I. (eds.) SCN 2008. LNCS, vol. 5229, pp. 309–326. Springer, Heidelberg (2008)
18. Patra, A., Cloudhary, A., Rangan, C.P.: Brief announcement: perfectly secure message transmission in directed networks re-visited. In: PODC 2009, pp. 278–279 (2009)
19. Patra, A., Shankar, B., Choudhary, A., Srinathan, K., Rangan, C.P.: Perfectly secure message transmission in directed networks tolerating threshold and non threshold adversary. In: Proc. CANS, pp. 80–101 (2007)
20. Rabin, T.: Robust sharing of secrets when the dealer is honest or cheating. J. of the ACM 41(6), 1089–1109 (1994)
21. Rabin, T., Ben-Or, M.: Verifiable secret sharing and multiparty protocols with honest majority. In: Proc. ACM STOC 1989, pp. 73–85. ACM Press, New York (1989)
22. Shamir, A.: How to share a secret. Communication of ACM 22(11), 612–613 (1979)
23. Shankar, B., Gopal, P., Srinathan, K., Rangan, C.P.: Unconditionally reliable message transmission in directed networks. In: Huang, S.-T. (ed.) SODA, pp. 1048–1055 (2008)
24. Srinathan, K., Narayanan, A., Rangan, C.P.: Optimal perfectly secure message transmission. In: Franklin, M. (ed.) CRYPTO 2004. LNCS, vol. 3152, pp. 545–561. Springer, Heidelberg (2004)
25. Srinathan, K., Rangan, C.P.: Possibility and complexity of probabilistic reliable communications in directed networks. In: Proc. ACM PODC 2006 (2006)
26. Wang, Y., Desmedt, Y.: Perfectly secure message transmission revisited. IEEE Transaction on Information Theory 54(6), 2582–2595 (2008)
27. Yang, Q., Desmedt, Y.: Cryptanalysis of secure message transmission protocols with feedback (full version). Cryptology ePrint Archive, Report 2009/632 (2009)

# Appendix

## A   Guessing Attack to Patra et al.'s Protocols

In [19], Patra et al. proposed three protocols for secure message transmission with feedbacks: *Protocol I* and *Protocol II* were claimed to be $(0,0)$-secure against a $k$-active threshold adversary, and *Secure Protocol* was claimed to be $(0,0)$-secure against a general adversary structure. We observe that neither of the three protocols enables 0-private message transmission when Guessing Attack takes place. We present our Guessing Attack against Secure Protocol (that tolerates an adversary structure) here, and the similar attacks against Protocols I and II in the full version of this paper [27]. Without loss of generality, we assume that the transmitted message $m \in_R \mathbb{F}$.

Now, we prove that Secure Protocol (SP), which is a three phase protocol tolerating a subset $\mathcal{B}$ of an adversary structure $\mathcal{Z}$ where $|\tilde{\mathcal{B}}| = 3$, is not 0-private. To show our Guessing Attack, we first sketch SP in the following.

**Conditions for SP.** Let $\tilde{\mathcal{B}} = \{Z_1, Z_2, Z_3\}$. (1) there is a PRMT (perfectly reliable message transmission) protocol from $A$ to $B$, and (2) if $\mathcal{P}_{Z_1 \cup Z_2 \cup Z_3} = \mathcal{P}$, then there exist two paths $q_\alpha \in \bar{\mathcal{Q}}_{Z_\alpha}, q_\beta \in \bar{\mathcal{Q}}_{Z_\beta}$ ($\alpha, \beta \in \{1, 2, 3\}$).

**Sketch of SP.** Due to the existence of PRMT, there exist three paths $p_1 \in \bar{\mathcal{P}}_{Z_2 \cup Z_3}$, $p_2 \in \bar{\mathcal{P}}_{Z_1 \cup Z_3}$, and $p_3 \in \bar{\mathcal{P}}_{Z_1 \cup Z_2}$ (see [6]). Let $m$ be the message that $A$ transmits to $B$.

    Phase I.   $A$ chooses a bivariate polynomial $Q(x, y) = \sum_{i=0}^{1} \sum_{j=0}^{1} r_{i,j} x^i y^j$ uniformly at random such that $Q(0,0) = m$. $Q(x, y)$ is symmetric; i.e., $Q(i, j) = Q(j, i)$. $A$ sends the polynomial $Q(x, i)$ to $B$ via path $p_i$, $1 \le i \le 3$.

    Phase II.   $B$ receives the polynomial $Q_i^B(x) = Q^B(x, i)$ on path $p_i$, $1 \le i \le 3$. Out of the three $Q_i^B(x)$-s, at most one is corrupted. $B$ then performs tests to determine which path $p_i$ is faulty.[5] According to the outcome of the tests:

        - if $B$ concludes that all $p_i$-s ($1 \le i \le 3$) are honest, then $B$ recovers $m$ and terminates the protocol;

        - if $B$ finds which $p_i$ ($1 \le i \le 3$) is faulty, then $B$ recovers $m$ and terminates the protocol;

        - if $B$ finds one of the two paths $p_i$ and $p_j$ ($1 \le i, j \le 3$ and $i \ne j$) is faulty but cannot distinguish which one, then $B$ sends a 4-tuple $(i, j, Q_i^B(j), Q_j^B(i))$ to $A$ via paths $q_\alpha$ and $q_\beta$.

    Phase III.   $A$ receives two 4-tuples: $(i_\alpha, j_\alpha, v_{i_\alpha}, v_{j_\alpha})$ on path $q_\alpha$ and $(i_\beta, j_\beta, v_{i_\beta}, v_{j_\beta})$ on path $q_\beta$.

        - Corresponding to $(i_\alpha, j_\alpha, v_{i_\alpha}, v_{j_\alpha})$, $A$ checks whether $v_{i_\alpha} = Q(j_\alpha, i_\alpha)$ and whether $v_{j_\alpha} = Q(i_\alpha, j_\alpha)$. Depending on the outcome, $A$ concludes which path $p_{i_\alpha}$ or $p_{j_\alpha}$ is faulty, and

---

[5] The details of the tests are not important here. For more details see [19, Secure Protocol].

The adversary $X$ chooses $Z_3$ to control; that is, $X$ corrupts both $q_1$ and $q_2$. In Phase I of SP, $X$ can only get $Q(x, 3)$, with which $X$ knows $Q(1, 3)$ and $Q(2, 3)$, thus it only needs the value of $Q(1, 2)$ to recover $m$. In each phase of SP, $X$ acts passive on paths in $\mathcal{P}_{Z_3}$. Thus $B$ does not use the feedback channel throughout the protocol. In Phase II of SP, $X$ chooses four distinct random numbers $v_1^X, v_2^X, v_3^X, v_4^X \in_R \mathbb{F}$, and transmits two 4-tuples $(1, 2, v_1^X, v_2^X)$ and $(1, 2, v_3^X, v_4^X)$ to $A$. Then in Phase III, if corresponding to a value $v_i^X$ $(1 \le i \le 4)$, no appended error message "Path $\gamma$ is faulty" ($\gamma$ is either $p_1$ or $p_2$) is broadcast by $A$, then $X$ knows that $v_i^X$ is correct (i.e., $= Q(1, 2)$), and hence recovers $m$; otherwise, $X$ uses a random guess over $\mathbb{F} \setminus \{v_1^X, v_2^X, v_3^X, v_4^X\}$ to get an $m'$.

**Fig. 4.** Guessing Attack to SP

> appends an error message "Path $\gamma$ is faulty" ($\gamma$ is either $p_{i_\alpha}$ or $p_{j_\alpha}$) to $(i_\alpha, j_\alpha, v_{i_\alpha}, v_{j_\alpha})$.
>  - $A$ performs similar computation to the other 4-tuple $(i_\beta, j_\beta, v_{i_\beta}, v_{j_\beta})$.
>  - $A$ broadcasts the two 4-tuples along with the appended error messages.

...

Next we show that the adversary $X$ can learn the message $m$ by performing Guessing Attack (contradict to [19, Lemma 12]).

We assume there exist a path $q_1 \in \bar{\mathcal{Q}}_{Z_1}$ and a path $q_2 \in \bar{\mathcal{Q}}_{Z_2}$, and $q_1, q_2 \in \mathcal{Q}_{Z_3}$. We show that by performing the Guessing Attack in Fig.5, $X$ can learn $m$ with probability better than $\frac{1}{|\mathbb{F}|}$.

In this Guessing Attack, the guess is successful if there is a $v_i^X = Q(1, 2) = Q(2, 1)$ $(1 \le i \le 4)$, so $A$ will broadcast the error message that indicates the value of $Q(1, 2)$ to $X$. Thus the probability $T$ that the guess is successful is

$$T = 4 \times \frac{1}{|\mathbb{F}|} = \frac{4}{|\mathbb{F}|}.$$

If the guess fails, then $X$ knows that neither of the four random numbers it chose is correct, so it will use a random guess over $\mathbb{F} \setminus \{v_1^X, v_2^X, v_3^X, v_4^X\}$ and with probability $\frac{1}{|\mathbb{F}|-4}$, it will learn the message $m$. Thus the total probability $G$ that $X$ learns $m$ using Guessing Attack is

$$G = T + (1 - T) \times \frac{1}{|\mathbb{F}| - 4} = \frac{4}{|\mathbb{F}|} + \left(1 - \frac{4}{|\mathbb{F}|}\right) \times \frac{1}{|\mathbb{F}| - 4} = \frac{5}{|\mathbb{F}|}.$$

It is straightforward that the probability that $X$ learns $m$ is much higher than expected (i.e., $\frac{1}{|\mathbb{F}|}$), thus SP is not 0-private.

# The Optimum Leakage Principle for Analyzing Multi-threaded Programs

Han Chen and Pasquale Malacaria

School of Electronic Engineering and Computer Science,
Queen Mary University of London
hanchen@dcs.qmul.ac.uk,
pm@dcs.qmul.ac.uk

**Abstract.** Bellman's optimality principle is a method for solving problems where one needs to find best decisions one after another. The principle can be extended to assess the information leakage in multi-threaded programs, and is formalized into the optimum leakage principle hereby proposed in this paper. By modeling the state transitions in multi-threaded programs, the principle is combined with information theory to assess the leakage in multi-threaded programs, as the result of an optimal policy. This offers a new perspective to measure the information leakage and enables to track the leakage at run-time. Examples are given to demonstrate the analysis process. Finally, efficient implementation of this methodology is also briefly discussed.

## 1 Introduction and Background

The quantitative analysis of multi-threaded programs and concurrent systems is recognized as an important challenge. A multi-threaded program may have more vulnerabilities when compared to a single-threaded one: not only from explicit and implicit information flows but also from the *timing channels* and *probabilistic timing channels* [26]. It is also a difficult problem because the leakage in the same program may vary due to the additional uncertainty in scheduling. For example, consider the following program:

```
l=h; | h=h & 0x07h;
```

Suppose the attacker observes the value of $l$ in every single step of execution [22]. If the second statement is run at first then 3 bits of h is leaked, otherwise every bit of h is leaked. In this case the channel capacity is $size(h)$ bits, which is achieved by running the first statement at first.

An early quantitative assessment of leakage in multi-threaded programs has been using the mutual information between the input and the output [13]. Further proposals using algebraic or approximation methods to derive the channel capacity as an leakage upper-bound include [12] and [29]. Recently, Smith [28] proposed to use minimum entropy to evaluate the leakage. However, these approaches have remained preliminary; also, all of them are static, unable to track

K. Kurosawa (Ed.): ICITS 2009, LNCS 5973, pp. 177–193, 2010.

the actual amount of information leaked when a program is run. Until today, there is not yet a feasible solution for dynamically tracking the (quantitative) information leakage of multi-threaded programs at run-time.

Now, by combining the Bellman optimality principle with recent progress on the quantitative information flow, a method is proposed in this paper to provide a more sensible analysis of the leakage (or the confidentiality) of programs as well as to allow the tracking of leakage dynamically.

To apply this method, firstly the target multi-threaded program is modeled by a state-transition automata. We consider a probabilistic scheduler (the Lottery scheduler) which represents a general case for a range of modern schedulers. The execution of the program can be seen as a Markov process and the state-transition can be represented as a tree, where each possible state of the execution is a node in the tree with non-negative values on the edges. We assume the attacker can observe each single step of the execution. Then by applying the Bellman equation, the optimal or the pessimal leakage, which represents the leakage generated using an optimal policy or a worst policy in the program execution, can be derived. These can be derived either from the start of the program, or from any point of execution.

The method has several unique qualities:

- general: it is generally applicable to analyze multi-threaded programs run by a probabilistic scheduler, as well as similar probabilistic state-transition systems;
- sensible: the Bellman equation gives the accurate optimal leakage bounds;
- flexible: it is able to track the current leakage bound at any point of the execution tree;
- simple: a simplification algorithm can be applied prior to the Bellman algorithm, such that only the state-transitions with interference between high and low variables need to be considered.

In the longer term, this is aiming to build a policy which quantitatively restrict and control the leakage. By applying such bounds decision can be made either to accept or to reject a program, while dynamic measurement can reassure that an attacker can not acquire a substantial quantity of information. Also, in a broader sense, we believe the method can also be a template for tracking information leaks in state transition systems.

The paper is organized as follows: the next subsection reviews existing literature and the background. Section 2 provides a short tutorial of the Bellman equation and the optimality principle, and Section 3 presents the definition of the information leakage in multi-threaded programs. In Section 4 we show how multi-threaded programs are modeled and we develop the theorems and propositions of optimal leakage analysis. Then we present an analysis of two sample programs. Finally, we investigate the complexity in the process and propose a simplification algorithm to accelerate the solution process. Section 5 concludes the paper and identifies our future work.

## 1.1   Related Work

Learning theory, statistics and information flow analysis are naturally tied together by Shannon's information theory [27]. A few pioneers have brought Bayesian methods into the field of quantitative information flow, such as [6,5]. In this paper, besides the application of the Bellman's optimality principle to this field, we hope to provoke discussions on identifying more interesting connections between quantitative information flow and the learning theory.

The Bellman equation is regarded as one of the most fundamental theories in reinforcement learning. It gives an accurate model of gaining information in a state-transition system and underpin a vast extension of optimality algorithms in various specific directions.

The other end of the connection is the quantification of information leakage. The use of conditional mutual information in the context of information leakage has been pioneered by Gray [11]. However his definition is not aimed to measure leakage but to define it. Other pioneers on the use of information theory in the context of security are Dennings, McLean and Millen [9,8,20,21]. In recent years, a theoretical framework has been established based on Shannon's information theory to allow static, quantitative program analysis that provides an expectation of leakage in programs [15,16,17,23]. The theory is preliminarily extended to multi-threaded programs [13]. Recently an automatic method for information flow analysis is developed in [18]. Lowe's work [19] defined quantitative channel capacity in the context of CSP. Further, the channel capacity of a leakage channel under constraints was worked out by using Lagrange multiplier methodology and Karush–Kuhn–Tucker conditions, which was also applied in programs and anonymity protocols [22,12,14].

Besides, various other different, albeit inherently relevant definitions and methods have been proposed to quantify the information leakage. Among them, Di Pierro et al. used the norm of a transition matrix as a measure of probabilistic confinement [10]. Recently, Smith et al. proposed the use of minimum entropy, and argued that it can better describe the risk of leakage in [28]. Moreover, the idea of quantitative leakage in the context of protocols has been investigated in [3]. A discussion of the relationship between min entropy and Shannon entropy relevant to the context of this work can be found in [24].

In comparison, what our results represent is based on adopting the Bellman's optimality principle as the rule-of-thumb: it is not representing the very worst case which may happen with a very rare chance, but instead representing the expectation from an optimal strategy (or a most dangerous one) with which a multi-threaded program can be set to run.

## 2   Bellman's Optimality Equation and Optimality Principle

### 2.1   Bellman's Optimality Equation

In reinforcement learning, a Bellman equation refers to a recursion for expected rewards. The expected reward in a particular state $s$ using a certain policy $\pi$ follows the Bellman equation:

$$V^\pi(s) = R(s) + \gamma \sum_{s' \in S} P(s'|s, \pi(s)) V^\pi(s')$$

where:

1. $S$ is the set of states.
2. $s, s'$ are states and $s, s' \in S$.
3. $R$ is the one-period return function (e.g., a utility function).
4. $\pi$ is a policy which maps from $S$ to $A$ which is the set of actions. A policy is hence a way to choose an action given a particular state of the system.
5. $P(s'|s, \pi(s))$ is a probability which describes the transition probability from the state $s$ to $s'$ with the action $a \in A$ following a policy $\pi$. In deterministic case, for each state and action, we specify a new state $S \times A \to S$ while in probabilistic case $S \times A \to P(S)$. For each state and action we specify a probability distribution $P(s|s, a)$ over next states.
6. $V^\pi$ is the value function representing the expected objective value obtained by following a policy $\pi$ from each state in $S$.
7. $\gamma$ is a weight value, we can take $\gamma = 1$ for simplicity.

This equation describes the expected reward for taking the action prescribed by a given policy $\pi$. It is used to show how to use a model of the environment to convert immediate rewards into values.

Value functions partially order the policies, but at least one optimal policy $\pi^*$ exists, and all optimal policies have the same value function $V^*$, which is solvable by Bellman optimality equations.

The equation for the optimal policy is referred to as the Bellman optimality equation:

$$V^*(s) = R(s) + \max_a \gamma \sum_{s' \in S} P(s'|s, a) V^*(s')$$

and

$$\pi^* = \arg\max_a \gamma \sum_{s' \in S} P(s'|s, a) V^*(s')$$

the optimality of $\pi^*$ can be proved via negation: if a policy $\pi$ selected an action $a$ does not give out the maximal value of

$$\gamma \sum_{s' \in S} P(s'|s, a) V^*(s')$$

then there exists another policy $\pi'$, which is the same as $\pi$ everywhere except at state $s$. At state $s$, $\pi'$ chooses the action $a'$ which maximize the above expression. Thus, $\pi$ can not be optimal and can not be chosen. Inversely, every optimal policy must choose actions to maximize the above one.

## 2.2  Bellman Optimality Principle

The Bellman optimality equation is central throughout the theory of Markov decision processes [25] (MDPs) and reflects the principle of optimality. The principle states:

**"Regardless of the decision taken to enter a particular state in a particular stage, the remaining decision made for leaving that stage must constitute an optimal policy"** [2].

There is another way of saying that: an optimal policy always achieves optimal value for every start state, or, in each state the optimal policy will always select the same action as an optimal policy for which the state is the start state.

Therefore, it means if we entered the terminal state of an optimal policy we can trace it back. The equation reflects the principle: in the solution process, the Bellman equation is written forwards from the initial state but can be solved backwards from terminal state. The following is a small example to show how this principle is used.

**Example of Bellman optimality principle.** Consider the following probabilistic state transition system. In this transition system we assume $s_0$ is the initial state and $s_{11}$ is the terminal state. We mark the probability and value of the transition in the path. Here the value of the transition is computed by the value function $V$ as mentioned in the Bellman equation. We are going to use Bellman's optimality principle to find the policies for both maximal and minimal profit for this transition system.

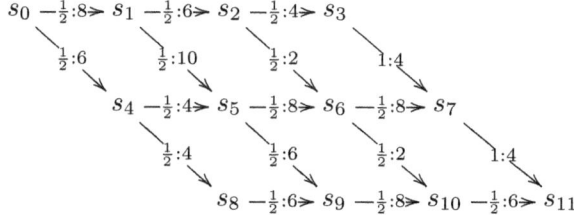

According to Bellman's optimality principle we start from the terminal state $s_{11}$ and mark it as 0. We can reach this terminal node from nodes $s_7$ and $s_{10}$. If we are at node $s_7$ the value at transition is 4 and it is the only possibility transition from $s_7$, so we write $s_7$ of "$1 \times 4 = 4$" using "$P(s'|s, a)V^*(s')$" where here we assume the factor $\gamma = 1$. Similarly the value of only transition from $s_3$ to $s_7$ is "$1 \times 4 = 4$" and we write $s_3$ of 4 as well. Likewise $s_{10}$ is marked by "3" because the only transition from $s_{10} \rightarrow s_{11}$ has the value "$\frac{1}{2} \times 6 = 3$". Not all node only has one possibility, some states in the system have two possibilities, for example $s_6$ there are two transitions: one is to $s_7$ with the value "$\frac{1}{2} \times 8 + 4 = 8$" where in the equation "4" is the old value of $s_7$ and "$\frac{1}{2} \times 8$" comes from the transition; the other is to $s_{10}$ with the value "$\frac{1}{2} \times 2 + 3 = 4$". Because $8 > 4$ we choose the transition to $s_7$ and write $s_6$ of 8. We leave the transition chosen as solid arrow and the transitions not chosen are marked with a dot arrow. Next we consider the previous node to $s_6$ which also has two possible transitions which are: one is to $s_3$ with the value "$\frac{1}{2} \times 4 + 4 = 6$"; the other is to $s_6$ with the value "$\frac{1}{2} \times 2 + 8 = 9$". At node $s_2$ we choose the transition to $s_6$ because $9 > 6$. We continue this procedure back to state $s_0$ with a value 21 which is the sought maximal profit.

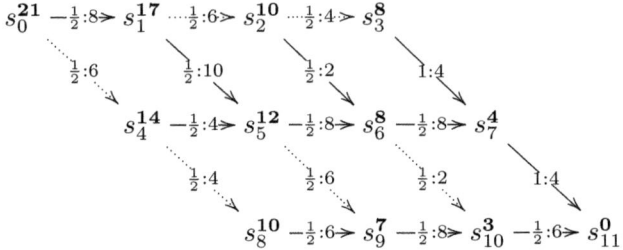

The maximal profit is achieved by the path:

$$s_0 \rightarrow s_1 \rightarrow s_5 \rightarrow s_6 \rightarrow s_7 \rightarrow s_{11}$$

Using the same principle and oppositely, if we choose minimal value at each stage, when there are more than one choices, we can find the solution which results in a minimal profit of the transition system. The solution is 12 where the details are showing below:

$$s_0^{12} - \tfrac{1}{2}{:}8 \rightarrow s_1^{8} - \tfrac{1}{2}{:}6 \rightarrow s_2^{5} \cdots \tfrac{1}{2}{:}4 \rightarrow s_3^{8}$$

and the selected path is

$$s_0 \rightarrow s_1 \rightarrow s_2 \rightarrow s_6 \rightarrow s_{10} \rightarrow s_{11}$$

# 3  Information Leakage of Multi-threaded Programs

Information theory can be used to quantify the leakage in programs [15,16,17,13]. Generally speaking, the leakage of a system is the difference between the amount of original confidential information and the amount of remaining confidential information after observations. In information theory, this difference is formulated by mutual information:

$$I(h; l) = H(h) - H(h|l)$$

where

1. $h$ is the high (confidential) information and $l$ is the low (public) one.
2. $H(h)$ is the Shannon's entropy defined as $H(X) = -\sum_{x \in X} \mu(x) \log \mu(x)$ in which $X = \{x_1, \ldots, x_n\}$ with probabilities $\mu(x_1), \ldots, \mu(x_n)$.
3. $H(h|l)$ is the conditional entropy defined as $H(X|Y) = -\Sigma_{Y=y}\mu(Y = y)\Sigma_{X=x}\mu(X = x|Y = y)\log(\mu(X = x|Y = y))$, where $\mu(X = x|Y = y)$ is the conditional probability of $X = x$ when $Y = y$.

Intuitively, mutual information $I(h; l)$ measures the information shared between $h$ and $l$. In other words, it measures how much uncertainty of a variable is reduced by knowing the other. An extreme case is if $h$ and $l$ are independent, then $I(h; l) = 0$.

Further, conditional mutual information, a form of ternary interaction will be used to quantify *interference*. Conditional mutual information measures the correlation between two random variables conditioned on a third random variable, which is defined as:

$$I(h; l|Z) = H(h|Z) - H(h|l, Z) = H(l|Z) - H(l|h, Z)$$

Given the leakage formula defined from mutual information and conditional mutual information, we can compute the leakage of the high variable $h$ coming from the observation of low variable $l$ in a program.

Now, we consider the multi-threaded programs with probabilistic scheduling, as in [13]. We assume the attacker has the ability to observe the value of $l$ in each single step; this represents the most conservative observational model in [22] and can be easily adapted to the other models such as the widely-used input-output model as in [16,23].

For example:

```
h=random(0, n); | l=h;
```

There are two threads and we assume each thread has probability $\frac{1}{2}$ to be chosen first and $h$ is a $k$ bit integer variable ($n = 2^k - 1$). The statement h=random(0, n) assigns a random number to $h$, while the other l=h leaks everything about $h$, which is $k$ bits. Due to different scheduling there are two possible kinds of observations with equal probabilities of $\frac{1}{2}$, which will lead to either 0 bit or k bits of leakage. Then the expected leakage (as in [23]) would be

$$\frac{1}{2} \times k + \frac{1}{2} \times 0 = \frac{k}{2}$$

while the upper bound is $k$ and lower bound is 0. For more complex multi-threaded programs, the computation of leakage could refer to the method in [13] and [22].

In comparison, we propose the optimal leakage principle below. We assume the attacker can make decision about the scheduling in the run time of multi-threaded programs and we give a methodology to evaluate the optimistic decision. The modeling of multi-threaded programs is described below, followed by theorems and propositions and then demonstrated by two program examples.

# 4  The Optimal Leakage Principle for Multi-threaded Programs

## 4.1  Modeling Multi-threaded Programs

Here we model a multi-threaded program using a probabilistic state-space transition system:

$$\langle \mathcal{S}, \mathcal{A}, \mathcal{P}, \mathcal{L} \rangle$$

where

1. $\mathcal{S}$ is a set of possible states in the system; we note the initial state as $s_0$.
2. $\mathcal{A}$ is a set of actions which are statements in multi-threaded programs and we write them as $a_i$.
3. $\mathcal{P}$ is a set of probabilities associated to $\mathcal{S}$, and we note the probability from $s_i$ to $s_j$ as $p_{ij}$. We assume determinacy, i.e. given $s_i$ and an action $a$ there is at most one $s_j$ s.t. $p_{ij} > 0$.
4. $\mathcal{L}$ is a set of values associated to $\mathcal{S}$, and we note the value from $s_i$ to $s_j$ as $L_{ij}$, where $L_{ij}$ is the information leaked in the state transition $s_i$ to $s_j$.

To this structure we can associate a state transition graph: we start from the initial state and select the statement from the program to reach a new state. We continue with this procedure until the last statement of the program. For example we first write the state transition of above example as

$$s_0 \xrightarrow{a_1} s_1 \xrightarrow{a_2} s_2$$
$$\searrow^{a_2}$$
$$s_3 \xrightarrow{a_1} s_4$$

where $a_1$="l=random(0,n)" and $a_2$="l=h". and we also have the $\langle \mathcal{S}, \mathcal{A}, \mathcal{P}, \mathcal{L} \rangle$
where $\mathcal{S} = \{s_0, s_1, s_2, s_3, s_4\}$;
$\mathcal{A} = \{a_1, a_2\}$;
$\mathcal{P} = \{p_{01} = 1 - p, p_{12} = 1, p_{03} = p, p_{34} = 1\}$;
$\mathcal{L} = \{L_{01} = 0, L_{12} = k, L_{03} = k, L_{34} = 0\}$.
    It is often easier to write the probabilities and values instead of actions in the transition system. Thus, the above state transition can be written as

$$s_0 \xrightarrow{1-p:0} s_1 \xrightarrow{1:k} s_2$$
$$\searrow^{p:k}$$
$$s_3 \xrightarrow{1:0} s_4$$

**A Note on Scheduler Sequence.** There are many well-known schedulers that provide a deterministic execution order, for example Round Robin and Shortest Time First, however the execution sequences of multi-threaded programs in most of today's computing systems are non-deterministic.

In this paper we specifically analyze probabilistic schedulers, also known as the Lottery scheduler. Since a probabilistic scheduler represents a probabilistic policy of choosing threads, almost all other simple schedulers can be seen as specific examples of that. The only difference between different schedulers is in the choice of statements in the execution sequence due to the different scheduling policies.

We use the scheduler sequence to denote the execution order of a multi-threaded program. After choosing a statement in each small step in the run time, there is only one execution sequence chosen from all possible scheduling sequences following a certain probability distribution. We assume there are $n$ threads and the scheduler sequence would be: $ijk...$ which means the $i^{th}$ thread is chosen first, followed by the $j^{th}$ thread, then the $k^{th}$ thread, where $0 \leq i, j, k \leq n - 1$.

Different outputs may come from different scheduler sequences, but one scheduler sequence can only produce one output. In the transition system, one path from the initial state to the terminal state represents a scheduler sequence.

We can now state an optimal leakage theorem.

## 4.2   Optimal Leakage Theorem

**Theorem 1.** *Optimal Leakage Theorem*
*In a transition system, the upper bound of leakage $L$ starting from a state $s$ is given by the optimality equation:*

$$L^*(s) = L(s) + \max_a \sum_{s'} P(s'|s, a)L^*(s')$$

*and the corresponding scheduler for achieving this upper bound is*

$$S^* = arg\max_a \sum_{s'} P(s'|s, a)L^*(s')$$

*where*

1. *$L$ is the leakage function, i.e. $\max_j L_{s,s_j}$ and*
2. *$P(s'|s, a)$ is the unique probability $p_{s,s'}$ given the action $a$*

*Proof:*
Proof by contradiction: if a scheduler sequence $S^*$ selected a statement $a$ which does not give out the maximal value of

$$\sum_{s'} P(s'|s, a)L^*(s')$$

then we can find another scheduler sequence $S'$, which is the same as $S^*$ everywhere except at state $s$. At state $s$, $S'$ chooses the action $a'$ which maximize the above expression.

Thus, $S^*$ can not be optimal and can not be chosen. Inversely, every optimal policy must choose actions to maximize the above one.

The proof completes.

Similarly we can have the following proposition to get the lower bound.

**Proposition 1.** *Pessimal Leakage Theorem*
*In a transition system, the lower bound of leakage $L$ is given by the optimality equation:*

$$L^*(s) = L(s) + \min_a \sum_{s'} P(s'|s,a)L^*(s')$$

*where*

$$S^* = \arg\min_a \sum_{s'} P(s'|s,a)L^*(s')$$

We can also easily prove this proposition via negation. The proof is omitted due to space limitation.

### 4.3   The Optimal Leakage Principle

Like the Bellman equation which reflects the optimal principle, Theorem 1 and Proposition 1 reflect the principle of information leakage under optimal exploit strategies. To build a transition system, we need to simulate all possible transitions for possible executions. As previously mentioned, in multi-threaded programs, different probabilistic scheduler may produce different outputs. Thus, there will be a set of terminal states, rather than one terminal state, in the transition system for a multi-threaded program. Suppose the set of terminal states is $\mathcal{T}$, each item in $\mathcal{T}$ is noted as $t_i$ where $t_i \in \mathcal{S}$ as well.

To find the optimal and pessimal leakage, every element in $\mathcal{T}$ needs to be accessed, then traced back to the initial state. Formally, we have the proposition below:

**Proposition 2.** *Optimal Leakage Principle*

1. *Firstly we start from the elements in $\mathcal{T}$. As these are terminal states, we mark them as 0.*
2. *Now trace back one level to look for previous nodes $s_i, s_j, ...$ adjacent to each element in $\mathcal{T}$. For each state, use Theorem 1 and Proposition 1 to compute the leakage at this stage and make the optimal or pessimal choice.*
3. *Repeat this process. At each stage compute the new value using Theorem 1 and Proposition 1 to make the optimal or pessimal choice. Trace backwards until arriving at the initial state, then we can achieve the optimal or pessimal leakage for the transition system.*
4. *Finally, the reverse path that starts from the initial state and constitutes of the chosen decisions above forms an optimal path.*

**Example I.** In the previous example:

$$\texttt{l=rand(n); | l=h;}$$

Here we use $p$ to represent the probability of choosing "l=h" first and we assume $p < 1$. With the transition system previously established in Section 4.1, we use Proposition 2 to solve the leakage bounds recursively. There are two terminal states in this automata $s_2$ and $s_4$ so we mark them as 0. Then we look for the previous level and find $s_1$ and $s_3$. We start from $s_1$, the only reachable state is $s_2$ and the only transition has a value of leakage $k$ with probability 1 so $L_{new}^{s_1} = k$; thus we mark $s_1$ to be $k$. For $s_3$, the only transition is $s_3 \to s_4$ which has a value of leakage of 0 with probability 1 so we mark $s_3$ as 0. We continue tracking back to $s_0$. $s_0$ has two possible choices: $s_0 \to s_1$ and $s_0 \to s_3$. $s_0 \to s_1$ has a leakage value of $k + 0 = k$ where $k$ is the previous leakage coming from $s_1$ while $s_0 \to s_3$ has $0 + p \times k = pk$. Since $pk \leq k$ we choose the transition $s_0 \to s_1$ and we mark $s_0$ as $k$. We mark the unchosen edge as dotted line.

$$s_0^{\mathbf{k}} \xrightarrow{\;0\;} s_1^{\mathbf{k}} \xrightarrow{\;k\;} s_2^{\mathbf{0}}$$
$$\overset{pk}{\searrow}$$
$$s_3^{\mathbf{pk}} \xrightarrow{\;0\;} s_4^{\mathbf{0}}$$

The optimal leakage is achieved by the path

$$s_0 \to s_1 \to s_2$$

Also, we can easily get the pessimal path in the transition system

$$s_0^{\mathbf{pk}} \dashrightarrow{\;0\;} s_1^{\mathbf{k}} \xrightarrow{\;k\;} s_2^{\mathbf{0}}$$
$$\overset{pk}{\searrow}$$
$$s_3^{\mathbf{pk}} \xrightarrow{\;0\;} s_4^{\mathbf{0}}$$

and the pessimal leakage $pk$ is achieved by the path

$$s_0 \to s_3 \to s_4$$

**Example II.** Let us consider another example from [26]. This is a nested multi-threaded program. In the outer two threads, we use $p$ as probability operator. There are two nested threads in one of them, reflected by the introduction of an additional probability operator $q$. Also, we assume that $h$ is $k$ bits long.

$$\texttt{l=h}|_p(\ \texttt{l=0}|_q\texttt{l=1})$$

Here we assume $p = q = \frac{1}{2}$ which is a coin-flip choice operator. Using the modeling method in Section 4.1 we can got the transition system:

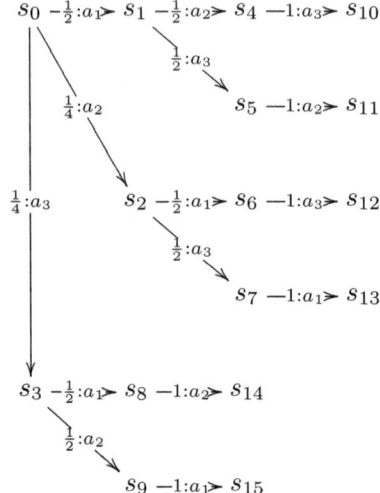

where $a_1=$ "l=h"; $a_2 =$ "l=0"; $a_3=$ "l=1". We can see from the statements that $a_1$ leaks $k$ bits while others do not leak. From this nested threads example, we also note that if the program has dynamic thread creation, then its transition system may similarly be constructed by reserving states and choices for the upcoming threads.

We are going to use Proposition 2 to solve the bounds of the leakage for this transition system. Firstly we consider the optimal leakage. At each stage we use Theorem 1 to achieve the optimal choice. We start from six possible terminal states $s_{10} \ldots s_{15}$ and we mark them to be 0. We track back one level to find the states $s_4 \ldots s_9$. In these states we first consider the node $s_4$, there is only one reachable state from $s_4$ which is $s_{10}$ and the leakage in this transition is 0 with a probability of 1 so we mark $s_4$ to be $1 \times 0 = 0$. Also we can easily find that $s_{11}, s_{12}, s_{13}, s_{14}, s_{15}$ can only be reached by $s_5, s_6, s_7, s_8, s_9$. The leakage values for these transitions are $0, 0, k, 0, k$ with the probability 1, because in the transitions $s_7 \rightarrow s_{13}$ and $s_9 \rightarrow s_{15}$, $a_1$ has $k$ bits leakage while in the other transitions, $a_2$ and $a_3$ has 0 leakage. So we mark $s_5, s_6, s_7, s_8, s_9$ with $0, 0, k, 0, k$ accordingly. We continue tracking back one level and find the states $s_1, s_2$ and $s_3$. $s_1$ can be reached by $s_4$ and $s_5$ where the leakage from the two transitions are both 0 so we mark $s_1$ as 0. Then we consider $s_2$, which can be reached by $s_6$ and $s_7$. The leakage in transition $s_2 \rightarrow s_6$ is $k$ with probability $\frac{1}{2}$ and in transition $s_2 \rightarrow s_7$ is 0. Considering the leakage previously we get $0 + \frac{1}{2} \times k < k + \frac{1}{2} \times 0$, thus at this stage we choose $s_2 \rightarrow s_7$ and we put $s_2 \rightarrow s_6$ as dotted line. Similarly we know that for $s_3$, the optimal choice is $s_3 \rightarrow s_9$ with the leakage $k$. We mark it as $k$ and put $s_3 \rightarrow s_8$ as dotted line. Then we arrive at the initial state $s_0$. There are three reachable states $s_1, s_2, s_3$ from $s_0$, the leakage for $s_0 \rightarrow s_1$ is $0 + \frac{1}{2} \times k$ while for the other two transitions is $k + \frac{1}{4} \times 0$, so we could choose either $s_0 \rightarrow s_2$ or $s_0 \rightarrow s_3$. The solution is showing in the following graph.

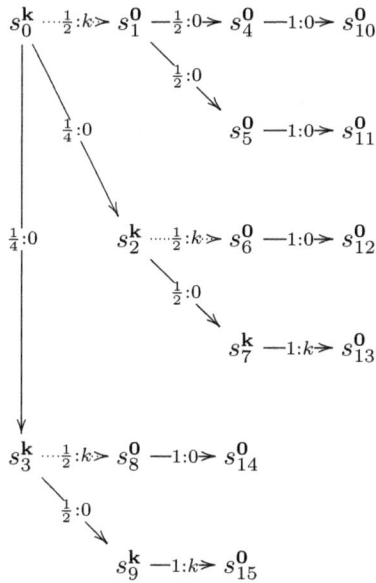

The optimal leakage $k$ is achieved by:

$$s_0 \to s_2 \to s_7 \to s_{13} \quad (\{a_2, a_3, a_1\}), \quad \text{or} \quad s_0 \to s_3 \to s_9 \to s_{15} \quad (\{a_3, a_2, a_1\})$$

Alternatively, using Proposition 2, at each stage we can choose the minimal value to get the pessimal leakage:

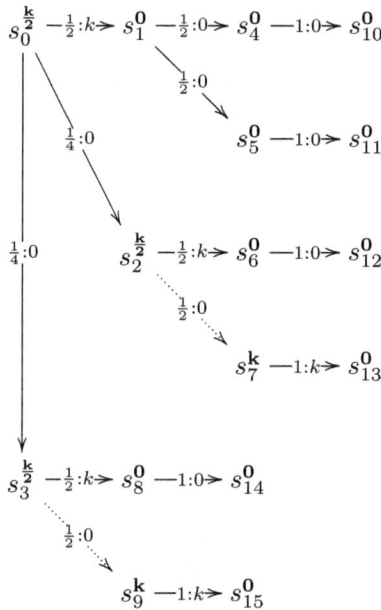

and the pessimal leakage $\frac{k}{2}$ is achieved by one of the following paths:

$$s_0 \rightarrow s_1 \rightarrow s_4 \rightarrow s_{10} \quad (\{a_1, a_2, a_3\})$$
$$s_0 \rightarrow s_1 \rightarrow s_5 \rightarrow s_{11} \quad (\{a_1, a_3, a_2\})$$
$$s_0 \rightarrow s_2 \rightarrow s_6 \rightarrow s_{12} \quad (\{a_2, a_1, a_3\})$$
$$s_0 \rightarrow s_3 \rightarrow s_8 \rightarrow s_{14} \quad (\{a_3, a_1, a_2\})$$

## 4.4   Complexity

Computational complexity is a very important factor for implementation and is considered a practical issue for the use of Bellman equation. We denote the computational complexity as $R$ here. Since the execution trees in our state tran- sition systems are acyclic and strictly nondecreasing backwards, the computa- tional complexity of the optimality leakage principle (Proposition 2) is bounded by the number of vertexes (nodes) or edges in the tree, which can be bounded by two factors: the number of choices at each stage and the other is the number of stages.

If the state transition system has $n$ stages[1], with two decisions taken at every stage, this requires $R = O(2^n)$ arithmetical operations. In the general case, if there are $n$ stages in the transition system and at each stage there are $m$ deci- sions, the complexity for the implementation is of the order of $O(m^n)$ arithmeti- cal operations. The computational complexity will increase significantly with the decisions at every stage. For example, if there are 20 stages and 3 decisions at every stage, we will get 3 486 784 401 operations; in a computer with a speed of 1 million arithmetical operations per second, it will take 3487 seconds i.e 0.97 hour to finish this computation. For this reason there is a strong motivation to simplify the computation otherwise the method would be rarely applicable. Then we have to consider the method to simplify the complexity.

Here we only consider the transition system without considering any transition probabilities. Firstly a transition system can be written as a set of transitions $\mathcal{T}$, in which an element $t_{ij}$ can be written as a triple

$$\langle s_i, \ a_k, \ s_j \rangle$$

where $s_i$ is a starting state and $a_k$ is an action on $s_i$ which transit $s_i$ to the state $s_j$.

We consider two kinds of improvements. Firstly, since the graph is a tree, there are existing standard algorithms which are much more computationally efficient than $O(m^n)$ for tree-search. Secondly, in the process of using Proposition 2 to solve the leakage bounds, if $L^*(s') = 0$ whatever $P(s'|s,a)$ is, the edge will not contribute to the new value of leakage. In the following algorithm, we are removing these edges whose weight is 0, where there is no interference between $h$ and $l$.

---

[1] In the examples, each line is seen as a stage. In reality however, instead of tracking every line of program, it is rational to only track the lines which has something to do with the high variable(s).

**Table 1.** Algorithm to simplify the transition system

| **Algorithm 1.** Simplification algorithm for transition system |
| --- |
| **Require:** $\mathcal{T}$ a set of transitions |
| **Ensure:** $\mathcal{T} \neq \phi$? |
| 1: Visited $= \phi$ |
| 2: Waiting $= \mathcal{T}$ |
| 3: **repeat** |
| 4:   Get $t_{ij}$ from Waiting |
| 5:   Visited $=$ Visted $\cup \{t_{ij}\}$ |
| 6:   **if** $L(t_{ij}) == 0$ |
| 7:     Remove $t_{ij}$ from Waiting |
| 8:     Modify $t_{j*} \in Waiting$ as $t_{i*}$ |
| 9:   **endif** |
| 10: **until** Visited $= \mathcal{T}$ |
| 11: Return Waiting; |

For example, in the example 4.3, there are 15 transitions (edges). Now if we use the above algorithm to cut some 0 weight edges, we can then simplify the transition system to be

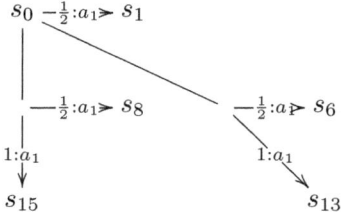

There are only 5 remaining edges after simplification and the number of edges has reduced by 67%.

## 4.5   Further Remarks

1. The optimality principle allows for an interesting characterization of leakage in multi-threaded programs, based on what can be leaked from an optimal or pessimal policy. In comparison, previous quantitative result for multi-threaded programs is an overall expectation [13].
2. Since state-transition forms a tree graph, in the program run-time the tree will continuously evolve into subtrees. This allows to track run-time leakage at each time spot, by finding the optimal leakage in the subtree with the knowledge of which previous steps have been taken. Further, this can hopefully allow automatic run-time leakage tracking of programs by attaching such a builtin state-transition tree into the program code segment.
3. Furthermore, we should repeat that we have assumed the attacker can observe the low-variable in every single step of execution, and we have modeled

the state transitions based on that. The stages thus can be seen as a super-set [22]. If other kinds of observational assumptions are desirable, our leakage optimality principle can also be easily adapted to those assumptions by considering a subset of the stages, which would lead to a somewhat simpler state transition graph.

4. Finally, the work remains preliminary with respect to real implementation. For programs following a Turing-complete language (with imperative statements, if statements and for loops) we can hopefully borrow experiences from previous works [16,23,13], although several problems have to be solved, for example, how to cope with non-terminating loops and breaks. This would be an open problem for the next step.

## 5   Conclusions and Future Work

By extending the Bellman's optimality principle into quantitative information flow, we propose a novel principle for characterizing information leakage and tracking the run-time leakage in multi-threaded programs.

This may create lots of exciting opportunities: according to the static results further actions can be made either to accept or to reject a program, while dynamic measurement can be used for alert or guarantee that an attacker can not acquire a certain quantity of information at run-time. Such a method can also serve as a template for tracking information leaks in state transition systems. Finally, we believe this work demonstrates an interesting perspective by connecting the field of information security with the theory of machine learning.

## References

1. Bhargava, M., Palamidessi, C.: Probabilistic Anonymity. In: Abadi, M., de Alfaro, L. (eds.) CONCUR 2005. LNCS, vol. 3653, pp. 171–185. Springer, Heidelberg (2005)
2. Bellman, R.: On the Theory of Dynamic Programming. In: Proceedings of the National Academy of Sciences (1952)
3. Braun, C., Chatzikokolakis, K., Palamidessi, C.: Quantitative notions of leakage for one-try attacks. In: Proceedings of MFPS 2009 (2009)
4. Chatzikokolakis, K., Palamidessi, C., Panangaden, P.: Anonymity Protocols as Noisy Channels. Postproceedings of the Symp. on Trustworthy Global Computing. LNCS. Springer, Heidelberg (2006)
5. Chatzikokolakis, K., Palamidessi, C., Panangaden, P.: On the bayes risk in information-hiding protocols. Journal of Computer Security 16(5), 531–571 (2008)
6. Michael, R., Clarkson, A.C.: Myers, and Fred B. Schneider: Belief in information flow. In: Proceedings of 18th IEEE Computer Security Foundations Workshop, pp. 31–45. Aix-en-Provence, France (2005)
7. Cover, T., Thomas, J.: Elements of Information Theory. John Wiley&Sons, Inc., Hoboken (2006)
8. Denning, D.E.: Cyptography and Data Security. Addison-Wesley, Reading (1982)
9. Denning, D.E.: A lattice model of secure information flow. Communications of the ACM 19(5) (May 1976)

10. Di Pierro, A., Hankin, C., Wiklicky, H.: Measuring the confinement of probabilistic systems. Theoretical Computer Science 340(1), 3–56 (2005)
11. Gray III, J.W.: Toward a methematical foundataion for information flow security. In: Proceedings of the 1991 IEEE Symposium on Security and Privacy, Oakland, California (May 1991)
12. Chen, H., Malacaria, P.: Quantifying Maximal Loss of Anonymity in Protocols. In: Proceedings of ASIACCS 2009, Sydney, NSW, Australia, March 10-12 (2009)
13. Chen, H., Malacaria, P.: Quantitative Analysis of Leakage for Multi-threaded Programs. In: Proceedings of ACM 2007 workshop on Programming languages and analysis for security (2007)
14. Chen, H., Malacaria, P.: Studying Maximum Information Leakage Using Karush–Kuhn–Tucker Conditions. In: Proceedings of the 7th International Workshop on Security Issues in Concurrency
15. Clark, D., Hunt, S., Malacaria, P.: David Clark, Sebastian Hunt, Pasquale Malacaria: A static analysis for quantifying information flow in a simple imperative language. Journal of Computer Security 15 (2007)
16. Clark, D., Hunt, S., Malacaria, P.: Quantitative Analysis of the leakage of confidential data. Electronic Notes in Theoretical Computer Science 59 (2002)
17. Clark, D., Hunt, S., Malacaria, P.: Quantified interference for a while language. Electronic Notes in Theoretical Computer Science 112, 149–166 (2005)
18. Backes, M., Kopf, B., Rybalchenko, A.: Automatic Discovery and Quantification of Information Leaks. In: Proceedings of the 30th IEEE Symposium on Security and Privacy, S&P 2009 (2009)
19. Lowe, G.: Quantifying information flow. In: Proceedings of the Workshop on Automated Verification of Critical Systems (2001)
20. Mclean, J.: Security models and information flow. In: Proceedings of the 1990 IEEE Symposium on Security and Privacy. Oakland, California (May 1990)
21. Millen, J.: Covert channel capacity. In: Proceedings of the 1987 IEEE Symposium on Research in Security and Privacy (1987)
22. Malacaria, P., Chen, H.: Lagrange Multipliers and Maximum Information Leakage in Different Observational Models. In: Proceedings of ACM SIGPLAN Third Workshop on Programming Languages and Analysis for Security (June 2008)
23. Malacaria, P.: Assessing security threats of looping constructs. In: Proceedings of ACM Symposium on Principles of Programming Language (2007)
24. Malacaria, P.: Risk Assessment of Security Threats for Looping Constructs. Journal of Computer Security (2009)
25. Puterman, M.L.: Markov decision processes: discrete stochastic dynamic programming., 2nd edn., illustrated. Wiley-Interscience, Hoboken (2005)
26. Sabelfeld, A., Sands, D.: Probabilistic noninterference for multi-threaded programs. In: Proceedings of IEEE Computer Security Foundations Workshop, July 2000, pp. 200–214 (2000)
27. Shannon, C.E., Weaver, W.: A Mathematical Theory of Communication. Univ. of Illinois Press, Urbana (1963)
28. Smith, G.: On the Foundation of Quantitative Information Flow. In: de Alfaro, L. (ed.) FOSSACS 2009. LNCS, vol. 5504, pp. 288–302. Springer, Heidelberg (2009)
29. Chatzikokolakis, K., Chothia, T., Guha, A.: Calculating Probabilistic Anonymity from Sampled Data (manuscript) (2009), http://www.cs.bham.ac.uk/~tpc/Papers/CalcProbAnon.pdf

# A General Conversion Method of Fingerprint Codes to (More) Robust Fingerprint Codes against Bit Erasure

Koji Nuida

Research Center for Information Security (RCIS), National Institute of Advanced
Industrial Science and Technology (AIST), Akihabara-Daibiru Room 1003, 1-18-13
Sotokanda, Chiyoda-ku, Tokyo 101-0021, Japan
k.nuida@aist.go.jp

**Abstract.** A $c$-secure fingerprint code is called robust if it is secure
against a limited number of bit erasure in undetectable positions in addition to usual collusion attacks. In this article, we propose the first
general conversion method of (non-robust) $c$-secure codes to robust $c$-
secure codes. It is also applicable to amplify robustness of given robust
$c$-secure codes. By applying our conversion to $c$-secure codes given by
Nuida et al. (AAECC 2007), we present robust $c$-secure codes with code
lengths of order $\Theta(c^2 \log^2 c)$ with respect to $c$. The code length improves
preceding results by Sirvent (WCC 2007) and by Boneh and Naor (ACM
CCS 2008) and is close to the one by Billet and Phan (ICITS 2008),
where our result is based on a weaker assumption than those preceding
results. As an application, the use of the resulting code in construction
by Boneh and Naor also improves their traitor tracing scheme against
imperfect decoders in efficiency of key sizes and pirate tracing procedure.

**Keywords:** Fingerprint code, robust c-secure code, general conversion,
traitor tracing scheme, information-theoretic security.

## 1 Introduction

### 1.1 Background

Recently, digital content distribution services have been widespread with support
of the progress of information processing/communication technology. Digitiza-
tion of contents and content distribution has been promoted convenience for
many people. However, it does also work better for malicious pirates, and the
number of illegal content copying/redistribution has increased very rapidly. Thus
technical countermeasures for such illegal activities are strongly desired.

Digital fingerprinting is a possible solution for the above problems. Here we
focus on code-based schemes; a content server first encodes each user's ID and
then embeds each codeword as a fingerprint into a content that will be sent to the
user. This intends to make the pirate traceable from the fingerprint embedded
in a pirated content, and this scheme would work effectively when a single pirate

K. Kurosawa (Ed.): ICITS 2009, LNCS 5973, pp. 194–212, 2010.
© Springer-Verlag Berlin Heidelberg 2010

redistributes the received content and the digital watermarking scheme used to embed the fingerprint is sufficiently robust. However, it has been pointed out that, if two or more pirates collude, then strong attacks (collusion attacks) to the embedded fingerprint are possible. Hence any fingerprint code should be equipped with a pirate tracing algorithm that determines a pirate correctly with an overwhelming probability even from an attacked fingerprint. Such a fingerprint code is called $c$-secure [5] if at least one of the pirates is traceable (in the above sense) provided the number of pirates is not larger than $c$. Note that usually no assumption is put on complexity of the attack algorithms of pirates, hence $c$-secure fingerprint codes provide information-theoretic security. The first concrete example of $c$-secure codes was given by Boneh and Shaw [5], and then several construction of $c$-secure codes have been proposed, e.g., [3,7,8,9,10,11,12,14,15,16].

Intuitively, the conventional assumption for $c$-secure codes (Marking Assumption [5]) is as follows. Suppose, for each (say, $j$-th) digit of the fingerprint code, that the place in the content where $j$-th digit of a user's codeword is embedded is common to all users. If the $j$-th digits of codewords for pirates are not the same, then by comparing their contents they will find some difference at that place (such a digit is called "detectable"). In this case, pirates would be able to create the pirated content in such a way that the $j$-th digit of the embedded fingerprint is either modified or erased (the latter being formalized as an erasure symbol '?'). On the other hand, if the $j$-th digits of codewords for all pirates are the same (called "undetectable"), then they cannot recognize the digit by comparing their contents in the above manner. In this case, the Marking Assumption states that $j$-th digit of the pirated fingerprint will remain not attacked so that it will be the same as the $j$-th digit of some (or equivalently, any) pirate's codeword. Based on this assumption, several $c$-secure codes have been proposed (e.g., [3,5,7,8,10,11,14,15,16]). However, it has also been pointed out that the strict Marking Assumption seems not practical. In fact, even if the undetectable digits in the above sense are really undetectable, it is still possible that pirates add some noise randomly to the content, which may make some undetectable digits not decodable. Thus some relaxation of Marking Assumption, allowing some undetectable digits to be attacked, have been introduced in various ways and several construction of $c$-secure codes under those assumptions, called robust $c$-secure codes, have been proposed, e.g., [9,11,12]. Recently, robust $c$-secure codes are also studied in connection with traitor tracing schemes against pirates with powerful decoders [13] or imperfect decoders [4]. Thus robust $c$-secure codes are important in both theoretical and practical viewpoints.

However, constructing robust $c$-secure codes, or modifying non-robust $c$-secure codes to make them robust, requires in general further intricate and scheme-dependent arguments, which would significantly increase the difficulty of the construction and understanding of the schemes. This tendency seems stronger for $c$-secure codes with combinatorial construction (e.g., [7,8,16]) and those with security highly depending on the characteristics of Marking Assumption (e.g., [3,10]).

## 1.2  Our Contribution and Organization of the Article

Concerning the problem mentioned in Sect. 1.1, in this article we present the first general conversion method of any $c$-secure fingerprint code to a robust $c$-secure code. The same method can also amplify the robustness of given $c$-secure codes, that is, our method converts less robust $c$-secure codes into more robust ones (i.e., allowing a larger number of undetectable digits to be attacked). Our method has the following good characteristics, for instance:

**Black-box treatment.** Our conversion requires *no* knowledge of specific properties for the target fingerprint code, except the relation between code length and tracing error probability.
**Information-theoretic security.** The security proof of our conversion method requires *no* computational assumptions, hence the resulting robust fingerprint code is also information-theoretically secure.
**Simplicity and efficiency.** Our conversion method is very simple, and the increase of computational costs induced by our conversion is not large.
**Generality.** Our conversion is applicable to very general $c$-secure fingerprint codes, including not only binary but also $q$-ary codes (e.g., [12,14]).
**Extendibility.** In our conversion method, the meaning of "error probability" can be flexibly modified to concern various situations. By the property, our method would also be applicable to some related schemes, such as two-level fingerprinting codes introduced very recently in [1].

Here we explain the essential idea of our conversion method. For simplicity, we assume that the target fingerprint code $\mathcal{C}$ is binary and not robust (the general case is similar). To resist erasure of undetectable bits, whose number is bounded by a certain fraction, denoted by $\delta$, of the total code length (that is allowed by our relaxed Marking Assumption), our method first expands each bit in each codeword of $\mathcal{C}$ to a block of $b$ identical bits, and appends $L$ dummy bits to every codeword that are common to all codewords. The resulting codewords are sent to the users, where the distribution of bits in the undetectable blocks is concealed from the pirates by using a random permutation and random bit flippings. Now, when a pirated word for the expanded code is given, even if a part of an undetectable block was erased, the undetectable bit corresponding to the block can be still recovered provided at least one bit in the block survives. Moreover, by choosing a sufficiently large block size $b$ and a sufficiently large number $L$ of dummy bits, it becomes sufficiently difficult for the pirates to erase all bits in an undetectable block. Thus a valid pirated word for the original code is obtained with overwhelming probability, therefore the resulting fingerprint code is equipped with the desired robustness (see Theorem 1).

We also investigate appropriate values of the parameters $b$ and $L$, and give formulae for these parameters (see Theorem 2). By using the result, we describe the asymptotic behavior of code lengths of the resulting robust $c$-secure codes in terms of those of the original $c$-secure codes. Moreover, by choosing the (less) robust $c$-secure codes proposed by Nuida et al. [11] as the original fingerprint code, we show that there exist robust $c$-secure binary fingerprint codes (for arbitrary $0 < \delta < 1$) with code lengths $\overline{m}$ satisfying

$$\overline{m} \sim 21.41244 \left(\frac{c \log c}{1 - \delta}\right)^2 \log(N/\varepsilon), \tag{1}$$

where $N$ denotes the number of users and $\varepsilon$ denotes the error probability (see Theorem 3). Comparing with the lower bound $\Omega(c^2 \log(N/\varepsilon))$ of code lengths of (non-robust) $c$-secure codes given by Tardos [15], it would be possible to say that our code length is of "nearly optimal" order. The constant factor 21.41244 in (1) is also not very huge; e.g., the constant factor for Tardos code [15] is 100.

We give a remark on efficiency of our conversion. In the implementation of fingerprint codes by embedding the codewords into digital contents by some digital watermarking scheme, embedding less robust watermarks, say, with decoding error probability 10%, requires less redundancy than embedding more robust watermarks, say, with decoding error probability 0.01%. Thus, although our conversion method increases the code lengths, the actual increase of the overall size of embedded objects in such implementation will be smaller than the apparent increase of the code lengths. Theoretical evaluations for increase of the amount of actual embedded objects would be a challenging research topic.

To be honest, the results of this article contain some points for improvement. First, our proposed conversion method can be interpreted as concatenating the original fingerprint code with a repetition code (and also some dummy digits); it can be expected that the use of more sophisticated erasure codes would improve the efficiency of the conversion method. Secondly, our analysis of code lengths is not fully optimized and a more detailed and complicated analysis would be able to reduce the resulting code lengths further. The reason of leaving such rooms for improvement is that the main purpose of this article is to pioneer the study of the general conversion methods by showing the first concrete, easy-to-understand idea and example, not to give the best result at once by an involved and intricate argument. Moreover, the relative simplicity of our formula of code lengths enabled us to determine the asymptotic behavior theoretically. The author hopes that some subsequent future research will realize the above-mentioned improvements for the current result. On the other hand, in this article we only concern bit erasure in undetectable positions, but in some practical situation one may wish for robustness against some bit flipping in undetectable positions as well (as the case discussed in [11]). It would also be an important future research topic to extend our conversion method to the more general situation, e.g., by using more sophisticated error correcting codes instead of our repetition codes.

This article is organized as follows. After some remarks on related works (Sect. 1.3) and notations and terminology (Sect. 1.4), in Sect. 2 we summarize the notion of fingerprint codes and the relaxed Marking Assumption (called $\delta$-Marking Assumption) on which our construction is based. In Sect. 3, we present the above-mentioned three main theorems of this article. Section 4 gives the proofs of main theorems, where some part is left to the forthcoming full version of this article. Finally, Sect. 5 shows some numerical examples of our results.

## 1.3    Related Works

As mentioned in Sect. 1.1, there have been proposed several kinds of relaxation of the Marking Assumption. Guth and Pfitzmann [9] considered the situation that each undetectable bit is erased (i.e., marked with '?') *independently* with a certain probability, and extended Boneh-Shaw codes [5] to their assumption. (Safavi-Naini and Wang [12] also considered the same assumption for $q$-ary fingerprint codes.) There seems no overall implication between our relaxed Marking Assumption and their relaxed one; however, our assumption would look weaker due to the lack of the above-mentioned independence condition.

In connection with traitor tracing schemes against imperfect decoders, Sirvent [13], Billet and Phan [2], and Boneh and Naor [4] considered another assumption that is more relevant to ours. In their relaxed Marking Assumption, the digitwise independence of erasure (assumed in [9]) is not required, but the number of erased digits *in the whole positions*, not *just in undetectable positions* as in our assumption, is bounded by $\delta$ fraction of the total code length (see e.g., Sect. 4.1 of [4]). Thus our relaxed Marking Assumption is readily weaker than theirs; i.e., our assumption allows a bounded number of erasure in undetectable positions and *arbitrarily many* erasure in detectable positions. In [13,4], they extended Boneh-Shaw codes to their relaxed assumption, with resulting code lengths $m = \Theta(c^4 \log(N/\varepsilon) \log(c^2 \log(N/\varepsilon)/\varepsilon))$ in [13] (where the dependence of $m$ on $\delta$ seems not clarified) and $m = \Theta((N^3/(1-\delta)^2) \log(2N/\varepsilon))$ in [4] (in the full-collusion case $c = N$). On the other hand, in [2], they extended Tardos codes [15] to their relaxed assumption, with resulting code lengths $m = \Theta((c^2/(1-\delta)) \log(N/\varepsilon))$. Despite that our code is based on a weaker assumption, its code length in (1), with $c = N$ when compared with [4], is significantly more efficient than [13,4] and is close to [2]. Moreover, by using our code instead of the extended Boneh-Shaw code in the traitor tracing scheme in [4] with constant size ciphertext, we can improve their scheme in efficiency of key sizes and pirate tracing procedure (see [4] for the details of their construction).

On the other hand, Nuida et al. [11] considered another relaxation of Marking Assumption; the number of undetectable bits that are *either erased or flipped* is bounded by $\delta$ fraction of the total code length. Their assumption is thus weaker than ours, and their $\delta$-robust $c$-secure codes have code lengths $m = \Theta(c^2 \log(N/\varepsilon))$ that are shorter than (1). However, in their scheme the parameter $\delta$ is restricted to be far from 1, i.e., $\delta = O(c^{-2})$ (see [11, Sect. 6.1]), while in our scheme the parameter $\delta$ can be arbitrarily close to 1. (In fact, the construction of our $\delta$-robust $c$-secure codes with code lengths in (1) is based on their codes, as mentioned in Sect. 1.2.) To extend our conversion method to their weaker assumption would be an interesting future research topic.

## 1.4    Notations and Terminology

In this article, $\log x$ denotes the natural (i.e., base $e$) logarithm of $x$. The expression "$x \to x_0$" means "$x$ converges to $x_0$" (or "$x$ diverges to $x_0$", when $x_0 = \pm\infty$). For $i, j \in \mathbb{Z}$, $(i)_j$ denotes the lower factorial: $(i)_j = i(i-1)\cdots(i-j+1)$.

The symbols $\lfloor x \rfloor$ and $\lceil x \rceil$ denote the largest $M \in \mathbb{Z}$ with $M \leq x$ and the smallest $M \in \mathbb{Z}$ with $M \geq x$, respectively. Moreover, $\Sigma_q = \{s_0, s_1, \ldots, s_{q-1}\}$ denotes a $q$-ary alphabet (including the binary case $\Sigma_2 = \{0, 1\}$), and for $s \in \Sigma_q$ and $j \in \mathbb{Z}$, the expression "rotate $s$ by $j$" means to convert $s = s_h \in \Sigma_q$ into $s_i \in \Sigma_q$, where $i \equiv h + j \pmod{q}$.

## 2    Robust Fingerprint Codes

In this article, each user is identified with the corresponding index $i$, $1 \leq i \leq N$. A $(q\text{-}ary)$ *fingerprint code* is a pair $\mathcal{C} = (\mathsf{Gen}, \mathsf{Tr})$ of a code generation algorithm $\mathsf{Gen}$ and a pirate tracing algorithm $\mathsf{Tr}$ with the following characteristics:

- The algorithm $\mathsf{Gen}$ takes a parameter $\varepsilon$ for error probability (and implicitly other relevant parameters such as the total number $N$ of users) as input, and outputs a collection $W = (w_1, \ldots, w_N)$ of $q$-ary codewords $w_i$ of common length $m$ and a certain element $\mathsf{st}$, called *state information*. The codeword $w_i$ is sent to the user $i$, while $\mathsf{st}$ should be kept secret.
- The algorithm $\mathsf{Tr}$ takes, as input, $W$ and $\mathsf{st}$ output by $\mathsf{Gen}$, and a word $y$ of length $m$ over an expanded alphabet $\Sigma_q \cup \{?\}$ called a *pirated word*. Then $\mathsf{Tr}$ outputs a (possibly empty) subset $\mathsf{Acc}$ of the user set $\{1, 2, \ldots, N\}$.

Here '?' signifies erasure of a digit. An example of the state information $\mathsf{st}$ is the collection of bias parameters $p_1, \ldots, p_m$, $0 < p_i < 1$, for Tardos codes [15].

Let $C$ be a subset of $\{1, 2, \ldots, N\}$; users in $C$ are called *pirates*. For $1 \leq j \leq m$, $j$-th position in a codeword is called *undetectable* if the $j$-th digits $w_{i,j}$ of codewords $w_i$ coincide for all $i \in C$; and *detectable* otherwise. A *collusion strategy* is an algorithm $\rho$ that takes the codewords $w_i$ for all $i \in C$ as input and outputs a pirated word $y$ (of length $m$ over $\Sigma_q \cup \{?\}$). In this article, we put one of the following two sorts of assumptions on the collusion strategies, where $0 \leq \delta < 1$ is a parameter (the classification follows from the one given in [14]):

$\delta$-**Marking Assumption (unreadable digit model).** We have $y_j \in \{w_{i,j} \mid i \in C\} \cup \{?\}$ for any $1 \leq j \leq m$. Moreover, the number of undetectable positions with $y_j = ?$ is not larger than $\delta m$.

$\delta$-**Marking Assumption (general digit model).** We have $y_j \in \Sigma_q \cup \{?\}$ for any detectable position, while we have $y_j \in \{w_{i,j} \mid i \in C\} \cup \{?\}$ for any undetectable position. Moreover, the number of undetectable positions with $y_j = ?$ is not larger than $\delta m$.

Which of the two assumptions is adopted is fixed throughout the argument. Note that these two assumptions are identical for binary case. Any of the two assumptions with $\delta = 0$ coincides with the *Marking Assumption* [5].

We say that a fingerprint code $\mathcal{C}$ is $\delta$-*robust c-secure* if, for any set $C$ of pirates with $1 \leq |C| \leq c$ and any collusion strategy $\rho$ satisfying $\delta$-Marking Assumption, we have:

$$Pr[(W, \mathsf{st}) \leftarrow \mathsf{Gen}; y \leftarrow \rho((w_i)_{i \in C}); \mathsf{Acc} \leftarrow \mathsf{Tr}(W, \mathsf{st}, y)$$
$$: \mathsf{Acc} \cap C = \emptyset \text{ or } \mathsf{Acc} \not\subset C] \leq \varepsilon.$$

Such a code $\mathcal{C}$ with $\delta = 0$ is called *c-secure* [5]. Intuitively, Acc signifies the set of users accused as a pirate by the tracing algorithm, and the events $\mathsf{Acc} \cap C = \emptyset$ and $\mathsf{Acc} \not\subset C$ correspond to false-negative (i.e., no pirate is accused) and false-positive (i.e., some innocent user is accused), respectively. The aim of this article is to propose the first general conversion method from given $\delta_0$-robust *c*-secure codes to $\delta$-robust *c*-secure codes, where $0 \le \delta_0 < \delta < 1$.

## 3   Main Results

In this section, we present the main results of this article. In Sect. 3.1, we describe our proposed general conversion method and state its validity. In Sect. 3.2, we give an appropriate choice of code lengths and relevant parameters for our conversion, and describe the asymptotic behavior of the resulting robust *c*-secure codes. An outline of the proofs will be given in Sect. 4.

### 3.1   The Conversion

To state our conversion method, let $\mathcal{C} = (\mathsf{Gen}, \mathsf{Tr})$ be an arbitrary $\delta_0$-robust *c*-secure *q*-ary fingerprint code ($0 \le \delta_0 < 1$), with code length denoted by $m$. We construct from $\mathcal{C}$ a $\delta$-robust *c*-secure *q*-ary fingerprint code $\overline{\mathcal{C}} = (\overline{\mathsf{Gen}}, \overline{\mathsf{Tr}})$, where $0 < \delta < 1$. Given a security parameter $0 < \varepsilon < 1$ for $\overline{\mathcal{C}}$, choose $0 < \varepsilon_1 < 1$ and $0 < \varepsilon_2 < 1$ such that

$$\varepsilon_1 + \varepsilon_2 \le \varepsilon. \tag{2}$$

The parameter $\varepsilon_1$ signifies the loss of security through our conversion, and $\varepsilon_2$ is a security parameter for the original code $\mathcal{C}$.

Let $b \ge 1$ and $L \ge 0$ be integer parameters. Then our conversion from $\mathcal{C}$ to $\overline{\mathcal{C}}$, where $\overline{\mathcal{C}}$ has code length $\overline{m} = bm + L$, is constructed in the following manner:

**Algorithm $\overline{\mathsf{Gen}}$**     Input: security parameter $0 < \varepsilon < 1$

(1) Perform $\mathsf{Gen}$, with input security parameter $\varepsilon_2$ chosen as above, to obtain a collection $W = (w_i)_{i=1}^{N}$ of codewords and the corresponding state information st.

(2) For every digit $w_{i,j}$ in $W$, replace it with a block of $b$ digits each of which is identical with $w_{i,j}$.

(3) Append $L$ '0's, called *dummy digits*, to the tail of every word obtained by the previous step. (Thus the resulting word has length $\overline{m} = bm + L$.)

(4) Choose a secret word $\mathsf{fl} = (\mathsf{fl}_1, \ldots, \mathsf{fl}_{\overline{m}})$, where $\mathsf{fl}_j \in \{0, 1, \ldots, q-1\}$, uniformly at random. Then for every word obtained by the previous step and for every $1 \le j \le \overline{m}$, rotate *j*-th digit of the word by $\mathsf{fl}_j$ (see Sect. 1.4 for the terminology).

(5) Choose a secret permutation $\mathsf{perm}$ of $\overline{m}$ letters $1, \ldots, \overline{m}$ uniformly at random, and permute the digits of every word obtained by the previous step according to $\mathsf{perm}$ (i.e., *j*-th digit of the word becomes $\mathsf{perm}(j)$-th digit of the resulting word).

(6) Output the collection $\overline{W} = (\overline{w}_i)_{i=1}^{N}$ of codewords and the corresponding state information $\overline{\mathsf{st}} = (\mathsf{st}, \mathsf{fl}, \mathsf{perm})$, where $\overline{w}_i$ is the word obtained from $w_i$ by Steps 2–5.

**Algorithm $\overline{\mathsf{Tr}}$** Input: $\overline{W}, \overline{\mathsf{st}}$ output by $\overline{\mathsf{Gen}}$, and a pirated word $\overline{y} = (\overline{y}_1, \dots, \overline{y}_{\overline{m}})$
(1) Permute the digits in $\overline{y}$ according to the inverse of $\mathsf{perm}$, and for every $1 \le j \le \overline{m}$, rotate $j$-th digit of the word after the inverse permutation by $-\mathsf{fl}_j$ if and only if it is not '?'. Let $\overline{y}'$ denote the resulting word.
(2) Generate a word $y = (y_1, \dots, y_m)$ in the following way: For each $1 \le j \le m$, put
  – $y_j = x \in \Sigma_q$, if $j$-th block of $\overline{y}'$ contains at least one digit $x$ and no digits different from $x$ and '?'.
  – $y_j = ?$, otherwise.
(3) For every $\overline{w}_i$, permute the digits in $\overline{w}_i$ according to the inverse of $\mathsf{perm}$; remove the last $L$ digits (i.e., the dummy digits); rotate $j$-th digit by $-\mathsf{fl}_j$ for every $1 \le j \le bm$; and replace the $j$-th block with its first digit for every $1 \le j \le m$. Let $w_i$ denote the resulting word.
(4) Perform $\mathsf{Tr}$, with $W = (w_i)_{i=1}^{N}$, $\mathsf{st}$ and $y$ as input, and output what this $\mathsf{Tr}$ outputs.

We give some intuitive explanation of the conversion method. First, the new code generation algorithm $\overline{\mathsf{Gen}}$ calls the original code generation algorithm $\mathsf{Gen}$ with slightly smaller security parameter as a subroutine. The expansion process in Steps 2–3 aims at making it difficult for pirates to erase all digits in an undetectable block randomly. The shuffle process in Steps 4–5 aims at concealing the distribution of blocks and dummy digits from the pirates, forcing the erasure strategy of pirates to be just random. The rotation of digits and permutation of positions should be kept secret against pirates, thus these together with the original state information form the new state information. Secondly, the new tracing algorithm $\overline{\mathsf{Tr}}$ first reverses the above shuffle process and expansion process to obtain the codewords and a pirated word for the original code $\mathcal{C}$, then performs the original tracing algorithm $\mathsf{Tr}$. If the parameters are appropriately selected, the obtained pirated word for $\mathcal{C}$ is valid with overwhelming probability, hence the overall error probability for $\overline{\mathcal{C}}$ will be bounded by the specified value $\varepsilon$.

In order to prove the security of our conversion, we assume that the above parameters satisfy the following condition:

$$L \ge \nu_1 \text{ and } \left(\frac{a}{\nu_2}\right) \frac{\binom{ba+L-b\nu_2}{\nu_1-b\nu_2}}{\binom{ba+L}{\nu_1}} \le \varepsilon_1 \text{ for every integer } 0 \le a \le m, \tag{3}$$

where $\nu_1 = \lfloor \delta(bm + L) \rfloor$ and $\nu_2 = \lfloor \delta_0 m \rfloor + 1$.

Note that some explicit choices of these parameters will be discussed in Sect. 3.2. Then we have the following result, which will be proven in Sect. 4.1:

**Theorem 1.** *In the above situation, the resulting fingerprint code $\overline{\mathcal{C}} = (\overline{\mathsf{Gen}}, \overline{\mathsf{Tr}})$ is $\delta$-robust $c$-secure with error probability not higher than $\varepsilon$.*

## 3.2    Code Lengths and Parameters

Here we give some concrete and appropriate choices of the parameters. Note that the following choices of parameters are not fully optimized yet, hence some improvement would be possible by more precise analysis, either theoretically or numerically, based on the conditions (2) and (3). The first priority in this article is to make the formulae of parameters simple and our theoretical analysis easier. A more tight and detailed analysis will be a future research topic.

We describe the choices of parameters. First, for parameters $\varepsilon_1$ and $\varepsilon_2$, put

$$\varepsilon_1 = \varepsilon_2 = \varepsilon/2,$$

satisfying the condition (2). Secondly, for parameter $L$, put

$$L = \max \left\{ \left\lceil \frac{b\nu_2}{1 - (1 - \nu_2/m)^{1/b}} \right\rceil - bm + b - 1, \left\lceil \frac{\delta bm}{1 - \delta} \right\rceil \right\}. \tag{4}$$

Moreover, for parameter $b$, if $\nu_2 = 1$ (i.e., the original fingerprint code $\mathcal{C}$ is not robust), then put

$$b = \left\lceil \frac{\log(m/\varepsilon_1)}{\log(1/\delta)} \right\rceil; \tag{5}$$

while, in a general case, put

$$b = \left\lceil \frac{\log(m/\nu_2) + 1 + \nu_2^{-1} \log(1/\varepsilon_1)}{\log(1/\delta)} \right\rceil. \tag{6}$$

Note that the former choice (5) is better than the latter one (6) with $\nu_2 = 1$; the reason is that in the case $\nu = 1$ some quantities that will appear in the analysis admit much simpler expressions than a general case, which allow us to perform sharper estimate that improves the choice of $b$. Now we have the following result, which will be proven in Sect. 4.2:

**Theorem 2.** *In the above situation, the parameters $b$ and $L$ satisfy the condition (3) for Theorem 1.*

Hence by Theorem 1, the resulting fingerprint code $\overline{\mathcal{C}}$ of length $\overline{m} = bm + L$ by our conversion method becomes $\delta$-robust $c$-secure with error probability $\leq \varepsilon$ by using the above parameters.

From now, we discuss the asymptotic behavior of the code length $\overline{m}$ of $\overline{\mathcal{C}}$ based on the above parameters; thus we consider (implicitly) sequences of $\delta_0$-robust $c$-secure fingerprint codes $\mathcal{C}$ and of the corresponding $\delta$-robust $c$-secure fingerprint codes $\overline{\mathcal{C}}$, rather than an individual fingerprint code. We may assume without loss of generality that the parameter $\delta_0$ converges to a constant $0 \leq d \leq 1$, by applying Bolzano-Weierstrass theorem (which implies that any infinite sequence of real numbers in a finite interval has a convergent subsequence) to the sequence of parameters $0 \leq \delta_0 < 1$. Moreover, we assume $d < 1$ further to simplify our argument. In what follows, we consider the asymptotic behaviors in the limit case $c \to \infty$, $N/\varepsilon \to \infty$, and $\delta \to 1$. Note that $m = \Omega(c^2 \log(N/\varepsilon))$ by the celebrated lower bound of code lengths of $c$-secure codes given by Tardos [15]. Now we have the following results, which will be proven in Sect. 4.3:

**Theorem 3.** *In the above situation we have the followings:*

1. *We have $\overline{m} = \Theta(b^2 m)$ for arbitrary $\delta_0$-robust c-secure fingerprint codes $\mathcal{C}$.*
2. *If there exist $\delta_0$-robust c-secure fingerprint codes $\mathcal{C}$ of length $m$ with error probability not higher than $\varepsilon_2 = \varepsilon/2$ such that $\delta_0 = \Omega(c^{-2})$, $\delta_0 \to d$, $0 \leq d < 1$ and $m = \Theta(c^2 \log(N/\varepsilon_2))$, then the corresponding $\delta$-robust c-secure fingerprint codes $\overline{\mathcal{C}}$ satisfy*

$$\overline{m} = \Theta\left(\left(\frac{c\log(1/\delta_0)}{1-\delta}\right)^2 \log(N/\varepsilon)\right).$$

*More precisely, if $m \sim Kc^2 \log(N/\varepsilon_2)$ for a constant $K > 0$, and*
*(a) if $\delta_0 = \Theta(g(c)^{-1})$ for an eventually positive function $g(c)$ such that $g(c) = O(c^2)$ and $g(c) = \omega(1)$, then we have*

$$\overline{m} \sim K\left(\frac{c\log g(c)}{1-\delta}\right)^2 \log(N/\varepsilon);$$

*(b) if $\delta_0 \to d$ and $0 < d < 1$, then we have*

$$\overline{m} \sim DK\left(\frac{c}{1-\delta}\right)^2 \log(N/\varepsilon),$$

*where*

$$D = \max\left\{\frac{-d(1-\log d)^2}{\log(1-d)},\ 1-\log d\right\} < \infty.$$

3. *There exist $\delta$-robust c-secure binary fingerprint codes $\overline{\mathcal{C}}$ of length*

$$\overline{m} = \Theta\left(\left(\frac{c\log c}{1-\delta}\right)^2 \log(N/\varepsilon)\right)$$

*with error probability not higher than $\varepsilon$. Moreover, the constant factor can be set to 21.41244; i.e., we have*

$$\overline{m} \sim 21.41244 \left(\frac{c\log c}{1-\delta}\right)^2 \log(N/\varepsilon).$$

The first part of Theorem 3 shows a general relation between code lengths of the original code $\mathcal{C}$ and the new code $\overline{\mathcal{C}}$. The second part deals with the special case that the original code $\mathcal{C}$ has code length of optimal order (with respect to $c$, $N$ and $\varepsilon$) and the parameter $\delta_0$ does not decrease too rapidly. The third part shows the existence of "nearly optimal" robust codes by virtue of our conversion method, which will be proven by applying the part 2(a) to the robust c-secure codes in [11]. Moreover, the part 2(b) says that to obtain $\delta$-robust c-secure codes for any $0 < \delta < 1$ with code lengths of order $\Theta(c^2)$ (with respect to $c$) matching the lower bound, it suffices to construct such codes for (arbitrarily small) *constant* $0 < \delta < 1$. This seems to reduce the difficulty of the construction of desired codes significantly. It is worthy to search for such construction, or to investigate whether such construction is actually possible or not. Moreover, if the construction is not possible, it is also interesting to find the tight lower bound of the code lengths of $\delta$-robust $c$-secure codes, lying between $\Omega(c^2)$ and $\Omega((c \log c)^2)$ (with respect to $c$) by virtue of our result.

# 4    Proofs of Main Results

In this section, we give (outlines of) proofs of three main theorems presented in Sect. 3. We describe the proof of Theorem 1, an outline of the proof of Theorem 2, and an outline of the proof of Theorem 3 in Sect. 4.1, Sect. 4.2, and Sect. 4.3, respectively. The omitted details for the proofs of Theorem 2 and Theorem 3 will be supplied in a forthcoming full version of this article.

## 4.1    Proof of Theorem 1

To prove Theorem 1, let $\overline{\rho}$ be an arbitrary collusion strategy, that satisfies $\delta$-Marking Assumption, for the fingerprint code $\overline{\mathcal{C}}$ obtained by our conversion. Then we construct from $\overline{\rho}$ a collusion strategy $\rho$ for the original $\delta_0$-robust $c$-secure code $\mathcal{C}$ in the following manner:

**Algorithm $\rho$**    Input: The collection $W_{\mathrm{pirate}}$ of pirates' codewords
**(1)** Convert $W_{\mathrm{pirate}}$ to a collection $\widehat{W}_{\mathrm{pirate}}$ of codewords for $\overline{\mathcal{C}}$ in the same way as Steps 2–5 of the algorithm $\overline{\mathsf{Gen}}$, using randomly chosen $\mathsf{fl}$ and $\mathsf{perm}$.
**(2)** Execute $\overline{\rho}$ with input $\widehat{W}_{\mathrm{pirate}}$ and receives a word $\widehat{y}$ output by $\overline{\rho}$.
**(3)** Convert $\widehat{y}$ to a word $\widetilde{y}$ of length $m$ in the same way as Steps 1–2 of the algorithm $\overline{\mathsf{Tr}}$, using the same $\mathsf{fl}$ and $\mathsf{perm}$ as the first step above.
**(4)** If the number of undetectable positions in $\widetilde{y}$ marked with '?'s is larger than $\delta_0 m$, then replace the '?' in every such position with the common digit of codewords in $W_{\mathrm{pirate}}$ in the same position. Otherwise, replace nothing. Then output the resulting word $\widetilde{y}'$.

By definition, the output $\widetilde{y}'$ of $\rho$ satisfies $\delta_0$-Marking Assumption with respect to $\mathcal{C}$. Intuitively, we show that the distributions of $\widetilde{y}'$ and the word $y$ constructed in Step 2 of the algorithm $\overline{\mathsf{Tr}}$ are sufficiently close to each other, hence the security of $\mathcal{C}$ implies the security of $\overline{\mathcal{C}}$. We summarize some notations:

- $(\overline{W}, \overline{\mathsf{st}})$: The output of $\overline{\mathsf{Gen}}$ with input $\varepsilon$
- $(W, \mathsf{st})$: The output of $\mathsf{Gen}$ with input $\varepsilon_2$, performed in Step 1 of $\overline{\mathsf{Gen}}$
- $\widetilde{y}$: The word of length $m$ generated by Step 3 of $\rho$, with input being the collection of pirates' codewords in $W$
- $\widetilde{y}'$: The word of length $m$ generated from $\widetilde{y}$ by Step 4 of $\rho$
- $\overline{y}$: The output of $\overline{\rho}$ of length $\overline{m}$, with input being the collection of pirates' codewords in $\overline{W}$
- $\overline{y}'$: The word of length $\overline{m}$ generated by Step 1 of $\overline{\mathsf{Tr}}$, with input $(\overline{W}, \overline{\mathsf{st}}, \overline{y})$
- $y$: The word of length $m$ generated from $\overline{y}'$ by Step 2 of $\overline{\mathsf{Tr}}$

In this situation, the definition of $\rho$ implies that the two triples $(W, \mathsf{st}, \widetilde{y})$ and $(W, \mathsf{st}, y)$ follow the same probability distribution. On the other hand, the tracing algorithm $\mathsf{Tr}$ against $\rho$ takes input $(W, \mathsf{st}, \widetilde{y}')$, not $(W, \mathsf{st}, \widetilde{y})$. This implies that the difference between the error probability of $\overline{\mathcal{C}}$ against $\overline{\rho}$ and the error probability of $\mathcal{C}$ against $\rho$, the latter being bounded by $\varepsilon_2$ since $\mathcal{C}$ is $\delta_0$-robust $c$-secure, is at most the probability that $(W, \mathsf{st}, \widetilde{y}')$ differs from $(W, \mathsf{st}, \widetilde{y})$. Thus the error probability of $\overline{\mathcal{C}}$ is bounded by $\varepsilon$ provided $Pr[(W, \mathsf{st}, \widetilde{y}') \neq (W, \mathsf{st}, \widetilde{y})] \leq \varepsilon_1$. Since $(W, \mathsf{st}, \widetilde{y})$ and $(W, \mathsf{st}, y)$ follow the same distribution, the definition of $\widetilde{y}'$ implies that the probability of the event $(W, \mathsf{st}, \widetilde{y}') \neq (W, \mathsf{st}, \widetilde{y})$ is equal to the probability that more than $\delta_0 m$ undetectable positions in $y$ (with respect to $W$) are marked with '?'s. Moreover, the latter event is equivalent to the event, denoted by $\mathsf{E}$, that more than $\delta_0 m$ undetectable blocks in $\overline{y}'$ (with respect to $\overline{W}$) are entirely marked with '?'s. By the above argument, it suffices to prove that $Pr[\mathsf{E}] \leq \varepsilon_1$.

We use the condition (3) in the proof. To prove the claim, it suffices to consider the case that pirates always mark as many undetectable positions in $\overline{y}$ with '?'s as $\delta$-Marking Assumption allows, i.e., they mark $\lfloor \delta \overline{m} \rfloor = \nu_1$ undetectable positions in total (note that there are at least $\nu_1$ undetectable positions in $\overline{y}$ by the condition $L \geq \nu_1$). For an integer $a$, let $S(a, \nu_2)$ denote the set of all subsets of $\{1, 2, \ldots, a\}$ with $\nu_2 = \lfloor \delta_0 m \rfloor + 1$ elements (note that $S(a, \nu_2) = \emptyset$ when $a < \nu_2$). Moreover, for each $J \in S(a, \nu_2)$, let $\mathsf{E}'(a, J)$ denote the event that the number of undetectable positions in $W$ (or equivalently, the number of undetectable blocks in $\overline{W}$) is $a$ and for every $j \in J$, the $j$-th undetectable block in $\overline{y}'$ is entirely marked with '?'s. By definition of the events, whenever the above-mentioned event $\mathsf{E}$ occurs, the event $\mathsf{E}'(a, J)$ also occurs in the same time for some $0 \leq a \leq m$ and $J \in S(a, \nu_2)$. This implies that

$$Pr[\mathsf{E}] \leq \sum_{a_0=0}^{m} Pr[a = a_0] \sum_{J \in S(a_0, \nu_2)} Pr[\mathsf{E}'(a, J) \mid a = a_0], \tag{7}$$

where $a$ denotes the number of undetectable blocks in $\overline{W}$.

Since the undetectable digits in pirates' codewords are completely shuffled by Steps 4–5 of $\overline{\mathsf{Gen}}$, every $\nu_1$-element subset of the $ba + L$ undetectable positions in $\overline{y}$ is chosen by pirates with the same probability to be marked with '?'s. Thus for each $a_0$, the probabilities $Pr[\mathsf{E}'(a, J) \mid a = a_0]$ for $J \in S(a_0, \nu_2)$ coincide with each other. Note that $|S(a_0, \nu_2)| = \binom{a_0}{\nu_2}$. When $\nu_2$ out of $a_0$ fixed undetectable blocks in $\overline{y}'$ corresponding to $J \in S(a_0, \nu_2)$ (containing $b\nu_2$ digits in total) are entirely marked with '?'s, there are $\binom{ba_0+L-b\nu_2}{\nu_1-b\nu_2}$ choices of the remaining $\nu_1 - b\nu_2$ digits out of the remaining $ba_0 + L - b\nu_2$ undetectable positions to be marked with '?'s. On the other hand, there are $\binom{ba_0+L}{\nu_1}$ choices of the $\nu_1$ undetectable positions to be marked with '?'s. Thus the right-hand side of (7) is equal to

$$\sum_{a_0=0}^{m} Pr[a = a_0] \binom{a_0}{\nu_2} \frac{\binom{ba_0+L-b\nu_2}{\nu_1-b\nu_2}}{\binom{ba_0+L}{\nu_1}} \leq \sum_{a_0=0}^{m} Pr[a = a_0] \varepsilon_1 = \varepsilon_1, \tag{8}$$

where we used the condition (3) in the first inequality. Hence we have $Pr[\mathsf{E}] \leq \varepsilon_1$ as desired, therefore the proof of Theorem 1 is concluded.

## 4.2  Proof of Theorem 2

Here we give an outline of the proof of Theorem 2. Let the parameter $L$ satisfy (4) and let the parameter $b$ satisfy (5) (in the case $\nu_2 = 1$) or (6) (in the general case). Our aim is to prove the property (3). First, the definition (4) of $L$ implies immediately that $L \geq \delta bm/(1 - \delta)$, therefore $L \geq \delta(bm + L)$ and $L \geq \nu_1$ by the definition of $\nu_1$. The main part of the claim is thus the second inequality in (3).

To prove the inequality, we may assume that $\nu_1 \geq b\nu_2$, as otherwise the target inequality is obvious. First, note that for any integer $0 \leq a \leq m$, we have

$$\frac{\binom{ba+L-b\nu_2}{\nu_1-b\nu_2}}{\binom{ba+L}{\nu_1}} = \frac{(ba + L - b\nu_2)!\nu_1!(ba + L - \nu_1)!}{(\nu_1 - b\nu_2)!(ba + L - \nu_1)!(ba + L)!}$$

$$= \frac{(ba + L - b\nu_2)!\nu_1!}{(\nu_1 - b\nu_2)!(ba + L)!} = \frac{(\nu_1)_{b\nu_2}}{(ba + L)_{b\nu_2}}$$

(see Sect. 1.4 for the notation). Now we present the following lemma on the left-hand side of the target inequality, whose proof is omitted here and will be given in the full version of this article:

**Lemma 1.** *In the above setting, $\binom{a}{\nu_2}(\nu_1)_{b\nu_2}/(ba+L)_{b\nu_2}$ is increasing for integer $0 \leq a \leq m$.*

Although we omit the proof of Lemma 1 here, we notice that the property (4) of $L$ is essential to prove this lemma. By virtue of Lemma 1, it suffices to prove that $\binom{m}{\nu_2}(\nu_1)_{b\nu_2}/(bm+L)_{b\nu_2} \leq \varepsilon_1$. To prove this, we use the following two inequalities:

**Lemma 2 ([6]).** *For integers $0 \leq k \leq n$, we have $\binom{n}{k} \leq (ne/k)^k$.*

**Lemma 3.** *For integers $h \geq i \geq j \geq 1$, we have $(i)_j/(h)_j \leq (i/h)^j$.*

*Proof.* Apply the inequality $(i - x)/(h - x) \leq i/h$ for every $0 \leq x \leq j$.

We consider the case of general $\nu_2$ first, therefore $b$ satisfies (6). By Lemma 2 and Lemma 3, we have

$$\binom{m}{\nu_2}\frac{(\nu_1)_{b\nu_2}}{(bm + L)_{b\nu_2}} \leq \left(\frac{me}{\nu_2}\right)^{\nu_2}\left(\frac{\nu_1}{bm + L}\right)^{b\nu_2}$$

$$= \left(\frac{me}{\nu_2}\left(\frac{\nu_1}{bm + L}\right)^b\right)^{\nu_2} \leq \left(\frac{me}{\nu_2}\delta^b\right)^{\nu_2}, \tag{9}$$

where we used the fact $\nu_1 \leq \delta(bm + L)$ (following from the definition of $\nu_1$) in the last inequality. By (6), we have

$$b\nu_2 \log(1/\delta) \geq \nu_2 \log(m/\nu_2) + \nu_2 + \log(1/\varepsilon_1),$$

therefore we have $\delta^{-b\nu_2} \geq (me/\nu_2)^{\nu_2}\varepsilon_1^{-1}$. This implies that the right-hand side of (9) is not larger than $\varepsilon_1$, therefore the claim holds in this case.

Secondly, we consider the case $\nu_2 = 1$, therefore $b$ satisfies (5). In this case, we use the precise value $\binom{m}{\nu_2} = m$ of the binomial coefficient $\binom{m}{\nu_2}$ instead of the bound in Lemma 2 to improve the result of analysis. Now we have

$$\binom{m}{\nu_2} \frac{(\nu_1)_{b\nu_2}}{(bm+L)_{b\nu_2}} \leq m \left( \frac{\nu_1}{bm+L} \right)^b \leq m\delta^b, \tag{10}$$

where we used the fact $\nu_1 \leq \delta(bm+L)$ in the last inequality. By (5), we have $b\log(1/\delta) \geq \log(m/\varepsilon_1)$, therefore the right-hand side of (10) is not larger than $\varepsilon_1$. Thus the claim also holds in this case, concluding the proof of Theorem 2.

### 4.3   Proof of Theorem 3

Here we give an outline of the proof of Theorem 3. To prove the first part of Theorem 3, let $L_1$ and $L_2$ denote, respectively, the first and the second terms in the "max" in the definition (4) of $L$, therefore $L = \max\{L_1, L_2\}$. First we present the following lemma, whose proof is omitted here and will be given in the full version of this article:

**Lemma 4.** *In the above setting, we have*

$$1 - \left(1 - \frac{\nu_2}{m}\right)^{1/b} \sim \begin{cases} \dfrac{\nu_2}{mb} & \text{if } d = 0, \\[2mm] -\dfrac{\nu_2 \log(1-d)}{mbd} & \text{if } 0 < d < 1. \end{cases}$$

By virtue of Lemma 4, we have

$$bm + L_1 \sim \begin{cases} b^2 m & \text{if } d = 0, \\[2mm] \dfrac{-d}{\log(1-d)} b^2 m & \text{if } 0 < d < 1, \end{cases} \tag{11}$$

On the other hand, to analyze $L_2$, we use the following property:

**Lemma 5.** *We have $\log(1/\delta) \sim 1 - \delta$ when $\delta \to 1$.*

*Proof.* Apply l'Hôpital's rule to derive $\lim_{\delta \to 1} \log(1/\delta)/(1-\delta) = 1$.

Let $B$ denote the numerator of the fraction in the ceiling function in (5) or (6), depending on which we have used to define $b$. Then we have $b \sim B/(1 - \delta)$ by Lemma 5, while $B = \Omega(1)$, therefore $1/(1-\delta) = O(b)$. Thus we have $L_2 = O(b^2 m)$ and $bm + L_2 = O(b^2 m)$. This implies that $bm + L_1$ is eventually dominant among the two values $bm + L_i$, $i \in \{1,2\}$, therefore we have $\overline{m} = \max\{bm + L_1, bm + L_2\} = \Theta(b^2 m)$. Hence the first part of Theorem 3 holds.

We prove the second part of Theorem 2. Here use the following lemma, whose proof is omitted here and will be given in the full version of this article:

**Lemma 6.** *Let $x_1$ and $x_2$ be eventually positive functions. If either $x_1 = \Theta(x_2)$ and $x_2 = \omega(1)$, or $x_1 \sim x_2$ and $\log x_2 = \Omega(1)$, then we have $\log x_1 \sim \log x_2$.*

We use the definition (6) for $b$, therefore the above-mentioned $B$ satisfies $B = \log(m/\nu_2) + 1 + \nu_2^{-1}\log(1/\varepsilon_1)$. We have $b \sim B/(1-\delta)$ by Lemma 5. First, we have $\delta_0 m = \Omega(\log(N/\varepsilon))$ by the properties of $m$ and $\delta_0$ in the statement (note that $\log(N/\varepsilon_2) = \log 2 + \log(N/\varepsilon)$ and $\log(N/\varepsilon_2) \sim \log(N/\varepsilon)$). Secondly, by the definition of $\nu_2$, we have $\nu_2^{-1}\log(1/\varepsilon_1) \leq (\delta_0 m)^{-1}\log(1/\varepsilon_1) = O(1)$ (note that we set $\varepsilon_1 = \varepsilon_2 = \varepsilon/2$). Moreover, we have $\nu_2 \sim \delta_0 m$ (hence $m/\nu_2 \sim 1/\delta_0$) since $\delta_0 m = \omega(1)$ as above, while $\log(1/\delta_0) = \Omega(1)$ by the property of $\delta_0$. Now the second part of Lemma 6 implies that $\log(m/\nu_2) \sim \log(1/\delta_0)$. By these results, we have $B \sim \log(1/\delta_0)$ and $b \sim \log(1/\delta_0)/(1-\delta)$, therefore

$$\overline{m} = \Theta\left(\left(\frac{c\log(1/\delta_0)}{1-\delta}\right)^2 \log(N/\varepsilon)\right)$$

by the first part of Theorem 3. From now, we prove claims (a) and (b).

For the claim (a), note that $d = 0$ by the property of $\delta_0$ specified in the statement, therefore $bm + L_1 \sim b^2 m$ by (11). Since $g(c) = \omega(1)$, we have $\log(1/\delta_0) \sim \log g(c)$ by the first part of Lemma 6. Now the argument in the previous paragraph implies that $b \sim (\log g(c))/(1-\delta)$. Hence we have

$$bm + L_1 \sim \left(\frac{\log g(c)}{1-\delta}\right)^2 m\,,\ bm + L_2 \sim \frac{bm}{1-\delta} \sim \frac{\log g(c)}{(1-\delta)^2}m.$$

Since $\log g(c) = \omega(1)$, this implies that we have eventually $\overline{m} = bm + L_1$. Hence the claim follows from the property of $m$ specified in the statement.

For the claim (b), it was shown in the second last paragraph that $\log(m/\nu_2) \sim \log(1/\delta_0)$, $\nu_2^{-1}\log(1/\varepsilon_1) \leq (\delta_0 m)^{-1}\log(1/\varepsilon_1)$ and $b \sim B/(1-\delta)$. On the other hand, since $\delta_0 \to d > 0$, we have $\log(1/\delta_0) \sim -\log d$ and $(\delta_0 m)^{-1}\log(1/\varepsilon_1) = o(1)$, therefore $B \sim 1 - \log d$. Thus we have $b \sim (1 - \log d)/(1-\delta)$, and the property (11) implies that

$$bm + L_1 \sim \frac{-db^2 m}{\log(1-d)} \sim \frac{-d(1-\log d)^2}{(1-\delta)^2\log(1-d)}m\,,\ bm + L_2 \sim \frac{bm}{1-\delta} \sim \frac{1-\log d}{(1-\delta)^2}m.$$

Thus we have eventually $\overline{m} = \max\{bm + L_1, bm + L_2\} \sim Dm/(1-\delta)^2$, therefore the claim holds by the property of $m$. Hence the second part of Theorem 3 holds.

Finally, to prove the third part, we apply the part 2(a) of Theorem 3 to the $c$-secure binary fingerprint codes given by Nuida et al. in [11]. Their fingerprint codes are in fact $c$-secure under $\delta_0$-Marking Assumption with $\delta_0 = \Theta(c^{-2})$ (see below). Now it follows from the argument in Sect. 6.1 of [11] that their code length $m$ satisfies $m \sim Kc^2\log(N/\varepsilon_2)$, $K = (j_1^2(A_0\log A_0 - A_0 + 1))^{-1}$, where $j_1 = 2.40482\cdots$ and $A_0 = 1 + 2(\pi^{-1} - \Delta_0)/j_1$ (see [11] for the precise definition of $j_1$), provided $0 \leq \Delta_0 \leq (2\pi)^{-1}$ and $2c^2\delta_0/j_1 \sim \Delta_0$. Since $K$ is a continuous function of $\Delta_0$, and we have $K \leq 5.35311$ when $\Delta_0 = 0$ (see [11, Theorem 6.3]) and $K > 5.35311$ when $\Delta_0 = (2\pi)^{-1}$, it follows that there exists a constant $0 < \Delta_0 < (2\pi)^{-1}$ such that $K = 5.35311$. Now by putting $\delta_0 = j_1\Delta_0 c^{-2}/2 = \Theta(c^{-2})$ to satisfy the above requirement, the part 2(a) of Theorem 3 implies that $\overline{m} \sim 4K(c\log c/(1-\delta))^2\log(N/\varepsilon)$ with $4K = 21.41244$. Hence the third part of Theorem 3 holds, concluding the proof of Theorem 3.

## 5    Examples

We have seen in Theorem 3 the asymptotic behavior of code lengths of $\delta$-robust $c$-secure fingerprint codes obtained by our conversion method. In this section, we give some numerical examples for the case of smaller $c$. Here we use the $\delta_0$-robust $c$-secure binary fingerprint codes in [11] as the target of our conversion method. We choose $c$ as $c \in \{2, 3, 4, 6, 8\}$, and we consider the following three choices of the user number $N$ and the error probability $\varepsilon_2$ for these original codes:

- Case 1: $N = 100c$ and $\varepsilon_2 = 10^{-11}$;
- Case 2: $N = 10^9$ and $\varepsilon_2 = 10^{-6}$;
- Case 3: $N = 10^6$ and $\varepsilon_2 = 10^{-3}$.

We deal with three families of the codes, referred to as "Original 1", "Original 2", and "Original 3", respectively, with various $\delta_0$ listed in Table 1. Now Original 1 is not robust at all; Original 2 is slightly robust (which appeared in the numerical examples in Sect. 5 of [11]); and Original 3 is most robust, in the sense that the values $\delta_0$ for Original 3 are maximal subject to the conditions given in [11]. The code lengths for the three families are shown in Table 2. Here the lengths for Original 1 and Original 2 are quoted from Table 4 and Table 5 in [11]. On the other hand, for Original 3, we chose the parameters $\beta$ for the formula [11] of error probability as in Table 3 which are optimized by numerical calculation.

**Table 1.** Parameter $\delta_0$ for the original codes in [11]

| $c$ | | 2 | 3 | 4 | 6 | 8 |
|---|---|---|---|---|---|---|
| | Original 1 | 0 | 0 | 0 | 0 | 0 |
| $\delta_0$ | Original 2 | 0.005 | $2.58556 \times 10^{-3}$ | $2.58556 \times 10^{-3}$ | $1.78017 \times 10^{-3}$ | $1.36437 \times 10^{-3}$ |
| | Original 3 | 0.0625 | $1.76067 \times 10^{-2}$ | $1.32044 \times 10^{-2}$ | $5.61077 \times 10^{-3}$ | $3.09638 \times 10^{-3}$ |

We apply our conversion to the three original codes, obtaining $\delta$-robust $c$-secure codes referred to as "Conversion $k$", $k \in \{1, 2, 3\}$, which result from "Original $k$". Here we set $\varepsilon = 2\varepsilon_2$ and $\delta = 0.5$ for the parameters, hence the resulting codes are much more robust than the original codes. The code lengths $\overline{m}$ for the resulting codes are also shown in Table 2, where we determined the parameter $L$ by (4) and the parameter $b$ by (5) for Conversion 1 and by (6) for Conversion 2 and Conversion 3. The block sizes $b$ are also included in Table 2.

Table 2 shows that both Conversion 2 and Conversion 3 are always more efficient than Conversion 1, however there is no overall superiority or inferiority between Conversion 2 and Conversion 3, thus starting from more robust original codes is not always a good strategy. Intuitively, if the original code becomes more robust, then the efficiency of our conversion itself is improved (indeed, in the table, the ratio of code lengths for Conversion 3/Original 3 is always better than that for Conversion 2/Original 2), while the code length of the original code increases. Hence there exists a trade-off between these two effects. To investigate how to find the optimal point would be a significant future research topic.

**Table 2.** Code lengths for conversion of $c$-secure codes in [11] (with $\delta = 0.5$)

| $c$ | code | Case 1 | Case 2 | Case 3 |
|---|---|---|---|---|
| 2 | Original 1 | 373 | 410 | 253 |
| | Original 2 | 403 | 444 | 273 |
| | Original 3 | 1,429 | 1,572 | 969 |
| | Conversion 1 | 788,278 ($b = 46$) | 344,432 ($b = 29$) | 81,836 ($b = 18$) |
| | Conversion 2 | 177,113 ($b = 21$) | 113,319 ($b = 16$) | 53,339 ($b = 14$) |
| | Conversion 3 | 50,082  ($b = 6$) | 55,094  ($b = 6$) | 33,963  ($b = 6$) |
| 3 | Original 1 | 1,309 | 1,423 | 877 |
| | Original 2 | 1,514 | 1,646 | 1,014 |
| | Original 3 | 4,973 | 5,404 | 3,330 |
| | Conversion 1 | 2,890,548 ($b = 47$) | 1,367,068 ($b = 31$) | 350,630 ($b = 20$) |
| | Conversion 2 | 604,859 ($b = 20$) | 322,174 ($b = 14$) | 198,484 ($b = 14$) |
| | Conversion 3 | 315,807  ($b = 8$) | 343,166  ($b = 8$) | 211,470  ($b = 8$) |
| 4 | Original 1 | 2,190 | 2,360 | 1,454 |
| | Original 2 | 2,671 | 2,879 | 1,774 |
| | Original 3 | 8,420 | 9,074 | 5,591 |
| | Conversion 1 | 5,044,682 ($b = 48$) | 2,416,177 ($b = 32$) | 641,024 ($b = 21$) |
| | Conversion 2 | 682,951 ($b = 16$) | 485,939 ($b = 13$) | 255,137 ($b = 12$) |
| | Conversion 3 | 677,987  ($b = 9$) | 577,375  ($b = 8$) | 355,754  ($b = 8$) |
| 6 | Original 1 | 5,546 | 5,909 | 3,640 |
| | Original 2 | 7,738 | 8,244 | 5,079 |
| | Original 3 | 21,300 | 22,691 | 13,980 |
| | Conversion 1 | 13,314,843 ($b = 49$) | 6,434,407 ($b = 33$) | 1,761,551 ($b = 22$) |
| | Conversion 2 | 1,515,387 ($b = 14$) | 1,186,157 ($b = 12$) | 730,727 ($b = 12$) |
| | Conversion 3 | 2,124,604 ($b = 10$) | 2,263,344 ($b = 10$) | 1,394,451 ($b = 10$) |
| 8 | Original 1 | 10,469 | 11,062 | 6,815 |
| | Original 2 | 16,920 | 17,879 | 11,015 |
| | Original 3 | 40,185 | 42,463 | 26,161 |
| | Conversion 1 | 26,171,387 ($b = 50$) | 12,787,166 ($b = 34$) | 3,604,908 ($b = 23$) |
| | Conversion 2 | 2,857,620 ($b = 13$) | 2,572,937 ($b = 12$) | 1,585,115 ($b = 12$) |
| | Conversion 3 | 4,855,517 ($b = 11$) | 4,240,366 ($b = 10$) | 2,612,417 ($b = 10$) |

**Table 3.** Parameter $\beta$ for codes in [11], the case of Original 3

| $c$ | 2 | 3 | 4 | 6 | 8 |
|---|---|---|---|---|---|
| $\beta$ | 0.093099 | 0.032980 | 0.019780 | 0.0085396 | 0.0047522 |

## 6   Conclusion

In this article, we proposed the first general conversion method of $c$-secure finger-print codes to robust $c$-secure codes. Our method deals with the target $c$-secure code as a black-box, and it is applicable for the sake of both converting non-robust $c$-secure codes to robust one and amplifying less robustness of the target $c$-secure codes to provide more robustness. We estimated appropriate values of parameters for our conversion method theoretically, deriving a closed-form formula of the resulting code length. By using the formula, we described the asymptotic behavior of the resulting code length. Moreover, by applying our conversion to some existing $c$-secure codes, we obtained robust $c$-secure codes with code lengths of order $(c \log c)^2$ with respect to $c$, which improves some preceding construction and is theoretically "nearly-optimal".

**Acknowledgments.** The author would like to thank Professor Hideki Imai and the anonymous referees for their precious comments.

# References

1. Anthapadmanabhan, N.P., Barg, A.: Two-Level Fingerprinting Codes. In: Proceedings of IEEE ISIT 2009. IEEE, Los Alamitos (2009), http://www.arxiv.org/abs/0905.0417v1, See also: arXiv:0905.0417v1 [cs.IT]
2. Billet, O., Phan, D.H.: Efficient Traitor Tracing from Collusion Secure Codes. In: Safavi-Naini, R. (ed.) ICITS 2008. LNCS, vol. 5155, pp. 171–182. Springer, Heidelberg (2008)
3. Blakley, G.R., Kabatiansky, G.: Random Coding Technique for Digital Fingerprinting Codes. In: Proceedings of IEEE ISIT 2004, p. 202. IEEE, Los Alamitos (2004)
4. Boneh, D., Naor, M.: Traitor Tracing with Constant Size Ciphertext. In: Proceedings of ACM CCS 2008, pp. 501–510. ACM, New York (2008)
5. Boneh, D., Shaw, J.: Collusion-Secure Fingerprinting for Digital Data. IEEE Trans. Inform. Theory 44, 1897–1905 (1998)
6. Cormen, T.H., Leiserson, C.E., Rivest, R.L., Stein, C.: Introduction to Algorithms, 2nd edn. MIT Press, Cambridge (2001)
7. Cotrina-Navau, J., Fernandez, M., Soriano, M.: A Family of Collusion 2-Secure Codes. In: Barni, M., Herrera-Joancomartí, J., Katzenbeisser, S., Pérez-González, F. (eds.) IH 2005. LNCS, vol. 3727, pp. 387–397. Springer, Heidelberg (2005)
8. Fernandez, M., Soriano, M.: Fingerprinting Concatenated Codes with Efficient Identification. In: Chan, A.H., Gligor, V.D. (eds.) ISC 2002. LNCS, vol. 2433, pp. 459–470. Springer, Heidelberg (2002)
9. Guth, H.-J., Pfitzmann, B.: Error- and Collusion-Secure Fingerprinting for Digital Data. In: Pfitzmann, A. (ed.) IH 1999. LNCS, vol. 1768, pp. 134–145. Springer, Heidelberg (2000)
10. Nuida, K., Fujitsu, S., Hagiwara, M., Imai, H., Kitagawa, T., Ogawa, K., Watanabe, H.: An Efficient 2-Secure and Short Random Fingerprint Code and Its Security Evaluation. IEICE Trans. Fundamentals E92-A(1), 197–206 (2009)
11. Nuida, K., Fujitsu, S., Hagiwara, M., Kitagawa, T., Watanabe, H., Ogawa, K., Imai, H.: An Improvement of Discrete Tardos Fingerprinting Codes. Designs, Codes and Cryptography 52, 339–362 (2009); Extended abstract appeared in: Boztas, S., Lu, H.-F. (eds.) AAECC 2007. LNCS, vol. 4851, pp. 80–89. Springer, Heidelberg (2007)
12. Safavi-Naini, R., Wang, Y.: Collusion Secure q-ary Fingerprinting for Perceptual Content. In: Sander, T. (ed.) DRM 2001. LNCS, vol. 2320, pp. 57–75. Springer, Heidelberg (2002)
13. Sirvent, T.: Traitor Tracing Scheme with Constant Ciphertext Rate against Powerful Pirates. In: Proceedings of WCC 2007, pp. 379–388 (2007)

14. Škorić, B., Katzenbeisser, S., Celik, M.U.: Symmetric Tardos Fingerprinting Codes for Arbitrary Alphabet Sizes. Des. Codes Cryptogr. 46, 137–166 (2008)
15. Tardos, G.: Optimal Probabilistic Fingerprint Codes. J. ACM 55(2), 1–24 (2008); Extended abstract appeared in: Proceedings of STOC 2003, pp. 116–125. ACM, New York (2003)
16. Tô, V.D., Safavi-Naini, R., Wang, Y.: A 2-Secure Code with Efficient Tracing Algorithm. In: Menezes, A., Sarkar, P. (eds.) INDOCRYPT 2002. LNCS, vol. 2551, pp. 149–162. Springer, Heidelberg (2002)

# An Improvement of Pseudorandomization against Unbounded Attack Algorithms – The Case of Fingerprint Codes*

Koji Nuida and Goichiro Hanaoka

Research Center for Information Security (RCIS), National Institute of Advanced Industrial Science and Technology (AIST), Akihabara-Daibiru Room 1003, 1-18-13 Sotokanda, Chiyoda-ku, Tokyo 101-0021, Japan
{k.nuida,hanaoka-goichiro}@aist.go.jp

**Abstract.** Recently, the authors proposed an evaluation technique for pseudorandom generator-based randomness reduction of cryptographic schemes against computationally unbounded attack algorithms. In this article, we apply the technique to the case of fingerprint codes and verify the effectiveness. Then we propose a technique that improves the randomness reduction by dividing the target randomness into suitable parts and using a separate pseudorandom generator for each part. Considering fingerprint codes as a typical example, we give a theoretical evaluation of the proposed technique, and also a numerical evaluation showing that our technique improves the effect of randomness reduction to about 29 times as good as the plain randomness reduction in a reasonable setting.

**Keywords:** Randomness reduction, fingerprint code, information-theoretic security, pseudorandom number generator, security evaluation.

## 1 Introduction

### 1.1 Backgrounds

Collusion-secure fingerprint codes [2] are an example of cryptographic schemes that aim at information-theoretic security. Usually, the standard security assumption (Marking Assumption [2]) restricts bit positions in codewords which the adversaries (pirates) can attack, while it allows the attack algorithm to have unbounded complexity. Such information-theoretic security seems especially desirable in this case, since fingerprint codes are usually not used alone but used as a building block in combination with digital watermarking schemes or other schemes such as traitor tracing schemes (e.g., [1,4]), and security assumptions for a building block are generally expected to be as minimal as possible.

Many existing fingerprint codes, such as plain Boneh-Shaw codes $\Gamma_0(n, d)$ [2], use random permutations of bit positions in codewords to conceal them from the

---

* A part of this work was supported by 2007 Research Grants of the Science and Technology Foundation of Japan (JSTF).

K. Kurosawa (Ed.): ICITS 2009, LNCS 5973, pp. 213–230, 2010.

214 K. Nuida and G. Hanaoka

pirates. Tardos [13,14] made use of further randomness in codeword generation for improving the performance. His fingerprint codes (Tardos codes) have code lengths of theoretically minimal order with respect to the maximal number of pirates, and the minimal order has been achieved so far only by that code and its variants. However, a drawback of Tardos codes is that auxiliary random elements used in the codeword generation should be recorded throughout, as those will be used in the pirate tracing process as well. This requires extra memories to store those auxiliary data as well as extra random bits to generate them. There have been given some results on reducing the extra memories (and also reducing code lengths) [7,10,11] by replacing the continuous probability distributions used in Tardos codes with finite (discrete) distributions. The replacement of probability distributions also results in randomness reduction of the schemes, since the new probability distributions are relatively simple and more efficient to implement.

A more naive and simple strategy for reducing such extra costs is to replace the perfect random source with pseudorandom generators (PRGs). This obviously reduces the required randomness, while the required memories are also reduced since now all the randomly generated data that should be recorded throughout can be recovered from the seed of the PRG. However, although the fingerprint code itself is information-theoretically secure, a naive evaluation method can prove the security of the consequent scheme only against computationally bounded attack algorithms as no information-theoretically secure PRGs exist. Very recently, the authors [12] proposed a security evaluation technique for the PRG-based randomness reduction applied to information-theoretically secure schemes. That technique can prove the security *against computationally unbounded attack algorithms* only by accepting an assumption on hardness of a problem *in a fixed computational model* that is irrelevant to the attack algorithms. The aim of this article is to give a concrete example of the above-mentioned evaluation technique, and moreover to propose another technique to improve the PRG-based randomness reduction.

## 1.2 Our Contributions

In this article, first we apply the above-mentioned evaluation technique in [12] to fingerprint codes in [10] that are an improvement of Tardos codes [13,14]. Then we propose a novel technique to improve the PRG-based randomness reduction.

To explain the essence of our proposed technique, first we briefly show the idea of the evaluation technique in [12]. Consider the following situation: Alice converts an output $x$ of a random source $\mathcal{R}$, either perfectly random or given by a PRG G, to an element $w \in W$ by an efficient algorithm H. Eve tries to distinguish the random and pseudorandom cases from the element $w$ (see Fig. 1(a)). Now the idea is that the difference of generation probabilities of a fixed element $w_0 \in W$ in random and pseudorandom cases is nothing but the advantage of a "distinguisher" for G that outputs 1 if $H(x) = w_0$ and 0 if $H(x) \neq w_0$, and the *statistical* distance of Eve's elements $w$ in the two cases is a half of the sum of those advantages taken over all $w_0 \in W$. Thus if G is sufficiently secure and the set $W$ is sufficiently small, then this statistical

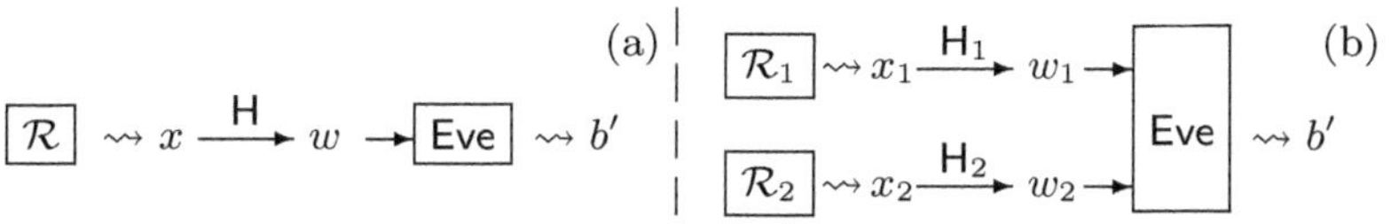

**Fig. 1.** An example of (a) the argument in [12] and (b) our improvement

distance is also sufficiently small, therefore the two cases are indistinguishable for Eve *even with computationally unbounded algorithms*. Intuitively, if $W$ is very small, then the amount of information on the output $x$ of $\mathcal{R}$ received by Eve via the element $w \in W$ is too scanty even for computationally unbounded attack algorithms. Although this is just a toy example, the technique in [12] enables one to perform a similar evaluation for more practical situations of PRG-based randomness reduction for information-theoretically secure schemes.

Now we explain our proposed technique. In the example, assume that $W$ consists of pairs $(w_1, w_2)$ of elements $w_i \in W_i$, $i = 1, 2$, and elements of each set $W_i$ are calculated from outputs of an *independent* random source $\mathcal{R}_i$ (see Fig. 1(b)). Then the difference between random and pseudorandom cases is bounded by the sum of the difference between the cases $(\mathcal{R}_1, \mathcal{R}_2) = (T, T)$ and $(\mathcal{R}_1, \mathcal{R}_2) = (P, T)$ and the difference between the cases $(\mathcal{R}_1, \mathcal{R}_2) = (P, T)$ and $(\mathcal{R}_1, \mathcal{R}_2) = (P, P)$, where T and P signify true random and pseudorandom sources, respectively. Now each of the two differences can be evaluated by using the technique in [12], where the evaluation result is much improved since the size of each $W_i$ is significantly smaller than $W$. Hence the total evaluation result is also significantly improved. Our proposed technique is also applicable to more general situations by finding a suitable decomposition as above.

We apply the above techniques to the case of fingerprint codes in [10], where we use a provably secure PRG recently proposed by Farashahi et al. [6] based on the DDH assumption. We describe a theoretical evaluation of the difference between random and pseudorandom cases. Moreover, we also give a numerical example showing that in a reasonable setting, our technique improves the effect of randomness reduction (more precisely, the ratio of the total seed length to the original number of required perfectly random bits) to about 29 times as good as the case of plain randomness reduction without our proposed technique.

## 1.3   Related Works

Before the work [12], Dubrov and Ishai [5] also studied randomness reduction of information-theoretically secure schemes by introducing a generalized notion of PRGs. Their technique also proves security of the randomness reduction *against computationally unbounded attack algorithms* only by accepting an assumption on hardness of a problem. However, the types of applications in [5], e.g., private multi-party computation, are restricted, and the technique in [5] is not effective for more general schemes such as fingerprint codes (see [12]). The essential difference mentioned in [12] is that the secret elements in multi-party computation (i.e., the local inputs for honest players) are *independent* of the target randomness of randomness reduction, while the secret elements in fingerprint codes (e.g., innocent users' codewords) *depend* on the target randomness. By this reason, our argument in this article is based on the result in [12] rather than [5].

On the other hand, Kuribayashi et al. [8] discussed implementation of Tardos codes in which the probability distributions used by Tardos codes are approximated by certain simple PRGs. However, security of the PRG used in [8] is not yet proven and their security evaluation is due to computer experiments only. They seem aiming at time and memory efficiency rather than provable security.

### 1.4   Organization of the Article, Notations and Terminology

In Sect. 2, we summarize a formulation of the notion of fingerprint codes and the concrete construction of fingerprint codes in [10]. In Sect. 3, we summarize some definitions relevant to PRGs and properties of the PRGs in [6, Sect. 4.1]. Our proposed technique is described in Sect. 4.1 for the case of fingerprint codes, followed by theoretical evaluation in Sect. 4.2 and Sect. 4.3. Then Sect. 4.4 gives a modification of PRGs in [6]. Finally, Sect. 4.5 presents some numerical examples.

Throughout this article, any algorithm is probabilistic unless otherwise specified. Let $U_X$ denote the uniform probability distribution over a (finite) set $X$. We often identify a probability distribution with the corresponding random variable. We write $x \leftarrow P$ to signify that $x$ is a particular value of a random variable $P$. We naturally identify the set $\mathbb{Z}_q$ of integers modulo $q$ with $\{1, 2, \ldots, q\}$. We put $\Sigma = \{0, 1\}$ and we identify the set $\Sigma^h$ of $h$-bit sequences with $\{0, 1, \ldots, 2^h - 1\}$ via binary expressions of integers. Let $|q|_2$ denote the bit length of an integer $q$.

## 2   Fingerprint Codes

In this article, we define a *fingerprint code* as a pair (Gen, Tr) of the *codeword generation algorithm* Gen and the *tracing algorithm* Tr that are considered in the following context. First, a *provider* runs the algorithm Gen that is given a random element $x \in X$ from a random source $\mathcal{R}$ as input and outputs *secret information* $s \in S$. (Note that Gen and Tr may vary with respect to security parameters or other parameters such as the number $N$ of users.) The secret information $s$ consists of $N$ codewords corresponding to the $N$ users, who are identified with the user IDs $1, 2, \ldots, N$, and some (possibly empty) element which we refer to as a *state element*. Here the codewords are binary and of common length $m$. Then the provider distributes each codeword to the corresponding user, either innocent or adversarial, the latter being called a *pirate*. Let $C \subset \{1, \ldots, N\}$ denote the unknown coalition of pirates. Since the innocent users play no active roles in the argument, we ignore them in the formalization and let Dist denote the map (or algorithm) that associates to $s$ the collection $w = \mathsf{Dist}(s) \in W$ of all codewords for the pirates. Then the pirates run an attack algorithm P to generate from $w$ a *pirated word* $y = \mathsf{P}(w) \in Y$ that is a word of length $m$ over an extended alphabet $\{0, 1, ?\}$, where '?' denotes an erasure symbol. The only assumption we put on P is the standard assumption called *Marking Assumption* [2]. The important feature

$$\mathcal{R} \rightsquigarrow X \xrightarrow{\ \mathsf{Gen}\ } S \xrightarrow{\ \mathsf{Dist}\ } W \overset{\mathsf{P}}{\Longrightarrow} Y \xrightarrow{\ \overset{\mathsf{Tr}}{\ }\ } A \xrightarrow{\ \mathsf{Ref}\ } \{0,1\}$$

**Fig. 2.** Flowchart for fingerprint codes (here the duplicated arrow signifies the attack algorithm with unbounded complexity)

is that Marking Assumption does *not* restrict the computational complexity of P. The provider receives $y$, and runs the algorithm Tr that takes $y$ and $s$ as inputs and outputs a (possibly empty) set $a = \mathsf{Tr}(y,s) \in A$ of accused users. Finally, an auxiliary third-party *referee* receives $a$ and $s$ and decides by an algorithm Ref whether or not the tracing process succeeded. Namely, we have $\mathsf{Ref}(s,a) = 0$ if the tracing succeeded (usually this means that $a$ contains at least one pirate and no innocent user) and $\mathsf{Ref}(s,a) = 1$ if it failed. The attack success probability $\mathsf{succ_P} = \mathsf{succ}_\mathsf{P}^\mathcal{R}$ is defined as the probability that $\mathsf{Ref}(s,a) = 1$ taken over the random source $\mathcal{R}$. The situation is summarized in Fig. 2, where the duplicated arrow means that the corresponding algorithm P has unbounded complexity.

In our argument, we deal with a fingerprint code in [10] that is an improvement of Tardos code [13,14] as an example of information-theoretically secure schemes. A main reason of considering the code in [10] rather than Tardos code is that the finite probability distribution used in [10] is much simpler than the continuous distribution in Tardos code, which can simplify our evaluation of randomness reduction technique. We apply the above formulation to the fingerprint code in [10]. In their fingerprint code, a state element consists of $m$ random values $0 < p_j < 1$, $1 \le j \le m$, each being independently generated according to the common probability distribution $\mathcal{P}$ specified below. The algorithm Gen first generates the state element. Then it generates each, say, $j$-th bit $w_{i,j}$ of $i$-th user's codeword $w_i$ independently by $Pr[w_{i,j} = 1] = p_j$ and $Pr[w_{i,j} = 0] = 1 - p_j$. On the other hand, the algorithm Tr first calculates the score $\mathsf{sc}_i = \sum_{j=1}^{m} \mathsf{sc}_{i,j}$ of $i$-th user, where the bitwise score $\mathsf{sc}_{i,j}$ for $j$-th bit is a function of $y_j$, $w_{i,j}$ and $p_j$ specified below. Then Tr outputs (any one of) the user(s) with highest score. Hence the output $a \in A$ is now a single user rather than a set of users.

We describe details of the choices of probability distributions $\mathcal{P}$ and scoring functions in the fingerprint codes in [10]. Here we consider only the case of three pirates ($c = 3$) for simplicity. First, let the probability distribution $\mathcal{P}$ take one of the two values $p^{(0)}$ and $p^{(1)}$ with equal probability $1/2$, where

$$p^{(0)} = 0.211334228515625 = (0.001101100001101)_2 \text{ and } p^{(1)} = 1 - p^{(0)} \ .$$

These values are approximations of values of the probability distribution given in [10, Definition 4] with approximation error less than $10^{-5}$ (here we require the values $p^{(0)}$ and $p^{(1)}$ to have short binary expressions rather than short decimal expressions; the same also holds for values $u_0$ and $u_1$ below). Secondly, for the scoring function, we define two auxiliary values $u_0$ and $u_1$ by

$$u_0 = 1.931793212890625 = (1.111011101000101)_2 \ ,$$
$$u_1 = 0.5176544189453125 = (0.1000010010000101)_2 \ ,$$

and define the bitwise score $\mathsf{sc}_{i,j}$ for $j$-th bit of $i$-th user in the following manner: If $p_j = p^{(\nu)}$, $\nu \in \{0,1\}$, then put

$$\mathsf{sc}_{i,j} = \begin{cases} u_\nu & \text{if } y_j = 1 \text{ and } w_{i,j} = 1 \ , \\ -u_{1-\nu} & \text{if } y_j = 1 \text{ and } w_{i,j} = 0 \ , \\ -u_\nu & \text{if } y_j \neq 1 \text{ and } w_{i,j} = 1 \ , \\ u_{1-\nu} & \text{if } y_j \neq 1 \text{ and } w_{i,j} = 0 \ . \end{cases}$$

These two values $u_0$ and $u_1$ are approximations of Tardos's scoring function $\sqrt{(1-x)/x}$ (that is also used in [10]) at $x = p^{(0)}$ and $x = p^{(1)}$, respectively, with approximation error $\Delta < 4.2 \times 10^{-6} < 10^{-5}$. Note that effects of such approximation errors are also considered in the security proof of [10].

In our numerical examples, we consider the case that the attack success probability $\mathsf{succ}_\mathsf{P}^\mathcal{R}$, that is now the probability that the output $a$ of $\mathsf{Tr}$ is not a pirate, for perfectly random source $\mathcal{R}$ is bounded by $\varepsilon = 10^{-3}$. We vary the number $N$ of users as $N = 10^3, 10^4, \ldots, 10^9$. Then by the bound for attack success probabilities given in the first part of [10, Theorem 1], we can calculate the code lengths for these cases as in Table 1, where we used auxiliary values $\Delta = 4.2 \times 10^{-6}$, $\eta = 1.93180$, $\mathcal{R} = 0.40822$, and $\beta = 0.0613461$ in the calculation.

**Table 1.** Code lengths of fingerprint codes in [10] with $c = 3$ and $\varepsilon = 10^{-3}$

| user number $N$ | $10^3$ | $10^4$ | $10^5$ | $10^6$ | $10^7$ | $10^8$ | $10^9$ |
|---|---|---|---|---|---|---|---|
| code length $m$ | 614 | 702 | 789 | 877 | 964 | 1052 | 1139 |

## 3   Pseudorandom Generators

In the following section, we will evaluate the security of fingerprint codes in the case that the perfect random source is replaced with a pseudorandom generator (PRG). This section summarizes definitions relevant to PRGs and some properties of PRGs recently proposed by Farashahi et al. [6]. For the purpose, first we clarify the meaning of the term "computational model" used in this article:

**Definition 1.** *A computational model $\mathcal{M} = (\mathcal{A}_\mathcal{M}, C_\mathcal{M})$ consists of a set $\mathcal{A}_\mathcal{M}$ of algorithms described in the model, and a map $C_\mathcal{M} : \mathcal{A}_\mathcal{M} \to \mathbb{R}$ that assigns to each $\mathsf{A} \in \mathcal{A}_\mathcal{M}$ its "complexity" $C_\mathcal{M}(\mathsf{A}) \in \mathbb{R}$.*

Here the "complexity" may take various meanings depending on the context, such as time complexity on a fixed Turing machine, average or worst-case running time on a fixed PC, and circuit complexity with fixed fundamental gates.

We define a PRG to be an algorithm $\mathsf{G} : S_\mathsf{G} \to O_\mathsf{G}$ with seed set $S_\mathsf{G}$ and output set $O_\mathsf{G}$. We deal with exact (concrete) security in this article rather than asymptotic security, thus $\mathsf{G}$ is a single algorithm rather than a sequence of algorithms with various seed sets. The following notion of indistinguishability for PRGs is a natural translation of the conventional notion to the case of exact security and has essentially appeared in the literature such as [6, Definition 1]:

**Definition 2.** *An algorithm* $D : O_G \to \{0, 1\}$ *is called a* distinguisher *for a PRG* $G$. *For any distinguisher* $D$ *for* $G$, *its* advantage $\mathsf{adv}_G(D)$ *is defined by*

$$\mathsf{adv}_G(D) = |Pr[D(G(U_{S_G})) = 1] - Pr[D(U_{O_G}) = 1]| \ .$$

**Definition 3.** *Let* $\mathcal{M}$ *be a computational model (see Definition 1) and* $R(t) \geq 0$ *a non-decreasing function. A PRG* $G$ *is called* $R(t)$-*secure in* $\mathcal{M}$ *if for any distinguisher* $D \in \mathcal{A}_\mathcal{M}$ *for* $G$, *its advantage is bounded by*

$$\mathsf{adv}_G(D) \leq R(C_\mathcal{M}(D)) \ .$$

An example of $R(t)$-secure PRGs is recently given by Farashahi et al. [6, Sect. 4.1] under the DDH assumption. The construction of their PRGs uses two prime numbers $p$ and $q$ such that $p = 2q + 1$, thus $p$ is a safe prime and $q$ is a Sophie-Germain prime. Let $\mathbb{G}_1$ be the multiplicative group of nonzero quadratic residues modulo $p$, therefore $|\mathbb{G}_1| = q$. We identify the set $\mathbb{G}_1$ with $\mathbb{Z}_q$ via the bijection $\mathsf{enum}_1$ used in [6, Sect. 4.1]. Under the identification, their PRG $G = G_{\mathrm{DDH}}$, called *DDH generator*, with parameter $k_0 > 0$ has seed set $S_G = (\mathbb{Z}_q)^3$ and output set $O_G = (\mathbb{Z}_q)^{k_0}$ (in their construction, two elements of $\mathbb{G}_1$ denoted by $x$ and $y$ are randomly chosen as well as the "seed" of the PRG denoted by $s_0$ [6, Sect. 3.1], and here we include the random $x$ and $y$ in the seed of the PRG). We omit further details of the construction since it is not relevant to our argument.

The argument in [6] yields the following description of the function $R(t)$ in Definition 3 for $G_{\mathrm{DDH}}$. Since the numerical observation in [6] is based on the experiments by Lenstra and Verheul [9], here we define the complexity function $C_\mathcal{M}$ for the computational model $\mathcal{M}$ by worst-case running times on a fixed Pentium machine that was used in the experiments in [9]. (Note that it is not clear in [6] whether the running times are in average-case or in worst-case, and here we adopt worst-case ones since our choice can avoid at least overestimation of security and it simplifies our argument than the case of average-case running times.) The unit of time is set to be 360 Pentium clock cycles that is approximately the time for one encryption in a software implementation of DES according to the experiment in [9] (see also [6, Sect. 2.4]). Now [6, Theorem 2] shows that if there is a distinguisher $D \in \mathcal{A}_\mathcal{M}$ for $G_{\mathrm{DDH}}$ such that $C_\mathcal{M}(D) \leq T$ and $\mathsf{adv}_{G_{\mathrm{DDH}}}(D) > \varepsilon$, then the DDH problem in $\mathbb{G}_1$ can be solved by some $A \in \mathcal{A}_\mathcal{M}$ such that $C_\mathcal{M}(A) \leq T$ with advantage larger than $\varepsilon/k_0$. Thus by assuming that the time-success ratio $T'/\varepsilon'$ for the complexity $T'$ and the advantage $\varepsilon'$ of any adversary in $\mathcal{M}$ for the DDH problem in $\mathbb{G}_1$ does not exceed a constant $R_{\mathrm{ts}}$, it follows that $G_{\mathrm{DDH}}$ is $R(t)$-secure in $\mathcal{M}$ with $R(t) = k_0 t / R_{\mathrm{ts}}$. In [6, Assumption 1], the value $R_{\mathrm{ts}}$ is assumed to be the complexity of the best known algorithm for solving the DDH problem in $\mathbb{G}_1$, which is estimated according to the data in [9] as $R_{\mathrm{ts}} = L(|q|_2)$ where

$$L(n) = 4.7 \times 10^{-5} \exp(1.9229(n \ln 2)^{1/3} (\ln(n \ln 2))^{2/3})$$

(see [6, Sect. 2.4]). These assumptions imply the following assumption which is adopted in our numerical examples given in the following section:

$$G_{\mathrm{DDH}} \text{ is } R(t)\text{-secure in } \mathcal{M} \text{ with } R(t) = k_0 t / L(|q|_2). \tag{1}$$

Note that this has been derived by an assumption on the hardness of the DDH problem *in a fixed (classical) computational model.*

## 4   Randomness Reduction and Its Evaluation

In this section, we evaluate the difference of attack success probabilities $\mathrm{succ}_{\mathsf{P}}^{\mathcal{R}}$ for fingerprint codes in Sect. 2 between the cases that $\mathcal{R}$ is a perfectly random source and that $\mathcal{R}$ is a PRG by using the evaluation technique in [12]. Moreover, we not only apply this evaluation technique straightforwardly but also introduce a technique for randomness reduction to improve the evaluation result.

### 4.1   A Technique to Improve Randomness Reduction

Our technique to improve the PRG-based randomness reduction is first dividing the set $\{1, 2, \ldots, m\}$ of bit positions in users' codewords into plural, say, $\ell$ parts $I_1, I_2, \ldots, I_\ell$ and generating each part $(w_{i,j})_{1 \le i \le N, j \in I_\nu}$ of users' codewords and each part $(p_j)_{j \in I_\nu}$ of the state element by a *separate* PRG. The new situation is shown in Fig. 3 (we exhibit the picture only for the case $\ell = 2$, but a general case is analogous). Namely, the $\nu$-th part $s_\nu = \mathsf{Gen}_\nu(x_\nu) \in S_\nu$ of the secret information is generated from $\nu$-th random sequence $x_\nu \in X_\nu$ given by $\nu$-th random source $\mathcal{R}_\nu$. We assume that the random sources $\mathcal{R}_\nu$, $1 \le \nu \le \ell$, are independent. Note that the $\nu$-th part of codewords depends solely on the $\nu$-th part of the state element. The $\nu$-th part $\mathsf{Dist}_\nu(s_\nu) \in W_\nu$ of pirates' codewords obviously depends solely on $s_\nu$. Roughly speaking, the main effect of our technique is to improve the dependence of the security evaluation result on the *product* of sizes of $W_\nu$ to dependence on the *sum* of sizes of $W_\nu$. Although we only consider the case of fingerprint codes here, our technique is applicable to other cases by finding a suitable decomposition of the randomness used in the scheme.

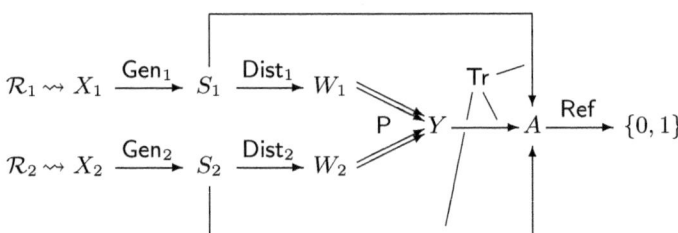

**Fig. 3.** Modified flowchart for fingerprint codes, with $\ell = 2$ (here the duplicated arrows signify the attack algorithm with unbounded complexity)

### 4.2   Security Evaluation for the Randomness Reduction

We apply the hybrid argument to the evaluation of the situation in Sect. 4.1. For each $1 \le \nu \le \ell$, let $\mathcal{R}_\nu^{\mathrm{rnd}}$ denote the perfect random source on $X_\nu$, and let $\mathcal{R}_\nu^{\mathrm{prnd}}$

denote the random source on $X_\nu$ produced by a separate PRG $\mathsf{G}^{(\nu)}$. Assume that each $\mathsf{G}^{(\nu)}$ is $R_\nu(t)$-secure in the computational model $\mathcal{M}$ given in Sect. 3. Now for each $0 \le \nu \le \ell$, let $\mathcal{R}_\nu^*$ be the collection of random sources $\mathcal{R}_{\nu'}$, $1 \le \nu' \le \ell$, such that $\mathcal{R}_{\nu'} = \mathcal{R}_{\nu'}^{\mathrm{prnd}}$ if $1 \le \nu' \le \nu$ and $\mathcal{R}_{\nu'} = \mathcal{R}_{\nu'}^{\mathrm{rnd}}$ if $\nu + 1 \le \nu' \le \ell$. Let $\mathsf{succ}_\mathsf{P}^{(\nu)}$ be the attack success probability with respect to the collection $\mathcal{R}_\nu^*$ of random sources. Now the difference $\mathsf{diff}_\mathsf{P}$ of attack success probabilities $\mathsf{succ}_\mathsf{P}^{(0)}$ and $\mathsf{succ}_\mathsf{P}^{(\ell)}$ in entirely random and entirely pseudorandom cases, respectively, is bounded by the sum of $\ell$ values $\mathsf{diff}_\mathsf{P}^{(\nu)} = |\mathsf{succ}_\mathsf{P}^{(\nu-1)} - \mathsf{succ}_\mathsf{P}^{(\nu)}|$, $1 \le \nu \le \ell$, owing to the triangle inequality. Thus our task is reduced to evaluation of each $\mathsf{diff}_\mathsf{P}^{(\nu)}$.

Put $\mathsf{succ}_\mathsf{P}^{\nu,\mathrm{rnd}} = \mathsf{succ}_\mathsf{P}^{(\nu-1)}$ and $\mathsf{succ}_\mathsf{P}^{\nu,\mathrm{prnd}} = \mathsf{succ}_\mathsf{P}^{(\nu)}$ for simplicity. Hence in the definition of $\mathsf{succ}_\mathsf{P}^{\nu,b}$ where $b \in \{\mathrm{rnd}, \mathrm{prnd}\}$, we have $\mathcal{R}_\nu = \mathcal{R}_\nu^b$ and each of the other random sources $\mathcal{R}_{\nu'}$ is common to the two choices of $b$. In what follows, let $Pr_P[v]$ denote the probability of a random variable $P$ taking a value $v$. Let $x_{\nu'}$, $s_{\nu'}$, $w_{\nu'}$, $y$, and $a$ denote elements of $X_{\nu'}$, $S_{\nu'}$, $W_{\nu'}$, $Y$, and $A$, respectively. Let $\boldsymbol{x}$ denote the tuple of all $x_{\nu'}$, $1 \le \nu' \le \ell$, and let $\boldsymbol{x}_{\neg\nu}$ denote the tuple of all $x_{\nu'}$, $1 \le \nu' \le \ell$, $\nu' \ne \nu$ (similarly for $\boldsymbol{s}$, $\boldsymbol{s}_{\neg\nu}$, $\boldsymbol{w}$ and $\boldsymbol{w}_{\neg\nu}$). Now by the evaluation technique in [12], we express $\mathsf{succ}_\mathsf{P}^{\nu,b}$ in the following form, where each index in each summation runs over the corresponding set (e.g., $\boldsymbol{x}$ runs over $\prod_{\nu'=1}^\ell X_{\nu'}$):

$$
\begin{aligned}
\mathsf{succ}_\mathsf{P}^{\nu,b} &= \sum_{\boldsymbol{x},\boldsymbol{s},\boldsymbol{w},y,a} Pr_{\mathcal{R}_\nu^b}[x_\nu] \prod_{\nu' \ne \nu} Pr_{\mathcal{R}_{\nu'}}[x_{\nu'}] \prod_{\nu'=1}^\ell \left( Pr_{\mathsf{Gen}_{\nu'}(x_{\nu'})}[s_{\nu'}] \, Pr_{\mathsf{Dist}_{\nu'}(s_{\nu'})}[w_{\nu'}] \right) \\
&\qquad \cdot Pr_{\mathsf{P}(\boldsymbol{w})}[y] \, Pr_{\mathsf{Tr}(y,\boldsymbol{s})}[a] \, Pr_{\mathsf{Ref}(a)}[1] \\
&= \sum_{y,\boldsymbol{x}_{\neg\nu},\boldsymbol{s}_{\neg\nu},\boldsymbol{w}} \prod_{\nu' \ne \nu} \left( Pr_{\mathcal{R}_{\nu'}}[x_{\nu'}] \, Pr_{\mathsf{Gen}_{\nu'}(x_{\nu'})}[s_{\nu'}] \, Pr_{\mathsf{Dist}_{\nu'}(s_{\nu'})}[w_{\nu'}] \right) Pr_{\mathsf{P}(\boldsymbol{w})}[y] \\
&\qquad \cdot \sum_{x_\nu,s_\nu,a} Pr_{\mathcal{R}_\nu^b}[x_\nu] \, Pr_{\mathsf{Gen}_\nu(x_\nu)}[s_\nu] \, Pr_{\mathsf{Dist}_\nu(s_\nu)}[w_\nu] \, Pr_{\mathsf{Tr}(y,\boldsymbol{s})}[a] \, Pr_{\mathsf{Ref}(a)}[1] .
\end{aligned}
\tag{2}
$$

To simplify the expression (2), we introduce auxiliary algorithms $\mathsf{D}_{y,w_\nu,\boldsymbol{s}_{\neg\nu}}^\nu$ : $X_\nu \to \{0,1\}$, that will play a role of distinguishers for the PRG $\mathsf{G}^{(\nu)}$, in the following manner according to the technique in [12] again:

**Algorithm** $\mathsf{D}_{y,w_\nu,\boldsymbol{s}_{\neg\nu}}^\nu$ $(1 \le \nu \le \ell, y \in Y, w_\nu \in W_\nu, s_{\nu'} \in S_{\nu'}$ for $\nu' \ne \nu)$
**Input:** $x_\nu \in X_\nu$    **Output:** 0 or 1
(1) Set $s_\nu \leftarrow \mathsf{Gen}_\nu(x_\nu)$
(2) Set $w' \leftarrow \mathsf{Dist}_\nu(s_\nu)$
(3) Set $a \leftarrow \mathsf{Tr}(y,\boldsymbol{s}) = \mathsf{Tr}(y, s_1, \ldots, s_\nu, \ldots, s_\ell)$
(4) Set $b' \leftarrow \mathsf{Ref}(a)$
(5) Output 1 if $w' = w_\nu$ and $b' = 1$; output 0 otherwise

Now for each $y$, $\boldsymbol{x}_{\neg\nu}$, $\boldsymbol{s}_{\neg\nu}$ and $\boldsymbol{w}$, we have

$$\sum_{x_\nu, s_\nu, a} Pr_{\mathcal{R}_\nu^b}[x_\nu]\, Pr_{\mathsf{Gen}_\nu(x_\nu)}[s_\nu]\, Pr_{\mathsf{Dist}_\nu(s_\nu)}[w_\nu]\, Pr_{\mathsf{Tr}(y,\boldsymbol{s})}[a]\, Pr_{\mathsf{Ref}(a)}[1]$$

$$= \sum_{x_\nu} Pr_{\mathcal{R}_\nu^b}[x_\nu] \sum_{s_\nu, a} Pr_{\mathsf{Gen}_\nu(x_\nu)}[s_\nu]\, Pr_{\mathsf{Dist}_\nu(s_\nu)}[w_\nu]\, Pr_{\mathsf{Tr}(y,\boldsymbol{s})}[a]\, Pr_{\mathsf{Ref}(a)}[1]$$

$$= \sum_{x_\nu} Pr_{\mathcal{R}_\nu^b}[x_\nu]\, Pr\big[\mathsf{D}_{y,w_\nu,\boldsymbol{s}_{\neg\nu}}^\nu(x_\nu) = 1\big] = Pr\big[\mathsf{D}_{y,w_\nu,\boldsymbol{s}_{\neg\nu}}^\nu(\mathcal{R}_\nu^b) = 1\big]\ .$$

By substituting this for (2), we have

$$\mathsf{succ}_\mathsf{P}^{\nu,b} = \sum_{y,\boldsymbol{x}_{\neg\nu},\boldsymbol{s}_{\neg\nu},\boldsymbol{w}} \prod_{\nu'\neq\nu} \big(Pr_{\mathcal{R}_{\nu'}}[x_{\nu'}]\, Pr_{\mathsf{Gen}_{\nu'}(x_{\nu'})}[s_{\nu'}]\, Pr_{\mathsf{Dist}_{\nu'}(s_{\nu'})}[w_{\nu'}]\big)\, Pr_{\mathsf{P}(\boldsymbol{w})}[y]$$

$$\cdot Pr\big[\mathsf{D}_{y,w_\nu,\boldsymbol{s}_{\neg\nu}}^\nu(\mathcal{R}_\nu^b) = 1\big]\ .$$

Now the triangle inequality implies that

$$\mathsf{diff}_\mathsf{P}^{(\nu)} \leq \sum_{y,\boldsymbol{x}_{\neg\nu},\boldsymbol{s}_{\neg\nu},\boldsymbol{w}} \prod_{\nu'\neq\nu} \big(Pr_{\mathcal{R}_{\nu'}}[x_{\nu'}]\, Pr_{\mathsf{Gen}_{\nu'}(x_{\nu'})}[s_{\nu'}]\, Pr_{\mathsf{Dist}_{\nu'}(s_{\nu'})}[w_{\nu'}]\big)\, Pr_{\mathsf{P}(\boldsymbol{w})}[y]$$

$$\cdot \big|Pr\big[\mathsf{D}_{y,w_\nu,\boldsymbol{s}_{\neg\nu}}^\nu(\mathcal{R}_\nu^{\mathrm{rnd}}) = 1\big] - Pr\big[\mathsf{D}_{y,w_\nu,\boldsymbol{s}_{\neg\nu}}^\nu(\mathcal{R}_\nu^{\mathrm{prnd}}) = 1\big]\big|$$

$$= \sum_{y,\boldsymbol{x}_{\neg\nu},\boldsymbol{s}_{\neg\nu},\boldsymbol{w}} \prod_{\nu'\neq\nu} \big(Pr_{\mathcal{R}_{\nu'}}[x_{\nu'}]\, Pr_{\mathsf{Gen}_{\nu'}(x_{\nu'})}[s_{\nu'}]\, Pr_{\mathsf{Dist}_{\nu'}(s_{\nu'})}[w_{\nu'}]\big)\, Pr_{\mathsf{P}(\boldsymbol{w})}[y]$$

$$\cdot \mathsf{adv}_{\mathsf{G}^{(\nu)}}(\mathsf{D}_{y,w_\nu,\boldsymbol{s}_{\neg\nu}}^\nu)\ .$$

We assume that the complexity of the distinguisher $\mathsf{D}_{y,w_\nu,\boldsymbol{s}_{\neg\nu}}^\nu$ for $\mathsf{G}^{(\nu)}$ is not larger than a value $T_\nu$ that is independent of $y$, $w_\nu$, and $\boldsymbol{s}_{\neg\nu}$. Then, since $\mathsf{G}^{(\nu)}$ is $R_\nu(t)$-secure, we have $\mathsf{adv}_{\mathsf{G}^{(\nu)}}(\mathsf{D}_{y,w_\nu,\boldsymbol{s}_{\neg\nu}}^\nu) \leq R_\nu(T_\nu)$, hence $\mathsf{diff}_\mathsf{P}^{(\nu)}$ is bounded by

$$R_\nu(T_\nu) \sum_{y,\boldsymbol{x}_{\neg\nu},\boldsymbol{s}_{\neg\nu},\boldsymbol{w}} \prod_{\nu'\neq\nu} \big(Pr_{\mathcal{R}_{\nu'}}[x_{\nu'}]\, Pr_{\mathsf{Gen}_{\nu'}(x_{\nu'})}[s_{\nu'}]\, Pr_{\mathsf{Dist}_{\nu'}(s_{\nu'})}[w_{\nu'}]\big)\, Pr_{\mathsf{P}(\boldsymbol{w})}[y]\ .$$

The summation in this expression is equal to

$$\sum_{\boldsymbol{x}_{\neg\nu},\boldsymbol{s}_{\neg\nu},\boldsymbol{w}} \prod_{\nu'\neq\nu} \big(Pr_{\mathcal{R}_{\nu'}}[x_{\nu'}]\, Pr_{\mathsf{Gen}_{\nu'}(x_{\nu'})}[s_{\nu'}]\, Pr_{\mathsf{Dist}_{\nu'}(s_{\nu'})}[w_{\nu'}]\big) \sum_y Pr_{\mathsf{P}(\boldsymbol{w})}[y]$$

$$= \sum_{\boldsymbol{x}_{\neg\nu},\boldsymbol{s}_{\neg\nu},\boldsymbol{w}} \prod_{\nu'\neq\nu} Pr_{\mathcal{R}_{\nu'}}[x_{\nu'}]\, Pr_{\mathsf{Gen}_{\nu'}(x_{\nu'})}[s_{\nu'}]\, Pr_{\mathsf{Dist}_{\nu'}(s_{\nu'})}[w_{\nu'}]$$

since $\sum_y Pr_{\mathsf{P}(w)}[y] = 1$. Similarly, the last value is also equal to

$$\sum_{w_\nu} \sum_{\boldsymbol{x}_{\neg\nu},\boldsymbol{s}_{\neg\nu},\boldsymbol{w}_{\neg\nu}} \prod_{\nu'\neq\nu} Pr_{\mathcal{R}_{\nu'}}[x_{\nu'}]\, Pr_{\mathsf{Gen}_{\nu'}(x_{\nu'})}[s_{\nu'}]\, Pr_{\mathsf{Dist}_{\nu'}(s_{\nu'})}[w_{\nu'}]$$

$$= \sum_{w_\nu} \prod_{\nu'\neq\nu} \sum_{x_{\nu'},s_{\nu'},w_{\nu'}} Pr_{\mathcal{R}_{\nu'}}[x_{\nu'}]\, Pr_{\mathsf{Gen}_{\nu'}(x_{\nu'})}[s_{\nu'}]\, Pr_{\mathsf{Dist}_{\nu'}(s_{\nu'})}[w_{\nu'}]$$

$$= \sum_{w_\nu} \prod_{\nu'\neq\nu} \left(\sum_{x_{\nu'},s_{\nu'}} Pr_{\mathcal{R}_{\nu'}}[x_{\nu'}]\, Pr_{\mathsf{Gen}_{\nu'}(x_{\nu'})}[s_{\nu'}] \sum_{w_{\nu'}} Pr_{\mathsf{Dist}_{\nu'}(s_{\nu'})}[w_{\nu'}]\right)$$

$$= \sum_{w_\nu} \prod_{\nu' \neq \nu} \sum_{x_{\nu'}, s_{\nu'}} Pr_{\mathcal{R}_{\nu'}}[x_{\nu'}] \, Pr_{\mathsf{Gen}_{\nu'}(x_{\nu'})}[s_{\nu'}]$$

$$= \sum_{w_\nu} \prod_{\nu' \neq \nu} \left( \sum_{x_{\nu'}} Pr_{\mathcal{R}_{\nu'}}[x_{\nu'}] \sum_{s_{\nu'}} Pr_{\mathsf{Gen}_{\nu'}(x_{\nu'})}[s_{\nu'}] \right)$$

$$= \sum_{w_\nu} \prod_{\nu' \neq \nu} \sum_{x_{\nu'}} Pr_{\mathcal{R}_{\nu'}}[x_{\nu'}] = \sum_{w_\nu} \prod_{\nu' \neq \nu} 1 = \sum_{w_\nu} 1 = |W_\nu|$$

(we used $\sum_{w_{\nu'}} Pr_{\mathsf{Dist}_{\nu'}(s_{\nu'})}[w_{\nu'}] = 1$ in the third equality, and $\sum_{x_{\nu'}} Pr_{\mathcal{R}_{\nu'}}[x_{\nu'}] = 1$ in the fifth equality). Hence we have

$$\mathsf{diff}_{\mathsf{P}}^{(\nu)} \leq |W_\nu| \cdot R_\nu(T_\nu) \; .$$

Summarizing, we have the following result:

**Theorem 1.** *Assume that for $1 \leq \nu \leq \ell$, the PRG $\mathsf{G}^{(\nu)}$ is $R_\nu(t)$-secure in $\mathcal{M}$ and the complexity $C_{\mathcal{M}}(\mathsf{D}_{y,w_\nu,s_{\neg\nu}}^\nu)$ of the distinguisher $\mathsf{D}_{y,w_\nu,s_{\neg\nu}}^\nu$ for $\mathsf{G}^{(\nu)}$ is not larger than $T_\nu$ for every $y$, $w_\nu$, and $s_{\neg\nu}$. Then the difference $\mathsf{diff}_{\mathsf{P}}$ of attack success probabilities for the fingerprint code in Sect. 2 between the two cases*

- *every random source $\mathcal{R}_\nu$, $1 \leq \nu \leq \ell$, is perfectly random; and*
- *each random source $\mathcal{R}_\nu$, $1 \leq \nu \leq \ell$, is produced by the PRG $\mathsf{G}^{(\nu)}$*

*is bounded by*

$$\mathsf{diff}_{\mathsf{P}} \leq \sum_{\nu=1}^{\ell} |W_\nu| \cdot R_\nu(T_\nu)$$

*even if the attack algorithm $\mathsf{P}$ of pirates has unbounded complexity.*

### 4.3   Complexity of the Distinguishers

To proceed the evaluation further, we estimate the complexity of the distinguisher $\mathsf{D}_{y,w_\nu,s_{\neg\nu}}^\nu$ for $\mathsf{G}^{(\nu)}$. For simplicity, we choose the partition $(I_1, \dots, I_\ell)$ of bit positions $\{1, \dots, m\}$ such that each $I_\nu$ consists of $j$-th positions with $\overline{m}_{\nu-1} + 1 \leq j \leq \overline{m}_\nu$, where $m_\nu = |I_\nu|$ and $\overline{m}_\nu = \sum_{\nu'=1}^{\nu} m_{\nu'}$ (hence $\overline{m}_\ell = m$). Let $1 \leq i_1 < i_2 < i_3 \leq N$ be the three pirates (recall that now $c = 3$).

We give a pseudo-program for the algorithm $\mathsf{D}_{y,w_\nu,s_{\neg\nu}}^\nu$ for the sake of complexity evaluation. For the purpose, we encode each digit $y_j$ of $y \in Y$ in such a way that 2-bit sequences 00, 01, and 10 represent '0', '1' and '?', respectively (hence one can determine whether $y_j = 1$ or not by just one comparison in the lower bit). Secondly, the element $w_\nu = w^{(\nu)} \in W_\nu$ consists of $w_{i,j}^{(\nu)} \in \{0,1\}$ with $i \in \{i_1, i_2, i_3\}$ and $\overline{m}_{\nu-1} + 1 \leq j \leq \overline{m}_\nu$. Thirdly, for each $\nu' \neq \nu$, the element $s_{\nu'} \in S_{\nu'}$ consists of the values $p_j$ ($\overline{m}_{\nu'-1} + 1 \leq j \leq \overline{m}_{\nu'}$) and $w_{i,j} \in \{0,1\}$ ($1 \leq i \leq N$, $\overline{m}_{\nu'-1} + 1 \leq j \leq \overline{m}_{\nu'}$). Since each $p_j$ is chosen from the two values $p^{(0)}$ and $p^{(1)}$ given in Sect. 2, here we encode each $p_j$ into $\xi \in \{0,1\}$ such that $p_j = p^{(\xi)}$. We also use the two values $u_0$ and $u_1$ given in Sect. 2. Now we describe a pseudo-program for $\mathsf{D}_{y,w^{(\nu)},s_{\neg\nu}}^\nu$ together with an estimate of its complexity (see below for details) as follows, where $\mathtt{next\_}n(x_\nu)$ denotes an operation to load the next $n$ bits from the input binary sequence $x_\nu$ (the subscript '$n$' is omitted in the case $n = 1$) and we put $\mathrm{sc}_0 = -mu_0$:

```
Input: xν ∈ Xν     Output: 0 or 1
01: for j in m̄ν−1+1,...,m̄ν do
02:   set pj := next(xν)      — 1 TU
03: end for      — 3mν + 2 TUs for 01 - 03
04: for i in 1,...,N do
05:   for j in m̄ν−1+1,...,m̄ν do
06:    if next_15(xν) < p⁽⁰⁾ then
07:     set wi,j := 1-pj      — 2 TUs
08:    else
09:     set wi,j := pj      — 1 TU
10:    end if      — 3 TUs for 06 - 10
11:    if i = i1 or i = i2 or i = i3 then
12:     if not wi,j = wi,j⁽ν⁾ then
13:      return 0
14:     end if      — 1 TU for 12 - 14
15:    end if      — 4 TUs for 11 - 15
16:   end for      — 9mν + 2 TUs for 05 - 16
17: end for      — (9mν + 4)N + 2 TUs for 04 - 17
18: set scmax := sc0      — 1 TU
19: for i in 1,...,N do
20:   set sc := 0      — 1 TU
21:   for j in 1,...,m do
22:    if yj = 1 then
23:     if wi,j = 1 then
24:      if pj = 0 then
25:       set sc := sc + u0      — 1 TU
26:      else
27:       set sc := sc + u1      — 1 TU
28:      end if      — 2 TUs for 24 - 28
29:     else
30:      if pj = 0 then
31:       set sc := sc - u1      — 1 TU
32:      else
33:       set sc := sc - u0      — 1 TU
34:      end if      — 2 TUs for 30 - 34
35:     end if      — 3 TUs for 23 - 35
36:    else
37:     if wi,j = 0 then
38:      if pj = 0 then
39:       set sc := sc + u1      — 1 TU
40:      else
41:       set sc := sc + u0      — 1 TU
```

```
42:      end if      — 2 TUs for 38 - 42
43:      else
44:       if p_j = 0 then
45:         set sc := sc - u_0      — 1 TU
46:       else
47:         set sc := sc - u_1      — 1 TU
48:       end if      — 2 TUs for 44 - 48
49:      end if      — 3 TUs for 37 - 49
50:     end if      — 4 TUs for 22 - 50
51:    end for      — 6m + 2 TUs for 21 - 51
52:    if not sc < sc_max then
53:      set sc_max := sc, a := i      — 2 TUs
54:    end if      — 3 TUs for 52 - 54
55:  end for      — (6m + 8)N + 2 TUs for 19 - 55
56:  if a = i_1 or a = i_2 or a = i_3 then
57:    return 0
58:  end if      — 3 TUs for 56 - 58
59:  return 1
```

Since it is infeasible to determine the precise running time of the pseudo-program executed on the machine used in the definition of $\mathcal{M}$ (see Sect. 3), in the above estimate we approximated the worst-case running time by the following two rules. First, we regard each of one substitution, one addition, one subtraction, and one comparison as taking one time unit (in the above description, "TU" stands for "time unit"). This would be justified since every such operation in the above pseudo-program is either an operation between fixed-point numbers with at most just 12-bit integer parts and at most just 16-bit fractional parts or an operation between at most just 30-bit integers (see Sect. 2 for the precise values of $p^{(0)}$, $p^{(1)}$, $u_0$, and $u_1$ and see Table 1 for the precise choices of $N$ and $m$), which would be much more efficient than one DES encryption. In fact, this estimate of complexity is likely to be overestimation. Secondly, we ignore the complexity of loading a next bit from the input (i.e., an operation $\texttt{next\_}n(x_\nu)$), outputting an element (i.e., an operation $\texttt{return}$), and jumping in the execution flow (that is implicitly used in $\texttt{for}$ loops and $\texttt{if}$ statements), which (together with any other unregarded issue on computational complexity) seems negligibly small and would be absorbed by the above overestimation. It follows from the two rules that the worst-case running time of a $\texttt{for}$ loop of the form "$\texttt{for CN in ST,...,EN do JOB}_{\mathsf{CN}}\texttt{ end for}$" is (over)estimated to be the sum of $2(\mathsf{EN} - \mathsf{ST} + 2)$ time units (i.e., 1 initialization of the counter $\mathsf{CN}$, $\mathsf{EN} - \mathsf{ST} + 1$ increments for $\mathsf{CN}$ and $\mathsf{EN} - \mathsf{ST} + 2$ checks for the terminating condition) and the sum of running times of $\mathsf{JOB}_{\mathsf{CN}}$ for all $\mathsf{ST} \leq \mathsf{CN} \leq \mathsf{EN}$. In particular, if the running time of $\mathsf{JOB}_{\mathsf{CN}}$ is constantly equal to $\mathsf{T}$ time units, then the estimated running time of the loop is $(\mathsf{EN} - \mathsf{ST} + 1)(\mathsf{T} + 2) + 2$ time units. The above estimates of running times of each line, each $\texttt{for}$ loop and each if statement are thus obtained. By summing the running times presented at lines 03, 17, 18, 55, and 58, we have $C_{\mathcal{M}}(\mathsf{D}^{\nu}_{y,w^{(\nu)},\boldsymbol{s}_{\neg\nu}}) \leq T_{\nu}$ where

$$
\begin{aligned}
T_{\nu} &= (3m_{\nu} + 2) + ((9m_{\nu} + 4)N + 2) + 1 + ((6m + 8)N + 2) + 3 \\
&= (6m + 9m_{\nu} + 12)N + 3m_{\nu} + 10 \ .
\end{aligned}
$$

Since $|W_{\nu}| = |(\Sigma^{m_{\nu}})^3| = 2^{3m_{\nu}}$, Theorem 1 implies that

$$
\mathsf{diff}_{\mathsf{P}} \leq \sum_{\nu=1}^{\ell} 2^{3m_{\nu}} R_{\nu}(T_{\nu}) \ . \tag{3}
$$

### 4.4  Modification of the DDH Generators

In our numerical examples below, we use the following modification of DDH generators $\mathsf{G}_{\mathrm{DDH}}$ described in Sect. 3. More precisely, the seeds and outputs of $\mathsf{G}_{\mathrm{DDH}}$ are sequences of finite field elements, and we convert them into binary sequences. For the purpose, for integer parameters $h_1$ and $h_2$, define two maps $\gamma : \Sigma^{3h_1} \to (\mathbb{Z}_q)^3 = S_{\mathsf{G}}$ and $\gamma' : O_{\mathsf{G}} = (\mathbb{Z}_q)^{k_0} \to \Sigma^{k_0 h_2}$ by

$$
\gamma(s_1, s_2, s_3) = (\gamma_0(s_1), \gamma_0(s_2), \gamma_0(s_3)), \ \gamma'(s_1, \ldots, s_{k_0}) = (\gamma_0'(s_1), \ldots, \gamma_0'(s_{k_0}))
$$

where $\gamma_0 : \Sigma^{h_1} \ni x \mapsto (x \bmod q) + 1 \in \mathbb{Z}_q$ and $\gamma_0' : \mathbb{Z}_q \ni x \mapsto (x \bmod 2^{h_2}) \in \Sigma^{h_2}$ (we let $x \bmod n$ lie between 0 and $n-1$). Intuitively, the map $\gamma$ approximates the seeds of $\mathsf{G}_{\mathrm{DDH}}$ by binary sequences, while $\gamma'$ converts the outputs of $\mathsf{G}_{\mathrm{DDH}}$ into binary sequences. Before evaluating the effect of these two maps, we recall the definition of statistical distances between two distributions:

**Definition 4.** *For two probability distributions $P_1, P_2$ over the same finite set $X$, their* statistical distance $\mathsf{SD}(P_1, P_2)$ *is defined by*

$$
\begin{aligned}
\mathsf{SD}(P_1, P_2) &= \frac{1}{2} \sum_{x \in X} |Pr[x \leftarrow P_1] - Pr[x \leftarrow P_2]| \\
&= \max_{E \subset X} (Pr[x \leftarrow P_1 : x \in E] - Pr[x \leftarrow P_2 : x \in E]) \ .
\end{aligned}
$$

Note that $\mathsf{SD}(F(P_1), F(P_2)) \leq \mathsf{SD}(P_1, P_2)$ for any (probabilistic) function $F$. Now the following property holds:

**Lemma 1.** *We have*

$$
\mathsf{SD}(\gamma(U_{\Sigma^{3h_1}}), U_{(\mathbb{Z}_q)^3}) \leq 3f(2^{h_1}, q) \ and \ \mathsf{SD}(U_{\Sigma^{k_0 h_2}}, \gamma'(U_{(\mathbb{Z}_q)^{k_0}})) \leq k_0 f(q, 2^{h_2}) \ ,
$$

*where*

$$
f(z_1, z_2) = \frac{(z_1 \bmod z_2) \cdot (z_2 - (z_1 \bmod z_2))}{z_1 z_2} \ .
$$

*Proof.* First, if $P_i$ and $P_i'$ are random variables on the same set for each $i \in \{1, 2\}$, $P_1$ and $P_2$ are independent, and $P_1'$ and $P_2'$ are independent, then we have

$$
\mathsf{SD}(P_1 \times P_2, P_1' \times P_2') \leq \mathsf{SD}(P_1, P_1') + \mathsf{SD}(P_2, P_2') \ .
$$

Owing to this fact, it suffices to show that

$$\mathsf{SD}(\gamma_0(U_{\Sigma^{h_1}}), U_{\mathbb{Z}_q}) = f(2^{h_1}, q) \text{ and } \mathsf{SD}(U_{\Sigma^{h_2}}, \gamma_0'(U_{\mathbb{Z}_q})) = f(q, 2^{h_2}) .$$

For the former claim, write $2^{h_1} = aq + b$ with $b = (2^{h_1} \bmod q)$. Then we have $|\gamma_0^{-1}(x)| = a + 1$ for $b$ out of the $q$ elements $x \in \mathbb{Z}_q$, while $|\gamma_0^{-1}(x)| = a$ for the remaining $q - b$ elements $x \in \mathbb{Z}_q$. This implies that

$$\begin{aligned}
\mathsf{SD}(\gamma_0(U_{\Sigma^{h_1}}), U_{\mathbb{Z}_q}) &= \frac{1}{2} \cdot \left( b \left| \frac{a+1}{aq+b} - \frac{1}{q} \right| + (q-b) \left| \frac{a}{aq+b} - \frac{1}{q} \right| \right) \\
&= \frac{1}{2} \cdot \left( b \cdot \frac{q-b}{q(aq+b)} + (q-b)\frac{b}{q(aq+b)} \right) \\
&= \frac{b(q-b)}{2^{h_1}q} = f(2^{h_1}, q) .
\end{aligned}$$

The latter claim is similarly proven. Hence Lemma 1 holds.

Let $\mathsf{G}' = \mathsf{G}'_{\mathrm{DDH}}$ denote the composition $\gamma' \circ \mathsf{G}$ of $\mathsf{G} = \mathsf{G}_{\mathrm{DDH}}$ followed by $\gamma'$, which is also a PRG with seed set $S_{\mathsf{G}'} = S_{\mathsf{G}} = (\mathbb{Z}_q)^3$ and output set $O_{\mathsf{G}'} = \Sigma^{k_0 h_2}$. Now the map $\gamma'$ just outputs some lower bits of the original output of $\mathsf{G}$, therefore the issue of complexity of $\gamma'$ may be practically ignored for simplicity. Then Lemma 1 and the assumption (1) imply (by ignoring complexity of $\gamma'$) that the PRG $\mathsf{G}'$ is $R'(t)$-secure in $\mathcal{M}$ with

$$R'(t) = k_0 \left( \frac{t}{L(|q|_2)} + f(q, 2^{h_2}) \right) . \tag{4}$$

The other map $\gamma$ will be used in the next subsection as well.

## 4.5   Numerical Examples

From now, we apply the above argument to the concrete choices of parameters $N$ and $m$ given in Table 1. For simplicity, we choose the parameters $m_\nu$ such that $|m_\nu - m/\ell| < 1$, and let each PRG $\mathsf{G}^{(\nu)}$ be a copy of the same $\mathsf{G}'_{\mathrm{DDH}}$ given in Sect. 4.4. Then we have $m_\nu \leq \lceil m/\ell \rceil$, and it follows from (3) and (4) that

$$\begin{aligned}
\mathsf{diff}_{\mathsf{P}} &\leq \sum_{\nu=1}^{\ell} 2^{3\lceil m/\ell \rceil} k_0 \left( \frac{T_\nu}{L(|q|_2)} + f(q, 2^{h_2}) \right) \\
&= 2^{3\lceil m/\ell \rceil} k_0 \left( \frac{(6\ell m + 9m + 12\ell)N + 3m + 10\ell}{L(|q|_2)} + \ell f(q, 2^{h_2}) \right) .
\end{aligned} \tag{5}$$

On the other hand, the above pseudo-program shows that the minimal length of the input $x_\nu$ is $(15N + 1)m_\nu$, therefore the number of required random bits in perfectly random case is $(15N + 1)m$ and the parameters $k_0$ and $h_2$ should satisfy $k_0 h_2 \geq (15N + 1)\lceil m/\ell \rceil$. For simplicity, we assume that the integer $k_0$ is as small as possible, namely we have $k_0 = \lceil (15N + 1)\lceil m/\ell \rceil / h_2 \rceil$.

Since the original bound of attack success probability is set to $\varepsilon = 10^{-3}$, the value diff$_P$ should be significantly smaller than $10^{-3}$ to make the scheme in pseudorandom case secure as well. On the other hand, to evaluate the effect of randomness reduction, we approximate the non-binary seeds in $S_{G'} = (\mathbb{Z}_q)^3$ by binary sequences via the map $\gamma : \Sigma^{3h_1} \to (\mathbb{Z}_q)^3$ given in Sect. 3. Now the new "seed set" is $\Sigma^{3\ell h_1}$ and the statistical distance between the distribution of an element of $(\mathbb{Z}_q)^{3\ell}$ induced by the map $\gamma$ and the uniform distribution on $(\mathbb{Z}_q)^{3\ell}$ is bounded by $3\ell f(2^{h_1}, q)$ by Lemma 1. Hence the value $3\ell f(2^{h_1}, q)$ should be significantly smaller than $10^{-3}$ as well. In the example below, we require the sum of $3\ell f(2^{h_1}, q)$ and the right-hand side of (5) to be smaller than $10^{-6}$.

Table 2 shows the evaluation results and the corresponding parameters for the PRG $G'$, where the case $\ell = 1$ coincides with the plain PRG-based randomness reduction (without our proposed technique of dividing the randomness). In the table, "difference" signifies the sum of $3\ell f(2^{h_1}, q)$ and the value in the right-hand side of (5) (written in scientific E notation), and "ratio" signifies the ratio of the seed length $3\ell h_1$ to the original number of random bits required in perfectly random case. The Sophie-Germain primes $q$ in the table are

$$q_{(1)} = 790717071 \times 2^{54254} - 1 \ , \ \ q_{(2)} = 2566851867 \times 2^{70001} - 1 \ ,$$

$$q_{(3)} = 18912879 \times 2^{98395} - 1 \ , \ \ q_{(4)} = 7068555 \times 2^{121301} - 1 \ ,$$

$$q_{(5)} = 137211941292195 \times 2^{171960} - 1 \ .$$

The last four primes are taken from the current (July 2009) version of a list by Caldwell [3], while the first one is taken from an old (September 2008) version of the list. On the other hand, for each case where no precise prime number $q$ is shown, an approximation was performed since the authors could not find a suitable Sophie-Germain prime in the literature. In such a case, we calculated the "difference" and the corresponding seed length as if both $f(2^{h_1}, q)$ and $f(q, 2^{h_2})$ vanish and $h_1 = h_2 = |q|_2$. This approximation seems not too bad since $h_1$ and $h_2$ are not significantly far from $q$ in the five cases with precise values of $q$. The table shows that our proposed technique for the randomness reduction (in cases $\ell = 2$ and $\ell = 5$) indeed improves the effect of randomness reduction from the plain case ($\ell = 1$), with the case $\ell = 5$ being better than the case $\ell = 2$. This table also shows that the new seed lengths are almost independent of the number $N$ of users, while the original numbers of required random bits are almost linear in $N$, therefore the "ratio" becomes significantly better as $N$ is getting larger.

Moreover, Fig. 4 shows a relation between the value $\ell$ and the approximated seed length for the case $N = 10^3$ calculated by the same rule as the previous paragraph. By the observation in the previous paragraph, the overall tendency would be similar for the other choices of $N$. In the graph, the approximated seed length takes the minimum value $236,220$ at $\ell = 31$, which is about 2.57% of the original number of required random bits (this ratio is further improved in the case of larger $N$) and is about 29 times as short as the case $\ell = 1$. Thus our proposed technique of dividing the randomness into plural parts and generating each part by a separate PRG indeed improves the effect of randomness reduction significantly. Moreover, as a by-product, our technique also reduces the

**Table 2.** Evaluation of randomness reduction and parameters for DDH generators

| user number $N$ | | $10^3$ | $10^4$ | $10^5$ | $10^6$ | $10^7$ | $10^8$ | $10^9$ |
|---|---|---|---|---|---|---|---|---|
| code length $m$ | | 614 | 702 | 789 | 877 | 964 | 1052 | 1139 |
| # of random bits | | 9.21E6 | 1.05E8 | 1.18E9 | 1.31E10 | 1.44E11 | 1.57E12 | 1.70E13 |
| $\ell = 1$ | $q$ | — | — | — | — | — | — | — |
| | $\|q\|_2$ | 2.29E6 | 3.24E6 | 4.41E6 | 5.82E6 | 7.47E6 | 9.41E6 | 1.17E7 |
| | $h_2$ | | | | | | | |
| | $h_1$ | | | | | | | |
| | difference | 1.48E-7 | 6.69E-7 | 2.63E-7 | 5.03E-7 | 5.81E-7 | 7.40E-7 | 1.15E-9 |
| | seed length | 6.87E6 | 9.72E6 | 1.33E7 | 1.75E7 | 2.25E7 | 2.83E7 | 3.51E7 |
| | ratio | 7.46E-1 | 9.26E-2 | 1.13E-2 | 1.34E-3 | 1.57E-4 | 1.81E-5 | 2.07E-6 |
| $\ell = 2$ | $q$ | — | — | — | — | — | — | — |
| | $\|q\|_2$ | 4.07E5 | 5.73E5 | 7.76E5 | 1.02E6 | 1.30E6 | 1.63E6 | 2.01E6 |
| | $h_2$ | | | | | | | |
| | $h_1$ | | | | | | | |
| | difference | 9.57E-7 | 8.66E-7 | 8.09E-7 | 5.15E-7 | 3.88E-7 | 4.43E-7 | 3.28E-7 |
| | seed length | 2.45E6 | 3.44E6 | 4.66E6 | 6.12E6 | 7.80E6 | 9.78E6 | 1.21E7 |
| | ratio | 2.67E-1 | 3.28E-2 | 3.95E-3 | 4.68E-4 | 5.42E-5 | 6.23E-6 | 7.12E-7 |
| $\ell = 5$ | $q$ | $q_{(1)}$ | $q_{(2)}$ | $q_{(3)}$ | $q_{(4)}$ | $q_{(5)}$ | — | — |
| | $\|q\|_2$ | 54,284 | 70,033 | 98,420 | 121,324 | 172,007 | 1.90E5 | 2.30E5 |
| | $h_2$ | 54,254 | 70,001 | 98,395 | 121,301 | 171,960 | | |
| | $h_1$ | 54,306 | 70,056 | 98,441 | 121,347 | 172,029 | | |
| | difference | 4.56E-7 | 8.24E-7 | 9.67E-7 | 3.66E-7 | 4.78E-7 | 4.39E-7 | 9.57E-7 |
| | seed length | 8.15E5 | 1.06E6 | 1.48E6 | 1.83E6 | 2.59E6 | 2.84E6 | 3.45E6 |
| | ratio | 8.85E-2 | 1.01E-2 | 1.26E-3 | 1.40E-4 | 1.80E-5 | 1.81E-6 | 2.03E-7 |

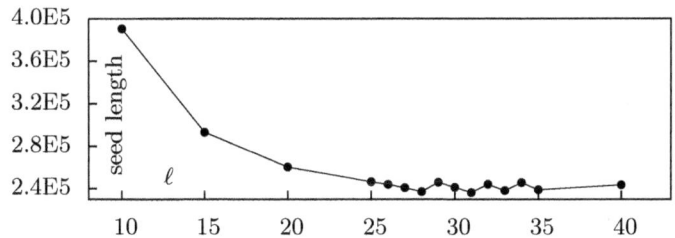

**Fig. 4.** Values of $\ell$ and approximated seed lengths, for $N = 10^3$

computational cost of the PRGs since the sizes of the primes $q$ used in the PRGs are also significantly decreased.

## 5    Conclusion

In this article, we applied the authors' recently proposed evaluation technique for PRG-based randomness reduction to the case of fingerprint codes and verified the effectiveness. Although we used a PRG, the evaluation result is effective even against computationally unbounded attack algorithms. We also proposed a novel technique for construction of the PRG-based randomness reduction to improve the evaluation result further. We proved a bound of loss of security through the improved randomness reduction method, and gave a numerical example showing that in a reasonable setting, our proposed technique improves the effect of randomness reduction to about 29 times as good as the case of plain randomness reduction. Applications of our proposed technique to other information-theoretically secure schemes will be a future research topic.

**Acknowledgments.** The authors would like to thank the anonymous referees for their precious comments.

# References

1. Billet, O., Phan, D.H.: Efficient traitor tracing from collusion secure codes. In: Safavi-Naini, R. (ed.) ICITS 2008. LNCS, vol. 5155, pp. 171–182. Springer, Heidelberg (2008)
2. Boneh, D., Shaw, J.: Collusion-secure fingerprinting for digital data. IEEE Transactions on Information Theory 44, 1897–1905 (1998)
3. Caldwell, C.: The Top Twenty: Sophie Germain (p),
   http://primes.utm.edu/top20/page.php?id=2
4. Chor, B., Fiat, A., Naor, M.: Tracing traitors. In: Desmedt, Y.G. (ed.) CRYPTO 1994. LNCS, vol. 839, pp. 257–270. Springer, Heidelberg (1994)
5. Dubrov, B., Ishai, Y.: On the randomness complexity of efficient sampling. In: Proceedings of STOC 2006, pp. 711–720. ACM, New York (2006)
6. Farashahi, R.R., Schoenmakers, B., Sidorenko, A.: Efficient pseudorandom generators based on the DDH assumption. In: Okamoto, T., Wang, X. (eds.) PKC 2007. LNCS, vol. 4450, pp. 426–441. Springer, Heidelberg (2007)
7. Hagiwara, M., Hanaoka, G., Imai, H.: A short random fingerprinting code against a small number of pirates. In: Fossorier, M.P.C., Imai, H., Lin, S., Poli, A. (eds.) AAECC 2006. LNCS, vol. 3857, pp. 193–202. Springer, Heidelberg (2006)
8. Kuribayashi, M., Akashi, N., Morii, M.: On the systematic generation of Tardos's fingerprinting codes. In: Proceedings of MMSP 2008, pp. 748–753. IEEE, Los Alamitos (2008)
9. Lenstra, A.K., Verheul, E.R.: Selecting cryptographic key sizes. Journal of Cryptology 14, 255–293 (2001)
10. Nuida, K., Fujitsu, S., Hagiwara, M., Kitagawa, T., Watanabe, H., Ogawa, K., Imai, H.: An improvement of discrete Tardos fingerprinting codes. Designs, Codes and Cryptography 52, 339–362 (2009)
11. Nuida, K., Hagiwara, M., Watanabe, H., Imai, H.: Optimization of Tardos's fingerprinting codes in a viewpoint of memory amount. In: Furon, T., Cayre, F., Doërr, G., Bas, P. (eds.) IH 2007. LNCS, vol. 4567, pp. 279–293. Springer, Heidelberg (2008)
12. Nuida, K., Hanaoka, G.: On the security of pseudorandomized information-theoretically secure schemes. In: The 4th International Conference on Information Theoretic Security (ICITS 2009), Shizuoka, Japan, December 4 (2009)
13. Tardos, G.: Optimal probabilistic fingerprint codes. In: Proceedings of STOC 2003, pp. 116–125. ACM Press, New York (2003)
14. Tardos, G.: Optimal probabilistic fingerprint codes. Journal of the ACM 55(2), 1–24 (2008)

# Statistical-Mechanical Approach for Multiple Watermarks Using Spectrum Spreading

Kazuhiro Senda and Masaki Kawamura*

Yamaguchi University, 1677–1 Yoshida, Yamaguchi-shi, Yamaguchi Japan
kawamura@sci.yamaguchi-u.ac.jp

**Abstract.** We formulated a Bayes optimum watermarking decoder and derived sub-optimum decoding algorithms for spread spectrum digital image watermarking. The optimum decoder can be obtained by considering the posterior probability under the Gaussian assumption for noise and attacks. The amount of calculation for the decoder is NP-hard. We, therefore, need to derive sub-optimum decoding algorithms in order to decode the watermarks. The proposed decoders are multiple watermark decoders that estimate multiple watermarks at the same time. These methods are based on the multi-stage demodulation method and the partial interference cancellation method, which are two CDMA multiuser demodulation methods. We applied them to the digital watermarking scheme. When the original image is blind, the image itself is regarded as noise. We, therefore, evaluated bit error rates both for cases when the original image is informed and blind. As a result, we found both the multi-stage watermark decoder and the partial interference cancellation decoder were effective for watermarking. The latter performed better than the former.

## 1 Introduction

Misuse of digital content is emerging as a social issue. The copyright information attached to additional headers of digital content does not work well for copyright protection. Digital watermarking is one solution to this problem.

The basic idea of digital watermarking is that hidden messages or watermarks are invisibly embedded in the cover of digital content. The cover content may be images, video, audio, and so on. There are many different embedding schemes. For images, watermarks are either simply embedded by adding them to the cover content, or the cover content is transformed by discrete cosine transform (DCT) or wavelet transform, and then the watermarks are embedded in the transform domain [1–4]. On the other hand, messages are encrypted or spread in order to hide them. Spectrum spreading is one efficient, robust method. The maximum

* This work was partially supported by Grant-in-Aid for Young Scientists (B) No. 21700255, the Yamaguchi University Foundation, and the Nakajima Foundation. The computer simulation results were obtained using the PC cluster system at Yamaguchi University.

K. Kurosawa (Ed.): ICITS 2009, LNCS 5973, pp. 231–247, 2010.

likelihood estimation [5, 6] and the maximum a posteriori probability (MAP) estimation [7, 8] have been used with existing methods.

Cox *et al.* [1–3] proposed a method based on the communication model. The watermark sequences are chosen independently in accordance with Gaussian distribution, and then they are embedded in the spatial or transform domain. Since embedded sequences can be generated independently and identically distributed [2, 9], *multiple* watermarks can be embedded into the same pixel, since they become almost orthogonal. The phrase "multiple watermarks" in this paper means that several spread messages or watermarks are accumulated on the same pixel. Cox *et al.* [1–3] performed multiple watermark by computer simulations. However, no decoder for multiple watermarks has been discussed in theory because of multi-watermark interference.

In this paper, we formulate the Bayes optimum watermarking decoder for spread spectrum digital image watermarking. The optimum decoder can be obtained by considering the posterior probability under the condition of the Gaussian assumption for noise and attacks. Unfortunately, the amount of calculation to decode all embedded watermarks is NP-hard. We, therefore, need to derive sub-optimum decoding algorithms. We derive sub-optimum decoding algorithms from the optimum decoder. In this manner, because of the theoretical difficulty, we consider a simple watermarking model in which watermarks are simply embedded into the image domain.

We consider decoding algorithms for the spectrum spreading method. This method is also now used in code division multiple access (CDMA)[10–13]. In CDMA, more than one user can transmit information at the same time and within the same cell. Therefore, multiuser interference needs to be considered for the CDMA multiuser demodulator problem. Bayes optimum solutions have been obtained by statistical mechanics. The maximum posterior marginal (MPM) estimation gives the Bayes optimum [14]. Tanaka has evaluated this problem using the replica method [14–16]. Methods of demodulating CDMA by applying a dynamical theory of the Hopfield model have been described [17–19]. As in the case of CDMA, statistical-mechanical approaches are progressing in several fields, e.g., image restoration [20, 21], coding theory [22, 23], and rate distortion [24]. Now, we are addressing theoretical analysis of the digital watermarking model. It is important for a better understanding of watermarking to model, formulate, and derive decoding methods.

By applying CDMA demodulation methods to watermarking, multiple watermarks can be decoded simultaneously. Moreover, since multi-watermark interference can be reduced, bit error rate for watermarks will be improved. From a theoretical viewpoint, the distinction between CDMA and watermarking is based on assumptions about noise. Channel noise in the CDMA is usually assumed to be independent, or thermal noise. In watermarking, artificial noise occurs as the result attacked by illegal users. They are correlated types of noise, e.g., image noise, block-noise, and distortion. Although the assumption for noise should not intrinsically be Gaussian, in almost all cases, models with these noises would be intractable. Moreover, when the type of attack might be blind, we could not formulate its model. Therefore, we have no other choice but to assume the noise is Gaussian. Then, we evaluate decoding performance of the proposed decoders theoretically and using simulations.

Section 2 outlines our watermarking model. Section 3 describes the Bayes optimum decoder for multiple watermarks, and Sec. 4 describes computable multiple decoders. Section 5 shows results obtained theoretically and using computer simulations. Section 6 concludes our methods.

## 2   Mathematical Model of Watermarking

### 2.1   Embedding Procedure

A gray scale image is divided into $N$ pixels per block. There are no constrains on how it is divided as long as there are no overlaps between blocks. For example, each block may consist of $8 \times 8$ pixels, or $64 \times 1$ pixels by raster scanning. We only assume the block length stays constant for all blocks. Since each block is processed in turn, we refer to only one block in detail.

An image block consisting of $N$ pixels is represented as $\boldsymbol{I} = (I_1, I_2, \cdots, I_N)^T$. Hereinafter, we refer to this image block simply as "image." $K$-bit messages $\boldsymbol{s} = (s_1, s_2, \cdots, s_K)^T$ are embedded in the original image in layers, where $s_i = \pm 1$. Figure 1 is a diagram of the embedding procedure. Each bit of the message, $s_i$, is spread by specific spreading code $\boldsymbol{\xi}_i = (\xi_i^1, \xi_i^2, \cdots, \xi_i^N)^T$. The chip rate, or length of the spreading codes is equal to $N$. Each element of the spreading codes $\xi_i^\mu$ takes $\pm 1$ with probability

$$P\left[\xi_i^\mu = \pm 1\right] = \frac{1}{2}. \tag{1}$$

Here, we notice $(\xi_i^\mu)^2 = 1$. The spreading codes are usually generated by a PN sequence generator. Any generating method is okay as long as it satisfies (1).

A watermark to be embedded at the $\mu$th pixel, $w_\mu$, is represented by

$$w_\mu = \sum_{i=1}^{K} \xi_i^\mu s_i \ , \quad \mu = 1, 2, \cdots, N, \tag{2}$$

which is the sum of the spread messages. The stego image $\boldsymbol{X}$ is made by adding the watermarks $\boldsymbol{w} = (w_1, w_2, \cdots, w_N)^T$ to the original image $\boldsymbol{I}$, that is,

$$X_\mu = F_0\left(I_\mu + w_\mu\right) \tag{3}$$

$$\simeq I_\mu + w_\mu + n_{0\mu}, \tag{4}$$

where a function $F_0$ is the function that limits each pixel value to interval $[0, 255]$. We assume embedding error can be represented as noise $n_{0\mu}$ by linear approximation. In this way, the stego image $\boldsymbol{X}$ is generated and is distributed widely.

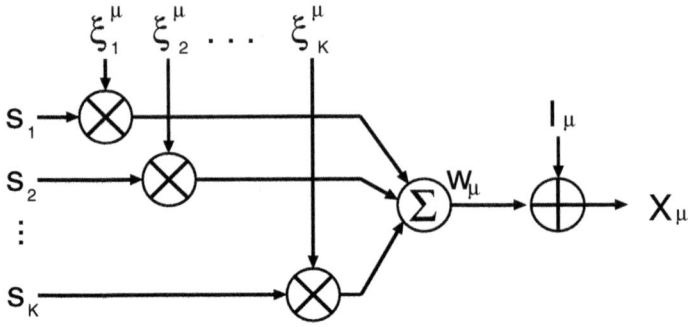

**Fig. 1.** Diagram of spreading and multiplexing of embedded watermarks

## 2.2    Attack

The stego image $X$ is usually attacked by illegal users. Attacks by lossy compression, band-pass filter, geometrical distortion, etc. are represented as noise. Since there are many different kinds of attacks, we should intrinsically consider each attacks individually. These effects cannot be represented as Gaussian distributions. Even if we can represent them by specific distributions, they may be intractable for many cases. Because we want to formulate the Bayes optimum decoder, we can introduce the Gaussian assumption. This condition is good case for decoder. So, now the tampered stego image $\widetilde{X}$ is given by

$$\widetilde{X}_\mu = X_\mu + n_{1\mu}. \tag{5}$$

From (4), by combining the noise $n_{0\mu}$ and $n_{1\mu}$, we obtain

$$\widetilde{X}_\mu = I_\mu + w_\mu + n_\mu, \tag{6}$$
$$n_\mu = n_{0\mu} + n_{1\mu}. \tag{7}$$

In the following discussions, we assume that noise $n_\mu$ obeys the Gaussian distribution $\mathcal{N}(0, \sigma_s^2)$ and that the noise is independent of both the original image $I_\mu$ and the watermark $w_\mu$.

## 2.3    Informed Decoder

The watermarks are decoded from the tampered image. When the original image is known, extracted information $r_\mu$ is calculated by subtracting the original image $I_\mu$ from the tampered image $\widetilde{X}_\mu$, that is,

$$r_\mu = \widetilde{X}_\mu - I_\mu, \tag{8}$$
$$= w_\mu + n_\mu. \tag{9}$$

By multiplying $r_\mu$ by the corresponding spreading code $\boldsymbol{\xi}_i$, the output of the correlator, $h_i$, is given by

$$h_i = \frac{1}{N} \sum_{\mu=1}^{N} \xi_i^\mu r_\mu \tag{10}$$

$$= s_i + \frac{1}{N} \sum_{\mu=1}^{N} \sum_{j\neq i}^{K} \xi_i^\mu \xi_j^\mu s_j + \frac{1}{N} \sum_{\mu=1}^{N} \xi_i^\mu n_\mu, \tag{11}$$

where the second term of the right-hand side in (11) is a multi-watermark interference term and the third one is the noise term. Then, the estimated value of the $i$th watermark, $\hat{s}_i$, is given by

$$\hat{s}_i = \mathrm{sgn}\,(h_i), \tag{12}$$

where a function $\mathrm{sgn}(h)$ is the signum function given by

$$\mathrm{sgn}(h) = \begin{cases} +1, & h \geq 0 \\ -1, & h < 0 \end{cases}. \tag{13}$$

The method of independently estimating each watermark is called a single decoder, like a single-user demodulator in CDMA.

## 2.4   Blind Decoder

When the original image is unknown, or blind, there are two ways to decode the watermarks: direct inference without estimating the original image and double inference with estimating the original image and watermarks. In the former case, the tampered image $\widetilde{X}_\mu$ itself becomes the extracted information $r_\mu$, that is,

$$r_\mu = \widetilde{X}_\mu \tag{14}$$

$$= w_\mu + n_\mu + I_\mu. \tag{15}$$

The output of the correlator, $h_i$, becomes

$$h_i = \frac{1}{N} \sum_{\mu=1}^{N} \xi_i^\mu r_\mu \tag{16}$$

$$= s_i + \frac{1}{N} \sum_{\mu=1}^{N} \sum_{j\neq i}^{K} \xi_i^\mu \xi_j^\mu s_j + \frac{1}{N} \sum_{\mu=1}^{N} \xi_i^\mu n_\mu + \frac{1}{N} \sum_{\mu=1}^{N} \xi_i^\mu I_\mu, \tag{17}$$

where the fourth term in (17), which differs from (11), is the image noise term. Since $I_\mu$ takes a larger value than the value of watermarks, it is hard to estimate the watermarks properly.

With the other method, we can infer an estimated image from the tampered image $\widetilde{X}_\mu$. The estimated image $\hat{I}_\mu$ can be reconstructed by some filtering and so on. Then, the extracted information $r_\mu$ is calculated by subtracting the estimated image $\hat{I}_\mu$ from the tampered image $\tilde{X}_\mu$, and is given by

$$r_\mu = \tilde{X}_\mu - \hat{I}_\mu \tag{18}$$

$$= w_\mu + n_\mu + I_\mu - \hat{I}_\mu. \tag{19}$$

Therefore, the output of the correlator, $h_i$, becomes

$$h_i = \frac{1}{N} \sum_{\mu=1}^{N} \xi_i^\mu r_\mu \tag{20}$$

$$= s_i + \frac{1}{N} \sum_{\mu=1}^{N} \sum_{j \neq i}^{K} \xi_i^\mu \xi_j^\mu s_j + \frac{1}{N} \sum_{\mu=1}^{N} \xi_i^\mu n_\mu + \frac{1}{N} \sum_{\mu=1}^{N} \xi_i^\mu \left( I_\mu - \hat{I}_\mu \right). \tag{21}$$

Whenever the estimated image $\hat{I}_\mu$ is sufficiently similar to the original image $I_\mu$, the image noise term of (21) can be reduced.

## 3 Optimum Multiple Watermarks Decoder

Since 1-bit messages are spread by $N$-bits spreading codes, the embedded capacity, or payload decreases to $1/N$. On the other hand, by spreading the messages, more than one message can be embedded in the same pixel in layers. In this case, multi-watermark interference cannot be eliminated. We, therefore, consider how to eliminate this interference.

The multi-watermarks interference term consists of messages $s_i$ and their corresponding spreading codes $\boldsymbol{\xi}_i$. The spreading codes are available for the owner, but information regarding the messages is blind. Therefore, the effect of the interference term can be decreased by using both estimated messages $\hat{s}$ and the spreading codes $\boldsymbol{\xi}_i$. Multiple watermark decoders in which all estimated messages are used to infer themselves simultaneously corresponds to the multiuser demodulator method in CDMA [14–16]. The Bayes optimum decoder can eliminate the multi-watermark interference. Next, we formulate a multiple watermark decoder under the Gaussian assumption. Let us start to calculate the posterior probability of messages $s$, given the extracted information $r$.

### 3.1 Posterior Probability

In the multiple watermark decoder, we start by obtaining the posterior probability. Since the estimated image $\hat{I}_\mu$ can be reconstructed by a mean filter or Wiener filter and we guess it is sufficiently similar to the original one, for simplicity, we assume the original image is informed. From (2) and (19), the noise term becomes

$$n_\mu = r_\mu - \sum_{i=1}^{K} \xi_i^\mu s_i, \tag{22}$$

and obeys Gaussian distribution,

$$P\left(n_\mu\right) = \frac{1}{\sqrt{2\pi\sigma_s^2}} \exp\left[-\frac{\left(n_\mu\right)^2}{2\sigma_s^2}\right].\tag{23}$$

The conditional probability of the extracted information $r$, given the true messages $s$, is given by

$$P\left(r|s\right) = \prod_{\mu=1}^{N} P\left(r_\mu|s, \xi\right)\tag{24}$$

$$\propto \exp\left[-\frac{\beta_s}{2N} \sum_{\mu=1}^{N} \left(r_\mu - \sum_{i=1}^{K} \xi_i^\mu s_i\right)^2\right],\tag{25}$$

where $\sigma_s^2 = N/\beta_s$. From Bayes' theorem, the posterior probability of messages $s$, given the extracted information $r$, is given by

$$P\left(s|r\right) = \frac{P\left(r|s\right)P\left(s\right)}{P(r)}\tag{26}$$

$$= \frac{P\left(r|s\right)P\left(s\right)}{\sum_x P\left(r|x\right)P\left(x\right)}.\tag{27}$$

The prior probability of the messages, $P(s)$, is assumed to have uniform distribution, that is,

$$P(s) = 2^{-K}.\tag{28}$$

Therefore, the posterior probability is given by

$$P\left(s|r\right) = \frac{P(s)}{Z(r)} \exp\left[-\frac{\beta}{2N} \sum_{\mu=1}^{N} \left(r_\mu - \sum_{i=1}^{K} \xi_i^\mu s_i\right)^2\right],\tag{29}$$

where we set in a parameter $\beta$ instead of the true parameter $\beta_s$, since the true parameter is unknown for the decoder. Also, $Z(r)$ is defined as

$$Z(r) = \sum_s P(s) \exp\left[-\frac{\beta}{2N} \sum_{\mu=1}^{N} \left(r_\mu - \sum_{i=1}^{K} \xi_i^\mu s_i\right)^2\right],\tag{30}$$

where summation over $s$ is defined as

$$\sum_s = \sum_{s_1=\pm 1} \sum_{s_2=\pm 1} \cdots \sum_{s_K=\pm 1}.\tag{31}$$

Therefore, the performance of the multiple watermark decoder can be evaluated in the same way as the multiuser demodulators in CDMA [14–16]. The maximum a posteriori (MAP) estimation and maximum posterior marginal (MPM) estimation can be applied to infer the messages $\boldsymbol{s}$. The MAP estimation is the method minimizing block error rate, and the MPM estimation is minimizing bit error rate. The estimated values by the MAP and MPM estimations are given by

$$\hat{\boldsymbol{s}}^{\mathrm{MAP}} = \arg\max_{\boldsymbol{s}} P\left(\boldsymbol{s}|\boldsymbol{r}\right), \tag{32}$$

$$\hat{s}_i^{\mathrm{MPM}} = \arg\max_{s_i} P\left(s_i|\boldsymbol{r}\right), \tag{33}$$

where probability $P\left(s_i|\boldsymbol{r}\right)$ is a marginal probability given by

$$P\left(s_i|\boldsymbol{r}\right) = \sum_{\boldsymbol{s}\backslash s_i} P\left(\boldsymbol{s}|\boldsymbol{r}\right), \tag{34}$$

where summation $\sum_{\boldsymbol{s}\backslash s_i}$ is the summation over $\boldsymbol{s}$ excepting $s_i$ and is defined as

$$\sum_{\boldsymbol{s}\backslash s_i} = \sum_{s_1=\pm 1} \cdots \sum_{s_{i-1}=\pm 1} \sum_{s_{i+1}=\pm 1} \cdots \sum_{s_K=\pm 1}. \tag{35}$$

The purpose of the MPM estimation is to find the code that maximizes the marginal posterior probability $P\left(s_i|\boldsymbol{r}\right)$.

Now, we consider decoding algorithms that infer the messages $\boldsymbol{s}$ by MPM estimation. From (33), estimated messages $\hat{s}_i^{\mathrm{MPM}}$ can be calculated by

$$\hat{s}_i^{\mathrm{MPM}} = \mathrm{sgn}\left(\sum_{s_i=\pm 1} s_i P\left(s_i|\boldsymbol{r}\right)\right) \tag{36}$$

$$= \mathrm{sgn}\left(\langle s_i \rangle\right), \tag{37}$$

where $\langle s_i \rangle$ is the average over the posteriori distribution and is defined as

$$\langle s_i \rangle = \sum_{s_i=\pm 1} s_i P\left(s_i|\boldsymbol{r}\right) \tag{38}$$

As mentioned, we were able to formulate the Bayes optimum multiple watermark decoder.

The estimation error is measured by the bit error rate $P_b$, which is defined as

$$P_b = \frac{1-M}{2}, \tag{39}$$

where $M$ is an overlap or degree of coincidence between the true messages $s_i$ and the estimated messages $\hat{s}_i$, and is defined as

$$M = \frac{1}{K}\sum_{i=1}^{K} s_i \hat{s}_i. \tag{40}$$

The estimation by (37) gives optimum solution, but unfortunately its computational complexity is NP-hard in the number of messages. Its proof is given in the same way as the case of CDMA [10]. In other words, to decode watermarks using (37), an enormous amount of computational time might be required to calculate the posteriori probability. Therefore, dynamics or computation algorithms such that it achieves an optimum or sub-optimum solution should be considered.

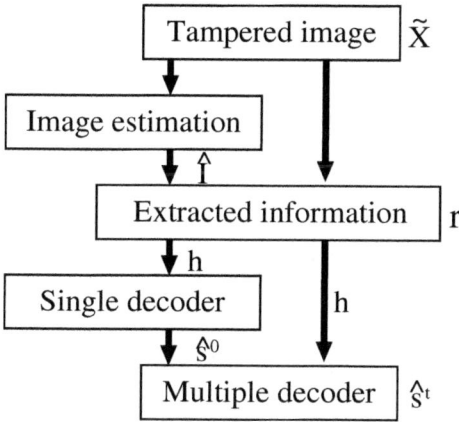

**Fig. 2.** Decoding procedure for multiple watermarks

## 4    Decoding Procedure

We propose multiple watermark decoders on the basis of the Bayes optimum decoder. The decoding procedure is shown in Fig. 2. We obtain the extracted information $r_\mu$ by (18) using the estimated image, $\hat{I}_\mu$, whose image is reconstructed by a mean filter. Then, the output of the correlator, $h_i$, is obtained by (20). At the initial states, the estimated message $\hat{s}_i^0$ is given using the single decoder by

$$\hat{s}_i^0 = \operatorname{sgn}(h_i). \tag{41}$$

Next, we consider how to reduce the multi-watermark interference. Since the optimum decoder is hard to compute, we need step-by-step algorithms that require relatively short computational time.

### 4.1    Multiple Watermark Decoders

From (29), we obtain the posterior probability in the form of a Hamiltonian or energy function, $H(s)$:

$$P(s|r) \propto \exp\left[-\beta H(s)\right], \tag{42}$$

$$H(s) = \frac{1}{2}\sum_{i=1}^{K}\sum_{j=1}^{K} J_{ij} s_i s_j - \sum_{i=1}^{K} h_i s_i, \tag{43}$$

where $J_{ij}$ is defined as

$$J_{ij} = \frac{1}{N}\sum_{\mu=1}^{N} \xi_i^\mu \xi_j^\mu. \tag{44}$$

According to (32) and (33), maximizing the posterior probability $P(s|r)$ corresponds to minimizing the Hamiltonian $H(s)$. We, therefore, obtain the following equation using the steepest descent method,

$$-\frac{\partial H(s)}{\partial s_i} = h_i - \sum_{j \neq i}^{K} J_{ij} s_j. \tag{45}$$

The steepest descent method can find one of the possible optimum or suboptimum solutions, since it stops at the local minimum.

We consider discrete dynamics, and introduce the multistage watermark decoder, which is obtained by

$$\hat{s}_i^{t+1} = \text{sgn}\left( h_i - \sum_{j \neq i}^{K} J_{ij} \hat{s}_j^t \right), \tag{46}$$

where $\hat{s}_i^t$ represents the estimated message at the $t$-th stage. The basic idea about multistage has appeared in the CDMA multiuser demodulation problem [11, 12, 18].

The reliability of estimation for early stages in the multistage watermark decoder (46) is low due to noise and use of the single decoder. Therefore, an interference cancellation parameter $P_t$ is introduced to the multi-watermark interference term. A partial interference cancellation method has been proposed for CDMA [13, 25–28]. The parameter $P_t$ is initially a small value, and then it becomes larger with time for increasing reliability. The estimated message at the $(t+1)$th stage, $\hat{s}_i^{t+1}$, in the partial interference cancellation decoder is given by

$$\hat{s}_i^{t+1} = \text{sgn}\left( h_i - P_t \sum_{j \neq i}^{K} J_{ij} \hat{s}_j^t \right). \tag{47}$$

At the initial stage, $\hat{s}_i^0$ is given by (41). When we put $P_t = 1$ for all stages, it is equivalent to the multistage watermark decoder (46).

## 4.2   Theory

In CDMA, the performance of the partial interference cancellation method is analyzed under the assumption that noise obeys Gaussian distribution [18, 19]. Mizutani *el al.*[18] proposed a decoding algorithm assuming that the last one-step correlation between stages is only effective, and correlations between other stages can be ignored.

In CDMA, we analyze the performance for multiple watermark estimation. The variance of the noise is $\sigma_s^2$. We consider the large-system limit $K \to \infty$ and $N \to \infty$, while the ratio $\beta \equiv K/N$ is kept finite. We define variance $V$ as the sum of the variance of the noise, $\sigma_s^2$, and the ratio $\beta$:

$$V = \beta + \sigma_s^2. \tag{48}$$

Under the random spreading assumption and the large-system limit, we redefine the bit error rate as $P_b^{t+1}$ for time evolution. The value of $P_b^{t+1}$ is to be evaluated by the following recursive formulas.

$$M_{t+1} = \sum_{\lambda=\pm 1} \frac{1 + \lambda M_{t-1}}{2} \operatorname{erf}\left(\frac{1 - (1 - \lambda P_{t-1})P_t U_t}{\sqrt{2V_t^2}}\right), \tag{49}$$

$$V_t^2 = V - 2P_t C_t + P_t^2 S_t^2, \tag{50}$$

$$U_{t+1} = \beta \sum_{\lambda=\pm 1} \frac{1 + \lambda M_{t-1}}{\sqrt{2\pi V_t^2}} \exp\left[-\frac{\{1 - (1 - P_{t-1}\lambda)P_t U_t\}^2}{2V_t^2}\right], \tag{51}$$

$$C_t = \beta M_t + U_t\left(V - P_{t-1}C_{t-1}\right), \tag{52}$$

$$S_t^2 = \beta + U_t^2 V_{t-1}^2 + 2\beta U_t M_t\left(1 - P_{t-1}M_{t-1}\right), \tag{53}$$

where $\operatorname{erf}(x)$ is the error function, which is defined as

$$\operatorname{erf}(x) = \frac{2}{\sqrt{\pi}} \int_0^x \exp\left[-u^2\right] du. \tag{54}$$

For the initial stage $t = 0$, equations are given by

$$M_{-1} = C_{-1} = S_{-1}^2 = 0, \tag{55}$$

$$M_0 = \operatorname{erf}\left(\frac{1}{\sqrt{2V_{-1}^2}}\right), \tag{56}$$

$$U_0 = \beta\sqrt{\frac{2}{\pi V_{-1}^2}} \exp\left[-\frac{1}{2V_{-1}^2}\right], \tag{57}$$

$$M_1 = \operatorname{erf}\left(\frac{1 - P_0 U_0}{\sqrt{2V_0^2}}\right), \tag{58}$$

$$U_1 = \beta\sqrt{\frac{2}{\pi V_0^2}} \exp\left[-\frac{(1 - P_0 U_0)^2}{2V_0^2}\right]. \tag{59}$$

The parameter $P_t$ for the partial interference cancellation decoder is given by

$$P_t = \frac{U_t V(P_{t-1} + 1) - C_t}{U_t C_t(P_{t-1} + 1) - S_t^2}, \tag{60}$$

and for the multistage watermark decoder it is $P_t = 1$. For a detailed derivation, refer to [18].

## 5    Simulation Results

We described decoding algorithms for multiple watermarks using spreading codes. To evaluate the performance of the multistage watermark decoder and the partial

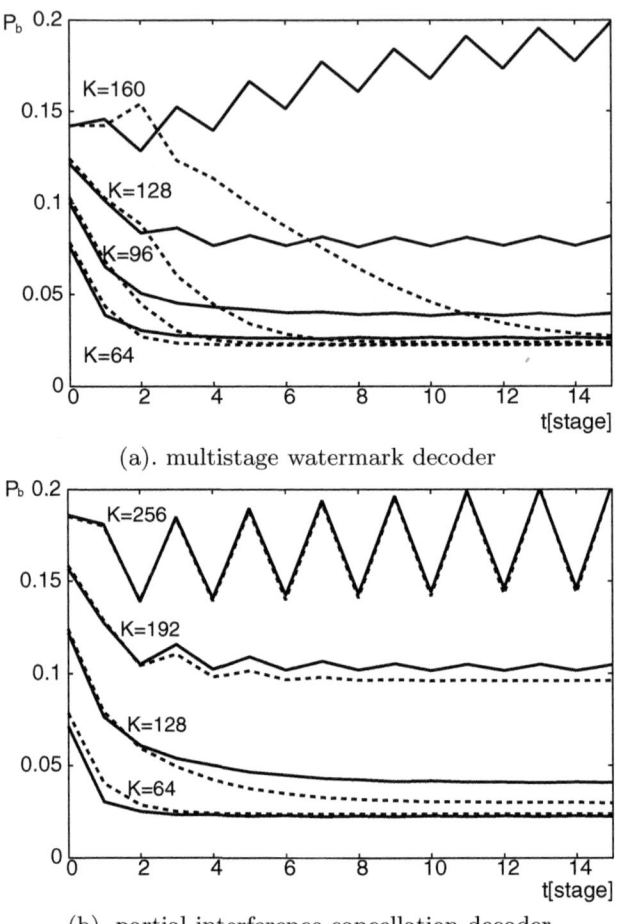

**Fig. 3.** Bit error rate $P_b$ for stage $t$ when the original image is known, where (a). $\beta = 0.25, 0.375, 0.50, 0.625$ ($K = 64, 96, 128, 160$) and (b). $\beta = 0.25, 0.50, 0.75, 1.0$ ($K = 64, 128, 192, 256$). Solid and broken lines represent results by computer simulations and theory, respectively.

interference cancellation decoder, we analyzed the bit error rate $P_b$ for several multiple $K$ using SIDBA GIRL. The length of the spreading codes was $N = 256 \times 1$, and the variance of noise was $\sigma_s^2 = 64$, i.e., the noise obeyed the Gaussian distribution $\mathcal{N}(0, \sigma_s^2)$.

## 5.1    Results for Informed Decoder

When the original image is known and attacks can be considered as additive white Gaussian noise (AWGN), the bit error rate $P_b$ is evaluated. Figure 3 shows $P_b$ for stage $t$. The solid lines in Fig. 3 (a) represent results obtained by computer

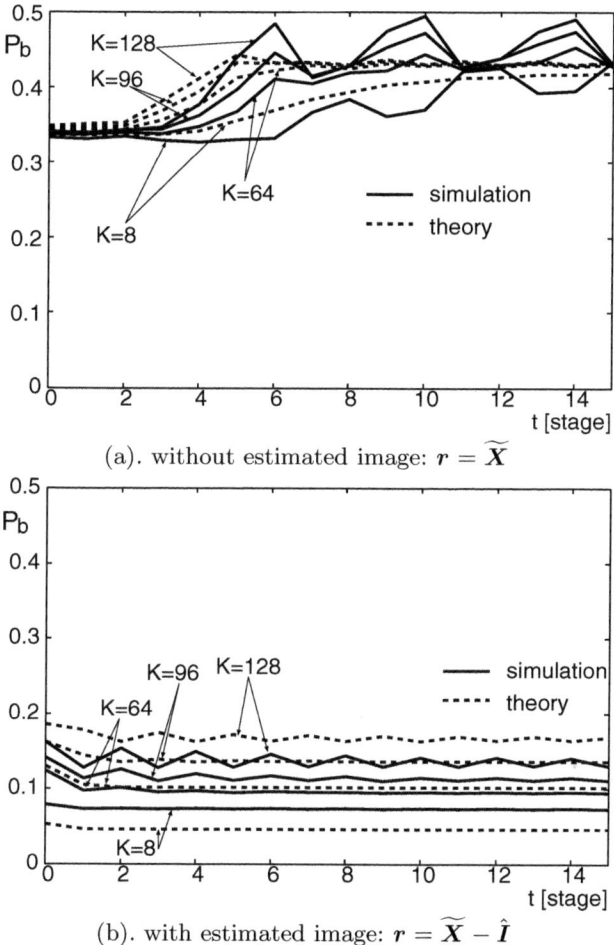

(a). without estimated image: $r = \widetilde{X}$

(b). with estimated image: $r = \widetilde{X} - \hat{I}$

**Fig. 4.** Bit error rate $P_b$ for stage $t$ when the original image is blind, (a). without estimated image, and (b). with estimated image. Solid and broken lines represent results by computer simulations and theory, respectively, where $\beta = 0.03125, 0.25, 0.375, 0.50$ ($K = 8, 64, 96, 128$).

simulations of the multistage watermark decoder. The broken lines represent theoretical values by time evolutions of the equations (49)–(53), where $P_t = 1$. The result of the initial stage, denoted by $t = 0$, was obtained by the single decoder. From Fig.3 (a), the multistage watermark decoder improved the bit error rate better than the single decoder for $\beta = K/N = 0.50$ ($K = 128$) or less. For $\beta = 0.625$, the single decoder gave the better result, since estimation error became large due to iterative calculation.

The solid lines in Fig. 3 (b) represent results obtained by computer simulations of the partial interference cancellation decoder. The broken lines represent theoretical values by time evolutions of equations (49)–(53), where $P_t$ is given

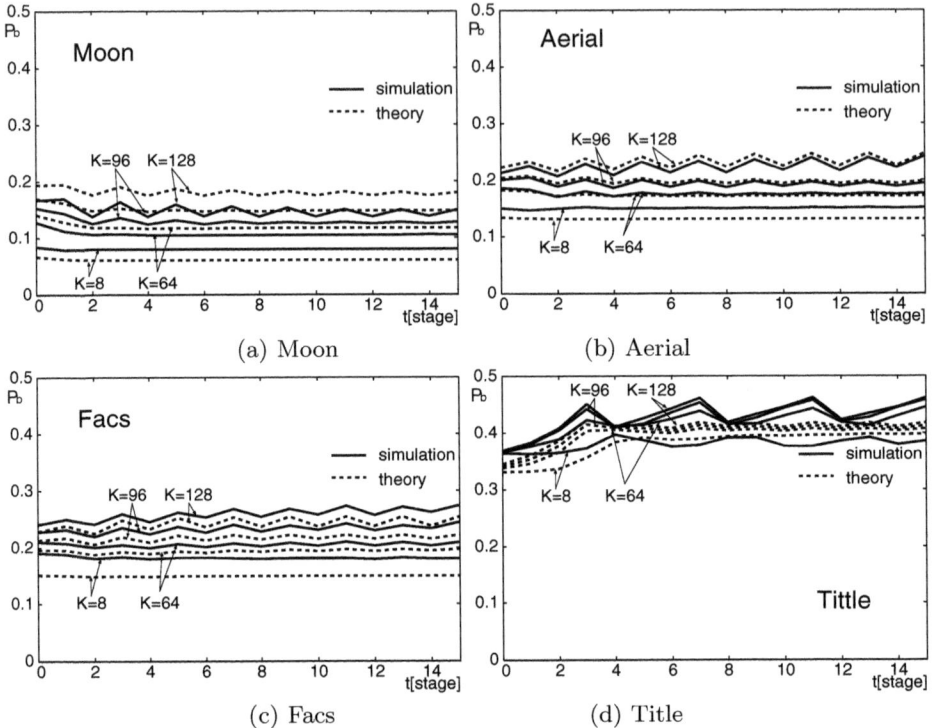

**Fig. 5.** Bit error rate $P_b$ with estimated image for various images; (a) Moon, (b) Aerial, (c) Facs, and (d) Title. Solid and broken lines represent results by computer simulations and theory, respectively, where $\beta = 0.03125, 0.25, 0.375, 0.50$ ($K = 8, 64, 96, 128$).

by (60). The result of the initial stage, denoted by $t = 0$, was obtained by the single decoder. As seen in Fig.3 (b), the partial interference cancellation decoder improved the bit error rate better than the single decoder for $\beta = 0.75$ or less. For $\beta = 1.0$, it cannot improve because of estimation error. Comparing these two decoders, the partial interference cancellation decoder was better than the multistage watermark decoder, because the interference cancellation parameter $P_t$ was introduced.

From Fig.3 (a) and (b), some differences occur due to approximation ignoring higher-order correlations. In other words, we have taken care of stages $t$ and $t-1$ in order to evaluate stage $t+1$. However, results of computer simulations agrees with ones of theory sufficiently.

## 5.2   Results for Blind Decoder

When the original image was blind, the bit error rate $P_b$ was evaluated. We applied a mean filter to the tampered image to obtain an estimated image $\hat{I}$. Figure 4 shows the bit error rate $P_b$ for stage $t$, using the partial interference cancellation decoder. Figure 4 (a) shows results of the case when no estimated image

**Table 1.** Bit error rate $P_b$ at stage $t = 0$ (single decoder) and $t = 14$ (multiple decoder)

| | | Girl | | Moon | | Aerial | | Facs | | Title | |
|---|---|---|---|---|---|---|---|---|---|---|---|
| $\beta$ | $K$ | $t = 0$ | $t = 14$ | $t = 0$ | $t = 14$ | $t = 0$ | $t = 14$ | $t = 0$ | $t = 14$ | $t = 0$ | $t = 14$ |
| 0.03125 | 8 | 0.075 | 0.068 | 0.085 | 0.080 | 0.150 | 0.150 | 0.190 | 0.181 | 0.364 | 0.379* |
| 0.250 | 64 | 0.117 | 0.091 | 0.128 | 0.106 | 0.186 | 0.175 | 0.210 | 0.203 | 0.366 | 0.430* |
| 0.375 | 96 | 0.140 | 0.113 | 0.153 | 0.126 | 0.201 | 0.189 | 0.227 | 0.234* | 0.368 | 0.445* |
| 0.500 | 128 | 0.162 | 0.130 | 0.167 | 0.139 | 0.213 | 0.223* | 0.240 | 0.262* | 0.368 | 0.446* |

was used, i.e., the extracted information was $r_\mu = \widetilde{X}_\mu$ from (14). Figure 4 (b) shows results using the estimated image $\hat{I}$, i.e., $r_\mu = \widetilde{X}_\mu - \hat{I}_\mu$ from (18). The solid lines represent results obtained by computer simulations, and the broken lines represent theoretical values by time evolutions of equations (49)–(53), where $P_t$ is given by (60). Since we take into account the one-step correlation in theory in 4.2, these results agree for the first few steps. Without an estimated image, the performance of the partial interference cancellation decoder became worse than the single decoder gradually, because the estimation error became large due to iterative calculation. Because an estimated image is used, it remains good performance.

We also evaluated our method using other images: SIDBA Moon, Aerial, Facs, and Title. Figure 5 shows results for these images by computer simulations using estimated images and by the partial interference cancellation decoder. Table 1 shows the bit error rate $P_b$ at stage $t = 0$ for the single decoder and at stage $t = 14$ for the multiple decoder by computer simulations. When the results using the multiple decoder become worse than those using the single decoder, we marked the values with *. For low load cases, namely, small $\beta = K/N$, the multiple decoder improved the bit error rate. Since we used a mean filter, the performance for natural images, e.g., Moon and Aerial, was better than artificial images which have many edges. The result for Title in Fig.5 (d) shows the worst case. The brightness of the image was 0 and 255 in many pixels, and embedding errors occurred. However, for many images, a multiple watermark decoder is effective as an estimated image in terms of the bit error rate.

## 6   Conclusions

By spreading watermarks using spreading codes, the watermarks can be concealed, and they can also have error-correcting capability. Although the payload decreases to $1/N$ without multiplexing, multiple watermarks can be embedded in the same pixel. We considered decoding algorithms for multiple watermarks and used the bit error rate to evaluate their performance.

For multiple watermarks, the problem is how to estimate all messages simultaneously. We formulated the Bayes optimum decoder under the Gaussian assumption. Since the optimum decoder is NP-hard, we derived dynamics or computation algorithms as multiple watermark decoders. We introduced a multistage watermark decoder and a partial interference cancellation decoder for watermarking. Since watermarks are embedded in an image, image noise needs to be taken into account in the blind case. Therefore, we analyzed cases both when the original image is informed and blind. We reconstructed estimated images by using a mean filter.

When the original image is informed, the partial interference cancellation decoder is better than the multistage watermark decoder, and both decoders together are better than the single decoder. When the bit error rate of the initial stage is large, the estimation error may become large. When the original image is unknown, or blind, the partial interference cancellation decoder is not effective without an estimated image. However, using the estimated image, which is reconstructed by a mean filter, the performance by the decoder can be improved sufficiently.

We consider simple watermarking models in order to discuss optimum or sub-optimum decoders. We show that finding one of the optimum solutions is computationally hard problem. When one will propose some decoders, it is necessary to consider theoretical limit. For practical use, more elaborate procedures are required. For a statistical-mechanical approach, these are interesting problems. Our approach can provide theoretical formulation of spectrum spreading watermarks.

# References

1. Cox, I.J., Kilian, J., Leighton, T., Shamoon, T.: Secure spread spectrum watermarking for images, audio and video. In: IEEE Int. Conf. Image Processing, vol. 3, pp. 243–246 (1996)
2. Cox, I.J., Kilian, J., Leighton, T., Shamoon, T.: Secure spread spectrum watermarking for multimedia. IEEE Trans. Image Processing 6(12), 1673–1687 (1997)
3. Cox, I.J., Miller, M., Bloom, J.A., Fridrich, J., Kalker, T.: Digital Watermarking and Steganography, 2nd edn. Morgan Kaufmann, San Francisco (2007)
4. Ruanaidh, J.J.K.Ó., Pun, T.: Rotation, scale and translation invariant spread spectrum digital image watermarking. Signal Processing 66, 303–317 (1998)
5. Hernández, J.R., González, F.P.: Statistical analysis of watermarking schemes for copyright protection of images. Proc. IEEE 87(7), 1142–1166 (1999)
6. Su, J., Hartung, F., Girod, B.: A channel model for a watermark attack. In: Proc. SPIE Security and Watermarking of Multimedia Contents, vol. 3657, pp. 159–170 (1999)
7. Kutter, M., Voloshynovskiy, S., Herrigel, A.: Watermark copy attack. In: Proc. SPIE Security and Watermarking of Multimedia Contents, vol. 3971, pp. 371–380 (2000)
8. Voloshynovskiy, S., Herrigel, A., Baumgaertner, N., Pun, T.: A stochastic approach to content adaptive digital image watermarking. In: Pfitzmann, A. (ed.) IH 1999. LNCS, vol. 1768, pp. 211–236. Springer, Heidelberg (2000)
9. Wong, P.H.W., Au, C., Yeung, Y.M.: A novel blind multiple watermarking technique for images. IEEE Trans. Circuits Syst. Video Technol. 13(8), 813–830 (2003)
10. Verdú, S.: Computational complexity of optimum multiuser detection. Algorithmica 4(1), 303–312 (1989)
11. Varanasi, M.K., Aazhang, B.: Multistage detection in asynchronous code-division multiple-access communications. IEEE Trans. Commun. 38, 509–519 (1990)

12. Varanasi, M.K., Aazhang, B.: Near-optimum detection in synchronous code-division multiple-access systems. IEEE Trans. Commun. 39, 725–736 (2001)
13. Divsalar, D., Simon, M.K., Raphelli, D.: Improved parallel interference cancellation for CDMA. IEEE Trans. Commun. 46(2), 258–268 (1998)
14. Tanaka, T.: A statistical-mechanics approach to large-system analysis of CDMA multiuser detectors. IEEE Trans. Info. Theory 48(11), 2888–2910 (2002)
15. Tanaka, T.: Statistical mechanics of CDMA multiuser demodulation. Europhys. Lett. 54, 540–546 (2001)
16. Nishimori, H.: Statistical physics of spin glasses and information processing. Oxford Univ. Press, Oxford (2001)
17. Kabashima, Y.: A CDMA multiuser detection algorithm on the basis of belief propagation. J. Phys. A: Math. Gen. 36, 11111–11121 (2003)
18. Mizutani, A., Tanaka, T., Okada, M.: Improvement of multistage detector with partial interference cancellation. IEICE Trans. Fundamentals (Japanese Edition) J87-A(5), 661–671 (2004)
19. Tanaka, T., Okada, M.: Approximate belief propagation, density evolution, and statistical neurodynamics for CDMA multiuser detection. IEEE Trans. Inf. Theory 51(2), 700–706 (2005)
20. Tanaka, K.: Statistical-mechanical approach to image processing. J. Phys. A: Math. Gen. 35(37), R81–R150 (2002)
21. Tanaka, K., Shouno, H., Okada, M., Titterington, D.M.: Accuracy of the Bethe Approximation for Hyperparameter Estimation in Probabilistic Image Processing. J. Phys. A: Math. Gen. 37(36), 8675–8696 (2004)
22. Skanzos, N., Saad, D., Kabashima, Y.: Analysis of common attacks inpublic-keycryptosystems based on low-density parity-check codes. Phys. Rev. E 68, 56125 (2003)
23. Kabashima, Y., Saad, D.: Statistical mechanics of low-density parity-check codes. J. Phys. A 43, R1–R43 (2004)
24. Murayama, T.: Statistical mechanics of the data compression theorem. J. Phys. A: Math. Gen. 35(8), L95–L100 (2002)
25. Sawahashi, M., Andoh, H., Higuchi, K.: Interference rejection weight control for pilot symbol-assisted coherent multistage interference canceler in DS-CDMA mobile radio. IEICE Trans. Fundamentals E81-A(5), 957–972 (1998)
26. Xue, G., Weng, J., Le-Ngoc, T., Tahar, S.: Adaptive Multistage Parallel Interference Cancellation for CDMA. IEEE J. Sel. Areas. Commun. 17(10), 1815–1827 (1999)
27. Buehrer, R.M., Correal, N.S., Woerner, B.D.: ADSP-based DS-CDMA multiuser receiver employing partial parallel interference cancellation. IEEE J. Sel. Areas. Commun. 17(4), 613–630 (1999)
28. Han, S.H., Lee, J.H.: Multi-stage partial parallel interference cancellation receivers multi-rate DS-CDMA system. IEICE Trans. Commun. E86-B(1), 170–180 (2003)

# Author Index